*Hamlet and Revenge*

# HAMLET
# AND REVENGE

Eleanor Prosser

SECOND EDITION

Stanford University Press
Stanford, California

For the second edition, the author has provided summaries of the assumptions dealt
with in Chapters 1–3, and a new appendix
on the relevance of political arguments to
*Hamlet*. She has also made revisions and
corrections throughout the text.

Stanford University Press
Stanford, California
© 1967, 1971 by the Board of Trustees of the
Leland Stanford Junior University
Printed in the United States of America
Cloth ISBN 0-8047-0316-7
Paper ISBN 0-8047-0317-5
LC 71-120745
First published 1967
Second edition, 1971

*To My Mother*

# Acknowledgments

I wish first to express my appreciation to the Lilly Foundation for its award of a Postdoctoral Fellowship in Religion for 1964–65, which made possible a year free from academic duties.

I am deeply grateful to Professors L. C. Knights, Robert Loper, Irving Ribner, and Virgil K. Whitaker, all of whom read the manuscript in various stages of preparation. Their suggestions have resulted in many major modifications of style, organization, and content.

The few names singled out here and in the text cannot begin to suggest the depth of my gratitude to hundreds of others: to generations of Shakespeare scholars, with whom I may sometimes disagree but for whom I have continually deepening respect; to my colleagues, who have encouraged me by their interest and stimulated me by their challenges; to my students, who have contributed not only their enthusiasm and their curiosity but also their healthy skepticism and common sense.

To Muriel Davison of Stanford University Press I owe a special debt for her meticulous and devoted job of editing.

I also wish to thank the staffs of the Huntington Library and the Stanford Library for their courteous help.

Quotations from Shakespeare are based upon the edition of Professor Hardin Craig (Chicago, 1951).

# Contents

# Introduction

The present investigation began quite by chance over a decade ago. At the time I was analyzing Shakespeare's use of the doctrine of repentance and was struck by the profound exposition of orthodox Christian concepts in the Prayer Scene of *Hamlet*. Suddenly, for the first time, I was appalled at Hamlet's reason for refusing to kill Claudius at prayer. I had always heard, and believed, that the desire to damn one's victim was merely a convention of Elizabethan revenge plays, a convention that Shakespeare's audience accepted without question. But was it possible, I now wondered, that Shakespeare expected his audience to approve of Hamlet's pagan vindictiveness when he had explicitly thrown the scene into a Christian context?

One question prompted another. At the time, I was buried in Elizabethan Christianity and knew that all the voices of Church and State inveighed against revenge. At the same time, I had always heard that revenge was to be accepted as a "sacred duty" in *Hamlet,* that the play's revenge code reflected a theatrical tradition that was frankly opposed to all religious, moral, and legal tenets. I had believed, in short, that the Elizabethan checked his morality at the door of the theater and that we should too. But is this possible when the play is packed with Christian references, when the Ghost is put into a Christian context—when, in fact, all evidence indicates that Shakespeare was alone responsible for putting the old barbaric story into a Christian framework?

At the time, these were but nagging questions that had to be set aside while I returned to my original subject: Shakespeare's use of Christian doctrine. In order to gain perspective, I turned to the medieval mystery cycles, and, over a period of several years, worked up to 1610, reading every play that might be relevant. When I came to the revenge plays, I was thrust back into the *Hamlet* quandary. My survey revealed not one example of a noble revenger who sought the damnation of his victim, not one example of a play in which revenge was clearly portrayed as a moral duty.

Gradually I was led to an uneasy suspicion. Might it be possible that the Elizabethan, even in the theater, felt the same qualms about murder that we feel? We have long assumed that "the first premise of *Hamlet* is that sons must avenge their fathers."[1] Is it possible, however, that Hamlet's implicit duty is *not* to kill Claudius? At first the idea seemed ridiculous to me, as it probably will to most readers. As Bradley notes, any theory suggesting that *Hamlet*'s audience is to view revenge as immoral "requires us to suppose that, when the Ghost enjoins Hamlet to avenge the murder of his father, it is laying on him a duty which *we* are to understand to be no duty but the very reverse."[2] Exactly. That is just what such a theory would require, and Bradley understandably dismissed it as a patent absurdity. Is the meaning of the action not clear? Hamlet prudently realizes that he must determine whether the Ghost is a good or evil spirit; he tests the Ghost and proves that it tells the truth; therefore, the Ghost is a good spirit. Thus it stands. Nonetheless, I now began to take serious notice of an apparent contradiction that had always bothered me. In *Macbeth*, Banquo warns that the instruments of darkness can tell us truths in order to win us to our harm. Was this idea new to Shakespeare in 1605? And would a spirit of health lay a sacred duty on a beloved son that leads to the destruction of two entire families? It became increasingly apparent that, in Dover Wilson's words, "the Ghost is the linchpin of *Hamlet*."[3] With these questions in mind, I plunged into Elizabethan ghost lore and the present project was under way.

---

[1] Harold Jenkins, "Hamlet and Ophelia," *Proceedings of the British Academy*, XLIX (1963), 137. Two early critics who questioned this premise were Hermann Ulrici in 1839 and Charlton Lewis in 1907. A few ambiguous hints in G. Wilson Knight's *The Wheel of Fire* suggest doubts, but it remained for Harold Goddard to challenge the premise in extended argument, in *The Meaning of Shakespeare* (1951). A similar challenge underlies the studies of Roy Walker, *The Time Is Free*; John Vyvyan, *The Shakespearean Ethic*; and L. C. Knights, *An Approach to Hamlet*.

[2] A. C. Bradley, *Shakespearean Tragedy*, 2d ed. (London, 1952), p. 100.

[3] *What Happens in Hamlet*, 3d ed. (Cambridge, Eng., 1961), p. 52.

I have outlined the evolution of this study in detail in order to help the reader over a rather formidable hurdle. As a glance at the Contents page will show, this book will retrace the path taken by my own investigation: first, defining conventional attitudes toward revenge in Shakespeare's day; next, attempting to determine audience attitudes toward revenge in the plays of Shakespeare and his contemporaries; then testing the Ghost according to criteria familiar to both Protestants and Catholics; and, finally, analyzing the play itself in the light of some surprising discoveries. The heart of the study of course lies in Part II. All of Part I is concerned with historical materials extrinsic to *Hamlet*.

Many readers may be loath to embark on yet another excursion into the "Elizabethan world picture." In the last few years such perceptive scholars as G. Wilson Knight and Robert Ornstein have launched an effective attack on the historical approach to Shakespearean criticism. Ornstein in particular has argued persuasively that historical criticism is invalid if it leads us to judgments of a work of art that conflict with our immediate intuitive impressions.[4] For this reason, it may not be amiss to anticipate the conclusions of the present study in the hope of putting Part I into perspective.

Despite the fact that one-third of this book is concerned with Elizabethan attitudes and codes and conventions, the investigation has led me to the conviction that our truest guide to understanding *Hamlet* is our intuitive response. This statement, and the epigraph to Part I, will probably seem ironic in light of the material to be covered. If historical facts are not essential to interpretation, why have they been analyzed in such detail? Only to correct a series of misconceptions.

In theory, a person who knows nothing of Elizabethan ethics or demonology or dramatic traditions should respond to a good production of *Hamlet* quite as naturally as did a spectator in the Globe. Unfortunately, no such person exists today, at least not in the English-speaking world. Our culture is permeated by the *Hamlet* myth. I would venture to say that no one can attend a performance of the play without knowing at least some of the traditional assumptions. Almost everyone enters the theater believing that Hamlet is excessively mel-

---

[4] "Historical Criticism and the Interpretation of Shakespeare," *Shakespeare Quarterly*, X (1959), 3–9.

ancholy, that the Ghost is his father, that the Ghost tells the truth, and that Hamlet is duty-bound to kill Claudius. Even a typical high-school student, reading the play for the first time, has surely heard of the "melancholy Dane," a man so paralyzed by his psychological problems that he "could not make up his mind" to do what any healthy, well-adjusted son should do. He has probably heard, if not himself mimicked, that morbid bit of posing (for so it seems in the popular tradition), "Alas poor Yorick," moaned in dismally funereal tones. As to the crucial soliloquy, who in the Western world has not heard "To be or not to be" droned in a sepulchral voice? In the popular imagination, the role of Hamlet is identified with an actor whose idea of profundity is dreary monotony and whose favorite pose is that of the tortured neurotic contemplating suicide. With all of these images and echoes so firmly established, can anyone respond to the play completely naturally? Moreover, really good productions of *Hamlet* are rare. Directors have long taken their cue from an established critical tradition that assumes we must ignore our contemporary moral response when approaching the revenge play, that both popular conviction and dramatic convention in Shakespeare's day unquestioningly approved of revenge as an obligation of honor that superseded all ethical considerations. The dominant critical tradition has explicitly told us: "Forget your own ethical code. The study of certain facts indicates that it is irrelevant in *Hamlet*." The facts, I submit, tell us exactly the opposite.

The purpose of Part I, then, is not to establish a necessary "Elizabethan perspective." On the contrary, it is solely to correct a series of faulty historical assumptions. If a reader could approach *Hamlet* with no preconceptions about its central ethical issue, he could, in fact, skip Part I entirely. The average reader, however, will encounter in Part II an approach to the play that will strike him as irresponsible scholarship unless he first accepts, or at least is willing to consider, some new assumptions about Elizabethan attitudes toward revenge, about dramatic conventions of the revenge play, and about the nature of audience response.

At the end of each chapter in Part I is a brief summary of these new assumptions. Unless the reader is particularly interested in historical backgrounds, I suggest that he turn immediately to each of these three concluding sections (beginning on pages 32, 70, and 93). If he suspects that the assumptions are based on incomplete or faulty evidence, he will wish to check for himself the detailed evidence in each chapter. If, however, he feels comfortable with the perspective established in each summary, I urge that he skip all the background material and move immediately to Part II and the discussion of *Hamlet*.

 PART I

# Elizabethan Attitudes toward Revenge

*I have always suspected that the reading is right, which requires many words to prove it wrong.*

Samuel Johnson

# CHAPTER I

# The Ethical Dilemma

Any critical study of *Hamlet* must at some time face a fundamental question: is the Ghost's command morally binding? Since the ethical question underlies the basic dramatic question it cannot be avoided. Is the play predicated on the assumption that Hamlet is morally obligated to revenge his father's death? With few exceptions, critics have long agreed that in Shakespeare's time the answer was an unqualified "yes," and that the modern reader must adjust to this Elizabethan premise even if it runs counter to his own ethical intuitions. To this day, many studies of *Hamlet* echo Bradley's dictum that—"whatever we in the twentieth century may think"—the "conventional moral ideas" of Shakespeare's audience endorsed blood revenge as an unquestioned duty.[1]

The persistence of this traditional assumption into our own time might, at first, seem surprising, for several modern scholars—notably Lily Bess Campbell, Willard Farnham, and Fredson Bowers—have firmly established that spokesmen for Elizabethan orthodoxy unanimously condemned private revenge.[2] Although their findings have borne fruit in some reevaluations of the revenge tradition and of

[1] *Shakespearean Tragedy*, 2d ed. (London, 1952), pp. 99–100. Northrop Frye's view of revenge as a "moral imperative" often endorsed by "the sanctions of religion" (*Fools of Time* [Toronto, 1967], p. 28) underlies such phrases as "pious task," "clear-cut filial obligation," and "imperative duty," encountered in many recent works. For similar views, see, among others, G. B. Harrison, *Shakespeare's Tragedies* (London, 1951), p. 90, and Harold Jenkins, "The Tragedy of Revenge in Shakespeare and Webster," *Shakespeare Survey*, XIV (1961), 47.

[2] Campbell, "Theories of Revenge in Elizabethan England," *Modern Philology*, XXVIII (1931), 281–96, and *Shakespeare's Tragic Heroes: Slaves of Passion* (Cambridge, Eng., 1930), pp. 3–24; Farnham, *The Medieval Heritage of Elizabethan Tragedy* (Berkeley, Calif., 1936), pp. 343–51; Bowers, *Elizabethan Revenge Tragedy, 1587–1642* (Princeton, N.J., 1940), pp. 3–61.

*Hamlet,*[3] most critics still hold that the average Elizabethan believed a son morally bound to revenge his father's death. The most thoughtful of these critics have not ignored the orthodox code; they have insisted, rather, that a popular code approving revenge had far more influence than the code of the Elizabethan Establishment.

A synthesis of their views might read as follows: "To be sure, the Establishment condemned private revenge, but history denies that its campaign had widespread influence. The tumultuous temper of the Elizabethan age stood in direct opposition to official platitudes about obedience, humility, resignation, patience. Far more influential than the orthodox code of the Establishment were two popular codes that placed the demands of revenge above the strictures of religion and law: an aristocratic counter-code of honor and a long-established folk code rooted deep in racial hungers. The popular Elizabethan revenge play arose in a theatrical tradition that appealed to popular, not official, attitudes. The Establishment's condemnation of those popular attitudes is surely no guide in determining either the playwright's intention or the audience's response."[4]

The argument is persuasive and has found many able proponents. The present investigation suggests, however, that the "popular" attitude toward revenge was far more complex than has been generally assumed. Popular literature and dramatic conventions indicate that the orthodox code did in fact have widespread influence. At the same time, they indicate that the average spectator at a revenge play was probably trapped in an ethical dilemma—a dilemma, to put it most simply, between what he believed and what he felt.

In order to define this dilemma, we must begin with what our average Elizabethan was taught. For the moment, let us set aside the question of whether or not he believed his teachers. Our sole concern at present is to become thoroughly familiar with the orthodox code—its ideas, its diction, its recurrent images. Only when we become alert to

[3] See, for example, Roy Walker, *The Time Is Out of Joint* (London, 1948); Harold C. Goddard, *The Meaning of Shakespeare* (Chicago, 1951); G. R. Elliott, *Scourge and Minister* (Durham, N.C., 1951); Paul N. Siegel, *Shakespearean Tragedy and the Elizabethan Compromise* (New York, 1957); Harold S. Wilson, *On the Design of Shakespearian Tragedy* (Toronto, 1957); John Vyvyan, *The Shakespearean Ethic* (London, 1959); Irving Ribner, *Patterns in Shakespearian Tragedy* (New York, 1960); and several significant articles by Bowers himself.

[4] I trust this is a fair treatment of the position taken by Helen Gardner, Hiram Haydn, Robert Ornstein, and several others. Specific points in the argument are treated in detail later in this chapter.

the language of orthodoxy will we be able to determine whether or not its words are echoed in the theater.

Our average Elizabethan could not have failed to hear the voice of the Establishment. Throughout the last half of the sixteenth century, Church, State, and conventional morality fulminated against private revenge in any form and under any circumstances. The vigorous campaign may perhaps best be seen as a response to the natural energies and contentiousness of the age, an age of new and unsettled political loyalties, new economic and class struggles, new fears, new hungers, new hopes. Conflicts were inevitable.[5] More specifically, the Establishment's denunciation of revenge was related to its recurrent fears of civil disorder. As Bacon was later to argue in prosecuting a dueling case, private revenge could lead to quarrels, thence to public tumult, thence to dissension between families, and thence to national quarrels.[6] Since punishment was the prerogative of the State, every possible argument was induced to convince the private citizen that he must leave revenge to God, and thus to the magistrates, His appointed agents.

The progressive intensity of the propaganda campaign reflects concern over a growing problem. In 1598, Sir Richard Barckley mourned the lost virtue of the previous age and the disparity between the professions of his contemporaries and their actions: "The trueth was never more knowne, and never lesse regarded: never better taught, and never worse followed.... All praise patience, and yet who resisteth the sweet passion of revenge?"[7] Again and again, moralists recognize that they are struggling against a powerful foe, for "to the nature of man, nothing is more Sweete then the passion of revenge."[8] The *lex talionis* has its roots deep in instinct: "Our corrupt nature, which ever striveth against thy blessed will, seeketh all means possible to be revenged, to requite tooth for tooth and eye for eye, to render evil for

---

[5] The violence of the age is vividly documented by Lawrence Stone in *The Crisis of the Aristocracy: 1558–1641* (Oxford, 1965), pp. 223ff.

[6] Bowers, *Elizabethan Revenge Tragedy*, pp. 11–12. The same concern underlies the important homily "Against Contention and Brawling." The second part is based entirely on two Scriptural texts customarily cited in arguments against revenge: Romans 12:19–21 and Deuteronomy 32:35. *Certaine Sermons or Homilies Appoynted to be read in Churches* (London, 1635), I, 92–96.

[7] *A Discourse of the Felicitie of Man: or his Summum bonum* (London, 1598), pp. 545–46. (When quoting from Renaissance works, I have retained the original punctuation and spelling, save that I have normalized the *u*'s, *v*'s, *i*'s, and *j*'s and have expanded contractions.)

[8] Geoffrey Fenton, *Golden Epistles* (London, 1577), fol. 40$^r$.

evil, when vengeance is thine and thou wilt reward; and by this means we grievously offend thee, and break the order of charity, and the bond of peace."[9] Recognition that the passion for revenge was a special problem in the period is reflected in Holland's translation of Plutarch's *Morals* (1603). Plutarch's essay arguing that man should not be moved to revenge when he sees God deferring punishment is deemed so important by Holland that his prefixed summary stresses its significance: "This treatise . . . of all others is most excellent, and deserveth to be read and perused over againe in these wretched daies, wherein Epicurisme beareth up the head as high as at any time before."[10]

Indeed, revenge became such a major concern that we often find it included in traditional lists of the sins: "We must purifie and cleanse our minds from our corrupt and uncleane affections. . . . They stirre up pride, envy, hatred, malice, desire of revenge, feare, and such like perturbations and unquietnesse of the mind."[11] Of special interest is Timothy Bright's list of the particular temptations Satan offers the melancholic: "Of this kinde are certaine blasphemies suggested of the Devill, and laying of violent handes of them selves, or upon others neither moved therto by hate or malice: or any occasion of revenge: of the same sort is the dispaire and distrust of gods mercy, and grace."[12] At times it almost seems as if revenge was considered the eighth Deadly Sin, and even, together with despair and suicide, one of the "sins against the Holy Ghost."

Revenge was a reprehensible blasphemy, as the most frequently cited Scriptural text made clear: "Dearly beloved, avenge not yourselves, but rather give place unto wrath: for it is written, Vengeance is mine; I will repay, saith the Lord."[13] Echoes of this divine command and promise reverberate throughout Elizabethan literature, and not merely in didactic works. It is heard as a direct quotation in Hieronimo's *"Vindicta mihi,"* and is paraphrased in John of Gaunt's

---

[9] Thomas Becon, "The Flower of Godly Prayers" (1551), *Prayers and Other Pieces of Thomas Becon,* ed. John Ayre for the Parker Society (Cambridge, Eng., 1844), p. 38.

[10] *The Philosophie, commonlie called, The Morals,* trans. Philemon Holland (London, 1603), p. 538.

[11] Barckley, *Felicitie of Man,* p. 472.

[12] *A Treatise of Melancholie* (1586), reprinted by the Facsimile Text Society (New York, 1940), p. 228.

[13] Romans 12:19. Deuteronomy 32:35 and Hebrews 10:30 were also frequently cited.

"God's is the quarrel." For private men to take revenge is not merely, like Lucifer, to seek to rival God; it is actually "to usurp Christ's office," "as if God had resigned his own right into their hands." Such rebellion against Divine Providence shows that man but little knows himself or his relation to his Maker. "Who art thou that so judgest another's servant? Is it not to his own master only to whom he stands or falls? Who art thou that takest such severity upon thee? that dealest so unmercifully with thy brother? He is a sinner: so thou either art, or hast been, or mayest be: judge therefore thyself, try and examine thine own works."[14]

The primary argument against revenge, therefore, was that the revenger endangered his own soul. No matter how righteous a man might think his motives, the act of revenge would inevitably make him as evil as his injurer in the eyes of God. "In so going about to revenge evill, we shew our selves to be evill, and, while we will punnish, and revenge another mans folly, we double, and augment our owne folly."[15] A revenger may honestly think he seeks justice, but the nature of revenge makes justice impossible. "It is a thing ... altogether to be detested, that thou shouldest revenge another mans maliciousnes with thine owne maliciousnes; & appointing thy selfe Judge in thine own cause, shouldest chastice another mans injustice with thine owne."[16] Not only is the revenger guilty of blasphemy and malice, he cuts himself off from the possibility of forgiveness and thus is damned forever:

For so doth Ecclesiasticus well teach us: "He that seeketh vengeance shall find vengeance of the Lord; and he will surely keep his sins. Forgive thy neighbour the hurt that he hath done to thee: so shall thy sins be forgiven thee also, when thou prayest. Should a man bear hatred against man, and desire forgiveness of the Lord? He will shew no mercy to a man that is like himself; and will he ask forgiveness of his own sins? If he that is but flesh nourish hatred, and ask pardon of God, who will entreat for his sins?"[17]

---

14 Edwin Sandys, *The Sermons* ... (1585), ed. John Ayre for the Parker Society (Cambridge, Eng., 1841), pp. 289, 228.

15 *Certaine Sermons*, I, 93.

16 Luis de Granada, *The Sinners Guyde*, trans. Francis Meres (London, 1598), p. 498.

17 Sandys, *Sermons*, p. 229. The implication that revenge was thus an unforgivable sin would seem to be homiletic license. When discussing repentance, all Elizabethan preachers insisted that no sin was too great to be forgiven, even the much discussed blasphemy against the Holy Ghost cryptically referred to in Matthew 12:31, Mark 3:29, and Luke 12:10.

Sinning man should meditate on this warning every time he says the Lord's Prayer, for in the sixth petition, "I am taught ... to see how thy children not only forgive all that offend them, but also pray for the pardoning of the offences of their enemies, and such as offend them; so far are they from maliciousness, pride, revengement, &c."[18] Eternal damnation was not the only penalty for revenge. An age devoted to temporal pursuits was constantly warned that there were penalties in this world as well. The ravages of revenge appear most clearly in the deterioration of the mind. At first, the revenger becomes distracted, shutting everything but revenge out of his consciousness; he "mindeth none other thinge, which reason and experience doth wel declare."[19] As he gives rein to his impatience, he "is therewith abstracte from reason and tourned in to a monstruous figure."[20] "To be short, after that anger hath once got the bridle at will, the whole mind and judgement is so blinded & caried headlong, that an angry man thinkes of nothing but of revenge, insomuch that he forgetteth himselfe, and careth not what he doth, or what harm will light upon himselfe in so doing, so that he may be avenged." At this point reason is totally eclipsed, and "a man in such a case is not much unlike to a mad dog," finally sinking to the most bestial crueltics.[21] Indeed, Gentillet insists that the revenger sinks even lower than wild animals:

Surely [revenge] is not onely farre from all Christian pietie, but also from all humanitie and common sence; yea, brute beasts, which have no reason,

---

[18] John Bradford, "Meditation on the Lord's Prayer" (1562), *The Writings* ..., ed. Aubrey Townsend for the Parker Society (Cambridge, Eng., 1848), I, 133.

[19] Jerome Cardan, *Cardanus Comforte*, trans. Thomas Bedingfeld (London, 1573), fol. L8ᵛ.

[20] Sir Thomas Elyot, *The Governour* (1531), ed. Ernest Rhys (London, 1937), p. 235.

[21] Peter de la Primaudaye, *The French Academie*, trans. T. B[owes] (London, 1618), pp. 497, 506. The four parts were published in translation in several editions, beginning with Part I in 1586, Part II in 1594, and Part III in 1601. In 1618 all three parts were reprinted and a fourth part added. All citations in this study are drawn from the first two parts as reprinted in the 1618 edition.

This compendium of Renaissance ethics is extremely valuable in determining norm attitudes (e.g., the humanist's distinction between Christian and pagan Stoicism, discussed below on pp. 11–12). Throughout, the author takes every opportunity to warn against private revenge. Especially pertinent is the discussion of patience in Part I, Chapter 29, and three essays treating revenge from three different perspectives: Chapter 36 in Part I ("Of an Enemy, of Injurie, and of Revenge"), and Chapters 55 and 58 in Part II ("Of anger, and of the vehemencie and violence thereof ... : of the affection of revenge ..." and "Of Revenge, Crueltie, and Rage").

are not so unreasonable: for a dog which we have offended, will be appeased with a piece of bread ... as much will an horse do and an oxe ...: and for such as say, that vengeance is lawfull by right of nature, are greatly deceived, as the beasts named before doe shew.[22]

Closely allied to dangers to the mind are dangers to the body. Psychological treatises by Bright, Grimestone, and Burton present the typical Renaissance view that physical health is dependent on the moderation of passion. La Primaudaye also connects the two; he warns that a pale man is more dangerous than a red-faced one, because the revenger's anger makes the blood leave the face and rush to the heart. Moreover, vehement anger often provokes a frenzy or the falling sickness.[23] These beliefs may underlie Caesar's fear of "pale Cassius" (*Antony and Cleopatra,* II.vi.15) and Othello's seizure. Any satisfaction a man may derive from punishing his enemy is more than outweighed by the utter misery he brings on himself:

[Revenge] maketh thee take no quiet rest in thine house, and thou hast no assurance to bee in the fieldes: shee tosseth thee with continuall cares, she tormenteth thee with ten thousand feares, shee carrieth thy judgement and reason cleane out of their proper seats, and playeth the tyrant over them. When thou thinkest thy selfe safest, then shee threatneth thee most: shee is importunate with thee, she gnaweth thee to the hart, she devoureth thee.[24]

If the potential revenger is undeterred by the threat of eternal damnation and of physical and mental illness, then, says the eminently moral Cardan, let him consider self-interest. "What can bee moore foolishe," he asks, "then to seeke revenge, when safelye it can not bee perfourmed?" Even if a man could get away with it, let him consider his reputation, for "the glory gotten by forgeving of foes, whom thou may oppresse is greater, then the pleasure of revenge."[25]

---

22 Innocent Gentillet, *A Discourse ... Against Nicholas Machiavell the Florentine,* trans. Simon Patericke (London, 1602), Part III, Maxim 6, p. 178. Didactic enthusiasm often trapped earnest writers into contradictions. Arguing that beasts live peaceably and therefore that man, who has no natural weapons such as horns, has even more obviously been created for peace, Luis de Granada then forgets where he started and adds: "Remember that anger and desire of revenge is proper unto wilde beasts." *The Sinners Guyde,* p. 407.

23 *The French Academie,* pp. 497–98.

24 B. de Loque, *Discourses of Warre and Single Combat,* trans. John Eliot (London, 1591), p. 54.

25 *Cardanus Comforte,* fols. L7ʳ–7ᵛ.

In short, Elizabethan moralists condemned revenge as illegal, blasphemous, immoral, irrational, unnatural, and unhealthy—not to mention unsafe. Moreover, not only did revenge violate religion, law, morality, and common sense, it was also thoroughly un-English. Gentillet's translator prays fervently that God will preserve England from the revolting practices of the Italians, for "indeed, there is nothing wherein they take greater delectation, pleasure, and contentment, than to execute a vengeance."[26] Bloodcurdling tales of "Italianate" revenge had trained Shakespeare's audience to shudder at the fiendishness of delayed vengeance and dissembling intrigue, practices befitting a nation that had produced such a monster as Machiavelli.

What recourse, then, does the orthodox code offer a man who has been grievously injured? He can take his case to the law—provided, however, he does so for the right reasons. "We must take heed that we go not to avenge ourselves upon our neighbour, with a vengeable heart. . . . When we will go to the law, we must beware that it be done charitably, not with a vengeable mind; for whosoever seeketh to be avenged, he shall not be blessed of God."[27] A man who institutes legal action out of anger and desire for retaliation may operate within the civil law, but he violates the laws of God and nature, and will suffer the same physical, mental, and spiritual penalties as the private revenger.

But what can the injured party do if he has no recourse to law? The orthodox code offers only one answer: nothing. "It will greatly help us, if when wee are mooved with anger, wee stay our tongue a certaine space, and delay a little while our owne revenge. For it is very certaine that a man promiseth, speaketh, and doth many things in his anger, which afterward he wisheth had never beene in his thought."[28] The wise man will first delay. Then he will proceed slowly, without anger, to take whatever steps justice demands.[29] If the stringent requirements of justice forbid any further action, his solace—and indeed his joy—must be patience.

The arguments for Christian patience in the face of adversity are too familiar to require summarizing here. A few recurring points,

---

[26] *Against Machiavell,* Part III, Maxim 6, p. 177.
[27] Hugh Latimer, "On the Gospel for All Saints" (1552), *Sermons,* ed. George Elwes Corrie for the Parker Society (Cambridge, Eng., 1844), p. 481.
[28] La Primaudaye, *The French Academie,* pp. 129–30.
[29] Plutarch, *The Philosophie,* p. 546.

however, have special relevance to the situation of the hero in Elizabethan revenge plays. Faced with an outright murderer who continues to thrive, how can a would-be revenger possibly convince himself that patience serves the ends of justice? The answer is hard. True justice demands that man's first concern should be not punishing the sin, but saving the sinner. Indeed, says Elyot, "the best waye to be advenged is so to contemne Injurie and rebuke, and lyve with suche honestie, that the doer shall at the laste be therof a shamed."[30] The just man must wait patiently, disdaining the injury and holding only charity in his heart, in the hope that eventually the sinner will repent and amend his evil life.[31]

But what if the evildoer is clearly beyond hope of redemption? Then waiting for him to repent is at best a frustrating discipline. Cardan offers an almost childishly pat answer: Rest assured that your enemy will die young or at least be miserable, for it is manifest that evil cannot be happy.[32] Other writers said much the same thing, but said it more thoughtfully. Plutarch devotes an entire chapter to this worrisome question: "How it commeth, that the divine Justice deferreth otherwhiles the punishment of wicked persons." His answer is that God begins punishing sin immediately, with "lamentable calamities, many terrible frights, fearfull perturbations and passions of the spirit, remorse of conscience, desperate repentance, and continuall troubles and unquietnesse."[33] Conscience is an inexorable judge that can never be stilled. A villain may refuse to follow its dictates, but he cannot ignore its torments. Thus even the most corrupt sinner must be left to Heaven's judgment.

Despite assurances that the wicked would eventually be punished in God's own time and way, no thoughtful Renaissance writer suggested that patience was easy. Few were able to accept the argument of the ancient Stoics, who required "such exactnesse and perfection ... that they would have a noble heart to be no otherwise touched with

30 *The Governour*, p. 236.
31 Plutarch, *The Philosophie*, p. 546.
32 *Cardanus Comforte*, fol. M5ʳ. Despite the respectful attention paid to Cardan, I find much in his consolations so superficially conventional as to be simpleminded.
33 Plutarch, p. 546. One of Plutarch's reasons for rejecting revenge is that one should stretch the vicious on the rack of life as long as possible. Moralists realized that patience had its human limits, and by interesting twists of reasoning tried to offer comfort. Here Plutarch seems to appeal to the vindictive malice of the injured party, while at the same time insisting that he should feel only charity for his injurer.

adversitie than with prosperitie.... Whereby it seemeth that these Philosophers delighted in painting out a picture of such patience, as never was, nor shall bee among men, except first they should be unclothed of all humane nature, or become as blockish and sencelesse as a stone." In thus distinguishing between Stoic endurance and Christian patience, La Primaudaye insists that man cannot, indeed should not, erase all traces of passion in himself, "for the abolishing of desire maketh the soule without motion, and without joy even in honest things."[34] The truly virtuous man may feel his injury deeply, but he subjects his fury to his reason.

No matter how grievously he is injured, the Christian must recognize that adversities—whether inflicted by man, nature, or Fortune—are inevitable, and that their remedy lies in the hands of Providence. "But he that is vexed with all these adversities, and will make head against them and remedie them, lette hym bee assured, that even then shall he laye the plotte of the ende, and dispatch of his life, when he begins to put order to these incurable harmes."[35] To be sure, the Christian must fight evil, but his proper enemy is his own sin, not the incurable ills that attend his life. He should welcome adversity as a loving gift of God. "Therefore true patience which wee ought to imbrace in all things, not as compelled and of necessitie, but cheerefully and as restoring in our welfare, is a moderation and tolerance of our evils, which ... cloth us in the meane while with a spirituall joy ... that in the end it worketh in us an affection of piety and godlinesse, joyned with a free and cheerefull mind."[36]

Perhaps the most moving appeal is that heard in Portia's mercy speech and in Isabella's plea to Angelo for her brother's life: he who "disdains" injuries and embraces patience with willing mind and charitable heart is "moste lyke unto God.... Whoe, or what is of greater force then God and Nature? and yet they delighte not in Revenge."[37] Patience is not merely the refusal to punish injury with further injury. It is spiritually active: the joyful giving of mercy and forgiveness. This appeal finds its most vivid expression in the recur-

---

[34] La Primaudaye, p. 127. This important distinction is clarified by John F. Danby in a valuable essay on *King Lear* in *Poets on Fortune's Hill* (London, 1952), pp. 108–27.

[35] Fenton, *Golden Epistles,* fols. 43ʳ–43ᵛ.

[36] La Primaudaye, p. 128. Note the parallel to Edgar's "Bear free and patient thoughts."

[37] *Cardanus Comforte,* fols. M2ʳ–2ᵛ.

ring example of Christ on the Cross. "After this manner ought all Christians to be affected, not to revenge, but ready to forgive; not to curse, but to bless; not to render evil for evil, but to overcome evil with goodness, leaving all vengeance to God, which saith: 'Vengeance is mine: I will reward.' "[38]

The orthodox position, then, is clear. Equally clear is the almost unanimous agreement in extant documents of the Elizabethan period. The code is upheld by Church and State, by preachers and philosophers, by sophisticated thinkers and men of common sense. But did the official code stand unchallenged? Fredson Bowers—along with Hiram Haydn, Curtis Watson, and many others—argues that a counter-code arose: "There can be little question that many an Elizabethan gentleman disregarded without a qualm the ethical and religious opinion of his day which condemned private revenge, and felt obliged by the more powerful code of honor to revenge personally any injury offered him."[39] Critics have generally agreed that such a counter-code led the Elizabethan audience to regard private revenge as an obligation of honor rather than an offense against God, as a virtue rather than a sin. There are several important objections to this view. On the simplest level, even if we grant that many members of the nobility adhered to a highly sophisticated counter-code of honor, can we assume that it was accepted or even recognized by the majority of the theatergoing public? It may be argued that Shakespeare and his contemporaries appealed primarily to the "judicious," not to the groundling. Undoubtedly there is some truth in this argument; any serious playwright knows that his audiences represent many degrees of comprehension. But is it conceivable that Elizabethan playwrights expected different members of their audiences to apply diametrically opposed moral judgments?

A more important objection, however, is that much of the most frequently cited evidence is of doubtful value in establishing that a counter-code was widespread even among the Elizabethan nobility. A case in point is the frequent reference to treatises on dueling. Although sev-

[38] *The Catechism of Thomas Becon* (1560), ed. John Ayre for the Parker Society (Cambridge, Eng., 1844), p. 179. See also the homily "For Good Friday," over half of which pictures Christ as an example of patience, charity, and mercy. *Certaine Sermons*, II, 175–80.

[39] Bowers, *Elizabethan Revenge Tragedy*, p. 37.

eral such treatises were published during the 1590's, dueling itself was not recognized as a serious problem in England until after the accession of James I and the influx of the Scots.[40] Material indicating an influential code of honor and arms comes not from England but from the Continent.[41] Moreover, arguments offered by apologists for dueling are scarcely proof that their views were commonly accepted. Such writers as Sir William Segar are not disinterested observers of the social conscience; they are propagandists endeavoring to change opinion. But even if dueling were widely accepted as morally justifiable, such evidence would be irrelevant to the immediate problem of the revenge play—the private killing of a defenseless man. Dueling is a highly conventionalized form of open combat between opponents of equal rank and training, equally forewarned and forearmed. No apologist for dueling ever argues that outright revenge murder is justified.

Indeed, the Elizabethan tracts on dueling offer some of the most emphatic arguments *against* revenge. The influential Vincent Saviolo, a fencing master, states explicitly that "Combat was ordayned for justifieng of a truth, and not to laye a waie for one man to revenge him of another, for the punishment of suche thinges resteth in the Prince." Under no circumstances does Saviolo justify blood revenge. It is true, as many have noted, that Saviolo sets aside "trecherie, or rape, or such like villainies" as base offenses that must be revenged, but his prescribed course of action would require the discipline of a saint. The "revenge," even for heinous crimes, must take the form of open combat in the lists, and the challenger's motives must be totally disinterested. He must proceed without hatred, solely "for love of vertue, and regarde of the universall good and publique profite." He must have no personal concern for the outcome—merely the wish to put himself

---

[40] Dueling never became a threat to order as it did in France. Not until the second decade of the seventeenth century did dueling reach its peak and the Crown become sufficiently disturbed to issue a proclamation against it. Even in the years between 1610 and 1619, only thirty-three deaths by dueling were recorded. For a full discussion, see Stone, *The Crisis of the Aristocracy*, pp. 242–50.

[41] Montaigne, for example, notes the irony involved in having a separate code for the nobility, so that "by the law and right of armes he that putteth up an injurie shall be degraded of honour and nobilitie; and he that revengeth himselfe of it, shall by the civill Law incurre a capitall punishment." *Essays*, trans. John Florio (1603), World's Classics (Oxford, 1904–6), I, 123. La Primaudaye also notes an influential—and, he thinks, dangerous—code practiced by many of the nobility (*The French Academie*, p. 129). I have found no such statement by an English writer of the Elizabethan period.

at the disposal of Providence. He must "be as it were, the minister to execute Gods devine pleasure."[42]

Sir William Segar's defense of blood revenge seems to be an exception, but his *Book of Honour and Armes* (1590) is hedged with qualifications and tangled with contradictions. On the one hand, Segar freely admits that Christian law requires the patient suffering of all wrongs and thus forbids single combat; on the other, he promises to show "the order of revenge and repulse, according unto Christian knowledge."[43] In the dedication, he insists that all martial minds scorn the infamous man who refuses to revenge an injury by single combat; in the text, he insists that a man should resort to trial by arms not for revenge but only for the discovery and justification of the truth.[44] The most flagrant contradiction in the work is found in the two passages most frequently cited. Surprisingly, in the midst of eminently solid arguments against revenging even the basest injury, he writes, "In mine opinion . . . for revenge of such cowardlie and beastiall offenses, it is allowable to use any advantage or subtiltie, according to the Italian proverbe . . . which is, that one advantage requireth another, and one treason may be with another acquitted."[45] In context, we may think he is arguing only that in such cases dueling is allowable, but he later repeats, unequivocally, that it then rests "in the choyce of the Injured, either to be revenged by challenge, which is more honorable, or with the like advantage."[46] Undeniably, here is an argument for blood revenge even by murder.

[42] *Vicentio Saviolo his Practise* (London, 1595), fols. Z4$^r$, P1$^v$, Y4$^v$, and Z1$^v$. Interestingly, the devoted martialist B. de Loque goes even further. In his *Discourses of Warre and Single Combat*, he flatly denies that there is any valid ground for private combat, and his detailed rebuttal of all possible arguments provides an excellent summary of the orthodox code. "Whosoever doth revenge himselfe, committeth sacriledge, appropriating unto himselfe that, which belongeth by right unto God himselfe. . . . If he who hateth his neighbour be a murtherer, how shall not he be one, that hating his neighbour, lifteth up his hand to be revenged of him?" (pp. 52–53). True honor is found only in obedience to God, in subduing the passions to reason. Though Saviolo would allow the combat, his arguments against revenge would be exactly the same.

[43] *Book of Honour and Armes,* fol. A3$^r$.

[44] *Ibid.,* fol. A2$^v$ and *passim.* Segar disallows the duel in cases of crime for several reasons: first, the dishonor of the injurer is manifest and thus needs no proof; second, a dishonorable injury places no burden of honor on the injured; third, "the punishment of wilfull acts contrarie to peace, is by civill authoritie to be performed"; fourth, by challenging such a criminal, "a man of good reputation dooth equall himselfe unto persons utterly unworthie." *Ibid.,* pp. 20, 31, 37.

[45] *Ibid.,* p. 20.

[46] *Ibid.,* p. 39.

We should not, however, overestimate the importance of these two sentences. Segar himself considers private revenge less honorable than open combat, and says that revengers inevitably put themselves on a level with their "utterly unworthie" victims. Furthermore, he stipulates that his defense of the right to take private revenge is his own opinion, thus suggesting that he stands against the majority. Apparently he does. The opinion not only of preachers and philosophers but even of worldly men like Saviolo, de Loque, and Count Romei is overwhelmingly against him.

If we eliminate apologies for dueling as valid evidence of a counter-code justifying revenge, what remains? Hiram Haydn's influential study, *The Counter-Renaissance,* argues that a courtly rebellion against the traditional humanistic ethic made wrath, the "ireful passion," into a virtue. In Haydn's judgment, the rebellion resulted in a masculine code that placed honor and wrath above reason, a courtly tradition holding "that there was a right revenge, not only just, but obligatory and above all authority of positive law."[47] However, most of the citations with which Haydn supports this concept of the "ireful virtue" have been taken out of context, with the result that they often convey exactly the opposite meaning from the one the original writer intended. On close inspection, the major spokesmen for this counter-code prove to be erring heroes (Rinaldo in Tasso's *Jerusalem Delivered*), satirized deviants and fools (Timotheo in Machiavelli's *Mandragola,* Shakespeare's Polonius, and Rabelais's Friar John), or patent villains (Cutwolfe in Nashe's *The Unfortunate Traveller* and Monsieur in Chapman's *Bussy D'Ambois*). No one either then or now could regard Machiavelli's ludicrous priest or Rabelais's "rash, hard-brained devil of a friar" as a norm for emulation, and, despite many odd contradictions in Chapman, the audience never doubts that Monsieur and all his twisted ideas are loathsome. We would not reconstruct an approved counter-code of Elizabethan statecraft by citing the policies and premises of Richard III.[48] Of course there were

---

[47] *The Counter-Renaissance* (New York, 1950), p. 595. See pp. 555–98 for Haydn's full discussion.

[48] The failure to note the speaker's purpose is apparent in Haydn's application of evidence from *Volpone.* In Celia's desperate attempt to dissuade her would-be ravisher, she pleads with Volpone to exercise not his lust but his "manly wrath," by destroying her beauty rather than

men who broke and even defied the conventional code, but the fact that sin existed does not prove that rational men called sin virtue.[49] Undoubtedly there were such men as Timotheo and Monsieur, and to this extent there was indeed a "counter-code," but on the basis of Haydn's evidence, it would appear to have been a code of villains and fools.

A final body of evidence remains to be considered. Many scholars have argued that most Elizabethans of all classes, not merely members of the nobility, considered blood revenge justifiable and even obligatory in certain special cases. Fredson Bowers, for example, argues that "few Elizabethans . . . would condemn the son's blood-revenge on a treacherous murderer whom the law could not apprehend for lack of proper legal evidence."[50] This view, however, appears to rest on several quotations that have been considered out of context. One of these is the passage supporting Bowers's argument that many Elizabethans believed a son was legally required to avenge his father's death in order to inherit his estate. Gentillet is arguing against Machiavelli's cynical statement that a prince can kill a man without fear of revenge if he does not confiscate his victim's goods, because children will bear their father's death but not the loss of their inheritance. To this, Gentillet responds: "If the successor, his sonne or other kinsman, despise and make no account to pursue by lawfull meanes, that justice bee done, for the unjust death of the slaine man, whom hee succeedeth, . . . he leeseth his honour, and by the civile lawes is cul-

---

her virtue. Such a frantic plea is scarcely proof that manly wrath was considered a true virtue by Celia, Jonson, or the audience. Had Volpone poured acid upon her, as she requests, surely no one in Jonson's audience would have considered him a noble convert to honor.

The importance of evaluating the spokesman is also apparent when we consider Bowers's citation of the evidence of one Sanquire, who had lost his eye in a bout with his fencing master and then, five years later, hired a gang of murderers to effect his revenge. In his defense, Sanquire insisted that no honorable man could brook such an injury, but surely we should not take this rationalization as evidence of an accepted code. His motive was suspect (he had not acted until James I expressed surprise that his injurer had survived the bloody bout), his method was despicable, and his hanging was thoroughly justified. Cf. Bowers, *Elizabethan Revenge Tragedy*, pp. 29–30.

[49] Sidney's distinction between true and false honor is pertinent. In the *Arcadia*, he defines true honor by the traditional method of showing what it is not—by rejecting the view of those who equate violence with valor. His discussion indicates that some men justified their faulty conduct by rationalization, not that there was an approved norm of the "Ireful Virtue." Cf. Haydn's discussion, *The Counter-Renaissance*, pp. 586–87.

[50] Bowers, p. 40.

pable and unworthie of the succession."[51] The key phrase is "by law-full meanes." Gentillet is defining (erroneously) a law requiring legal appeal, not blood revenge. A few people may have mistakenly be-lieved that a son had to seek legal punishment of his father's murder to ensure his inheritance, but I have found no evidence to indicate that Elizabethans believed the law required blood revenge.

The law was absolute: murder, as such, was never justified. Even if a man's entire family had been brutally massacred by the most vicious criminal, even if the magistrates themselves were so corrupt that they knowingly would let the guilty go free—even then, the man who planned and executed the death of the murderer would be equally a murderer in the eyes of the law. English law allowed only one excep-tion. Instant retaliation for an injury was adjudged manslaughter, on the grounds that it was unpremeditated, and in the Elizabethan pe-riod might be forgiven by royal pardon. To be considered manslaugh-ter, the killing had to be an immediate reaction to immediate injury. Any delay at all indicated premeditation, and Elizabethan law de-fined murder as unlawful killing by a sane adult with "malice pre-pensed." According to Chief Justice Sir Edward Coke, the standard authority on Elizabethan law, "This is said in law to be malice fore-thought, prepensed, *malitia praecogitata*." Moreover, "this malice is so odious in law, although it be intended against one, it shall be ex-tended towards another."[52] If Hamlet planned to kill Claudius when he entered his mother's bedchamber and thought it was Claudius be-

---

[51] *Against Machiavell*, Part II, Maxim 11, p. 221. The same view is reflected in an anony-mous argument against dueling written about 1612. Insisting that "the lawe meanes judiciall and ordinar meanes," the writer rules out dueling as a legitimate recourse. He is not sug-gesting that anyone believes the law to require murder. Cf. Bowers, pp. 38–39.

[52] As quoted by Bowers, p. 9. See pp. 8–12 for a full discussion of legal considerations. This distinction in Elizabethan law between instinctive retaliation and premeditated revenge casts doubt on the recent argument of S. F. Johnson that Shakespeare's audience accepted pri-vate revenge as a religious duty enjoined by the Old Testament. On the basis of Numbers 35:12, 19, and 30, Johnson concludes that "Hieronimo's duty is clearly spelled out in the Mosaic code, which Protestants believe to be quite as much the word of God as anything else in the two testaments."

In discussing laws for cities of refuge, the cited verses do indeed speak of a requirement that the "revenger of blood" slay the murderer, but verses 20 and 21 clearly stipulate that the revenger is guilty of murder if he strikes in hatred or lies in ambush. Even in that primitive code, retaliation had to be without delay and without malice to be justified. Although it is theoretically possible that the command of vengeance was known out of context, I have never encountered a reference to this Biblical warrant in an Elizabethan source. For Johnson's dis-cussion, see "*The Spanish Tragedy*: Babylon Revisited," *Essays on Elizabethan Drama in Honor of Hardin Craig*, ed. Richard Hosley (Columbia, Mo., 1962), pp. 29–30.

hind the arras, he was guilty of murder. The modern argument that he was not guilty of premeditated murder because he did not intend to kill Polonius would have been dismissed by Elizabethan courts.[53]

The Renaissance distinction between premeditated murder and instantaneous retaliation has not been sufficiently noted in studies of the revenge play. Lodowick Bryskett, for example, has been thought to endorse a pagan revenge code because he states that a man "may perchance at the instant repulse [an injury], or revenge himself in hot bloud without any great reproach." On the contrary, Bryskett's qualifying phrases—"at the instant repulse" and "in hot bloud"—both reflect the legal definition of manslaughter.[54] Count Annibale Romei makes the same distinction in *The Courtier's Academy*. Since Romei's discussion takes the form of an extended dialogue, spot passages may seem to justify revenge under many conditions: if the laws are insufficient, if no friend or relative can effect his own revenge, if the injury is especially base. Romei, however, unmistakably rejects all such excuses. Gualinguo, his norm spokesman, condones only instantaneous retaliation; but when asked whether it is not legitimate to recover honor by combat if for some reason retaliation is not immediate, he is adamant. The injured party "must not repell injurie, with a meane unjust, but just, according as the lawes commaund: Wherefore occasion once past, it is not convenient, that in cold bloud, as we usually say, he performe any other matter with his proper valor: for in suche case, the condition of the injurier is far worse, than of him injuried."[55] A faulty inference has also been drawn from William Perkins's well-known statement that "God puts the sword into the private mans hands" when the magistrate is absent. The context shows that Perkins is discussing instantaneous reaction—specifically, the instantaneous

---

53 One might argue that if Hamlet was merely lashing out instinctively at an unknown threat behind the arras, an Elizabethan court would judge him guilty only of manslaughter. It is doubtful, however, that the court would have considered suspected eavesdropping sufficient injury to warrant such violent retaliation.

54 *A Discourse of Civill Life* ... (London, 1606), pp. 76–77. Moreover, Bryskett is condoning retaliation only for the man "that is not come to that degree of vertue as to be magnanimous." He is not defining an obligation of the virtuous. Plutarch and La Primaudaye also insisted that the truly good man would restrain himself at the moment of injury until his anger cooled.

55 Trans. John Keper (London, c. 1598), p. 144. It should also be noted that the question at issue throughout the dialogue is open single combat in the lists, voluntarily entered into by equal opponents. There is no suggestion that anyone is defending revenge by murder. Indeed, even the retaliation condoned by Gualinguo is to take the form of open combat.

repulse of violence in self-defense.[56] Not only does Perkins repeat the legal position, he emphasizes the more stringent ethical position: there must be no malice at all, whether prepensed or otherwise, no desire for revenge.

The importance of context is perhaps most striking when we turn to a familiar passage by Francis Bacon. Almost every modern justification of the revenge ethic in Elizabethan drama cites Bacon's famous statement that "revenge is a kind of wild justice." If one reads only this first clause of the first sentence from the essay "Of Revenge" (1625), Bacon's approval seems obvious. This inference, however, is seriously misleading, as the complete introductory passage makes clear:

Revenge is a kind of wild justice; which the more man's nature runs to, the more ought law to weed it out. For as for the first wrong, it doth but offend the law; but the revenge of that wrong putteth the law out of office. Certainly, in taking revenge, a man is but even with his enemy; but in passing it over, he is superior.... This is certain, that a man that studieth revenge keeps his own wounds green, which otherwise would heal and do well. Public revenges are for the most part fortunate.... But in private revenges it is not so. Nay rather, vindictive persons live the life of witches; who, as they are mischievous, so end they unfortunate.[57]

The essay is an unequivocal condemnation of private revenge under any circumstances. To be sure, Bacon says that revenge when there is no recourse to law is "the most tolerable sort," and that revenge for a particularly base injury is less horrible than murder for private gain, but he is merely noting that different types of revenge will arouse different degrees of sympathy. He condemns all types as flatly wrong,

---

[56] Highly pertinent are the criteria by which Perkins establishes this defense as "just": "I. It must be done incontinent and forthwith so soone as ever violence is offered. For if there be delay, and it come afterward, it loses the name of a just defence, & becomes a revenge, a rising of prepensed malice, as the Lawyers use to speake. II. There must be an intention, not to revenge principally, or to kill, but onely to defend himselfe. III. There must be a just and equall proportion of weapons; therefore it is no just defence to shoote a naked man through with a musket, or other peece of ordinance, when he offers violence" ("Cases of Conscience," *The Works of ... William Perkins*, London, 1613, II, 120). Even less demanding moralists such as Gentillet insisted that instant repulse of violence was justified only if it was impossible to avoid: only, in other words, if the returned violence was self-defense, not revenge. *Against Machiavell*, Part III, Maxim 6, p. 178.

[57] *The Works of Francis Bacon*, ed. James Spedding, Robert Leslie Ellis, and Douglas Denon Heath, new ed. (London, 1890), VI, 384–85.

and on exactly the same grounds as the Establishment. Bacon would sympathize with the blood revenge of a son for a father, but he would firmly condemn it. On this issue, Bacon was in complete accord with the best minds of his day. Law, Church, State, and accepted morality were unanimous in their condemnation of private premeditated revenge under any circumstances.

Almost all the evidence cited thus far has been drawn from the frankly didactic works of preachers and Christian humanists. To what extent their exhortations met agreement among the common people can never be known beyond doubt. It does, however, seem indicative that the conventional ideas permeated all types of literature. Since the writers of "imaginative," as against purely didactic, literature aimed not merely to teach but to delight, we can assume they used ideas they thought would appeal to their audiences. An Elizabethan playwright who made his supposedly virtuous hero a disciple of Machiavelli would have been foolhardy indeed. Let us briefly consider, then, a few Elizabethan works arising from aims other than those of men like Plutarch, La Primaudaye, Sandys, and Becon.

The conventional code seems to infiltrate all poetry, from the most primitive to the most sophisticated. On the simplest level, we find an old ballad, "The Bellman's Good-morrow," reflecting the contemporary concern with revenge. A general opening admonishing man to strip himself of all wickedness is followed by a series of stanzas on various sins. The first, and seemingly the most urgent, reads:

> And ryse not to revenge thee
> of any trespas past;
> Thou knowest not of a certaintie
> how longe thy life will last.[58]

Typically, man is urged to forgive his injurer even as did Christ. No less conventional, though much more sophisticated, is Spenser's use of Ate in the *Faerie Queene*: she is the malicious mother of dissension, Hell's firstborn, who was nursed by furies and now dwells "hard by the gates of hell."[59] Though to Homer Ate had been the goddess

---

[58] Hyder E. Rollins, ed. *Old English Ballads: 1553–1625* (Cambridge, Eng., 1920), p. 231.
[59] IV.i.19, 20, 31. Note also the prologue to *Locrine* and Antony's prediction that Caesar's ghost will come "hot from hell," "with Ate by his side."

of mischief, Aeschylus made her specifically the goddess of revenge, and it is in this role that Elizabethan writers found her most useful.

Thomas Nashe's *The Unfortunate Traveller* (1594) is of particular interest because it is frequently cited to prove that a thriving code justified revenge, and more specifically that Hamlet spared Claudius at prayer merely because of an accepted belief that the revenger had to damn his victim for eternity. The problem of the Prayer Scene is discussed in Chapter VII. Here it is important to correct the general misconception. Cutwolfe, Nashe's revenger, is so fiendish as to border on the grotesque. Exulting over his defenseless victim, he revels in his blasphemy. "Though I knew God would never have mercy upon me except I had mercie on thee, yet of thee no mercy would I have. Revenge in our tragedies is continually raised from hell: of hell doe I esteeme better than heaven, if it afford me revenge." Sentenced to death for the ensuing murder, he mounts the scaffold to horrify his listeners with an "insulting oration":

This is the falt that hath called me hether; no true Italian but will honor me for it. Revenge is the glorie of armes, & the highest performance of valure: revenge is whatsoever we call law or justice. The farther we wade in revenge, the neerer come we to the throne of the almightie. To his scepter it is properly ascribed; his scepter he lends unto man, when he lets one man scourge an other. All true Italians imitate me in revenging constantly and dying valiantly. Hangman, to thy taske.

This satanic sophistry is too much even for the Italians. "Herewith all the people (outragiously incensed) with one conjoyned outcrie yelled mainely, Awaie with him, away with him. Executioner, torture him, teare him, or we will teare thee in peeces if thou spare him."[60] Every Elizabethan had heard many times that a "scourge" of God was a complete reprobate. With the most perverted logic, Cutwolfe confounds Heaven and Hell and then glories in his own damnation. By no stretch of the imagination can Nashe or his readers be understood to approve of his revenge.

How thoroughly the orthodox code infiltrated the literary mind is shown by Samuel Brandon's *Virtuous Octavia,* a closet drama published in 1598. Octavia's virtue, expounded in an endless series of long,

---

[60] *The Works of Thomas Nashe,* ed. Ronald B. McKerrow (London, 1910), II, 324–27.

Senecan speeches, lies in her refusal to take action against Antony despite his faithlessness. In a long debate with Octavius Caesar, she rejects his arguments for revenge.[61] Her strength lies in patience: "The heavens are just, let them revenge the wrong." He argues that inaction will dishonor her; she answers that she would dishonor herself if she gave in to rage. He charges her with cowardice; she answers that revenge springs not from courage but "from malice and disdaine":

> One wound doth not an others balme procure.
> Flame is not quencht with flame. . . .

Antony's sin merely reveals the frailty of man and warns her against falling into like temptation. At this Octavius offers his best argument: it is a sin to let a man persist in lewdness. But Octavia chooses a higher virtue: if she pardons the sinner, he may repent. This scene, and indeed the entire play, relies on a series of familiar precepts. At this point, the reader may be troubled by an unanswered question. In the words of Robert Ornstein, these "official and semi-official pieties" are undeniable, but how accurately do they reflect the attitude of Shakespeare's audience?[62] The question is eminently fair. Despite the almost unanimous condemnation of revenge in the Elizabethan period, history records that brawling increased, dueling began to capture interest, lawsuits flooded the courts, and the revenge tragedy flourished. As Ornstein notes, in the Elizabethan age, as in our own, popular platitudes stood in marked contrast to reality. The mid-twentieth century is ravaged by war and prejudice as it preaches peace and equality. The late sixteenth century was torn by religious and political dissension and yet talked endlessly of its belief in natural order and harmony.

On these grounds, Helen Gardner has suggested that it is pointless for the dramatic critic to concern himself with the orthodox condemnation of revenge. A much more significant guide to the temper of the times, she believes, is the threat of blood vengeance implicit in the Bond of Association of 1584, in which the government pledged, in the name of God, to counter any attack on Elizabeth by summarily exe-

---

61 Ed. Ronald B. McKerrow for the Malone Society (1909), ll. 1024-1311.
62 *The Moral Vision of Jacobean Tragedy* (Madison, Wis., 1960), pp. 15-16.

cuting any possible successor who might benefit from her death.[63] Such an ironic action on the part of an avowed agency of God may indeed suggest the turbulent passions of the time that constantly threatened to break loose, but in determining the ethics of revenge we are concerned with moral judgment, not with the emotional response that can lead a man or a nation to violate its best judgment. The temper and even the actions of an age may be in constant rebellion against its own ethics.

Admittedly, then, we cannot find the reality by defining the ideal. At the same time, however, we cannot define the reality and then call it the ideal. The high rate of alcoholism in the United States does not indicate that the average man approves of drunkenness. Indeed, very few drunkards would argue that their actions are governed by any code of morality, even their own. A man may hate his next-door neighbor and yet believe wholeheartedly in the brotherhood of man. Today we might say that natural instinct rebels against established mores; the Elizabethan preacher would say that original sin rebels against divine law.

Many Renaissance documents reflect this human conflict—the constant struggle between what Elizabethan man wanted to do, and did, and what he knew he should do. *Timon of Athens* neatly defines the dilemma. No analysis of revenge can ignore this extremely curious play, and yet, because of the rough condition of the text and the problem of ascertaining the playwright's intentions, it can prove nothing about Shakespeare's attitude. The play as a whole has thus been dismissed from the review of the Shakespearean canon that follows in Chapter III, but one scene is discussed here to illuminate the problem of simultaneous sympathy and judgment.

In Act III, Scene v, Alcibiades approaches the Senate to beg mercy for a friend who in single combat has killed a man for dishonoring him. The language of the scene establishes that the friend is guilty not of murder but of fighting an unauthorized duel, and thus, as

---

[63] *The Business of Criticism* (Oxford, 1959), p. 36. It seems doubtful that any Elizabethan would have viewed the Bond of Association as a warrant for private revenge. The threat was made by duly authorized legal authority, and the Elizabethan distinguished carefully between the rights of law, which was the arm of divine punishment, and the rights of private man.

noted, the issue is different from the problem of the revenge play.[64] Nonetheless, the debate between Alcibiades and the Senators on the relative merits of revenge and forbearance is highly relevant. Alcibiades defends the duel on the grounds that his friend's manifold virtues would have been soiled by cowardice had he not defended his reputation, that his fury was "noble," that he acted "in hot blood" yet with "sober and unnoted passion." The Senate castigates him for "striving to make an ugly deed look fair"—for laboring "to bring manslaughter into form and set quarrelling / Upon the head of valour"—and presents the familiar doctrine that "to revenge is no valour, but to bear." Alcibiades' heated rejoinder has special significance for the present study:

> Why do fond men expose themselves to battle,
> And not endure all threats? sleep upon't,
> And let the foes quietly cut their throats,
> Without repugnancy? If there be
> Such valour in the bearing, what make we
> Abroad? why then, women are more valiant
> That stay at home, if bearing carry it,
> And the ass more captain than the lion, the felon
> Loaden with irons wiser than the judge,
> If wisdom be in suffering.

To Alcibiades, the orthodox view would make cowards of us all. He is the man of action who scorns an ethic of passivity—for to him patience and endurance seem no more but so. Such an ethic condemns the very force that spurs the man of action to great enterprise. Alcibiades is quite willing to pay his respects to the Idols of the Theater, but he is a realist:

> To be in anger is impiety;
> But who is man that is not angry?

---

[64] I am indebted to G. K. Waggoner for this clarification ("*Timon of Athens* and the Jacobean Duel," *SQ*, XVI [1965], 303–11), although I am not fully convinced that the audience would accept Alcibiades' arguments without question. He first defends his friend as a man whose valor was attested by his noble fury, then as a man who entered combat with "sober and unnoted passion"; later he argues that "rashness in cold blood" is to be condemned but that his friend struck in anger and in defense. Undeniably the Senators are self-

Perhaps nowhere in Renaissance drama is the moral conflict inherent in revenge stated so explicitly: the conflict between an ethical absolute and a directly opposed human instinct.

The same conflict underlies a delightful passage in *The Arte of Poesie* (1589), in which Puttenham is defining "a certaine auncient forme of poesie by which men did use to reproach their enemies":

> There be wise men, and of them the great learned man *Plutarch* that tooke upon them to perswade the benefite that men receive by their enemies, which though it may be true in manner of *Paradoxe,* yet I finde mans frailtie to be naturally such, and alwayes hath beene, that he cannot conceive it in his owne case, nor shew that patience and moderation in such greifs, as becommeth the man perfite and accomplisht in all vertue: but either in deede or by word, he will seeke revenge.... This made the auncient Poetes to invent a meane to rid the gall of all such Vindicative men: so as they might be a wrecked of their wrong.... And this was done by a maner of imprecation, or as we call it by cursing and banning of the parties, and wishing all evill to a light upon them, and though it never the sooner happened, yet was it a great easment to the boiling stomacke.

Of course, Puttenham hastens to add, "We Christians are forbidden to use such uncharitable fashions, and willed to referre all our revenges to God alone."[65] Of course. And yet, despite all precepts and paradoxes, natural man is cursed with a "boiling stomacke."

This specific dilemma was a matter of real concern, and not only to closet philosophers—a fact most interestingly attested by the *Essayes* of William Cornwallis the Younger (1600). A husband at sixteen, a father of eleven children by the time of his death at thirty-five, a follower of Essex, a reformed prodigal, a scholar and writer—he is a fascinating representative of a turbulent era. Bankrupted by his profligate extravagances at the age of eighteen, Cornwallis went off with Essex in 1599 to Ireland, where he was knighted, and returned to England with high resolutions. At twenty, he said, "he vomited much that he had drunk at nineteen."[66] His essay "Of Patience" shows a very young man struggling to come to terms with himself. It is a

---

seeking usurers, repellent figures in their complacency and rigid absolutism. At the same time, the sophistries and contradictions in Alcibiades' argument, despite his moving plea for mercy, leave me uncertain as to the audience's response.

[65] Ed. Gladys Doidge Willcock and Alice Walker (Cambridge, Eng., 1936), p. 57.
[66] Ed. Don Cameron Allen (Baltimore, Md., 1946), p. xv.

highly personal, and painful, debate, and bears extensive quoting:

About nothing doe I suffer greater conflicts in my selfe then about induring wrongs; for other duties—though perhaps I seldome performe them, yet I am resolved they should be done; and it is not the fault of my meditation but of my negligent flesh. But heere is set up Reputation as the Garland appointed, and he that revengeth not is not capable of this glorie.

Heere hath crueltie borrowed the apparrell of wanton Vanitie and makes foolish youth her Agent. I know what Divinitie, what Philosophie perswades; I knowe these wrong-doers to be wretched creatures, rather in truth to be pittied then maliced; and yet for all this, I dare not yeeld. The cause: there is too much safetie in following this Advise; the bodie by this prevents an adventure; therefore, that respect makes mee obstinate. I know againe this idle breath should not divert me from Vertue; but having no present occasion wherein I may exercise valour and manifest my worth, I dare not take day [that is, put off payment] in any thing so nearly concerning me. But all this time I finde not my selfe angrie but, in trueth, somewhat subject to vaineglory, which is a worse disease because lesse violent and therefore of more continuance. I have not yet any outward witnesse of my valour, but this is my determination: not to refuse the first good quarrell and to performe it as well as I can. After which I will serve Vertue, beare and forbeare. And this I will doe in humilitie to please the world and to shew them I scorne not altogether their customes. . . . Upon the receipt of a wrong and an honest determination to forgive, I am whispered in the eare that this lenitie is injustice, that I nourish sinne with not cutting it up when I see it grow, that though I effect revenge, and revenge coulde doe no more, yet it is not revenge—it is justice. Pittifull abuse.

Thus far the tempting "adventure" envisioned would seem to be a duel, some "good quarrell" whereby a young man might "exercise valour and manifest [his] worth." In his conclusion, however, Cornwallis adds a puzzling comment:

Even in the behalfe of Truth & mercy, I will combat against a received tradition. I think nothing but murther should bee punished. For these pettie matters of theft and such trespasses, they are the effect of neede or wantonnesse, veniall faults. Age commonly reclaymeth the one, and the other is punished by the setter Povertie. For any thing lesse offensive—a coole reproofe, no chollerick revenge.[67]

[67] *Ibid.*, pp. 14–15.

Suddenly the issue has shifted, for theft motivated by need is scarcely the type of injury to be redressed in the open combat of honor.

It is probable, as Bowers notes, that we do find here a unique justification of private revenge for murder, although the context is difficult to understand and must be weighed carefully. Throughout the essay, Cornwallis is not so much transcribing his considered view as jotting down a stream of twisting, confused thoughts. (Would it "please the world" to serve virtue or welcome a quarrel? We cannot tell.) Nonetheless, it is clear that although Cornwallis may embrace the first temptation to revenge, he will be plagued by guilt. He may be able to defy his conscience, but he will not be able to silence it. His struggle to submit the promptings of instinct to the demands of conscience is evidence that the official "platitudes" were rooted deep.

Of particular interest in a study of the revenge tradition as it relates to *Hamlet* is Anthonie Copley's *A Fig for Fortune* (1596),[68] a tedious, undisciplined allegory obviously modeled on Spenser. Its diction is awkward, its grammar barbarous, its sentences often unintelligible, and its metrics chaotic. Despite these crudities, it has a curiously appealing vigor in the violence and vividness of its imagery, and echoes in Shakespeare of diction, phrasing, and ideas found throughout Copley's poem suggest that Shakespeare may have read it with lively interest. Discussion of the poem's significance for the structure of *Hamlet* must be reserved for later.[69] Our present concern is with Copley's delineation of the ethical dilemma facing a potential revenger.

An "Elizian out-cast of Fortune," vested in sable, ranges through the night on his jade, Melancholy. Suddenly he spies a ghastly figure, half angel, half serpent, who is wildly stabbing his bleeding body again and again. It is Cato's ghost. He tells how he had refused to be subjected to Caesar's "tyrant-whip," and, in a long passage of exhortation, advises Elizian man to follow him in committing suicide. Elizian man is drawing his sword when the ghost suddenly vanishes, leaving such a stench of sulphur that our despairing wanderer realizes the counsel was demonic. Remounting Melancholy, he rides on, down

---

[68] Printed for the Spenser Society (1883). All quotations are from this edition.

[69] See below, pp. 231–33. Copley is generally recognized as the source for Macbeth's image of "dusty death." Typical echoes include Copley's presentation of suicide as felicity because "One stab will send thee to eternity," closely followed by the usual comparison of death to sweet sleep, and the words in which Cato's ghost enjoins suicide: "Out with thy candle, let it burne no more." With the exception of the phrase "dusty death," none of the echoes is a conclusive parallel since the same ideas and diction were available in other sources, but the close juxtaposition of so many parallels suggests at least the possibility of direct influence.

into a gloomy, hell-black dale, until suddenly the rush of a "fatall blast" drives the enraged horse and terrified rider into the presence of an even more horrifying figure, who appears in a flash of sulphurous flame. Elizian man is frozen in "deadly horror of so dread a Bug," for her eyes are fires, her body is as pale as death, and her hair is "Snake-incurl'd *Medusa* like." At last, in a terrible roar of anger, she announces that she is Revenge, the "pith of Tragedies." After boasting of the famous men she has incited to criminal actions, she begins her exhortation:

> To be faire Fortunes ever Carpet-darling
> Is femall glorie: But Reveng'd disgrace
> That's truly Masculine, and rich triumphing:
> Al peace-content is too too cheap and base:
> > What manhood is it still to feed on Chickins
> > Like infant nurse-boys in nice Fortunes kitchins?...
>
> T's brave to plunge adowne into the deep
> *A*nd so up-bound againe above the wave,
> To be continually a mountain-sheep
> Is Cockrell-like, it is a dung-hill brave:
> > The cravin Cocke is hartlesse from his hill,
> > Shame to be so that hast a manly will....
>
> Be not as is the coward Scorpion
> That rounded all about with ashie embers
> Dispaires and dies in selfe destruction
> Renting with fierce enrage his venym members:
> > But if that *Jove* nill ayde thy fortitude
> > Downe to all *Acharon,* and the Furie brood....
>
> *H*eaven is the Arbiter, and wils it so,
> I and the Furies are the instruments
> To act that justice in all tragicke woe,
> Now is it in this case our good intents
> > To joyne with us thy manuall act heerin
> > That more then pristin glory thou maist win....
>
> Nature hath given you male and female willes,
> The one wherwith to covet meriments,
> The other to detest all adverse ils,
> Now is almightie *Joves* great woonderments
> > More in his Thunder-boltes then in his sweetes,
> > To shew Revenge more woorth then Pleasures greets.

> Then arme thy selfe Revenges Champion,
> To bandie away thy foes, and all disgrace
> With polliticke dissimulation
> Of contrarie language, and contrary face:
>     As the Camelion changeth still his hue
>     With every object cullor: so change thou.
>
> So maist thou close Camelion-like conceale
> Thy tragicke shape of Horror and Revenge,
> Whiles' they misdoubting not thy false reveale
> Are caught unwares like Woodcocks in a sprenge,
>     Such is the honour of Adversitie,
>     With sleightes to undermine Prosperitie. . . .
>
> T'is Heavens attaine to send thy foes to Hell
> With mutuall murthers in Seditions field:
> The upper Buckets fall into the well
> The lowers faire amount we see doth yeeld:
>     Such is the merit of Revenges deed,
>     With others wrack to work thine own good speed.
>
> At least to die in well appeased wrath
> And in survive of all thine enemies
> Is stately dying: t'is faire lie downe and laugh,
> And an up-rise to *Joves* benignities,
>     *Elizium* and Fame in after ages,
>     Revenges blessed Rightes and Appennages.

As Revenge is promising Elizian man glory in both this world and the next, dawn begins to break. Suddenly stopping in the middle of a sentence and staring about with terror, she vanishes just as the cock crows.

> Even so (quoth I) is it Revenges guize
> To be in force by Night, be gone by Day?
> Such is not the instinct of Paradize,
> God graunt it be no Plutonicke affray:
>     Oh what it is to be a mortall man
>     Subject to all the guiles and sleights of Satan.
>
> Yet for her speech was consonant to Nature,
> I wisht sh'had been an Oracle of truth;

So credulous is *A*ngers moodie vigure
When once it is in-Caesared in youth:
  And hand in-handed with a quaint Disdaine
  Injurious disglorie to sustaine.

Yea what is not the miser apt to doe,
What not beleeve to mittigate his evill?
Well may he faine a patient outward hue,
But not exile his inward damned devill. . . .

The voice of the cock has also terrified the jade Melancholy, and now, "unsprighted, and unnighted," he tears out across hedge and field in one last enraged flight until he faints—"such is the end of Rages ryotize." At that, a snow-white jennet, Good Desire, approaches and takes Elizian man to the cave of Devotion.

As he arrives, he sees an ancient hermit kneeling in prayer before a death's-head full of worms, the picture of a grave, and similar objects of inspiration. Catechrysius welcomes the outcast and begins the expected exhortation with traditional *de contemptu mundi* arguments. In this context he answers the temptation to suicide, and then for some eighty stanzas argues against Revenge: revenge attempts to usurp God's power; adversity may be God's punishment of the wicked or His test of the virtuous, and in either case it should be embraced with joy; a good conscience is man's only glory; the injuries of this world are merely the frowns of fickle Fortune, but naught can touch the blessed of God. The argument is summarized in the following description, typical in its vigor and grotesque imagery:

Such is Revenge: It is a haggard yll,
A Luciferiall ranke uncharitie:
The venym, and black-*Santus* of our will
Unreasons rage; spawne of Impietie,
  Breath of Despaire, Prime-brat of Envies brood,
  And all good Natures Satyr-*Antipode*.

Catechrysius' exhortation culminates in two familiar appeals: "Think on Christ," he urges:

Behold his image yonder on the Crosse,
See how he droops and dies and damnes Revenge

> Yeelding his whole humanity in grosse
> A pendular reproch on woodden henge.

And "Think on Death." If Elizian man but remembers that death de-
feats all, he will realize that the accidents of Fortune are meaningless
in eternity:

> Death is the gulfe of all: and then I say
> Thou art as good as *Caesar* in his clay.

As Catechrysius closes his "catechism," Elizian man begins to abhor
his "black and impious" melancholy, and swears to "be a beast no
more."

Any reader of Spenser can finish the story. Elizian man is led to
Sion, the Temple of Peace, where an angel gives him the armor of
virtue. Doblessa (Fortune), the "rampant Hagg and whoore of Babylon," assaults the Temple with her devils, but is repulsed by the Sion-
ites. The poem culminates in festivities of praise and thanksgiving,
and the joyful catechumen wends homeward, praying blessings on
his queen.

The reader has probably noticed several passages suggesting scenes
in *Hamlet,* and to these we shall return. At this point we are concerned only with Copley's attitude toward revenge, and of that there
can be no doubt. Revenge is a horrible emissary of Satan, loosed from
Hell to tempt man to damnation. Although Copley is clearly on the
side of the angels, he understands Satan's arguments and makes Revenge a far more compelling debater than Catechrysius. Catechrysius
speaks from the book. Revenge speaks from experience, with the voice
of human fears and desires and frustrations. The "plutonick sprite" is
a potent tempter, for its words are undeniably "consonant to Nature."

---

In the light of all this testimony, are we justified in assuming that
the Elizabethan "disregarded without a qualm" the familiar ethical
and religious injunctions of his day: that he felt bound by a counter-
code of honor and by popular tradition to seek private revenge?
Against the weight of opinion expressed by such different men as
Bishop Sandys and Francis Bacon, reflected in such different works
of literature as *The Unfortunate Traveller* and *The Faerie Queene,*
and confirmed even by arguments for dueling and handbooks for
courtiers, stand a few frankly atypical views. Can such doubtful evi-

dence outweigh the overwhelming mass of testimony from so many representative figures?

In the course of my investigation I have tried to come to terms with all the available evidence that might be thought to support an approved code of private revenge. If new evidence should be found, I would urge the posing of several questions to determine its relevance to the Elizabethan revenge play. Does the evidence come from the Elizabethan period, or from a time when attitudes may have differed? Does it come from England, or from the Continent, where there was indeed a thriving aristocratic code of honor enjoining revenge? Does it refer to actual murder, delayed and premeditated, or to manslaughter: instantaneous retaliation for an injury? Does it argue for attack on a defenseless enemy, or for open combat between forewarned and forearmed opponents? If the evidence is from a work of fiction, are the words those of an approved spokesman or those of a villain? If it is from a treatise in dialogue form, do the speaker's views prevail, or are they rejected? When the given passage is viewed in context, is it relevant to the specific issues underlying the revenge play?

Subjected to this kind of close analysis, the evidence from Elizabethan England suggests not an approved counter-code of revenge that seems foreign to the modern mind, but an ethical dilemma that obtains even today. In Anthony Copley's *A Fig for Fortune,* the dilemma is treated at length from an Elizabethan perspective. The argument of the poem is unequivocally orthodox. Revenge is a terrifying force from Hell; it is blasphemy against God, a rejection of Christ's Atonement; it begins in malice and ends in despair; it poisons the reason and perverts the will. No matter how appealing it may seem, it will destroy the mind, soul, and body of the man who embraces it. Copley, however, is sensitive to the frustrations imposed by an ethic of patience, and his allegorical figure of Revenge—an "inward damned devill"—uses almost every argument by which man justifies his instinctive hunger for revenge. Revenge is masculine and courageous; patience is effeminate and cowardly. The man who destroys evil partakes of the nature of God; the man who endures evil is no more than a beast. He who punishes the wicked follows Heaven's will that sin be punished; he who lets the wicked flourish is himself guilty of nourishing vice. The command to revenge arises from an ethic of action and leads to great enterprise; the command to pa-

tience arises from an ethic of passivity and leads to physical, intellec-
tual, and spiritual dry rot.

All of these arguments are significant for understanding the enduring appeal of the revenge play. Few audiences in any age would
be unsympathetic to a man who risks his life in a battle against corruption. Few would fail to understand a young hero who feels he
must prove his manhood when taunted with cowardice. Few would
fail to respond to the rebel who, frustrated by the prohibitions of
civil, moral, and divine law, rejects passive endurance of evil as the
highest goal to which man can aspire.[70]

But—and this point cannot be stated too strongly—we must not
make the error of equating sympathy with moral approval. No figure
in folklore and literature is more fascinating than the rebel. We identify with Faustus and even with Satan, but we know that they must
both be hurled into Hell. We sympathize with Hotspur, but our emotional involvement does not cancel our judgment. We identify even
with Macbeth, yet we still condemn him on moral grounds: indeed,
our knowledge that he is violating moral law increases our compassion. The same is even more true of the revenge play, for the revenger's dilemma is closer to us than that of Macbeth. Few of us have been
led by ambition to consider murder, but all of us have been prompted
by an injury to consider "getting even."

Undoubtedly, the average Elizabethan sympathized strongly with
a revenger, but we cannot assume that he therefore ignored all the
ethical and religious precepts he heard daily and which, according to
the available evidence, he generally accepted. The "willing suspen-
sion of disbelief" does not imply that an audience leaves all of its
knowledge, its ethics, its religious faith, at the box office. Is it not at
least possible that the Elizabethan audience could instinctively identify with the revenger and yet—either at the same time or later, when
released from emotional involvement—judge him, too?[71]

None of the preceding has been intended to argue that the audience
did in fact automatically condemn all dramatic revengers, no matter

[70] For further discussion of the strong appeal in Copley's treatment of revenge, see Farnham, *Medieval Heritage,* p. 347.

[71] For parallel discussions of this double response, see J. J. Lawlor, "The Tragic Conflict
in *Hamlet,*" *Review of English Studies,* New Series, I (April, 1950), 97–113; Philip Edwards,
ed., *The Spanish Tragedy,* Revels Plays (Cambridge, Mass., 1959), pp. lvii–lxi; and Goddard,
*The Meaning of Shakespeare,* p. 334.

what the circumstances. As Robert Ornstein has warned, we must not assume that creative dramatists cannot incorporate unfamiliar and even radical ideas in their plays.[72] A skillful playwright can make even heresy attractive. *Tamburlaine* may be a case in point. An even better example, if my analysis is valid, is *Bussy D'Ambois*. By the clever use of Christian signs that had become theatrical conventions, Chapman seems to be tricking his audience into accepting patently non-Christian ideas.[73]

In an age when so many conventional ideas had been stated and restated in similar language, certain words and ideas could be counted on to arouse certain specific responses. Words such as *Heaven, angel, grace,* and *charity* seem clearly intended to arouse a favorable response. *Hell, devil, damnation,* and *malice* are signs of evil. Forgiving one's enemies, acknowledging the justice of a punishment, retiring to a monastery—such actions suggest virtue. Stabbing an enemy in the back, approving of Machiavelli, equating oneself with God—such actions are signs of a villain. If a playwright wished to overcome his audience's qualms about revenge, no doubt he could do so with careful plotting and controlled diction.

Let us, then, take a new look at the Elizabethan revenge play, but without any prior assumptions. Of course we must admit one fact: the audience was at least nominally Christian. Any discussion of *Hamlet* that dismisses Horatio's "flights of angels sing thee to thy rest" as irrelevant to the tragic resolution is ignoring the audience for whom the play was written. Any interpretation of Tamburlaine as wholly corrupt ignores his freeing of the Christians enslaved by the savage Turks. The Christian orientation of the audience is undeniable, but let us erase any assumptions about its moral judgment of a given play. The Elizabethan audience may have entered the theater doubting that revenge was justified, but it was probably ready to be convinced.

---

[72] *The Moral Vision of Jacobean Tragedy,* pp. 12–18.

[73] Note the use of popular Christian signs to gain moral approval for the dying Bussy; he refuses to kill Montsurry; he forgives his enemies; he urges Tamyra to agree to Christian reconciliation with her husband; the ghost of the Friar hails his ascent to Heaven. Similarly, Tamyra speaks words that sound like contrition and then retires to the desert, two signs of the redeemed penitent. Actually the audience is tricked by Christian symbols into approving of her decision. Tamyra's words indicate Chapman's thoroughly non-Christian view; Tamyra now has the courage to refuse reconciliation with her husband and remain faithful to her lover.

# CHAPTER II

# Revenge on the English Stage, 1562–1607

Although a study of the Elizabethan revenge play normally deals only with "Kydian formula" plays as defined by Fredson Bowers, our present concern is with the Elizabethan moral response to revenge itself. If we can assess the audience's reaction to revenge motifs in any type of play (in a Biblical drama like *David and Bethsabe,* a chronicle history like *Edward II,* or a comedy like *The Dumb Knight,* as well as in a revenge play proper like *The Spanish Tragedy*), we should be better prepared to recognize established conventions. A given convention evokes a given audience response: a bastard son chafing at his lowly state is dangerous, whether in *Much Ado About Nothing* or *King Lear.* Thus we shall examine all plays produced between 1562 and 1607 in which private revenge is a clearly defined motive.[1]

To understand the full impact of the revenge motif on the Elizabethan audience, we should probably start with the medieval drama. Both Satan and his offspring, the Vice, are prototypes of the demonic revenger. In the mysteries and moralities, both characters resort to crafty dissimulation, delight in ironic wordplay, and revel with confidence in villainy.[2] Although many such traits of the Vice were to be-

---

[1] *Gorboduc* (1562) marks the first important use of revenge in the native English drama. After 1607, a possible *terminus ad quem* for *The Atheist's Tragedy,* the condemnation of revenge by both playwrights and audiences is relatively clear. Although our ultimate concern is the response of *Hamlet*'s original audience, later plays can show which devices of plot, character, and diction had evolved into fixed conventions. Plays in which open warfare is accompanied by vows of revenge have been eliminated from discussion when the issues are national and political rather than private and moral. In *Caesar's Revenge,* for example, the issue is not private revenge but public punishment of traitors. Caesar's Ghost really functions as a dramatic metaphor for Nemesis. Closet drama, having no audience, has not been considered.

[2] See Bernard Spivak's *Shakespeare and the Allegory of Evil: The History of a Metaphor in Relation to His Major Villains* (New York, 1958) for an excellent study of Elizabethan dramatic conventions evolving from the medieval Vice.

come useful in establishing conventions and will be noted, Satan and the Vice were revenging themselves on good, and there is no doubt about the audience's moral response. Let us, then, eliminate from extended consideration their direct successors on the Elizabethan stage: villains who would have pursued an evil course even if they had never had occasion to revenge. Some, like the Vice, take revenge on the virtuous simply because virtue is a threat. Piero relentlessly pursues Andrugio and his son, Antonio, throughout *Antonio and Mellida* (1599–1600) for no other discernible reason. Some pursue revenge for completely invalid reasons. In *Antonio's Revenge* (c. 1600), Piero becomes a vengeful maniac ostensibly because years ago Antonio's father had married a woman he himself had coveted. Similarly, Monsieur in *Bussy D'Ambois* (c. 1604) is an avowed revenger even though his only motives are his hatred of Bussy's virtue and resulting rise in royal favor and his anger at Tamyra's yielding to a better man. None of these revengers-for-assumed-injury causes a problem. All are loathed.

Another group of revengers are equally damnable even though they have suffered genuine injury. Both Montsurry in *Bussy D'Ambois* and Pietro in *The Malcontent* (1604) have been cuckolded, but they are too corrupt and vicious to arouse any sympathy. The same may be true of Barabas in *The Jew of Malta* (1589–90) and Alexander in *Alphonsus, Emperor of Germany* (c. 1594–97). Barabas arouses some sympathy at first because of the outrageous confiscation of his estate and the hypocritical scorn of the Christians, but once he embarks on his campaign of Machiavellian villainy, all sympathy vanishes. A modern audience might see him as a man of some stature and courage who is driven to revenge, but the Elizabethan audience probably took its cue from the prologue spoken by Machiavelli, from Barabas's gloating over his wealth (a sure sign of vice, harking back to an old morality tradition), and from the mere fact that he is a Jew venting his anger on Christians. It is more difficult to decide how Alexander was portrayed in the opening scenes of *Alphonsus*. Unless the actor relied on a stereotype, the audience may have first seen a grief-stricken youth, mourning the death of his murdered father. His pain is aggravated when, surrounded in a foreign country by those who hate him, he is taunted by the Electors, who revile his father, openly applaud his murder, and ridicule the young page as "boy." Alexander is helpless, aching for the day when he can become a man and take revenge. Sympathy for him might well be great. But Alphonsus, who is in fact the unknown murderer, plays on the boy's grief and rage, tricking him into taking revenge on all of Alphonsus's own enemies. Immediately Alexander turns into the most grotesque of Spanish villains, raping, poisoning, and stabbing. When he has finally narrowed the field to his true enemy, he forces Alphonsus to forswear God before killing him, and thus triumphantly destroys the soul along with the body. One might consider him a virtuous young man corrupted by his desire for revenge, but the play's sensationalism, together with the well-known Elizabethan loathing of all things Spanish, suggests that the actor portrayed him as a villain from the start.

One other group of villains require brief attention: those whose revenge motives are totally unimportant to the plot. Periodically they vow revenge, but their real motivation is ambition or general viciousness. Two pairs of Machiavellian monsters are typical. Acomat and Selimus, the rival brothers of *Selimus* (1594), are really involved in a power struggle, as are Borgias and his tool, Mulleasses, in *The Turk* (1607–8). In each case revenge is a fitfully alleged motive for villainous acts that would have taken place even without the provocation of some real or assumed injury. The same is true of many characters who set out on a course of revenge but once under way forget their original motive. Mendoza in *The Malcontent,* furious at the Duchess for jilting him and at her husband for having, quite rightly, suspected the affair, roars "My hart cries perish all" and sets out to take revenge (II.i).[3] But after killing the hapless lover, he forgets all thought of revenge to become an ambitious schemer. In *The Dumb Knight* (1607–8), Epire is immediately established as a villain when he vows revenge on a young hero who has fairly defeated him in chivalric combat, but a jumble of motives shortly develops until the revenge is forgotten in his intrigue to depose the King. He professes that "Revenge now rules as sovereign of my blood" only because the playwright uses every device to emphasize his viciousness.[4] In the tangle of perhaps thirteen different revenge actions launched in *The Revenger's Tragedy* (1606–7), several are immediately forgotten and at least five have no motivation whatsoever. The nonsense of much of the plot is epitomized by the furious vow of Ambitioso and Super-vacuo to revenge the execution of their brother, even though it is they themselves who have accidentally caused his death. These characters for whom revenge is merely a device imposed by the playwright are significant because they indicate how useful the motive could be in arousing revulsion. They seek vengeance solely because they are villains. According to ethics, revengers are evil; according to theatrical tradition, evil men are *ipso facto* revengers.

In attempting to determine the audience's attitude toward such hero-revengers as Hieronimo, Antonio, Vindici, and Hamlet, we find that all these villain-revengers are significant for still another reason. Conventions of diction and action became associated with such characters as Barabas, Piero, and Mendoza. Since we are certain of the audience's attitude toward these villains, we have a useful guide to its attitude toward the dramatic conventions associated with them. If, for example, we found that only villains dip their hands in the blood of their victims (a statement I cannot yet make with assurance), we would do well to pause before pronouncing Brutus's actions after Caesar's death to be evidence of his virtue. Of course a skillful playwright can transform a convention, but if he uses an established device, he inevitably awakens a certain response. He may capitalize on the audience's associations; he may consciously modify them. But he cannot ignore them.

Several of these conventions are fairly rigid by the time of *Lust's Dominion* in 1600. Eleazar, the Moor, sets out to destroy the entire Spanish aristocracy, apparently to revenge his own capture and his father's slaying. Typically, his vows of revenge serve merely to heighten his demonic nature, for his true motive is Tamburlainian ambition. Many familiar conventions are used to establish him as the epitome of evil; of these, three deserve special note. Appropriately, other characters are reminded of Hell when they but look at Eleazar's face.[5] As black in spirit as in complexion, he not only dares damnation, he embraces it. He swears that "Revenge and I will sail in blood to hell" (II.iii.192)—and they do.[6] The second convention is closely related.

---

[5] In *Othello,* Shakespeare's portrayal of the Moor, by convention a figure of unrelieved evil, is ample proof that a skilled playwright could transform a convention if he chose, putting the associations to work in a new way.

[6] Quotations are from *The Dramatic Works of Thomas Dekker,* ed. Fredson Bowers (Cambridge, Eng., 1961), Vol. IV.

As a creature of blackness, Eleazar invokes the aid of night as he begins his campaign of murder (II.ii.163-65). The conventional night speech became extremely popular to indicate the villain's affinity to evil. He may actually invoke the powers of night to aid him in his dark deed, like Eleazar, or he may welcome night as congenial to his evil spirit and intentions, like Piero (*Antonio's Revenge*, I.i) and Mendoza (*The Malcontent*, II.v). Speeches became so stereotyped that they could be interchanged: night is the time of owls, ravens, mandrakes, ghosts, and open graves; night will hide my evil with its gloomy shades, and sleep will be my ally by closing the eyes of witnesses. Macbeth's invocation of night is original in its subtle imagery, but conventional in its concept and purpose. A third convention is Eleazar's almost hilarious enjoyment of his own villainy, a trait found in varying degrees in Barabas, Piero, and Mendoza. All three of these conventions—the association with Hell, the affinity to night, the delight in intrigue—are part of a long-established tradition with its roots in the medieval Vice.

This brief survey of some two dozen villain-revengers appears to justify Cutwolfe's assertion that "revenge in our tragedies is continually raised from hell." However, as noted earlier, these characters are all totally corrupt. By nature committed to evil, they would be loathed by the audience even if they did not attribute their crimes to vengeance. They serve our present investigation only by revealing the general horror that revenge aroused and by indicating the audience's response to a series of conventions.

In the Elizabethan and Jacobean drama produced by 1607, we find at least fifteen non-Shakespearean plays in which characters face a dilemma analogous to that of Hamlet: a basically good man sustains an injury so severe that the law would execute the evildoer or would pardon his immediate slaying by a private citizen. The hero-revenger may have flaws of character, but, at least until he must decide whether or not to take private revenge, his primary commitment is to virtue.

*Gorboduc* (1562) shows how useful even early playwrights found revenge motifs to be in intensifying the miseries of civil and domestic chaos. When Gorboduc, in a rash move anticipating King Lear, resigns his crown and divides the kingdom equally between his two sons, Ferrex, the elder, understandably resents being deprived of half his rightful inheritance. Rejecting the temptation to take revenge,

Ferrex staunchly affirms his obedience to the gods, but unwisely accepts his parasite's crafty suggestion that he arm against possible attack by his brother. The younger brother, Porrex, is furious at what he assumes to be preparation for an attack on himself, and, similarly incited by a parasite, wrathfully vows to reward mischief with mischief. His decision initiates a cycle of horrors.

From that point on, Norton and Sackville take every opportunity to name revenge as the cause of all the ensuing chaos. Hearing that his sons are in arms, Gorboduc loses all control, wildly invoking the curse of Jove on both boys. Jove answers immediately: a messenger reports that Ferrex has killed his brother, and Gorboduc calls on heaven to send down flames of revenge. The motif is reinforced by a dumb show of the three Furies, immediately followed by a long plaint in which the Queen, Videna, rages for revenge against her surviving son. We feel no sympathy for her eventual murder of Ferrex, who is deeply repentant, because she stabs him when he is asleep and defenseless, and because we learn that he died raising his hands in prayer to heaven. When the long-suffering people finally rise and kill both Gorboduc and Videna, the playwrights attribute their rebellion once again to revenge, rather than to the more obvious political motives. The court is appalled:

> Shall subjects dare with force
> To worke revenge upon their princes fact?
> (V.i.17–18)[7]

Here, as in Carlisle's speech in *Richard II,* the question of revolt against a king is different from the question of private vengeance. Even so, it is significant that the playwrights treat every possible evil act as if it were revenge. In *Gorboduc* revenge is seen as the uncontrolled force that can tear the state apart.

In John Pikeryng's *Horestes* (1567), we encounter the first of several puzzling ambiguities. The problem is inherent in the source story. To Aeschylus, the revenge was wrong but Orestes was right. Ordered by Apollo to kill his mother, Orestes is vindicated on the grounds that the divine command itself was wrong, that the gods must learn and change. If Pikeryng read the *Oresteia* (which seems

---

[7] Joseph Quincy Adams, ed., *Chief Pre-Shakespearean Dramas* (New York, 1924).

doubtful), he probably did not even grasp the point. Bound by a familiar plot, he was forced to justify Horestes at the end of the play, but his Christian outlook led him to treat the revenge itself in the conventional manner. As a result, the play splits in two. The first half is a medieval morality in which Horestes falls to the temptation of vice and commits a shocking crime; the second half is a chivalric romance in which Horestes, as rightful ruler, purges the commonwealth of evil and is rewarded with a convenient princess. Since the play is often cited as proof of a theatrical tradition justifying revenge, we must consider the action in some detail.

The first character to enter would immediately be recognized by the audience as the medieval Vice. After boisterously threatening the audience in traditional fashion, he meets a pair of rustics, announces that his name is "Patience," and promptly reveals his real nature by losing his temper. He provokes the two fools into a revenge fight against each other, takes the occasion to beat up both of them, and exits before they can turn on him. Thus before Horestes enters, the Vice is revealed as the traditional tempter: he gives as his name the virtue that opposes the vice he really is; he instigates discord, turning friend against friend; he revels in the dissension he causes. Already we guess that his real name is "Revenge," although he will not admit the fact until the middle of the play.

Horestes now enters. Remembering his mother's evil deed, he cannot pity her, but he knows that Nature commands him to forgive. Trapped by his dilemma, he prays for guidance; at that moment the Vice enters, announcing that he is the messenger of the gods. Horestes is doubtful, but the Vice insists that he was in heaven when the gods agreed that Horestes must revenge Agamemnon's death. His name, he now announces, is "Courage," and his appeal frees Horestes of all qualms. He is eager to act; his "hart doth boyle in ded, with firey perching heate" (1.251).[8] The Vice urges him to act immediately in the heat of excitement, for he might repent of his decision if he delays. To this point, the audience could have no doubt that Horestes has been misled. We know the Vice lies when he says he is "Courage," and we have no reason to believe he was at the council in heaven.

[8] Quotations are from the Malone Society Reprint, ed. Daniel Seltzer (1961).

Although Idumeus and his Council both approve the proposed campaign against Clytemnestra, Horestes is forced once again to struggle with the moral issue. Leading his men to battle, thirsting for blood, he pauses to pray that his "courage" will not fail him, that the gods will help him. This time the gods do answer: Nature appears to argue that she is unequivocally opposed to matricide. It is inconceivable that we are to reject Nature's arguments as invalid, but Horestes shuts off the debate by insisting that the laws of god and man demand blood for blood.

As Horestes gathers his troops, the Vice reveals to the audience for the first time that his true name is "Revenge," and exults in all the carnage he is causing. When Horestes at last faces his mother and begins to weaken, Revenge craftily begins to weep: "O oo oo, you care not for me, nay, sone I have don I warrant ye" (894). That traditional appeal of the medieval tempter snaps Horestes out of his hesitation. Though Clytemnestra prays for mercy, he pronounces judgment. She kneels in a final desperate appeal for pity, but Revenge drags her to her death.[9]

After the killing, Revenge revels in his success. Horestes now "doth rew" his decision: "And was it not yll / His mother to kyll?" (1022–25). But repentance has come too late. Lest we have any doubt of the audience's judgment at this point, Fame enters to trumpet Horestes' new reputation: he has joined Nero and others of like "enterpryse" (1072).

Suddenly we find ourselves in another play. Going to Athens to seek judgment, Horestes pleads before Menalaus that he had piously obeyed the gods. Although the audience knows otherwise, his defense is accepted by all, and the play closes as Truth and Dewty crown him king and he is married to Menalaus' daughter. Revenge, however, has

---

[9] David M. Bevington has suggested that Horestes' character "is cleansed by the transfer of his avenging nature to an allegorical abstraction" (*From "Mankind" to Marlowe,* Cambridge, Mass., 1962, p. 179). I doubt, however, that the Elizabethan audience would see this distinction. In *Everyman,* the entrance of Knowledge indicates Everyman's own knowledge of his sin; the revival of Good Deeds marks a change in his spiritual state. In the morality tradition, still vital to the end of the sixteenth century, allegorical vices and virtues were not conceived of as having separate identities apart from the everyman figure in whom they operated. In the same way, Horestes kills his mother at the instigation of Revenge, a personification of his own desire. Had Pikeryng intended otherwise, he could have created a figure called "Justice" to serve as Horestes' executioner instead of the Vice.

not vanished. He is still up to his old Vice's tricks, but he fails when he finds Menalaus and Horestes accompanied by Amyte and Dewty. At the end of the play, revenge is still a vice, but Horestes is clearly virtuous.

Pikeryng is either a very confused moralist or a very careless playwright. The latter seems more likely. Several changes from his source suggest that he intended to follow the usual morality pattern: a good man yields to vice but repents and returns to virtue. In Caxton's *Recuyell of the Historyes of Troye,* Horestes was explicitly obeying a divine command and there is no suggestion of moral guilt. Pikeryng treats the command as a demonic lie and makes Horestes immediately repent of the murder. The ambiguity of *Horestes* thus seems to lie only in the plot resolution, not in the moral issue. The role of the Vice, the arguments of Nature, and the witness of Fame all make it clear that Pikeryng yielded to dramatic expediency in the end of the play, but that he consistently condemned revenge itself. The full title of the play reveals his intention: *A Newe Enterlude of Vice Conteyninge, the Historye of Horestes with the cruell revengement of his Fathers death, upon his one natur[a]ll Mother.*[10]

Ambiguity presents a more significant problem in Kyd's *The Spanish Tragedy* (c. 1587). Understanding the attitude of both Kyd and his audience is especially important in light of the play's popularity and its widespread influence. Unfortunately, moral issues are so tangled that some critics can view Hieronimo as a fully justified hero, pursuing his sacred duty of revenge with the sanction of the gods and the sympathy of the audience, while others see him as a good man

---

[10] E. B. de Chickera agrees that the Vice is lying but suggests that Horestes actually decides on revenge only when Idumeus, the king and thus God's magistrate, and his Council approve, thus implying divine sanction. Therefore "Horestes' revenge is now no longer a private revenge but a public revenge on Egisthus and Clytemnestra" ("Horestes' Revenge—Another Interpretation," *Notes and Queries,* n.s., VI, 1959, 190). If this was Pikeryng's intention, he is even more careless than I have suggested, since the debate with Nature and thus Horestes' final decision to reject the exhortations of virtue both follow the meeting with Idumeus, and since the Vice's role as evil motivator remains unchanged throughout. These facts also cast doubt on interpretations of the play as an allegory based on the life of Mary Queen of Scots. Among those who hold this view, James E. Phillips suggests that Pikeryng reshaped the old legend to argue that the deposing of an adulterous queen was politically, legally, and morally justified ("A Revaluation of *Horestes* (1567)," *Huntington Library Quarterly,* XVIII, 1955, 227–44). It is true that a strong case is made by Idumeus and his Council, but the allegorical interpretation cannot account for the function of both Nature and the Vice.

who turns villain.[11] Although there is solid evidence for both positions, the present study suggests that the play is less contradictory
than it appears.

Until the moment when Hieronimo confirms the identity of his
son's murderers, his dilemma is carefully defined and his character
consistently developed. He refers his actions to standards of which the
audience could thoroughly approve, and his character and situation
arouse increasing sympathy. At the same time, his emotional state increasingly warns of danger.

When Hieronimo discovers the body of Horatio hanging in the
arbor, he longs for revenge but will take no action. He will wait,
trusting to the justice of the heavens to unmask villainy. In the mean-
time, he and his wife, Isabella, must hide their grief. There is nothing
crafty in the decision to dissemble, merely recognition of the need for
rational control. Though Hieronimo yearns for death, he rejects suicide. Our response is completely sympathetic. Unless, however, we attribute the wild lamentations to Kyd's rhetorical extravagance, Hieronimo's excessive grief may be a sign of danger. Two other hints
may be planted intentionally. Hieronimo longs for revenge solely as
a means of relieving his own misery: he says nothing of duty to Horatio. And surely the audience would be at least vaguely uneasy when
he decides to leave the corpse unburied so that he may feed his grief
until he can take revenge. In the prologue we have heard that the
spirit of Don Andrea could not cross Acheron until his corpse was
buried, and in Pedringano's sentence later in the play we are reminded that only the foulest of criminals go unburied.[12] Traditionally,
there can be no worse desecration of a corpse.

Sympathy for Hieronimo and warnings of danger both increase in
III.ii. An intervening scene in Portugal has suggested a lapse of time,

11 For example, C. V. Boyer argues that Hieronimo's cause is legitimate because no legal
redress is available and because Revenge and the ghost of Don Andrea "heighten the sense
of revenge as a sacred duty" (*The Villain as Hero in Elizabethan Tragedy*, New York, 1914,
p. 100). In direct opposition, Bowers insists that by the end of the play Hieronimo's Machiavellian and Italianate actions would have made the Elizabethan audience view him as a villain (*Elizabethan Revenge Tragedy*, pp. 65–83). For an excellent analysis of the ambiguities,
see Philip Edwards's introduction to his edition for the Revels Plays. All quotations are from
this edition.

12 In the *Vindicta mihi* soliloquy, Hieronimo refers in passing to the belief that "Heaven
covereth him that hath no burial" (III.xiii.19), but the counter-evidence receives greater
emphasis.

and Hieronimo enters in an agony of frustration. He has trusted to the justice of the heavens, but the heavens have failed him. Night and the wounds of Horatio's corpse solicit him to consider, for the first time, a course that he knows to be unnatural:

> The ugly fiends do sally forth of hell,
> And frame my steps to unfrequented paths,
> And fear my heart with fierce inflamed thoughts.
> (III.ii.16-18)

We cannot doubt that a Christian response is encouraged in this speech. To Kyd's audience, the dreadful implication would seem clear: if Heaven does not act, Hieronimo will turn to Satan. At that precise moment, Heaven does act, as Bel-Imperia's letter naming Lorenzo and Balthazar as the murderers drops at Hieronimo's feet. Only the sudden intervention of Heaven prevents him from taking the first step on a fearful road. Despite the most intense provocation, Hieronimo is still trying to obey divine will, and we approve of his sensible doubts about the letter and his determination not to risk his life by acting upon what may be a trick. To confirm the murderers' identity, he decides to visit Bel-Imperia, but is immediately thwarted by Lorenzo. Although Hieronimo dissembles with Lorenzo, he uses no mockery, no ironic double meanings. He has our sympathy as a man who, in an apparently helpless situation, is exercising tight control.[13]

We next see Hieronimo functioning in his official capacity as Marshal, appearing in court to sentence Pedringano for murder. He is painfully aware of the irony of his situation. As a magistrate, he can effect justice for others:

> But shall I never live to see the day
> That I may come, by justice of the heavens,
> To know the cause that may my cares allay?
> (III.vi.5-7)

The brazen impudence of Pedringano further lacerates him, for he sees that Horatio's murder was not an isolated crime. The times have

---

[13] My analysis is based on the original play. The revisions, which first appear in the Quarto of 1602, merely extend Hieronimo's madness and move it forward in the play so that he begins raving immediately upon discovering the body. The reviser may in places give evidence of being a better poet, but Kyd had a more interesting concept of Hieronimo's character.

become monstrous if murder can be so insolently dismissed. In the name of God he sentences Pedringano to death, but he himself must wait on God's good time. He still refers his cause to the will of Heaven, but his agonized questioning makes us wonder how long his patience can last.

In the ensuing soliloquy, Hieronimo has reached the breaking point. His laments have driven the winds to break "through the brazen gates of hell," but in vain do they

> Beat at the windows of the brightest heavens,
> Soliciting for justice and revenge . . .
> I find the place impregnable. . . .
> (III.vii.9–17)

Again Heaven intervenes at a crucial moment, this time by means of Pedringano's intercepted letter confirming Bel-Imperia's charge. Now Hieronimo sees that Heaven has not been deaf. Though the sequence of accidents had before seemed mere chance, "now I feelingly perceive / They did what heaven unpunish'd would not leave" (III.vii.55–56). But the moment of calm acceptance is brief. Suddenly he gives way to fury, raging against Lorenzo, uttering dire imprecations against Balthazar, and even cursing Lorenzo's father, though the audience knows Castile to be guiltless in the murder. Just as his passion is about to shatter his reason, he catches himself. Railing is pointless; he will take his case before the King.

The sympathy of the audience is probably at its highest. Hieronimo has referred his cause to Heaven, has been rewarded, and is continuing to follow the proper course by deciding to appeal to the law. At the same time, there is another sign of danger. Before, grief alone had suggested Hieronimo's instability, but now rage has been added. What if he fails to convince the King? He says that his only alternative will be to haunt the court with dire threats. If denied, he may devote himself to nursing his hatred and grief, and the suggestion has been firmly planted that he may destroy his own reason.

On his next entrance, we are not surprised to see that Hieronimo's mind is indeed slipping. Meeting two Portingales who ask for directions to Lorenzo's home, he directs them to a left-hand path that leads from a guilty conscience down to Hell. There he pictures Lorenzo boiling in lead and the blood of innocents over a sulphur flame. He breaks into mad laughter and exits, to reappear immediately with a poniard and a rope, the conventional weapons of suicide. The King may be willing to hear him, but what if members of the court prevent him from speaking? If he cannot find justice on earth, he will descend to seek aid of Hell. As before, however, he determines to live to avenge Horatio's death. Now the King enters. His chance has finally come.

Though Hieronimo's grief and rage have ample cause and though the prolonged tension of waiting and inactivity has been extreme, the danger suggested in earlier scenes has now become explicit. Hieronimo's passion has led him into a madness that threatens both body and soul. Heaven is forgotten. Now he is wholly devoted to revenge, not justice, as he longs for Lorenzo's damnation (pictured in Christian terms) and again considers invoking Hell. Highly significant is Kyd's use of a fixed device, long since established in the moralities, to indicate damnable despair, the lowest point to which sin could lead Everyman: armed with weapons of self-destruction, usually a rope and a knife, Everyman would be about to commit suicide when a grace figure would enter to stop him.[14] Of course, Kyd does not put Hieronimo's thoughts of suicide into a Christian context, but his increasing desire to invoke Hell, his shift from grief to rage, and his incipient madness—all these, together with the audience's familiarity with the dangers of melancholy and with theatrical conventions, strongly suggest that the Elizabethan would now view Hieronimo with urgent apprehension. Moreover, Hieronimo has all but admitted defeat even before he approaches the King. Had the King been revealed as corrupt or had Hieronimo been out of favor at court, we would understand his despair of success. Unless Lorenzo can prevent access to the King, however, we have every reason to expect a fair hearing. In his speech to the Portingales and in his soliloquy on suicide, Hieronimo has indicated that his own state of mind is his greatest danger.

The following scene justifies our fears. Though the King seems completely willing to hear him, Hieronimo is so distracted by Loren-

---

[14] In *A Looking Glass for London and England* (1587–91), a Usurer, tempted to despair by an Evil Angel, enters with a halter and dagger but is restrained by the Good Angel's promise of mercy. The scene may have been directly influenced by *The Spanish Tragedy*, but the convention, rooted in treatments of Judas in the medieval mysteries, had long been established. In *Magnyfycence* (1515–23), for example, Myschefe presents the sinner with a halter and a knife, but both he and Dyspayre flee when Good Hope enters.

zo's two minor attempts to quiet him that his fury breaks forth in a fit of total insanity. He madly digs at the earth and rages:

> [I] here surrender up my marshalship:
> For I'll go marshal up the fiends in hell,
> To be avenged on you all for this.
>                                   (III.xii.76–78)

No wonder that the King calls for men to restrain him! Hieronimo would still be given a hearing if he could regain his reason, but he exits, driven—as he himself says—by devils. He has been thwarted not by Lorenzo but by his own madness. As if to emphasize this fact, the King expresses amazement at Hieronimo's inexplicable behavior. He even rejects Lorenzo's advice to remove the Marshal from office, compassionately refusing to "increase his melancholy" and determining to discover the cause. Kindly old Castile himself might give a hearing to the case against his son, for he later inquires closely into rumors that Lorenzo has wronged Hieronimo, making it clear that he would not tolerate any dishonorable behavior (III.xiv). Had Kyd wished to justify Hieronimo's forthcoming actions on the grounds that he had no recourse to law, he could easily have made the King and Castile vicious.

The scene also casts doubt on the argument that because of his role as Marshal, Hieronimo is to be justified as the official magistrate empowered to punish.[15] He has resigned his marshalship, vowing, in a total inversion of values, to marshal up the fiends in Hell to effect his revenge. Moreover, as Hieronimo knows, the fact that a magistrate is responsible for judging lawbreakers scarcely authorizes him to effect his own private revenge by non-legal means.

Hieronimo's mad outburst before the King might easily have served as the turning point of the play, but, lest we have any doubts at all about the moral question, Kyd gives Hieronimo one more soliloquy in which he debates the issue in explicit terms (III.xiii.1–45). In a return to calm and sanity, he is reading a book, trying to check his own descent into Hell. Despite the many pagan references in the play, the issue is unmistakably between the Christian Heaven and Hell, as Hieronimo's first words make clear: "*Vindicta mihi!*" This is, of

---

[15] S. F. Johnson, "*The Spanish Tragedy*: Babylon Revisited," pp. 30–31.

course, the Biblical injunction against revenge, familiar to every member of the audience. His following words echo the equally familiar divine promise—*ego retribuam*—that immediately follows in Scripture.

> Ay, heaven will be reveng'd of every ill,
> Nor will they suffer murder unrepaid;
> Then stay, Hieronimo, attend their will;
> For mortal men may not appoint their time.

At this point, however, Hieronimo apparently turns to the book he is carrying. His eye lighting on two quotations from Seneca, he distorts the meaning of each to serve his own ends and finally and irrevocably rejects patience, determining to wait no longer upon the will of Heaven. Clytemnestra's line from Seneca's *Agamemnon*—"The safe way for crime is always through crime"—is the rationalization of a hardened villainess, but Hieronimo defies this implicit warning.[16] Ironically, he reads it as a justification of revenge:

> Strike, and strike home, where wrong is off'red thee;
> For evils unto ills conductors be....

From the *Troades,* he reads Andromache's tender words of comfort to her son, whom she has hidden from the Greeks in Hector's tomb: "If the fates assist, you will have a safe retreat; if the fates deny life, you will have a tomb." Again Hieronimo reads a distorted meaning into the line: whether he lives or dies in effecting his revenge, he will be content. His decision is now firm. All that remains is to formulate a plan. He resolves to dissemble—not merely, as before, to hide his grief. Rather, he will play the affable courtier with his foes in order to watch and wait.

On superficial consideration, Hieronimo's subsequent actions follow the pattern we have been led to expect. An old man enters to

---

[16] John D. Ratliff suggests that Hieronimo quotes only the first part of Clytemnestra's argument but that we are to understand her further justification that she must kill Agamemnon before he kills her. Thus, he argues, Hieronimo acts out of self-defense ("Hieronimo Explains Himself," *Studies in Philology,* LIV, 1957, 112–18). Ratliff's interpretation would seem to overlook two objections. Even if a majority of the audience knew Seneca's *Agamemnon* that intimately (which is doubtful), the reading of one brief line does not allow time for tangential associations to rise to the conscious mind. And even if the audience did recall Clytemnestra's situation, it would also recall the fact that in Seneca she is a villainess who rationalizes her evil intent.

beseech justice for his murdered son, and Hieronimo again slips into madness, lacerating himself for inaction, swearing to descend to Hell and marshal a troop of Furies to torture Lorenzo, going berserk as he tears up the old man's petition with his teeth, running wild, and finally taking leave of reality as he mistakes Bazulto first for Horatio and then for a Fury. We sympathize as his rage subsides into broken grief, but we have been forewarned of the nightmare in store.

Throughout the final scenes, Hieronimo is a different man. Joining forces with Bel-Imperia, planning with his intended victims the fatal play that is to be his instrument of revenge, and settling important last-minute details with Castile, he is coolly efficient and eagerly confident. The struggle is over; he has surrendered himself wholly to his purpose. When Isabella, who has also gone mad from grief, commits suicide, Hieronimo expresses no sorrow for her death. Nor does he grieve for his son. On the contrary, he acts very much like a medieval Vice figure, enjoying his dissembling role, teasing his enemies with tricks of language, making fulsome protestations of friendship, grimly delighting in ironic lines of double meaning (III.xiv.120ff, IV.i. 52ff).

His revenge is as total and as bloody as we now expect. His defense to the court makes no mention of the law's failure, of his duty to his son, of his authorization as Marshal to punish, or of any other conceivable justification. He speaks only of his own pain. He does not declare his satisfaction that justice has triumphed; he says rather that his "heart is satisfied," that he is "eas'd with their revenge" (IV.iv. 129, 190). Though he expresses passing regret that Bel-Imperia has played her part too realistically in killing herself, he glories in the deaths of Lorenzo and Balthazar, and, for no reason whatsoever, stabs gentle old Castile before killing himself.[17]

On the surface, the play seems an emphatic portrayal of the ravages of revenge, arousing increasing apprehension and horror in the audience as Hieronimo moves from excessive grief to rage to madness to

[17] The killing has been justified on the grounds that Castile opposed the love of Don Andrea and Bel-Imperia, but the argument is not convincing. In the play itself, Castile is a sweet old man who does not deserve blame, much less sudden death. Equally savage and pointless is Hieronimo's biting out of his tongue. It has not been cited above as further evidence of his deterioration, however, because Kyd may originally have intended Hieronimo to have some secret he could not divulge even under torture. In the revised version extant, the sole reason seems to be Kyd's desire for another bit of sensation.

crafty intrigue to demonic barbarism. Unfortunately, there are several contradictions. Although Hieronimo progressively aligns himself with Hell, he believes that "all the saints do sit solliciting / For vengeance on those cursed murderers" (IV.i.33–34). Kyd may intend this confident assumption to be ironic, for it is Hieronimo's response to Bel-Imperia's announced determination to send the hateful souls of their enemies to Hell. But a reference to his forthcoming revenge as "wrought by the heavens" (IV.ii.196) and the Ghost's announcement at the close of the play that Hieronimo will find joy in Elysium (IV.v.23–26) cannot be dismissed. We find the same contradiction reflected in the constant references throughout the play both to Heaven as the abode of justice and to the wise judges of Hell. The ambiguity is minor but unavoidable, and, as a result, we can never be sure exactly how the Elizabethans judged Hieronimo. Nonetheless, Kyd's explicit appeal to Christian judgment in "*Vindicta mihi*," the association of revenge with night, Hell, and the fiends, and the manifest relationships between revenge and passion, madness, despair, and savagery—all these make it extremely doubtful that Kyd's audience viewed Hieronimo as wholly justified.

Three plays produced in the late 1580's reflect the immediate influence of *The Spanish Tragedy*: *The Misfortunes of Arthur* (1588), *Locrine* (published in revised form in 1591 but produced earlier in a lost version), and *David and Bethsabe* (c. 1588–94).[18] All three plays are unified by the revenge motif, even though the issue of private vengeance is irrelevant, or at most tangential, to the source story. In all three plays the audience is clearly intended to view revenge as deplorable.

*The Misfortunes of Arthur* offers striking proof that great works of art are rarely produced by a committee. Taking the relatively simple story of the struggle between Arthur and Mordred, Thomas Hughes and his fellow playwrights produced a series of dissertations on several popular dramatic motifs and philosophical themes, many of which are in conflict.[19] On only two things are they agreed: the

---

18 I suggest a later date than is customary for *David and Bethsabe* to allow for the possible influence of *Tamburlaine*. See below, p. 56.

19 Arthur blames the pagan fates and Fickle Fortune for his downfall, but then calls it divine punishment for his sin. After convincing us that he dies a sinner, he then launches into a patriotic glorification of his career. Guenevora's retirement to a cloister is alternately attributed to repentance, despair, and revenge.

horror of civil war and of revenge. Indeed, revenge is forced into the play solely to intensify the atmosphere of misery and doom. Gorlois, a prologue ghost, calls for revenge, but the specific revenge he invokes is irrelevant to the play. He merely establishes the atmosphere of wild hatred and the general theme. Throughout the play, revenge, the work of "cursed imps," is seen as the cause of all calamities. Typical is the treatment of Guenevora. Hearing of Arthur's return, she rages for revenge, calling on the fiends as does Lady Macbeth. Fronia urges her to calm her passion and banish such unnatural thoughts, for "A Ladies best revenge is to forgive" (I.ii.57).[20] At this, Guenevora turns her wrath inward and decides to kill herself. Her choice is presented in outlandishly contradictory terms. She is presented as a despairing Christian who commits "suicide," but chooses, as the means of death, to take "revenge" on herself by retiring to a cloister,

> Where dayly pennance done for each offence,
> May render due revenge for every wrong.
> (I.iii.72–73)

The state of her soul will not bear close scrutiny. All that matters is the emotional impact. Throughout the play, motives of despair and revenge are capriciously attributed to all of the major characters, whether relevantly or not, merely to emphasize their misery.

Even Arthur's decision to defend his kingdom against Mordred is attributed to a desire for private revenge. As King, Arthur obviously has not only the right but the duty to crush rebellion, but the playwrights carefully avoid the political justification. Once the irrelevance of the revenge motive is granted, the treatment of Arthur's dilemma, unlike that of Guenevora, is surprisingly consistent. In two extended debates, he effectively counters the argument that he should take just "revenge" on his rebel son. He rejects every appeal to justice, fame, and honor by citing the conventional precepts and determines to "leave the Heavens revengers of my wrong" (III.i.34). But when Mordred sends a challenge that taunts him with cowardice, Arthur at last decides to fight. The result is disastrous for both the principals and the country. Even though Arthur is the legal ruler defending

---

[20] Quotations are from *Early English Classical Tragedies*, ed. John W. Cunliffe (Oxford, 1912).

himself against rebellion, his choice is judged as wrong. When dying, he takes all the blame on himself. He should have endured and lived abroad or even have accepted death at Mordred's hands.

> But wrong incensing wrath to take revenge
> Preferred chaunce before a better choyse.
>
> (V.i.33–34)

Anything, argue the playwrights, is better than civil war. They emphasize their point by treating all misfortunes as the inevitable harvest of private vengeance.

*Locrine* is a miserable revenge hash of even more confused motives. The familiar figure of Ate opens and closes the play, and revenge is forced in at every opportunity. The ghost of Albanact enters to pursue Humber throughout four supposedly hair-raising scenes—even though he has already been revenged. Typically, the children of Corineus take revenge on Locrine for their father's death—even though Corineus was killed in battle by Locrine's enemy. Whenever a revenge motif is initiated, the victims automatically become pathetic and the revengers become fiends, no matter what their prior roles have been. When he is pursued by Albanact's ghost, Humber, the erstwhile barbaric invader of Britain, becomes the pitiable victim of a malevolent power. The virtuous Guendoline, cast off by the lustful, arrogant Locrine, in ten lines changes from a model of patience to a screaming harpy, eagerly envisioning some strange and hideous death for Sabren, the innocent daughter of Locrine and his paramour, Estrild. Conversely, once Locrine and Estrild are pursued by revenge, they become the virtuous and oppressed hero and heroine. Any values one might find in the blank verse of the play are more than offset by the shoddy sensationalism and sentimentality, the very features that tell us where the audience's sympathies lay.

A much more thoughtful condemnation of revenge is found in George Peele's *David and Bethsabe*. From the second book of Samuel, Peele selected the three unrelated episodes of David's lust for Bathsheba, Absalom's killing of Amnon for raping Tamar, and Absalom's revolt against David. Lesser playwrights would have written a disjointed chronicle merely to cram in the popular elements suggested by the Bible. Peele retains them all—rape, incest, adultery, murder, pitched battles, suicide, and morally edifying speeches—but gives his plot considerable unity by focusing on the parallel themes of revenge and repentance.

The Bible suggests no such pattern of cause and effect, and the three episodes are separated by considerable intervals of time. Peele intersplices the three to create one plot. David only desires, but has not yet taken, Bethsabe when, in a vaguely parallel situation, Ammon lusts for and rapes his sister, Thamar. Immediately, in a scene not in the Bible, Absolon goes to David to demand that his brother be punished, and David orders that revenge be left to him. Although Absolon now plans his revenge, it is delayed while we return to the killing of Urias, the union of David and Bethsabe, their repentance, the death of their child, and David's rousing himself to battle—and thus, by dramatic convention, to virtue.

We now return to the Biblical sequence, although Peele adapts it to fit his theme. Absolon invites Ammon to a feast and deliberately waits until his brother is drunk before killing him and then fleeing the country. At the moment David hears of the murder, the Widow of Thecoa enters to forestall any desire for vengeance. In the Bible, she convinces David merely to bring Absalom back from exile, but he refuses to see his son for two years. Peele relates the episode to specific Christian doctrine: David affirms that "to God alone belongs revenge" (947), and he immediately welcomes back Absolon with love.[21] Despite the reconciliation, Absolon treacherously plans his conspiracy, and the last half of the play portrays David's continuing repentance and Absolon's rebellion and death. Peele's unifying plan is clear. David views Ammon's lust and Absolon's murder and subsequent revolt as God's just punishment for his own sin. Even when Absolon attacks, David continues to love his son and abjure revenge. He knows that the rebellion must be quelled, but he orders his commander not to touch a hair of his beloved son's head. Thus he becomes a model of patience, who follows the pastoral injunction to look first at his own sin and leave revenge to God.

In contrast, Absolon is the man who does take revenge and is destroyed. By adding David's command that punishment of Ammon be left to him, Peele emphasizes Absolon's wrong. Moreover, he intensi-

21 Quotations are from the Malone Society Reprint, ed. W. W. Greg, 1912.

fies Absolon's guilt in the murder itself. In the Bible, his servants do the actual killing, while Amnon is "merry" and thus vulnerable. In the play, Absolon waits until Ammon is thoroughly drunk—and thus spiritually unprepared—and strikes the fatal blow himself. Peele turns the young man of great beauty described in the Bible into an ambitious, strutting egomaniac, who may echo Tamburlaine when he envisions the "glorie of a crowne" (1214) and marvels at his own beauty:

> ... heaven shall burne in love with Absolon,
> Whose beautie will suffice to chast all mists,
> And cloth the suns sphere with a triple fire....
> (1173-75)

He ever professes to serve God, but his swelling pride reveals blasphemous arrogance:

> [God's] thunder is intangled in my haire,
> And with my beautie is his lightning quencht,
> I am the man he made to glorie in....
> (1224-26)

Peele arouses considerable compassion for Absolon in his death, but there can be no doubt that the revenger has been corrupted, whereas David, in his enduring love and willing obedience to divine law, has been redeemed.

In a crucial scene in *Edward II* (c. 1592), Marlowe also capitalized on his audience's response to the revenge theme. In the middle of the play, Edward hears that his beloved favorite, Gaveston, has been killed, and he vows revenge on his enemies. Despite Gaveston's corrupting influence, his murder is a flagrant act of rebellion, and Edward, as King, has not only the legal authority but the duty to punish rebels. Still, his vow of vengeance is frightful. Earlier it has been made clear that England means nothing to him. He has dismissed the French invasion as "a trifle" (II.ii.10) and has sworn to chop up all England if he could but be alone with Gaveston (I.iv.47-50 and 69-73).[22] The threat of the greatest of Elizabethan terrors—civil

---

[22] Quotations are from *The Complete Plays of Christopher Marlowe*, ed. Irving Ribner (New York, 1963).

war—has been hovering. Now Edward kneels and vows a bloodbath of revenge. He will drag the headless trunks of his enemies "in lakes of gore" (III.ii.135), drenching his royal standard so that his "bloody colours may suggest / Remembrance of revenge immortally" (139–40). And immediately he adopts a new favorite, the corrupt parasite who had urged him to revenge. By a familiar device, Marlowe reduces audience sympathy for Edward to its lowest point in the play.

The ambiguity of *Horestes* and *The Spanish Tragedy* seems minor in comparison with the fantastic puzzle of *Antonio's Revenge*. After a career of butchery rivaled by few villain-revengers, Antonio is hailed as the sanctified savior of his country. The impossible grotesqueries are so revolting that one is tempted to embrace the interesting theory of R. A. Foakes that the play is a parody, a deliberately comic burlesque of melodramatic posturing by boy actors. Unfortunately, the excessive bombast on which Foakes bases much of his argument is also found in other plays acted by boys in which satire cannot possibly be intended. Therefore, although there is additional evidence for the theory, let us here assume that the play is serious.[23] Since most critics agree that Marston's sympathies lie with Antonio, it is necessary once again to pause for a detailed analysis of the action.[24]

Throughout the first two acts, before he learns that Piero is the author of the many catastrophes that devastate him, Antonio is undoubtedly sympathetic. As he suffers blow after blow in swift suc-

---

[23] Foakes also notes several unmistakable reminders in the play that the actors are boys ("John Marston's Fantastical Plays: *Antonio and Mellida* and *Antonio's Revenge*," *Studies in English Drama Presented to Baldwin Maxwell*, ed. Charles B. Woods and Curt A. Zimansky, Iowa City, 1962, pp. 229–39). The opening of the play seems undeniably comic. Piero enters dripping with blood, gurgling with glee over his first murder and his plans to defame his own daughter. In an ensuing dialogue, Strotzo, his tool, keeps trying to speak, only to have his words choked off again and again by Piero's torrent. By the end of the scene, Strotzo gives up even trying to answer Piero's volley of questions and merely grunts a throttled "Yes" or "No"—only to be blasted as a "dull lump" for not speaking up. Surely the audience howled.

[24] Even a casual reading of the play leaves one gasping at Parrott's assertion that there is no moral blurring in the work of John Marston (*The Plays and Poems of George Chapman*, London, 1910–14, II, 841). In light of the glaring contradictions in the play, it is little wonder that Fredson Bowers considers Antonio a villain whereas Levin L. Schücking believes him to have been viewed sympathetically by his audience, even in the slaughter of the innocent boy Julio (Bowers, *Elizabethan Revenge Tragedy*, p. 124; Schücking, *The Meaning of Hamlet*, London, 1937, p. 138). The critical problem is epitomized by the analysis of Samuel Schoenbaum, who believes Marston's sympathies to lie with the revengers even though he himself finds the play "a prolonged sadistic fantasy." "The Precarious Balance of John Marston," *PMLA*, LXVII (1952), 1071.

cession—the murder of his friend, the defamation of his beloved, Mellida, and the news of his father's death—he understandably becomes
frenzied. The world is cracking beneath him. Alberto, a norm voice,
urges that he moderate his grief, but Antonio responds violently:

> Patience is slave to fools, a chain that's fix'd
> Only to posts and senseless log-like dolts....
> Confusion to all comfort! I defy it.
> Comfort's a parasite, a flatt'ring Jack,
> And melts resolv'd despair.
> (I.ii.271–72, 284–86)[25]

He rushes out, distracted. Like Hieronimo, Antonio arouses sympathy for his grief, but his wild defiance of all conventional counsel and
his frantic determination to pursue a course of "resolv'd despair" are
familiar warnings.

In the first scene of Act III, when the ghost of his father appears
from the tomb to tell Antonio that Piero is the cause of all his woes—
the same Piero who is to marry his mother the next day—the madness
hinted at earlier becomes explicit, and for the rest of the play Antonio
will slip into and out of insanity.[26] After the ghost has vanished, he
rouses himself from his distraction and vows his vengeance:

> By the astoning terror of swart night,
> By the infectious damps of clammy graves,
> And by the mold that presseth down
> My dead father's skull, I'll be reveng'd!
> (ll. 76–79)

When Maria, his mother, urges him to bed, he refuses to leave the
graveyard:

> May I be cursed by my father's ghost
> And blasted with incensed breath of heaven,
> If my heart beat on ought but vengeance! ...

---

[25] Quotations are from G. K. Hunter's edition for the Regents Renaissance Drama Series
(Lincoln, Neb., 1965).

[26] The striking similarities to *Hamlet* are of little help in understanding either play since
it is impossible to know which play was written first or whether both were written simulta-
neously under the influence of the "Ur-Hamlet."

> May I be fetter'd slave to coward chance,
> If blood, heart, brain, plot ought save vengeance!
> (ll. 85–92)

Again entreated by the voice of his father's ghost, he swears he will "suck red vengeance / Out of Piero's wounds" (ll. 129–30). Immediately he has his chance. Piero enters and Antonio is about to stab when he suddenly stops. Everything is too easy. "I'll force him feed on life / Till he shall loathe it" (ll. 140–41).

No matter how confused Marston may have been (and there is a limit to the confusion we can allow a man shortly to take religious orders), it seems impossible at this point that he intended his audience to accord Antonio its moral approval. As conventional ethics warned, Antonio's grief has led him into madness, and, although he temporarily regains control, his vow to wipe everything but revenge from his mind indicates dangerous unbalance. His grisly oath is sworn by the forces of evil: by night, infection, death, and putrefaction.[27] He vows to suck blood, a diabolic practice commonly associated with witches. He rejects an obvious opportunity for immediate retaliation solely because he wants to torture his enemy.

At this precise moment, Julio, Piero's young son, conveniently takes a walk through the graveyard (one cannot guess why) and is delighted to find his beloved friend, whom, he protests, he loves better than his father. Antonio leaps on the hint:

> Thy father! Gracious, O bounteous heaven!
> I do adore thy justice: *venit in nostras manus*
> *Tandem vindicta, venit et tota quidem.*
> (ll. 150–52)

He is transported with ecstatic glee. Everything is perfect: the time (midnight), the place (the graveyard), and the victim. Under the circumstances, it is inconceivable that we are to regard with sympathy his determination to usurp God's function:

---

[27] The ludicrous reference to the "blasting" breath of Heaven may be intended to indicate the chaos of Antonio's mind. If not, one is again tempted to see evidence of parody in the violence of the imagery that confounds Hell in Heaven. Unfortunately, such exaggeration in defiance of logic is all too typical of Marston's work.

> Methinks I pace upon the front of Jove,
> And kick corruption with a scornful heel,
> Griping this flesh, disdain mortality.
>
> (ll. 161–63)

He sizes up his victim like a roast to be carved. If only he knew which part were father, he would rip out that alone; but since mother is inevitably compounded with father in every limb, "Have at adventure, pell-mell, no reverse!" (l. 168). In a standard speech hailing darkness, he offers the boy as a sacrifice to night and stabs him, crying "Behold I spurt warm blood in thy black eyes" (l. 194). Dipping his hands in gore, he sprinkles it as a libation around his father's tomb, praying that the restless spirit will suck the incense of Piero's blood. But his revenge is only begun. He exits crying, "More! / My heart hath thirsting dropsies after gore" (ll. 212–13).

Is it possible that an audience in any age could sympathize with Antonio in this scene, much less approve of his actions? Julio is made sentimentally sympathetic by his desire for a kiss from his friend, his fearful, childish cry of "I'll tell my father" (l. 172), his willing acceptance of the death stroke if only Antonio will still love him. Antonio, in contrast, is an inhuman monster, capering with joy as he hits on this perfect device, eyeing the boy as would a butcher, wallowing in the slaughter of a pathetic child, officiating at a sort of Black Mass. He has had his chance to inflict instinctive retaliation, but hatred has led him to ally himself with night, toads, gaping graves, and diseases, and to do the very deed pledged by Faustus as a token of his service to Beelzebub: to offer up the blood of innocent babes.

When the ghost next appears, in a closet scene paralleling the one in *Hamlet,* Antonio is again transported with ecstasy. Holding up his bloody arms in triumph, he now can dare "the horrid'st object of the night" without fear:

> Look how I smoke in blood, reeking the steam
> Of foaming vengeance. O, my soul's enthron'd
> In the triumphant chariot of revenge.
> Methinks I am all air and feel no weight
> Of human dirt clog. This is Julio's blood;
> Rich music, father! this is Julio's blood.
> Why lives that mother?
>
> (III. ii. 78–85)

Even though his mother has been Piero's innocent dupe, it is clear that Antonio would kill her on the spot if the ghost did not restrain him.

During the fourth act, as Antonio joins with two other revengers to lay plans for trapping Piero, we find further clues to guide our reactions. In explaining why he has disguised himself as a fool, Antonio pointedly allies himself with "Deep, deep-observing, sound-brain'd Mach'avel" (IV.i.24)—a comment scarcely intended to endear him to Elizabethans. Moreover, the revengers invoke Hecate and delight in their intrigue with all the fervor of Barabas.

The eventual murder of Piero may be the most extravagantly savage and grotesque scene in the Elizabethan drama. Tricking Piero into dismissing his attendants, the conspirators bind him in a chair and carry out their detailed plan to torture him to death. Antonio first plucks out Piero's tongue, glorying in the fresh gore on his fist. Then Balurdo, a fool, hurls ludicrous taunts. All take turns triumphing as Piero weeps and then bring him Julio's body to eat, appropriately butchered and roasted. They form a chorus, hurling Piero's crimes at him, and then take turns stabbing him again and again. They are careful, however, to hold off the deathblow as long as possible, "till he hath died and died / Ten thousand deaths in agony of heart" (V.iii. 106–7). Finally, cursing Piero to Hell, the revengers rush at him "pell-mell."

In light of all that has preceded, we are stunned to find ourselves thrust into a moral never-never land in the final scene. Facing the senators and courtiers, all the revengers contend for full responsibility. Antonio eagerly asserts his claim to full credit:

> I will not lose the glory of the deed
> Were all the tortures of the deepest hell
> Fix'd to my limbs.
>
> (V.iii.120–22)

In a responsible play, such a resolve to dare damnation would be conclusive, but to our surprise the senators heartily approve these sentiments and hail the murder as the work of divine ministers:

> Bless'd be you all; and may your honors live,
> Religiously held sacred, even for ever and ever.
>
> (V.iii.127–28)

Although our heroes decide to retire to a religious order, there is no suggestion that they do so in order to expiate their guilt. Rather they have seen enough of the corrupt world and find themselves, apparently, too pure to be further sullied by it.

What does Marston intend by this "sardonic travesty of Christian sentiment"?[28] The foregoing analysis leaves little doubt that he consciously used familiar conventions to arouse the horror of his audience, even to the point of nausea. At the same time, we cannot doubt that he intended us to sympathize with Antonio in the last scene, for it is Antonio who enjoins the courtiers to purge their hearts of hatred and who closes the play with a lament for his dead beloved. In the fantastic inversion of the final scene, the temptation to regard *Antonio's Revenge* as a parody is almost overwhelming.

A cursory reading of *Lust's Dominion* (c. 1600) might suggest that the audience approved the revenge of the protagonists, while condemning that of the villainous Moor, Eleazar. The Queen of Spain, infatuated with Eleazar, conspires with him and Cardinal Mendoza to overthrow the King and have her son, Philip, proclaimed a bastard. At the height of his power, Eleazar is trapped and killed by Philip, the Infanta, and Hortenzo (whose sister has been murdered). The Queen and the Cardinal are forgiven and order is restored. Viewed externally, the plot incidents suggest that the three protagonists have acted in self-defense: they plan to trick Eleazar only after they are imprisoned, facing immediate execution (and, in the case of the Infanta, imminent rape). Surprisingly, however, the playwright goes out of his way to define their plot as "revenge," not self-defense. Does the fact that they are the successful protagonists, approved by all in the play, mean that the Elizabethan audience, too, approved and sympathized?

The present study of theatrical conventions suggests the opposite. Throughout the play, Philip rants like a villain-revenger, swearing that to regain his kingdom he would "venture to hell-gates" (IV.ii. 87). The Infanta glories in the fact that their "revenge is hot," that their "plot is cast, / Into the mold of Hell" (V.ii.149–51). The Queen—guilty of perjury, adultery, treason, and murder—is forgiven, as is the corrupt Cardinal, and all blame is cast on Eleazar. In an extravagant scene that sums up the moral atmosphere of the play, all

---

[28] Ornstein, *The Moral Vision*, p. 155.

of the principals, bound in chains, ferociously curse each other and then turn their vitriolic hatred on Eleazar, cursing him with "worse than damnation" (V.ii.75)—whatever that might be. The entire play is an appallingly tasteless scream of rage at Spain and the Papacy. Though the play is extremely puzzling, it is hard to believe that the average Elizabethan gave such characters either approval or sympathy.

Thus far, we have considered thirteen plays written before *Hamlet* or at about the same time. In nine of these, revenge is almost unmistakably condemned. In four of the nine, revenge is undertaken only by the most flagrant villains: *The Jew of Malta, Selimus, Antonio and Mellida,* and *Alphonsus, Emperor of Germany.* In the other five, the revenge motives of good men, or of men whose will is not wholly perverted, are clearly reprehensible: *Gorboduc, Locrine, David and Bethsabe, The Misfortunes of Arthur,* and *Edward II.* In only four is it even remotely possible that private vengeance was considered justified: *Horestes, The Spanish Tragedy, Antonio's Revenge,* and *Lust's Dominion.* Even in these four, however, although the revengers are vindicated in the final scene (Hieronimo, to a certain extent, by the ghost of Don Andrea), revenge itself is treated as unmistakably evil. Horestes is incited by the demonic character "Revenge"; Hieronimo, Antonio, Philip, and the Infanta all align themselves with the powers of Hell. Although the four plays are slightly ambiguous in their outcome, there is no serious doubt about the audience's attitude toward revenge itself. Prior to *Hamlet,* then, nothing suggests that Shakespeare's audience was conditioned to regard private revenge as a "sacred duty" either in the theater or out of it.

In the first decade of the seventeenth century, the condemnation of revenge becomes progressively explicit in the theater. Ambiguities vanish as private revenge becomes the prerogative of outright villains. In fact, among the six plays remaining to be considered, only two arouse any sympathy whatsoever for their revengers: *Hoffman* and *The Revenger's Tragedy.*

The hero of *Hoffman* (c. 1602) gains our sympathy on his first entrance for his rejection of melancholy, his grief for his dead father, and his determination to seek only just revenge. Before five minutes have passed, however, we learn that his cause is tainted, for his father has been legally executed. Moreover, he joins forces with an obvious villain and swears to kill all who have even one ounce of his enemy's blood. From this point on, the audience is never in doubt. Hoffman rapidly degenerates into a demonic intriguer, imitating Barabas in his trickery and the medieval Vice in his gloating delight in evil. He is a devil incarnate, who dies refusing to call on Heaven. Although some scholars have viewed *Hoffman* as a transitional play, marking an early reaction against an assumed theatrical code approving revenge, the present study indicates that it is, instead, a further step in a tradition rooted in conventional ethics. From Horestes through Hieronimo and Antonio to Hoffman, the condemnation of revenge has become progressively intensified.

Superficial consideration of *The Revenger's Tragedy* (1606–7) might suggest that Vindici merits our approval. He is the playwright's spokesman for the satiric attack on corruption, he has suffered a serious injury for which there is no legal recourse, and he is convinced throughout that he is acting on the side of justice. As scholars have increasingly agreed, however, close study of Vindici's language and actions shows that he becomes almost as corrupt as the evil he sets out to purge.[29] His lashing of vice goes to such lengths that his views become jaundiced, his values twisted. He wallows in filth.

It might be argued that the playwright, obviously a man of deplorable taste if not of sick mind, intends neither the perverted values nor the gratuitous obscenities to suggest unbalance in Vindici. His constant use, however, of one rigid theatrical convention shows unmistakably that he intends us to see Vindici as a villain. Throughout the play, Vindici capers with glee at his own ingenuity, as did the medieval Vice. When the Duke blindly walks into a trap, Vindici is ecstatic: "O sweet, delectable, rare, happy, ravishing!" (III.v.i).[30] Utterly delighted at finding a way to torture the Duke before killing him—

---

[29] Ornstein, for example, notes the fact that Vindici is a different man at the end of the play. He sees the major irony in the fact that Lussurioso "hired Vindici to kill himself and Vindici does so, because he comes to love the game of evil for its own sake and to relish the murder rather than its 'moral' purpose" (*ibid.,* p. 115). Similarly, to Ribner, Vindici "represents the inevitable fate of man who would take upon himself the justice of God, embracing evil in a vain attempt to destroy evil" (*Jacobean Tragedy,* London, 1962, p. 80). Bowers agrees that Vindici is portrayed as a villain. *Elizabethan Revenge Tragedy,* pp. 132–38.

[30] Quotations are from R. A. Foakes's edition for the Revels Plays (Cambridge, Mass., 1966).

"I'm in a throng of happy apprehensions" (III.v.30)—he eagerly anticipates forcing his victim to witness the incestuous embraces of the Duchess and Spurio, "which most affecting sight will kill his eyes / Before we kill the rest of him" (III.v.23–24).

The extended torture of the Duke cannot be the work of a sympathetic hero. Vindici glories in the "malice" of the plot (III.v.109), both he and his brother proclaim themselves villains, and the murder itself is particularly abhorrent, even in this period of theatrical monstrosities. The Duke, thinking he is embracing Vindici's sister, kisses the poisoned skull of Vindici's dead mistress and shrieks as the poison eats out his tongue and teeth. Our heroes stamp on him, Vindici exulting in the fact that the slow spreading of the poison enables them to extend the torture. As the illicit lovers approach, Vindici orders his brother to nail down the Duke's tongue (or what is left of it), and with his own dagger forces his dying victim to watch the lovers embrace and express their loathing of him. In the final act Vindici approves the execution of two completely innocent men who have been caught up in his trickery, and his killing of Lussurioso entails the additional slaughter of three more nobles. Not content, he pounces on a survivor of the massacre, demanding that he confess to all the murders, and the unlucky man is hustled off to immediate execution. In light of all these villainous actions, we cannot possibly share Vindici's shock when the court greets his arrogant confession with a death sentence.[31]

Although Hoffman and Vindici both arouse a certain degree of sympathy before they embark on their vindictive and bloody campaigns, they nonetheless represent a dominant trend in the first decade of the seventeenth century. These years saw the development of the

---

[31] A curious scene in the play deserves brief note because it might seem contradictory. In I.iv, Antonio and the nobles vow to revenge the rape of Antonio's wife. The scene is pointless because the plot is stillborn. The rapist is accidentally killed while in jail awaiting trial. However, the audience's response to the vow itself is important because Antonio is the noble figure who eventually sentences Vindici. In the vow scene, the point is stressed that the nobles will take action only as a last resort. The accused has already been condemned by the court, but the Duke, at the insistence of the Duchess and her sons, has postponed sentence until the next session. All see that his judgment may cool, but they determine to act only on the condition that the court give clear evidence it has been bribed by freeing the guilty boy. The audience would undoubtedly sympathize with the determination to wait on legal justice. Fortunately for Antonio's position as noble hero at the end of the play, he never has to act upon his vow.

villain-revenger as protagonist, a development culminating in such monsters as Borgias in *The Turk* and Isabella in *The Insatiate Countess*. At the same time, the increasing relegation of revenge to villains led inevitably to the emergence of a new type of hero: the man who suffers base injury but whose major virtue is his explicit refusal to take revenge. A brief survey of four such heroes—Frankford in *A Woman Killed with Kindness,* Malevole in *The Malcontent,* Venice in *The Turk,* and Charlemont in *The Atheist's Tragedy*—is useful in further defining theatrical conventions and in determining the probable audience response to certain characters, speeches, and actions.

Although *A Woman Killed with Kindness* (1602) is shot through with ethical absurdities, the major appeal of the play assumes that its audience approves of and sympathizes with patience, even in the face of outrageous provocation.[32] Frankford's major claim to virtue is his refusal to take revenge on his adulterous wife and her lover. Surprising the guilty pair in bed, he rushes out of the chamber to pray for patience. Although Elizabethan law and the audience would probably have pardoned him for killing them both on the spot, he has touched neither. Even in that moment of anguish and distraction, he would not kill them in their guilty sleep, for then their unprepared souls would go to Hell. When Wendoll rushes forth in his nightgown and Frankford instinctively runs after him with sword drawn, we would again pardon him for immediate retaliation, but the maid restrains him. Frankford is grateful for the angel's hand that has prevented a bloody sacrifice, and properly contents himself in the knowledge that Wendoll's own guilty conscience will provide sufficient revenge. Facing the contrite Anne, he prays again for patience and retires to compose himself before deciding what to do. Of course the audience is to sympathize fully with Frankford's decision to send Anne into retirement. His determination to "kill her with kindness" is to be accepted as Christian patience, as a refusal to usurp God's

---

[32] The high-flown idiocy of the subplot, in which a virtuous young man is eager to pay a debt of "honor" by sacrificing his sister's chastity to a villain, has often been noted. In a play intentionally rooted in Christian ethics, it is surprising to find similar nonsense in Anne's extravagant statements of repentance: to undo her wrong, she would gladly hazard the redemption of her soul (i.e., in order to return to a state of grace, she would "dare damnation"); her husband, being a good Christian, of course could not be so "base" as to forgive sin; Heaven is powerless to forgive her unless her husband does. Heywood sacrifices all sense to sentimentality in attempting to make Anne as contrite and miserable as possible.

function, not as a desire to make her suffer.[33] If we had any doubt about the playwright's intention, it vanishes in the final scene when Frankford's course is approved by all as the only means of bringing Anne to repentance.

In *The Malcontent* (1604) we find another hero whose role consists of doing nothing. Although one finishes the play with the impression that Malevole has been extremely busy, he is, despite his voluminous and vivid talk, almost completely passive. His most notable decisions are, indeed, not to act: not to take revenge on the man who deposed him, not to follow the orders of a villain. His only actions are to lead his enemy to repentance and to reveal villainy by means of an innocuous masque. Considering the bitter taste that the play leaves, it is a surprise to discover on close investigation that Malevole aligns himself with wholly conventional ethics. He vows to take "just revenge" against Pietro by tormenting him, but his "torture" merely takes the form of taunting Pietro with the obvious truth that his wife is an adulteress. For two and a half acts, he does nothing but bide his time, waiting for the legal restoration of his dukedom. By the middle of Act III, his patience seems to be wearing thin as he asks Heaven why divine retribution is so long in coming. But instead of taking matters into his own hands, Malevole turns his attention from righting his own wrong to foiling the plots of a second villain, Mendoza. When Pietro is overthrown, solely as a result of Mendoza's intrigue, Malevole, instead of triumphing over his enemy, guides him to true repentance. Now he sees that the heavens have not been deaf to his pleas, for Pietro's conversion is proof of the hand of Providence. Malevole's "revenge" against Pietro is thus the salvation of his injurer. His revenge against the Machiavellian Mendoza is merely kicking the villain out of court. One would scarcely say that Malevole is a paragon of Christian charity, but he is an approved hero for his loathing of corruption, his conversion of and reconciliation with his enemy, and his unwavering determination to leave punishment to Heaven.

*The Turk* (1607–8) neatly exemplifies the evolution of the revenge play in the early seventeenth century. Three types of characters are contrasted: the villain-protagonist, Borgias, whose revenge intrigues

---

[33] As we read the play, a question nags insistently: "But what of Christian forgiveness of the penitent, what of mercy?" Heywood kept his audience too busy sopping up tears to think clearly.

provide the major interest of the play; the virtuous man, Ferrara, who turns revenger and thus deserves his death; and the patient hero, Venice, who leaves revenge to Heaven and is rewarded. Again, the Christian code is explicit. Incited by the supposed ghost of his beloved, the noble Duke of Venice is moved to take private revenge against her murderer but restrains himself on the grounds that he must not usurp Heaven's function. Instead he resolves to indict Borgias before the senate, thus effecting "revenge" by publicly denouncing the villain. In a parallel scene, the noble Duke of Ferrara faces the same decision, but he chooses revenge and becomes evil. He resolves to operate in secret, to spy at night, to effect an especially gory revenge, and finally to make all Venice swim in blood. The playwright thus solves the problem of what to do with two suitors for one heroine: Ferrara must die, so the "poetic justice" of his death is fixed by the revenge convention.

In light of the evolution traced in the preceding pages, *The Atheist's Tragedy, or The Honest Man's Revenge* (c. 1607–11) is not so radical a departure in its explicit condemnation of revenge as is often supposed. In Charlemont's decision to leave D'Amville's punishment to Heaven, Tourneur merely gives extended treatment to a hero who exemplifies patience, as against the more familiar villain, or hero-turned-villain, who exemplifies the rejection of patience. Moreover, such characters as Frankford, Malevole, Venice, and Charlemont are scarcely new on the English stage. The patient hero is found in Peele's *David and Bethsabe* and, as we shall note, in several plays by Shakespeare. What is unique about the play is Tourneur's creation of a ghost who appears specifically to warn against revenge.

The spirit of Montferrers puts his son in a state of agonizing frustration. He tells Charlemont that he has been murdered and Charlemont disinherited, and then in the same breath commands his son to do nothing:

> Attend with patience the success of things,
> But leave revenge unto the King of kings.
> (II.vi.22–23)[34]

Charlemont's ensuing struggle between his natural desires and his conscience reflects exactly the dilemma we have found debated in the

---

[34] Quotations are from Ribner's edition for the Revels Plays.

non-dramatic literature of the period. Driven by grief, and further tortured when his mistress is forced to marry the diseased son of D'Amville, the villain-protagonist, Charlemont finds his burden too heavy to endure with patience and determines to face his enemy. His purpose, however, is deflected by divine intervention. Attacked by D'Amville's son, Charlemont defends himself and is about to deal the deathblow, dedicating it to revenge, when his father's ghost suddenly reappears to restrain him:

> Hold, Charlemont!
> Let him revenge my murder and thy wrongs
> To whom the justice of Revenge belongs.
> (III.ii.32–34)

Charlemont understandably cries out in pain:

> You torture me between the passion of
> My blood and the religion of my soul.
> (III.ii.35–36)

Immediately arrested and imprisoned before his passion can drive him to defy his father's command, Charlemont is given a moment of calm to ponder his dilemma. In a prayer of expostulation, he struggles with the eternal question of why the virtuous suffer. Surely Heaven punishes a man only to the extent of his sins, for how could it be just if it overburdened man with undeserved affliction and yet bound him not to presume on Heaven's function? Such flagrant injustice, he pleads, encourages evil and drives good men to barbarous actions. Charlemont is in torment, his nature warring with his faith, but he rejects such logic as a "profane conceipt, / Against the sacred justice of my God!" (III.iii.13–14).

Submitting to divine will, Charlemont does nothing for the rest of the play but hope for death. Since suicide is impossible for a Christian, he welcomes the chance to be legally executed when, ambushed in the dark, he kills D'Amville's servant in self-defense. At the moment of execution, as the distraught D'Amville seizes the axe from the headsman to strike the fatal blow himself, Providence intervenes, and the villain, by an astounding miscalculation, strikes out his own brains. Charlemont attributes all to Heaven,

Whose gracious motives made me still forbear
To be mine own revenger. Now I see,
That *patience is the honest man's revenge.*
(V.ii.276-78)

If, as the title page claims, the play was often acted "in divers places," we can understand why, even though we today find it alternately dull and outlandish. The audience could have their cake and eat it too. In the atheist D'Amville they had the ultimate in stage villains, whom they could watch in delighted if horrified fascination, while in Charlemont they found the ultimate in patient heroes, with whose struggle they could sympathize and of whose Christian resolve they could thoroughly approve. Fortunately, Charlemont's role is minor compared with that of D'Amville, for the suffering of a patient man, though morally admirable, is not the stuff of drama.

*The Atheist's Tragedy* marks a fitting terminus for our inquiry into audience attitudes toward revenge on the Elizabethan stage. From 1607 to the closing of the theaters, Charlemont's philosophy triumphs in the drama. Issues become obvious. The honest man is the patient man; the villain is the revenger. Ambiguities vanish because the sympathetic revenge protagonist vanishes. Beginning almost fifty years before, his position had become increasingly untenable as, one by one, revenge heroes from Absolon and Hieronimo to Hoffman and Vindici surrendered more and more to villainy. By 1607 *Hamlet* probably could not have been written.

On the basis of this reevaluation of the revenge tradition on the popular stage, what conclusions can we draw? The mass of evidence would seem to deny categorically that the Elizabethan audience viewed blood revenge in the theater as a "sacred duty."

Of the twenty-one plays analyzed in the present chapter, only four are even slightly ambiguous in their condemnation of revenge. The evidence is even more striking when we consider the judgment on specific characters. We have encountered almost forty who are faced with the decision of whether or not to take revenge: of those who take action, only six are vindicated (whether by civil authorities, as in *Antonio's Revenge,* or by supernatural sanction, as in *The Spanish Tragedy*). These six would hardly represent the dominant theatrical tradition even if they were acting as the ministers of God. But they are not. Horestes, Hieronimo, Antonio, and the trio of revengers in *Lust's Dominion* all explicitly align themselves with Hell. The ambiguity of these plays lies in the contradictory vindication applied externally by the playwrights at the end, rather than in the treatment of the revenge itself. Not one of the six characters is motivated to or guided in his revenge by divine authority, or by any principle to which the Elizabethan audience could grant its moral approval.

The dominant theatrical tradition seems unmistakable when we consider the witness of six virtuous characters who explicitly reject revenge, five originally virtuous characters who turn villain when they embark on a course of vengeance, seventeen out-and-out villain-revengers, and many others whose threats or advice to pursue revenge are clearly judged as evil. The trained response of the audience to a series of conventions would also seem unmistakable. If a character willfully defies patience/Heaven and invokes fiends/Hell or is aligned with demonic forces (Hieronimo, Eleazar, Antonio), if he aligns himself with night/darkness/corruption (Piero, Eleazar, Antonio, Mendoza, Ferrara), if he imitates the medieval Vice in his ecstatic delight in intrigue and brutality (Eleazar, Barabas, Piero, Mendoza, Hoffman, Vindici), if he avidly hungers to spill/drink/suck blood (Edward II, Piero, Eleazar, Antonio, Ferrara)—if he does any one of these things he necessarily aroused the suspicions of the audience. All twenty-one plays analyzed, even those that seem ambiguous in their final judgment of the revenger, suggest unequivocally that Nashe's Cutwolfe knew his theater when he asserted that "Revenge in our tragedies is continually raised from hell."

Is there a chance that the present study is overemphasizing the importance of the moral issue? The traditional critical position has been capably stated by Robert Ornstein. He denies that the ethical question of revenge has any relevance to the Elizabethan and Jacobean drama, concluding that "there is not one great tragedy of the period in which the ethical attitude toward blood revenge is a central moral issue."[35] If we set Shakespeare aside for the moment, we have few "great tragedies" left and, of these, even fewer that deal with revenge. Even so, the present study suggests that in those few—perhaps *The Spanish*

[35] Ornstein, p. 23.

*Tragedy, The Jew of Malta, A Woman Killed with Kindness,* and *The Revenger's Tragedy*—the ethical question is, indeed, central. In all the plays we have considered, a study of dramatic conventions indicates that the established ethics of the period were, at the very least, relevant: in some, the hero debates with himself or another character the specific issue of private revenge versus Christian patience; in many, the dramatically operative code is explicitly Christian even though the issue is not debated; in all the others, the orthodox condemnation of revenge would seem to be implicit.

Here lies the problem. We have not recognized the familiar ethical and religious foundation upon which the plays were constructed because it is buried so deep. I would agree with Ornstein that the ethical question of revenge is rarely central in Elizabethan and Jacobean drama, but it is not central, I submit, precisely because it was not a "question" to the average playwright or to most of his audience. The issue was settled. Revenge was a sin against God, a defiance of the State, a cancer that could destroy mind, body, and soul—and that was that. It took a profound mind to cut through accepted platitudes and struggle anew with questions that had long since received official answers, and few of the playwrights we have discussed here were profound thinkers. The majority were practical men of the theater. It probably did not even occur to the author of *The Revenger's Tragedy* to have Vindici debate with himself the moral validity of private revenge. To his audience, the issue would be obvious. A character needed only to say *"Vindicta mihi"* or "To God alone belongs revenge" or "Patience is a slave to fools" or "My heart hath thirsting dropsies after gore" or "Revenge and I will sail in blood to hell." Such clues would suffice to indicate that the audience was to apply its familiar code of judgment.

None of the foregoing has been intended to suggest that the Elizabethan automatically rejected a revenger emotionally because it rejected revenge morally. Human instinct is on the side of the rebel who refuses to submit to injustice. Few dramatic themes are so appealing to man in any age, especially to the Elizabethan—full of energy, aware of the many evils about him, frustrated at the law's delay, yet operating under a code that required him to do nothing. The revenger was an ideal character with whom to identify. In the revenger, he found a man like himself, surrounded by evil and bound by the laws of God and man that said "Thou shalt not" at every turn; but he also saw an exceptional man who, unlike himself, somehow asserted a hidden potential in his willful rebellion against established order, in his defiant refusal to let corruption go unpunished.

The preceding extended discussion of ethical attitudes and dramatic conventions might suggest that the Elizabethan revenge play demands a special historical perspective. However, I believe that historical study validates our intuitive response to the basic issues involved. The dominant Western ethic still condemns private revenge, and the conventions of the revenge play arouse similar responses. When Hieronimo vows to "marshal up the fiends in hell," when Vindici chortles in anticipation of his bloody triumph, we are uneasy. Our emotional reactions and ethical judgments may differ in degree from those of the Elizabethan, but apparently not in kind.

Many of the conventions are, in fact, still vital in the modern theater, and our response to the popular revenge drama of today may be illuminating. Consider a television Western. The son of a good small homesteader learns that a bad big rancher's hired gunman has killed his father. He turns to the sheriff and then to the citizens but finds that the rancher "owns" both law and town. He need not debate his right to take the law into his own hands. The answer is assumed. Although our sympathy is with him, we know that he must not rush out and gun down the killer. The climax comes as our hero, driven by fury and frustration, traps his quarry, raises his gun—and suddenly stops short. In a traditional Western, he takes the killer to the nearest marshal or shames the paralyzed town into action. In an "adult Western," he is gradually consumed by his passion for revenge—alienating the town, rejecting his girl, pursuing his course by any means available—until he kills his man. We know he must be condemned to death, but we and the town regret the waste.

The plot is admittedly crude, evoking the most primitive emotions and the most obvious ethical judgments. That is exactly the point. In its barest outlines the modern plot reveals an archetypal pattern that also underlies the Elizabethan revenge play. May not the Elizabethans' reaction to a revenger have been as mixed as ours? Caught up in the performance, they too may have sympathized strongly with the very actions that later, in ensuing scenes or after the play, they strongly, if sadly, condemned.

# CHAPTER III

# Shakespeare and Revenge

Even though revenge was generally condemned in the Elizabethan and Jacobean drama, theatrical convention is not a certain guide in interpreting a given play. Obviously Shakespeare was not bound by a tradition that saw King John as a pre-Reformation hero or Hal as a raucous, thieving wastrel. We cannot understand Shakespeare's Lear by analyzing audience reaction to the sentimental penitent of the old *King Leir.* In these and other cases, Shakespeare transformed an old convention. The extended analysis of non-Shakespearean revenge plays just completed has had only one purpose: to correct the assumption that Shakespeare's contemporaries automatically considered revenge a duty of both piety and honor. His audience and other playwrights on the whole clearly did not. But what of Shakespeare himself? If it were true, as Bertram Joseph asserts, that "in Shakespeare's work in general we cannot find an overwhelming condemnation of revenge," such a break with the dominant ethical, religious, and even dramatic code of his day would be of great significance.[1] But is it true?

A comprehensive study of revenge motifs throughout the Shakespearean canon would deserve an entire book, for the elements of revenge—injury with its accompanying retaliation, whether intended or actually inflicted—appear in almost every play.[2] For our purposes,

---

[1] *Conscience and the King* (London, 1953), p. 44.

[2] To my knowledge, no comprehensive study has been made of revenge motifs in Shakespeare's plays. Fredson Bowers's important study, *Elizabethan Revenge Tragedy*, was concerned primarily with the Kydian convention and thus discussed only *Hamlet* and *Titus Andronicus.* The chronicle histories provided a focus for *Divine Vengeance*, by Sister Mary Bonaventure Mroz (Washington, D.C., 1941). Sister Mary compiled a valuable history of the re-

a brief survey of the characters who face a situation in some way analogous to that of Hamlet will suffice. To this end, let us first eliminate all out-and-out villains: characters whose motive for revenge is flimsy at best (Iago, Shylock), wholly invalid (Cornwall and Regan), or merely rhetorical (Aaron, Duke Frederick, Don John).[3] Such characters are personifications of evil, merely revenging themselves on virtue, and thus are irrelevant to the case of a virtuous character who has sustained a real injury. It is worth noting, though, how useful a motive Shakespeare found revenge to be. Aaron has no defined motive, and yet he rivals any genuine revenger in his rhetoric:

> Vengeance is in my heart, death in my hand,
> Blood and revenge are hammering in my head.
> (II.iii.38–39)

Perhaps we are to assume that his capture provides sufficient cause, but apparently the matter of motive is unimportant in the play. Aaron is a villain; therefore Aaron seeks revenge.[4]

Just as villainous revenges on virtue are irrelevant for our purposes, so too are comic revenges on folly. In passing, though, we should note that even in such cases as the revenges on Malvolio in *Twelfth Night*, on Falstaff in *Merry Wives of Windsor*, and on Parolles in *All's Well That Ends Well*, compassion tempers retribution. In such cases, moreover, we see a social unit exposing a wrong in order to restore social health, not a private man inflicting pain in order to revenge a wrong. The sanity of Windsor welcomes Falstaff back with laughter; Illyria

venge motif from pagan times to the Renaissance, but her analysis of the plays should be approached with caution. Attitudes are often attributed to Shakespeare on the authority of atypical views or early Renaissance codes repudiated in Elizabeth's day.

[3] Concern about anti-Semitism has too often led us to gloss over Shylock's real motives for exacting revenge. Yes, he has been taunted, but, it is emphasized, for his usury. He is thoroughly frank about his motives: Antonio has hurt his thriving business by lending money without interest (III.i.50–52) and, an even greater injury, has helped to save Shylock's debtors from impending foreclosure (III.iii.21–24). His revenge is motivated solely by malice, not by any desire for justice, and thus is villainous in intent.

[4] Shakespeare's early sensitivity to the association of revenge with villainy may be seen in a minor change in *King John*. In the source play, the Bastard's anger at the imposed peace with France is motivated primarily by his own desire for personal revenge against Austria (for dishonoring his father, Coeur-de-Lion). Shakespeare apparently cut the vindictive personal motive in order to strengthen the Bastard as a hero devoted solely to his country's cause. Though the change is a small one, it suggests that Shakespeare questioned the wisdom of associating revenge with a norm figure.

seeks only Malvolio's goodwill, and with such charming people it may win him over; under Lafeu's tender care, there may even be hope for Parolles.

The many revenge motives of warring factions, most clearly seen in the tangled threads of the Henry VI plays, are also tangential to our discussion. For the most part, the issues in war are not private revenge, but power—despite the passionate vows of vengeance that echo across Shakespearean battlefields.[5] Remove the rhetoric of revenge and the wars would continue. This fact, however, indicates once more how useful Shakespeare found the motive to be in establishing an atmosphere of horror. One has only to think of "fell" revenging Clifford slaughtering the boy Rutland, or of the "she-wolf" Margaret, glorying in York's tears and offering him a napkin dripping with the blood of his son (3 Henry VI, I.iii, I.iv). Or consider the ambiguous Antony of Julius Caesar. He has not yet assumed his role as Shakespeare's spokesman when he kneels by the dead body of Caesar and speaks the bloodcurdling prophecy of impending chaos:

> Caesar's spirit, ranging for revenge,
> With Ate by his side come hot from hell,
> Shall in these confines with a monarch's voice
> Cry 'Havoc,' and let slip the dogs of war.
>
> (III.i.270–73)

Surely this speech does not indicate moral approval of revenge. The monstrous power shortly to be unleashed is seen as rising from hell, rising "hot" with rage to cry for wanton destruction. That this speech is not merely colorful rhetoric in the classical tradition, and thus inadmissible as evidence of the play's ethical perspective, is made clear by Antony's tactics at the funeral. He appeals to the mob not to save Rome from the pollution of the murderers, not to effect justice, not even to punish: he appeals solely to personal motives, arousing his listeners by presenting Caesar as a friend who has deserved their loves and thus their loyalty. We immediately see the results in the maddened shrieks "Revenge! About! Seek! Burn! Fire! Kill! Slay!" (III.ii.208) and in the insane butchery of Cinna the poet. At

---

[5] The campaign planned by Coriolanus, the wars of Hotspur, Malcolm, and Macduff, and the combat of Edgar and Edmund are special cases, to be discussed below.

this point in the play we have little doubt that Antony is a ruthless demagogue who has tricked the mob into serving his own terrible purpose, and tricked them by appealing to one of man's most dangerous emotions: the desire for revenge.

Despite the several clues noted, the three types of revenge motif discussed—villainous revenges on virtue, comic revenges on folly, and revenge motives incidental to power struggles—are all irrelevant to the problem that Hamlet faces. Our concern is with the basically virtuous character who sustains (or thinks he sustains) a serious injury but has (or thinks he has) no recourse to the law. Three groups of characters are relevant: those faced with a supposed injury (Othello, Leontes, and Posthumus); those faced with a genuine injury, ranging from an affront to honor to the death of a close friend (Romeo, Hotspur, Henry V, the Trojans in *Troilus and Cressida,* Lear, Coriolanus, and Prospero); and those faced with the wanton murder of immediate kin (Titus, John of Gaunt, Isabella, Edgar, Macduff, and Hermione).[6]

Moving from the least to the most relevant, let us first touch upon the trio of revengers-for-false-cause: Othello, Leontes, and Posthumus. At first glance, it may seem pointless to consider these three. Obviously each man is dreadfully wrong to doubt his wife's faithfulness. Obviously the audience deplores each man's "revenge," for, like the villain-revenger, each is in reality attacking virtue. For that reason, the ethics of revenge would seem to be beside the point. But what if the three wives in question were indeed as faithless as their husbands' black imaginings have painted them? Would we then watch the ensuing events with satisfaction? I do not think so. In each play, the error is not merely the gullible belief in an obvious falsehood; it is the violence in each man that leads him not to seek punishment with justice but to inflict revenge.

Consider the close connection of the destructiveness of revenge with the destruction of Othello himself. At the climax of the temptation scene, Othello is finally overcome. In a wild roar, he delivers his will to the "demi-devil" Iago as he utters a terrible vow:

---

[6] Edgar sits uncomfortably in this list, for of course Gloucester was not "murdered." However, if we were to put Laertes in Edgar's position, I think we would grant him the potential motives of a blood revenger. On the other hand, Malcolm is omitted because he never has positive knowledge that his father was murdered. He will be touched on only incidentally in the discussion of Macduff.

Look here, Iago;
All my fond love thus do I blow to heaven.
'Tis gone.
Arise, black vengeance, from the hollow hell![7]
Yield up, O love, thy crown and hearted throne
To tyrannous hate!

(III.iii.444-49)

And then, his "bloody thoughts" swelling "like to the Pontic sea,"
with horrible irony he takes a sacred vow by Heaven never to pause
"till that a capable and wide revenge / Swallow them up" (453-60).
Were Desdemona guilty, I doubt that our horror and pain at the
complete disintegration of Othello would be any the less.

So too with Leontes. His mad jealousy awakens a greedy obsession
with revenge, not a desire for justice. When obscene images first rise
in his seething mind, he immediately orders the murder of his wife's
supposed lover; when that plot fails, he decides, "for present vengeance, / Take it on her" (*The Winter's Tale*, II.iii.22-23). The purpose of the "just and open trial" he announces is not to determine
Hermione's guilt, for in the same breath he adds that his heart will
be burdened until she is dead (II.iii.205-6). As in *Othello*, doubting
a faithful wife is folly, but taking upon oneself the right to punish is
madness.

*Cymbeline* might almost be considered an answer to those critics
who see Othello's and Leontes' error primarily in terms of their
credulity. Posthumus too believes a lie; he too tortures himself with
lewd imaginings; he too rages for revenge; he too devotes himself to
the service of hate. But he honestly and deeply repents. If this change
were merely a convention Shakespeare used because he was then in
his "reconciliation period," he might easily have had Posthumus repent after learning the truth, a familiar expedient in the seventeenth-

---

[7] Craig and Qq: *thy hollow cell*. The Folio reading seems much more probable. Shakespeare's frequent reference to "hollow earth" and "hollow ground" makes the adjective a logical description for Hell (e.g., *Taming of the Shrew*, Induction, ii, 48; *Richard III*, III.ii.140,
and *Othello*, IV.ii.79). Either reading obviously means Hell, but the present study suggests
that Shakespeare probably used the explicit word. As noted in Chapter II, a conventional vow
of revenge often took the form of defying Heaven and invoking Hell. Later in this chapter we
will note Shakespeare's use of the same convention in *Titus Andronicus* and a modification of
it in *Romeo and Juliet* and other plays. Othello is not merely contrasting "vengeance emerg-
ing from its lair and love enthroned and crowned" (M. L. Ridley, new Arden *Othello*, Cambridge, Mass., 1958, p. 120). He is flinging his love back to Heaven and invoking Hell, sur-
rendering his will to the service of hate.

century drama. He does not. Still believing Imogen guilty, Posthumus comes to see that his guilt in ordering her death was the greater.[8] The extended repentance scenes, including the "forgiveness" masque, are usually drastically cut in performance, and with good reason. They can pull the play out of focus. Instead of relying on last-minute conversion, Shakespeare develops Posthumus's penitence into two full scenes, writing for it some of his most moving lines (V.i.1–17, V.iv. 3–29). The conclusion seems unavoidable that his interest in the ethical issues outweighed his dramatic instinct.

Nonetheless, it might be argued that the cases of Othello, Leontes, and Posthumus cast no light on the audience's attitude toward revenge *per se,* since their attention, as well as the playwright's, is focused on the fact that each man's revenge is predicated on an untruth. More relevant to the issue in *Hamlet* are several primarily virtuous characters who have sustained a real and serious injury. Let us first turn to those whose injury, though severe, is less so than Hamlet's; less severe, that is, than the murder of immediate kin.

The tragedy of *Romeo and Juliet* has its roots in the Italian vendetta, the blood feud nourished by revenge. The almost reflex action of Lady Capulet in demanding an eye for an eye shows the vendetta to be a way of life to her (III.i.181–86). With complacent ease, she promises vengeance on Romeo for killing Tybalt, contentedly assuming that the mere assurance of bloody retaliation will stop the tears of a grieving young girl (III.v.88–93). Her perversion of values is chilling. It is this code of death and hate that dooms the lovers—and not wholly as an external force over which they have no control. Romeo himself makes the tragedy inevitable by doing the one thing he fervently did not want to do: he surrenders his will to the claims of his emotions and kills a Capulet. From the moment that Romeo throws rational patience back to Heaven and gives himself to rage, the lovers are doomed:

> Away to heaven, respective lenity,
> And fire-eyed fury be my conduct now!
> (III.i.128–29)

Benvolio later tells us that Romeo had not desired to take revenge on Tybalt until that very moment; but that one moment of fury does,

---

[8] In his penitence Posthumus recognizes that Imogen should have been saved to repent. This is one of the explicit arguments offered against revenge by most Renaissance thinkers.

indeed, make him "fortune's fool" (141). The destruction of the lines of both Montague and Capulet is fittingly viewed as "a scourge" that Heaven has "laid upon [their] hate" (V.iii.292).

In Hotspur, we have another fool of fortune whose anger provides the fuel for his own destruction. Even though he is a highly sympathetic character, the determination of this "wasp-stung and impatient fool" to "revenge the jeering and disdain'd contempt" of his King gives impetus to the forces of rebellion (*1 Henry IV,* I.iii.236, 183). No matter whose side has the greater justice in the issue of ransoming Mortimer, the ensuing civil war is, at best, born of a desperate gamble for honor over an eggshell. Of course, Hotspur's motives of "honor" differ from those of Worcester and Northumberland. The point is that this glowing young hothead's passion for revenge allows him to be manipulated.

When the issue is not an eggshell but a country, and the motive and cue for passion thus infinitely greater, Henry V responds not with fury, but with reason and humanity. In the increasingly popular attempt to blacken the character of Henry, several critics have viewed the traitors' scene as evidence of Henry's egotism and vindictiveness (II.ii.12–181). Nothing could be further from my reading of the scene. It is quite clear that Scroop, Cambridge, and Grey must be executed for the abortive plot to murder their King, and in Holinshed Henry summarily pronounces sentence when he learns of their treachery. In Shakespeare, the "trick" by which Henry gets the men to sentence themselves is not to be viewed as a petty cat-and-mouse game. It is a device by which the traitors, in their own malice, pronounce their own doom. Throughout the scene, as I envision it, Henry is struggling to rise above his personal feelings, and on the whole he succeeds. Of course he is human. Of course he is hurt. But his "I will weep for thee" to Scroop betrays no anger. "Touching our person seek we no revenge," he insists, and the context suggests that we are to believe him. When he dismisses the traitors to death, he expresses no satisfaction that they are going to the Hell they richly deserve; instead, he prays that God forgive them, that He grant them "patience to endure, and true repentance."

The entire scene is constructed to make it clear that genuine repentance has been awakened in each of the traitors, and awakened precisely because of Henry's control and compassion. Before Henry's speech detailing their guilt, the three men have shown only hypocrisy and malice. After his speech, they are different men. Scroop, Cambridge, and Grey all repent their guilt in heavily doctrinal language familiar to every member of the audience.[9] In all their speeches, they recognize that it is the greater mercy of God to punish the sinner rather than let him continue in evil, a theme that later would prompt some of Shakespeare's richest poetry.[10] They are thankful that Divine Providence has arrested their evil ("Our purposes God justly hath discover'd.... But God be thanked for prevention"). They repent their treason because it was a sin, not because they fear punishment ("I repent my fault more than my death.... My fault, but not my body, pardon, sovereign"). They rejoice in their contrition and punishment ("I in sufferance heartily will rejoice.... I do at this hour joy o'er myself"). These three professions are each voiced twice, in the manner of a musical fugue. We know nothing of the men themselves or their motives. Seemingly the only motivation for repentance is their impending death—which motivation they deny—and the King's speech. The extended scene thus serves to show the kingly grace of Henry instilling the love that must be added to fear before man can truly repent.[11] In Henry's situation, he could be enraged at treason without alienating audience sympathy. As God's vice-regent on earth, he is the agent of divine revenge. Yet the movement of the scene implies that the "sacred duty" here is not to inflict revenge on the man but to aid in the salvation of his soul.

[9] There is abundant evidence that both Shakespeare and his audience would have recognized the specific points of doctrine used in this scene. The same matters are repeated again and again, and in remarkably similar language, not only in such treatises as Hooker's *Laws of Ecclesiastical Polity* but in popular manuals for meditation and prayer (such as Thomas Becon's *The Sick Man's Salve,* John Norden's *A Progress of Piety,* and William Perkins's *A Golden Chaine*), in the familiar *Book of Common Prayer,* and in countless sermons (see especially the works of Bradford and Sandys, and, of course, the extremely influential homilies appointed to be read in the churches). With only minor differences, the same points were familiar to Catholics. Moreover, it is impossible that the language used in this scene is chance rhetoric. A recognizable core of repentance doctrine is heard throughout the plays: e.g., in the Prayer Scene in *Hamlet,* in Edgar's healing of his father's despair, and in the penitent speeches of Angelo, Leontes, and Posthumus.

[10] E.g., Posthumus's prayer in *Cymbeline* (V.iv.11–28).

[11] "Fear worketh no man's inclination to repentance, till somewhat else have wrought in us love also." Richard Hooker, *Of the Laws of Ecclesiastical Polity, The Works...,* ed. the Rev. John Keble, 3d ed. (Oxford, 1845), III, 9. Apparently we are to believe in *As You Like It* that Orlando's "kindness, nobler ever than revenge," not only saved Oliver's life but also effected his miraculous conversion (IV.iii.129). In *Rosalynde,* the evil brother fully repents before entering the forest.

As scholars have increasingly remarked, the debate between Troilus and Hector in Act II, Scene ii, of *Troilus and Cressida* is directly relevant to Hamlet's dilemma.[12] Also deserving attention is the revenge theme at the core of the play. The original cause of the pointless conflict was not Paris's lust for Helen, but simple revenge. Paris had been commissioned merely to take a Greek captive, any captive, in retaliation for the Greeks' capture of an old "aunt," who is never even named in the play. Hector voices the play's perspective on all ensuing events when he charges that "pleasure and revenge / Have ears more deaf than adders to the voice / Of any true decision" (II. ii. 171–73). The issue was tainted from the beginning.

Throughout the play, revenge is the nurse of barbarism and irrational frenzy. Troilus, scorning Hector's "vice of mercy" in granting life to Greeks he has downed in battle, dedicates himself to "venom'd vengeance"—a policy that the temperate Hector rejects as "savage" (V.iii.37–49). A few moments later Hector's position is vividly confirmed. Achilles, "arming, weeping, cursing, vowing vengeance" (V.v.30–35), is so maddened by Patroclus's death that he descends to bestial savagery, setting his rat-pack of Myrmidons on the defenseless Hector. We cannot hope that the insanity is over when, at the play's end, Troilus takes new strength in "hope of revenge" (V.x.31).

The association of revenge with madness is highly significant. Though Achilles may not be clinically insane, he loses all rational control as he rages forth, "crying on Hector." In a brief emblematic parallel, Ajax, who has also lost a friend, "foams at the mouth," "roaring for Troilus" (V.v.35–36). So too with Othello. In the moment that he vows revenge, he loses his power to reason, his self-possession. Indeed, Othello loses his mind, in a symbolic sense at least, in a violent seizure. Thus it is especially significant that in *King Lear,* Shakespeare's one major treatment of true madness, we can identify the exact moment at which the mind begins to crack—and that moment coincides with the first vow of vengeance. As his two daughters stand revealed before him, Lear first sees the abyss begin to open. Though he prays to the heavens for patience, he defies tears—"women's weapons," the only consolation that resignation would offer—and surrenders himself to rage:

---

[12] See below, pp. 169–70.

> No, you unnatural hags,
> I will have such revenges on you both,
> That all the world shall—I will do such things,—
> What they are, yet I know not; but they shall be
> The terrors of the earth.
>
> II.iv.281–85)

His mind is sputtering as if short-circuited. And at this point the storm breaks.

Though many questions of "right" and "wrong" are ambiguous in *Coriolanus*, its hero's plan to take revenge on all Rome seems clearly judged. The decision to embrace his enemy as a means to that revenge is hopelessly, even childishly, stupid. But more: the decision to take such revenge, whatever the means, is morally wrong. It is, as in *King Lear*, "unnatural." It leads him to reject all natural ties ("Wife, mother, child, I know not" [V.ii.88]), to humiliate his dearest friend, to embrace his and Rome's enemy, and to plot the destruction of his native land. Though the issues are not black and white, we cannot for a moment believe that the argument of the play vindicates Coriolanus against all the bonds of kin and country.

In all of the cases discussed thus far, revenge—both the child and the nurse of rage—inevitably leads to mental, physical, and spiritual destruction. The health of man and society requires patience. But on what is patience based? Stoic elimination of the emotions that feed revenge? The most familiar Shakespearean quotation on revenge denies the Stoics' view. Prospero, challenged by the compassion of Ariel, is finally moved to pardon his enemies:

> Though with their high wrongs I am struck to the quick,
> Yet with my nobler reason 'gainst my fury
> Do I take part: the rarer action is
> In virtue than in vengeance....
> (*The Tempest*, V.i.25–28)

This rather cryptic speech is illuminated by a passage from Montaigne's essay "Of Crueltie"; in fact, several parallels of diction and idea (here italicized) suggest that Florio's translation was Shakespeare's actual source.

Methinks Virtue is another manner of thing, and *much more noble* than the inclinations unto Goodnesse, which in us are engendered.... He that through a naturall facilitie and genuine mildnesse should neglect or contemne injuries received, should no doubt performe a *rare action,* and worthy commendation: but he who being *toucht and stung to the quicke* with any *wrong* or offence received, should arme himself with *reason against* this *furiously* blind desire of *revenge,* and in the end after a great conflict yeeld himselfe master over it, should doubtlesse *doe much more.* The first should doe well, the other *vertuously*: the one action might be termed Goodnesse, the other *Vertue.* For it seemeth that the very name of Vertue presupposeth difficultie, and inferreth resistance, and cannot well exercise itself without an enemie.

Editors of *The Tempest* often gloss Prospero's use of "virtue" as "forgiveness," but such a gloss is slightly misleading.[13] Shakespeare's meaning is that Prospero's specific type of forgiveness is a "rarer action" than that of a patient Griselda, who forgives easily because she feels no anger. Prospero is no Stoic. He deeply feels the injury, yet his reason is now in command. In electing to take the part of his "nobler reason" against the claims of his fury, he has acted with the "virtue" defined by Montaigne. As was noted with *Cymbeline,* the rejection of vengeance has often been dismissed as irrelevant to Shakespeare's earlier plays and considered an attitude limited to his later "reconciliation period." When we recall Henry V speaking words of compassion to the traitors, even though he too is "struck to th' quick," we find exactly the same spirit of mercy and forbearance.

Let us turn now to those characters who face a situation closely analogous to that of Hamlet: Titus Andronicus, John of Gaunt, Isabella, Macduff, Edgar, and Hermione. Each of them is, at least at the opening of the play, predominantly virtuous; each has suffered the murder of a close member of his family, knows the identity of the killer, and has no recourse to the law.

*Titus Andronicus* is a very curious play, and its hero a very puzzling character.[14] At first glance it seems ludicrous to speak of Titus and

---

[13] *Montaigne's Essays,* trans. John Florio, II, 119. Of course, Montaigne's point is slightly different: he is distinguishing true patience from the passivity of an amiable nature. See my article on "Shakespeare, Montaigne, and 'the Rarer Action,'" *Shakespeare Studies,* I (1966), 261–64.

[14] For our purposes, let us consider that the play is by Shakespeare. Even if he had no hand in it at all (which seems impossible), an analysis of it is pertinent in our understanding of the early Elizabethan attitude toward revenge.

Hamlet as related, yet they are at least cousins, if not brothers: as Fredson Bowers has shown, both are direct offspring of the Kydian revenge play.[15] Although few scholars would offer Titus as evidence that Shakespeare and his audience unquestioningly approved of personal revenge, the character is sufficiently ambiguous to require close attention.

The first act offers either a very fuzzy characterization of Titus as a noble hero or a very subtle characterization of him as a rash and self-indulgent man who is potentially dangerous. It is difficult to determine which. A useful guide may be found in an eighteenth-century chapbook in the Folger Library: *The History of Titus Andronicus, The Renowned Roman General....* It appears to be a late descendant of a very old version, and may even represent Shakespeare's source. If it does, Shakespeare made several significant additions and changes. Not one of Titus's decisive actions in the first scene is based on the chapbook. Each of them seems to have been added to establish a specific characterization.

First, Titus's decision to resign his title and bestow it on Saturninus is clearly unwise. In a twenty-line exchange immediately preceding Titus's entrance, the characters of the two candidates have been revealed to the audience: Saturninus is violent and arrogant; Bassianus is dignified and humble. Although Titus's decision seems motivated by humility and patriotism, his choice of Saturninus is fraught with danger. Second, Titus's decision to sacrifice Alarbus is seen as barbarous, even though it is ascribed to pious motives. The audience's pity would align it with Tamora: not only because she is a terrified mother (automatically the odds are on her side), but also because her noble plea for mercy is juxtaposed to the vicious eagerness of Lucius to "hew [her son's] limbs."[16] We agree with Tamora that even if Titus's motives are religious, the sacrifice is a "cruel, irreligious piety" (I.i.129–30). Third, Titus's killing of his own son Mutius is also treated unsympathetically. In theory, one might justify the act as a sign of Titus's loyalty, on the grounds that Mutius has just defied his newly established sovereign by helping to steal the emperor's intended bride for Bassianus. In production, however, I doubt that the audience

---

[15] Bowers, *Elizabethan Revenge Tragedy*, pp. 109ff.

[16] Tamora herself requires no close attention here. Though she is introduced sympathetically, from Act II on she is revealed as a mere pawn of the demonic Aaron. Her revenge-for-a-son motive is dropped. As a villain-revenger she is thus eliminated from discussion.

would see the killing in this light. Saturninus is an embryonic tyrant. Bassianus, though rash in seizing his betrothed, is clearly a wronged hero. No matter how good Titus's motives, our sympathy is with Bassianus and Mutius. Moreover, even Titus's motives are suspect. As he attempts to stop the escaping lovers, Mutius bars his way. In a swift reflex action, he stabs his son, crying "What, villain boy! / Bar'st me my way in Rome?" (I.i.290–91). The deathblow is not the necessary but regretted stroke of justice; it is a brutal retaliation for an affront to Titus's prerogatives. He later attributes his action to honorable motives, but his concern is with having been personally dishonored. Although I do not think that Titus is intended to be as "overbearingly proud and haughty" as Bowers suggests, he is surely to be interpreted as rash, headstrong, and self-centered.[17]

Despite the suggestion of certain negative traits in Act I, Titus moves through the next three acts in the role of oppressed virtue. He suffers blow upon blow, each successive torture undeserved, each inflicted by the most fiendish villainy. This virtuous posture is marred only by excessive grief, which is explicitly judged by all as dangerous. In the first scene of Act III, we find the first hint that his passion exceeds the bounds of moderation. Pleading to the senators and tribunes of Rome for mercy to his falsely accused sons, he "lieth down," a movement of abandon that Shakespeare later found useful for Constance and Richard II. When Titus sees his ravished, mutilated daughter, understandably his grief "disdaineth bounds" (III.i.71). Left to his own instincts, no member of the audience would coolly judge the wails of lamentation as irrational; nonetheless, Shakespeare warns both the audience and Titus through Marcus:

> O brother, speak with possibilities,
> And do not break into these deep extremes....
> But yet let reason govern thy lament.
> (III.i.215–19)

Finally, when Saturninus scornfully returns Titus's severed hand and the heads of his sons, he throws off all control and breaks into mad laughter. Throughout these first three acts, Titus is primarily a good

---

[17] Bowers, p. 112. Bowers suggests a parallel with Lear in Titus's decision to relinquish his title, but Titus's choice is not so flagrantly for reasons of personal gratification as Lear's. Even so, the decision is imprudent at best.

man whose genuine wrongs have led him to excessive grief and thus to madness. The audience is undoubtedly sympathetic, but it must be uneasy when Titus shows Lavinia how to commit suicide without using her hands, when he stabs wildly at a fly, when he shoots his arrows with messages to the gods—Marcus, all the while, commenting on his frenzy.

Despite his wrongs, his grief, and his madness, Titus withstands the temptation to revenge for three and a half acts. Even when two of his sons are killed, he does not turn to private revenge. True, he sends his exiled son Lucius to raise an army among the Goths, but he himself does nothing. Seeking the aid of Rome's enemy is scarcely the act of a patriotic Roman, but the assault by the Goths never takes place. That thorny problem is kept offstage and thus outside the audience's real awareness. Even when Lavinia reveals the names of her ravishers, Titus does not act. Marcus, our norm, makes it clear that we are not to attribute his inaction to cowardice, sloth, or madness (IV.i.123–29). No matter how great Titus's cause, how great his sorrows, he is "yet so just that he will not revenge. / Revenge, ye heavens, for old Andronicus!" Making a clear allusion to the Biblical injunction against private revenge, Marcus cries out to the heavens to "hear a good man groan," for Titus himself is still trusting to heaven, despite the inexplicable delay of divine justice. He continues to bide his time, relieving his tortured spirit by sending riddling taunts to his enemies.

But the heavens delay too long. IV.iii is a scene of choice that explains how we are to view Titus's bloodthirsty revenge in the fifth act. Now wholly insane, Titus has brought his family and friends to the fields, all of them equipped with bows and arrows. Justice, he tells them, has fled the earth. Some he sends to cast nets for her in the ocean; others he orders to dig down to Pluto's kingdom and seek her there. Humoring his lunacy and hoping, with Marcus, to convince Titus to join with the Goths, the digging kinsmen return him Pluto's message: Justice is not in hell,

> but Pluto sends you word,
> If you will have Revenge from hell, you shall:
> Marry, for Justice, she is so employ'd,
> He thinks, with Jove in heaven, or somewhere else,
> So that perforce you must needs stay a time.

At this, Titus finally rebels:

> He doth me wrong to feed me with delays.
> I'll dive into the burning lake below,
> And pull her [Revenge] out of Acheron by the heels.
>
> (IV.iii.37–44)

With that decision, he begins wildly shooting arrow-borne messages to the gods, and the scene closes as he sends a clown to Saturninus with another riddling letter, an action that results in the death of the innocent fool.

When we next see Titus, he is completely "rational" in the modern sense (that is, in contact with reality); he sees through Tamora's disguise as "Revenge," coolly tricks her into leaving her sons as hostages, and forthwith slits their throats. From this point on he is, if not a "villain-revenger," at least a tainted revenger who has forfeited our sympathy. The murder of Tamora's two vicious cubs would, in itself, undoubtedly call for our instinctive applause. But when Titus, not content with merely slaying them, stops their mouths to prevent any pleas (a typical villain's device in Renaissance drama) and then taunts them with his ghastly plans to make mush of their bones and blood, mold it around their severed heads, and serve the tempting "pasties" to their mother—the stomach of the most hardened spectator would surely rise.

This grisly speech is nothing, however, compared to the final catastrophe. First, Titus's killing of Lavinia is treated in such a way as to alienate sympathy. In the chapbook, Lavinia begs her father to kill her. In the play, Shakespeare treats her killing as a sudden, shocking slaughter, not as a requested act of mercy. To be sure, Titus recalls the example of Virginius, generally epitomized as a noble Roman father compelled by love and honor to kill his daughter. Nonetheless, Titus's argument is that the living presence of a dishonored daughter would bring constant shame and sorrow not to the suffering girl, but to the father. Even before the final horror, Titus has lost all claim to virtue.

But there is one more blow that, when reading the play, we may overlook. As Titus turns to the banquet table to gloat over Tamora, we read that she "hath daintily fed" *already* of the two loathsome "pasties" (V.iii.61). Without seeing a production, we can only dimly sense the impact of this scene. In the excitement of Lavinia's death, we have forgotten the bloody banquet already begun. Now we are reminded—and in a sudden wave of nausea remember that Tamora has already eaten.[18] Mercifully, Titus immediately stabs her (an actress could not maintain the required violent reaction for long) and, again mercifully, Titus is immediately killed. The audience could stand no more.

Any assumption that Shakespeare automatically conceived of blood revenge as a "sacred duty" must grapple with *Titus Andronicus*. It must also face the fact that among all the potential revengers-for-murdered-kin remaining to be considered, not one is so portrayed as to suggest that vengeance is commanded by God, required by honor, or expected by custom.

The decision facing John of Gaunt in *Richard II* is not strictly relevant to *Hamlet*. Gaunt is urged to rebel against an anointed king whose right to the throne is unquestioned. The issue is clearly political.[19] Nonetheless, Gaunt's argument against killing the man who ordered his brother's murder is pertinent to our investigation:

> Since correction lieth in those hands
> Which made the fault that we cannot correct,
> Put we our quarrel to the will of heaven. . . .
>
> (I.ii.4–6)

When the Duchess of Gloucester charges that his forbearance is not patience but "pale cold cowardice" and despair, he answers, "God's is the quarrel" (l. 37). Though the primary issue here is civil obedience, Gaunt echoes the traditional injunction against private revenge.

The relevance of Isabella in *Measure for Measure* is apparent. Few critics today would argue that she is either a paragon of virtue or the epitome of selfish prudery. Somewhere between the two extremes,

---

18 I have never seen a production of the play but wonder if the killing of Lavinia might not be almost ignored by the audience, once the actual feast has started. The scene requires very careful direction.

19 As Lily Bess Campbell has noted, all of Act I, Scene ii, of *Richard II* is Shakespeare's invention, a scene inserted solely to emphasize the doctrine of passive obedience (*Shakespeare's "Histories,"* San Marino, Calif., 1947, pp. 195–97). In Holinshed, Gaunt and York plan vengeance on Richard but wait to see if he might reform. Shakespeare has Gaunt explicitly reject all thought of revenge.

wherever we see the truth to lie, most would agree that the basic plot line is concerned in some way with a change in Isabella for the better. And however we define that change, it is expressed by a decision to reject revenge. Hearing of her brother's supposed execution, our gentle novitiate explodes in an extravagant threat against Angelo: "O, I will to him and pluck out his eyes!" The Duke cautions her with the familiar exhortation to patience: "Give your cause to heaven" (IV.iii.124,129). She endeavors to control her vindictiveness, but her fury breaks forth when she publicly confronts Angelo with his perfidy. It is against this violence that we see the full significance of her eventual plea for mercy to Angelo. All human instinct understandably urges her to demand a life for a life. The Duke makes this point emphatically:

> Against all sense you do importune her:
> Should she kneel down in mercy of this fact,
> Her brother's ghost his paved bed would break,
> And take her hence in horror.
>
> (V.i.438-41)

Family loyalty, natural emotion, common sense—all human considerations preclude charity. But Isabella takes that suprahuman step to the "rarer action," forgiveness.

*Macbeth* and *King Lear* both provide test cases, for they have been cited as evidence that Shakespeare unquestioningly accepted the morality of revenge. Patrick Cruttwell is not alone in believing that "the whole moral weight of *Macbeth* is behind the personal and bloody vengeance which Macduff vows and takes on the man who has killed his wife and children, and the whole moral weight of *Lear* is no less behind Edgar's challenging and killing of Edmund."[20] This study suggests that, on the contrary, Shakespeare carefully avoided imputing motives of personal vengeance to either character.

In *Macbeth*, only one passage can be offered in support of a revenge ethic. In his soliloquy on the battlefield, Macduff roars for Macbeth to show himself, swearing that if someone else has stolen from him the right to kill the tyrant, "my wife and children's ghosts will haunt me

---

[20] "The Morality of Hamlet—'Sweet Prince' or 'Arrant Knave'?" *Stratford-upon-Avon Studies* 5 (London, 1963), p. 119.

still" (V.vii.14–23). In the light of the rest of the play, I find the speech a contradiction. Elsewhere, the denial of personal revenge motives to Macduff is explicit. The dominant note is struck when we hear that Macduff has joined Malcolm in England, where he has gone to beg the King's help in liberating Scotland. In the messenger's report, there is no hint of vengeful vows or of righteous fury aching to be unleashed. There is only the hope—"with Him above/To ratify the work" (III.vi.32–33)—of freeing the bleeding land from tyranny in the name of the legitimate heir. Lennox gives the mission religious sanction: he will send "some holy angel" to England to warn that caution is needed to hasten the day when "a swift blessing" returns to Scotland (III.vi.45–59).

In the extended dialogue between Malcolm and Macduff, the emphasis is entirely on love of country. We hear not one word of vindictive hatred for Macbeth. He is called "treacherous," "untitled tyrant," and "devilish," but the most objective observer could say no less. Almost all the emotion in the first part of the scene is aroused by grief for Scotland. Even when Macduff learns of the slaughter of his wife and children, his major reaction is stunned grief. He is angry at himself for exposing them to danger, not at the man who murdered them. The nearest thing to a vow of personal revenge is Macduff's prayer that the heavens give him the opportunity to kill "this fiend of Scotland" in battle (IV.iii.230–33). It is clear, however, that all is surrendered to the will of Heaven. The forthcoming campaign is to be seen as a divine mission, not as a campaign of personal vengeance.[21]

A word should perhaps be said about Malcolm. It is true that he offers the "medicines of our great revenge" as comfort to the stricken Macduff (IV.iii.214), but in context the word has no force. Malcolm is treated solely as the divinely appointed agent of God's punishment. Had Shakespeare wished, he could easily have given Malcolm a blood revenge motive. Following the murder, he has an uneasy suspicion of Macbeth, but Shakespeare never makes his suspicion explicit. As with Macduff, Shakespeare seems to be avoiding an obvious motive.

In *King Lear,* the case of Edgar is unequivocal. He neither desires nor takes revenge in any way whatsoever, other than to effect the

---

21 Later Menteith says that "revenges burn" in Malcolm and Macduff, but he is reporting on offstage action (V.ii.3). When we see the two men leading their forces at Dunsinane, both are unemotional and efficient, devoting full attention to battle plans.

"revenge" of outraged order on evil. There is not one suggestion in his wanderings as poor Tom that he awaits an opportunity for personal vengeance. On the contrary, his is the voice of patience despite the most painful afflictions (III.vi.109–17). When he intercepts Goneril's letter revealing the plot on her husband's life and Edmund's role in it, he resolves to go to the British camp solely to expose the treachery. It is for this reason alone that he enters the lists. Edgar's purpose is not to kill the brother who wronged him but to prove by combat that Edmund is a traitor to his King. That his motive is in no way vindictive is shown by his first words when he reveals himself to the dying Edmund: "Let's exchange charity" (V.iii.166). Saviolo, it will be recalled, believed single combat legitimate only for the justifying of a truth and only if the challenger proceeded in the proper spirit. Edgar fulfills these criteria. He proceeds without hatred, motivated by "love of virtue, and regarde of the universall good and publique profite." Edgar acts, "as it were, the minister to execute Gods devine pleasure."[22]

In *The Winter's Tale* we have another of Shakespeare's late "reconciliation plays," and again the reconciliation is not effected by the mere trickery of romance conventions but motivated by the familiar ethical and religious concepts with which we have been concerned. Leontes' repentance is couched in thoroughly orthodox terms, and Hermione's forgiveness is carefully prepared. If one wished to be hard-headed about the play—and who does?—one might wonder what on earth could possess the woman to forgive her husband. On the other hand, if one were Christian enough to expect her to forgive Leontes, one might ask why she waited for so many years. The answers are found in Hermione's magnificent defense in the trial scene. No one could accuse her of having no "objective correlative" for her grief and outraged dignity. She minutely inventories Leontes' many wrongs, culminating, as she believes, in the outright murder of her newborn child. She is proud, even gloriously defiant, as she stands unbending, secure in the conviction of her known integrity. This regal creature, made of steel, is no sentimental Griselda who will welcome her penitent husband with clucks of tenderness one minute after he learns of his error. She will wait until the wound heals. And

[22] See above, pp. 14–15.

yet, fully aware of her husband's guilt and mitigating it not one jot, she closes her defense with words of charity:

> The Emperor of Russia was my father:
> O that he were alive, and here beholding
> His daughter's trial! that he did but see
> The flatness of my misery, yet with eyes
> Of pity, not revenge!
>
> (III.ii.120–24)

---

In all this evidence—over thirty characters, drawn from most of the Shakespearean canon—we find no suggestion that Shakespeare expected his audience to accept without question the validity of private blood revenge. The evidence suggests, rather, that his plays rely on the orthodox ethical and religious injunctions against it. Despite a maturing of both dramatic skill and thought between *Titus Andronicus* and *The Tempest,* the portrayal of the revenger seems to remain constant. Titus and Prospero are two sides of the same coin: Titus in his madness embracing revenge and thus descending to the hell of barbarism and destruction; Prospero in his sanity exercising his nobler reason and thus rising to forgiveness and reconciliation.

Revenge motifs recur throughout the plays. Again and again the surrender to revenge is seen as the surrender of reason, the surrender at least to rashness and at most to madness. Similarly, a decision to take revenge is often accompanied by an explicit rejection of some clear virtue or good. Just as Lear denies his daughters, Coriolanus predicates his revenge on the total rejection of the natural bonds of family ("Wife, mother, child I know not"). The rejection may take the form of symbolically flinging virtue back to heaven before vowing vengeance: Othello blows "all [his] fond love ... to heaven" and Romeo cries, "Away to heaven respective lenity."

Of special pertinence is the frequency with which revengers associate their motives and actions with Hell and the demonic. In *Titus Andronicus* we hear that the man who seeks private revenge must dive to the bowels of hell. In his madness, Titus takes that plunge. Antony envisions Caesar's spirit, an epitome of revenge, rising "with Ate by his side come hot from hell." Othello calls up "black ven-

geance, from the hollow hell." Coriolanus resolves to pursue his revenge "with the spleen/Of all the under fiends." None of these characters is originally demonic in purpose, as are Iago and Aaron. The
language is not the mere rhetoric of villainy.

In none of the foregoing do I intend to suggest that Shakespeare
was a dour, inflexible moralist, consigning his revengers to Hell with
grim satisfaction. At a given moment in a play—the moment when
Romeo stabs Tybalt, when Coriolanus defies the screaming mob,
when Hotspur rages at personal insult—we often instinctively identify with the very action that later, when we are released from emotional involvement, we see in ethical perspective. Shakespeare's plays
show a deeper penetration into the nature of the ethical dilemma involved in revenge and a greater compassion for the revenger than do
the plays of his contemporaries. Even so, they bear out Cutwolfe's
view that revenge in Elizabethan drama was "continually raised from
hell."

With—let us note—the possible exception of *Hamlet*. In his treatment of the Ghost, Shakespeare breaks new ground, demanding a
fresh response by transforming a theatrical convention. If we approach the play with certain preconceptions, we may be blind to a
radical change in ethical perspective. This chapter has not attempted
to use Shakespeare's other plays to interpret *Hamlet*. It has merely
questioned one particular preconception: that Shakespeare's plays in
general reflect an approved code of private blood revenge.

On the contrary, on the subject of revenge, his plays reflect agreement with sermons, moralist tracts, poetry, and other plays of his day.
No matter how base the injury, no matter how evil your enemy, no
matter how dim all hope of legal redress, leave the issue to Heaven;
"God's is the quarrel." In *Richard III*, Clarence's words to his murderers succinctly state a plea implicit in play after play:

> If God will be revenged for this deed,
> O, know you yet, he doth it publicly:
> Take not the quarrel from his powerful arm;
> He needs no indirect nor lawless course
> To cut off those that have offended him.
>
> (I.iv.221–25)

# PART II

# Hamlet's Revenge

*They say miracles are past; and we have our philosophical persons to make modern and familiar, things supernatural and causeless. Hence is it that we make trifles of terrors, ensconcing ourselves into seeming knowledge, when we should submit ourselves to an unknown fear.*

All's Well That Ends Well, II.iii.1–6

# CHAPTER IV

# Enter Ghost

No comfortable figure steps forward to speak the Prologue to *Hamlet,* adjusting us to a "play" world. We see no spirited crowd of familiar London figures. We do not find ourselves suddenly eavesdropping on a thoroughly human squabble or hear two apparently solid citizens conversing about family or business or politics. We are not excited by a flourish of trumpets heralding the colorful procession of a bustling court. A single figure in military garb paces the large platform alone, in silence. Every sense alert, he darts nervous glances to the side, behind him. He shivers—or is that an involuntary shudder? Perhaps, but he is obviously cold, for he pulls his mantle more closely about him. As he retraces his steps and a distant bell strikes twelve, we realize that he is a sentry keeping midnight watch in some cold, desolate, and for some reason terrifying place. Though a soldier accustomed to the monotony of sentry duty, he is obviously uneasy about something out there in the void.[1]

Suddenly a voice sounds from the dark. Although, as we immediately learn, Bernardo has come to take over the watch—a routine assignment—he too is uneasy. He neither waits for the customary challenge nor calls out his partner's name in confidence. Instead we hear a startled voice cry "Who's there?" Who should be there but Francisco?

---

[1] The theatrical tradition of tolling the midnight hour is justified by Francisco's first remark to Bernardo, "You come most carefully upon your hour," and Bernardo's reply, " 'Tis now struck twelve." (All citations from *Hamlet* are taken from Hardin Craig's *Complete Works of Shakespeare,* Chicago, 1951.) The tendency to dress the sentries in court garb, however, is unwise. Military costume suggests that Francisco's nervousness is not typical. He should not pace with firm tread, weapon poised to repel a possible human ambush. His movements and stance should make it clear that although he is a soldier trained to defend himself, he would be helpless against whatever danger it is that he fears.

Both men are edgy. Francisco is sick at heart. Bernardo, unwilling to stand this particular watch alone any longer than necessary, hopes that his expected companions will make haste. Even before Horatio enters with Marcellus to ask if "this thing" has again appeared, we are aware that the black night harbors something fearful, something portending evil.

What can the "thing" be? Horatio says it is but "fantasy"; it is some kind of "apparition"; it is a "dreaded sight" that has appeared twice before, last night just at the close of the witching hour. This is all we know of it, and we wait expectantly as everyone sits to hear Bernardo's detailed account. Our attention is riveted on the little cluster of men down on the forestage when suddenly, behind them—probably appearing as if miraculously from the trap—"Look, where it comes again!"

It is a ghost. But our question is still not answered. "It" looks "like the king that's dead." Horatio, who had dismissed early reports, is harrowed with fear and wonder. The soldiers believe that only a scholar can speak to it. No one seems to think it is actually the ghost of the dead King. Indeed, when Horatio gathers courage to address it, he assumes that some malign power not merely has taken on the familiar form but has wrongfully stolen it:

> What art thou that usurp'st this time of night,
> Together with that fair and warlike form
> In which the majesty of buried Denmark
> Did sometimes march? by heaven I charge thee, speak!

The "thing's" reaction is startling. Though it had been about to speak, it shows that it is offended—perhaps jerking back suddenly while frowning (as Horatio later tells us) with anger—and turns and stalks away.

Why is the Ghost "offended"? A critical tradition going back to Carl Rohrbach in 1859 holds that Hamlet's father is offended because Horatio doubts his identity. Why, then, doesn't it leave the moment Horatio charges it with "usurping" the dead King's form, instead of waiting until the last line of his speech? And why does it appear again, and again attempt to speak? The most obvious explanation is that the spirit is offended only when Horatio charges it "by heaven" to speak. At that invocation, the Ghost must react suddenly, even violently.

If directors and actors followed every clue in these first fifty lines alone, the modern audience would be suspicious of the Ghost already. It is a "dreaded sight," a "usurping" apparition, a "thing" associated with sickness of heart and terror and midnight. It is "warlike," frowning and angry, moving with "martial stalk" (not "tread" or "pace"). It is "offended" by the name of Heaven and swiftly retreats.

Before the second appearance of the Ghost, the atmosphere of foreboding is increased. The spirit has appeared thrice "at this dead hour" and apparently for some purpose. May it be a portent of disaster to the uneasy State? Even so had unnatural harbingers given omen of great Caesar's fall. Any such shattering of the natural order can bode only ill.

All of these ominous impressions are reinforced by the second appearance of the Ghost. Horatio determines to "cross it," daring the possibility that it may "blast" him—that is, with the fires of Hell. He does not hail it as "most noble King." He cries, "Stay, illusion!" even though he now knows it is no mere fantasy. He begs it to speak only

> If there be any good thing to be done,
> That may to thee do ease and grace to me. . . .

Suddenly again the spirit is startled and vanishes. This time it seems to be offended by the sound of the cock, for at the crowing, Horatio tells us, "it started like a guilty thing / Upon a fearful summons." The Ghost reacts to the cock just as it did to Horatio's invocation of Heaven. Apparently it cannot be abroad during daylight.

This fact alone is not necessarily significant, for Horatio is but repeating a common folk belief when he says that wandering spirits are warned by the cock that it is time to return to their "confines." But Marcellus throws the Ghost's action into a Christian context. During the season of Advent, he has heard,

> The bird of dawning singeth all night long:
> And then, they say, no spirit dare stir abroad;
> The nights are wholesome; then no planets strike,
> No fairy takes, nor witch hath power to charm,
> So hallow'd and so gracious is the time.

The cock in some way is the voice of grace; at its song, no evil spirits can remain abroad. Marcellus clearly assumes that the Ghost is exactly this type of unwholesome spirit.

Thus far, how would a modern audience react? Without any knowledge of Elizabethan ideas, we would be extremely suspicious— if, of course, we were fortunate enough to see a production that followed closely Shakespeare's many hints. The Ghost is assumed to be malign and we can see why. A usurping thing of the night—armed, angry, frowning—it is offended by the invocation of Heaven and starts like a guilty thing at the voice heralding the light of day and of grace. By the end of the first scene, would we trust it?

Elizabethans would have been even more suspicious. Some extremely important evidence from the great ghost debate between Protestants and Catholics in the late sixteenth century, as well as from popular literature, has been long overlooked. Beginning with the assumption that the Ghost is a good spirit (partly because it tells the truth, partly because it urges Christian forbearance with Gertrude, but primarily because we identify sympathetically with Hamlet), we have sought corroboration, not fact. We have found support in half-truths ("Catholics believed in Purgatory ghosts") and in sheer guesswork ("All ghosts should be addressed by scholars, who know Latin"). Although the relevant materials would seem to have been covered many times (most thoroughly by J. Dover Wilson), it thus becomes necessary to reconsider the beliefs about ghosts in Shakespeare's day.[2] I do not mean to suggest that we can understand *Hamlet* only if we are accomplished scholars in the history of ideas. On the contrary, it is scholarship, in my opinion, that has confused the issue. It has bequeathed to the director and the reader a tradition that seems but-

---

[2] Wilson's introduction to his edition of Lavater's *Of Ghostes and Spirites Walking by Nyght* (1572) (Oxford, 1929), and Campbell's analysis in *Shakespeare's Tragic Heroes*, closely followed by John Erskin Hankins's summary in *The Character of Hamlet and Other Essays* (Chapel Hill, N.C., 1941), represent the first serious attempts to interpret the Ghost in *Hamlet* in terms of Elizabethan religious beliefs. Growing interest has been evidenced by many studies, among the most significant being the following: Roy W. Battenhouse, "The Ghost in *Hamlet*: A Catholic 'Linchpin'?" *Studies in Philology*, XLVIII (1951), 161–92; Monsignor I. J. Semper, "The Ghost in *Hamlet*: Pagan or Christian?" *The Month*, n.s., IX (1953), 222–34; Robert H. West, "King Hamlet's Ambiguous Ghost," *PMLA*, LXX (1955), 1107–17, reprinted in *Shakespeare and the Outer Mystery* (Lexington, Ky., 1968); and Sister Miriam Joseph, "Discerning the Ghost in *Hamlet*," *PMLA*, LXXVI (1961), 493–502, an argument given an astute answer by Paul N. Siegel, *PMLA*, LXXVIII (1963), 148–49. I am especially indebted to Professor Battenhouse for raising the questions that originally prompted this study.

tressed by the incontestable authority of fact but that is actually the product of rationalization and wishful thinking. If the modern director, actor, and reader each followed his own instincts, I am convinced that their response would approximate that of the Elizabethan. The excursion in sixteenth-century pneumatology that follows is necessary only because scholarship has mistakenly led us to distrust our own responses.

What, then, is the Ghost in Shakespeare's *Hamlet?*[3] On one point all critics have agreed. It is not a mere folk ghost: a graveyard spook of popular imagination, returned from the charnel house, wandering among tombs, guarding treasure, haunting its earthly abodes. It is not a mere pagan ghost: a forlorn soul seeking proper burial, an errant soul still stained with the lusts of the world, hovering over the grave, the spirit of a murdered man pursuing his murderer or wandering until the day when he would have died naturally.[4] The first scene of *Hamlet* puts the Ghost into Christian perspective. The possibility that the Ghost is a hallucination is eliminated immediately. The educated, rational, doubting Horatio learns by the witness of his own eyes that this "thing" is no "fantasy." Moreover, his response, as well as that of the sentries, makes it clear that this is no mere conventional ghost of the popular theater. It is addressed in the name of Heaven; it is an ambiguous "illusion" that may "blast" or be the instrument of "grace." The nature of the Ghost is thrown into question as it is in no other play of the Elizabethan or Jacobean period, and Shakespeare may

---

[3] The most useful sources for Protestant beliefs include Lewes Lavater's *Of Ghostes and Spirites Walking by Nyght* (1572), in Dover Wilson's edition; James I, *Daemonologie* (1597), Bodley Head Quartos, ed.'G. B. Harrison (London, 1924); John Deacon and John Walker, *Dialogical Discourses of Spirits and Divels* (London, 1601); George Gifford, *A Discourse of the Subtill Practises of Devilles by Witches and Sorcerers* ... (London, 1587); [Pierre Viret], *The Second Part of the Demoniacke Worlde* (London, 1583); William Perkins, "A Discourse of the Damned Art of Witchcraft," *The Works*, Vol. III. The skeptical position, together with interesting, if often inaccurate, summaries of contemporary beliefs, is found in Reginald Scot, *The Discoverie of Witchcraft* (1584), ed. Montague Summers (London, 1930). The primary sources for Catholic beliefs are Thomas More, *The Supplication of Souls* (1529, trans. 1557), ed. Sister Mary Thecla, S.C. (Westminster, Md., 1950); Pierre Le Loyer, *IIII Livres des Spectres* (Angers, 1586); and Father Noel Taillepied, *A Treatise of Ghosts* (1588), trans. Montague Summers (London, 1933). The first book of Le Loyer's *IIII Livres* was published, in the translation of Z. Jones, in London in 1605, under the title *A Treatise of Specters or Straunge Sights*. In the following pages, English translations of passages from Book I are taken from the *Treatise*. Translations of passages from *IIII Livres*, Books II–IV, are mine.

[4] Agrippa, *Three Books of Occult Philosophy* (1510), trans. J. F[riske] (London, 1651), pp. 489–90.

well have intended to jolt his audience into a fresh response to what had become a hackneyed convention.[5] For the first time, they were to consider whether a stage ghost was a good spirit or an evil one, and they were to do so on religious principles. Marcellus's speech on the cock and the Advent of "our Saviour's birth" makes the play's Christian context unmistakable, and obliges us to give close attention to the exact beliefs of Shakespeare's audience.

The sixteenth-century controversy between Catholics and Protestants over the nature of ghosts arose out of Protestant attacks on the Catholic belief in the efficacy of good works and thus of prayers for the dead. Because man is justified by faith alone, the Protestants argued, either he is in a state of grace at the moment of his death and goes immediately to Heaven or he is damned and goes immediately to Hell. Since the issue of salvation or damnation was settled at the moment of death, there could be no Purgatory, no possibility that the good works of the living could deliver a soul from God's just punishment. To the Protestant, Purgatory was "but a scar[e]-babe," "a wicked device of the devil, which darkeneth, yea, and maketh void the cross and merits of Christ," a blasphemous plot of the papists to hold the ignorant in their power.[6] Both Protestants and Catholics agreed that a soul could not return from Heaven or Hell. By banishing Purgatory, the Reformation thus eliminated any possibility that the soul of the dead could return to earth.

The Protestants argued further that it would be inconceivable for God to allow the dead to return:

For if many dead persons had retourned backe again into this life, the wicked spirit the divell would easily have devised many sleights & wiles, & brought in much deceit into the life of man. And therfore god hath

---

[5] Although stage tradition helps us to see the Ghost in *Hamlet* in proper perspective, specific insights are so minor and require such detailed discussion that a summary at this point would merely distract. See Appendix A, "The Relevance of Religious Tests to the Stage Ghost, 1560–1610," pp. 255–60.

[6] Henry Smith, "The Pilgrims Wish," *Sermons* (London, 1609), p. 260; Henry Bullinger, *The Decades,* ed. for the Parker Society by the Rev. Thomas Harding (Cambridge, Eng., 1849), III, 391. That the ghost controversy was rooted in the dispute over prayers for the dead is clear in Father Taillepied's attack on Calvin: "All those writers who have drunk of the muddy and stinking waters of the Lake of Geneva incline absolutely to deny apparitions and ghosts, and this lie they have brewed out of their superstitious hatred of Prayers for the Dead." *A Treatise,* p. 5.

cleane shut up this dore of deceit, & not permitted any dead man to returne hither & shewe what things be done in the other life, least the divell might gredely catch this occasion to plant his fraudulent policies.[7]

The average Elizabethan was bombarded with these arguments. Again and again he was warned in sermons and meditational works that "a soul separated from the body cannot wander in these regions. ... [Souls] go a journey, chancing into unknown countries ... from whence they cannot return."[8]

Since a ghost could not be a human soul, it could be only a good or evil spirit, an angel or a devil. Thus Brutus asks the ghost of Caesar: "Art thou some god, some angel, or some devil ... ?" (*Julius Caesar,* IV.iii.279). To the two Protestant alternatives, Shakespeare adds a pagan possibility for the sake of decorum, but neither Brutus nor the ghost suggests that the spirit is actually the soul of Caesar. Spenser widens the range of possibilities in Arthur's combat with Maleger. When Maleger, though dealt many mortal wounds, still stands, Arthur is terrified:

> He doubted, least it were some magicall
> Illusion, that did beguile his sense,
> Or wandring ghost, that wanted funerall,
> Or aerie spirit under false pretence,
> Or hellish feend raysd up through divelish science.
> (*The Faerie Queene,* II.xi.39)[9]

Here we have the three Protestant possibilities—hallucination, angel, and devil—with a pagan alternative added for good measure.

The possibility of angelic intervention, however, was considered extremely slight.[10] Both Catholics and Protestants agreed that an angel could visit man as a result of divine intervention, but the Prot-

---

[7] Lavater, *Of Ghostes,* p. 122.

[8] Bullinger, *The Decades,* III, 402. That the "vain error of purgatory" was a recurrent pastoral concern is attested by extended discussions in the third part of the homily on prayer (*Certaine Sermons,* II, 118–23) and in the highly influential *Decades* of Henry Bullinger (III, 395–400), which served as a study manual for Elizabethan preachers. See also Sandys's *Sermons,* pp. 162–63, James I, *Daemonology,* p. 41, and Lavater, pp. 98ff.

[9] Quotations are from *The Poetical Works of Edmund Spenser,* ed. J. C. Smith and E. de Selincourt (London, 1950).

[10] Lavater, pp. 193–94.

estant contended that the age of miracles had passed. Indeed, majority opinion held that all ghosts were devils. King James had no doubt: "Since the comming of Christ in the flesh, and establishing of his Church by the Apostles, all miracles, visions, prophecies, & appearances of Angels or good spirites are ceased."[11] He was joined in this conviction by many, including Sir Thomas Browne: "I believe ... that those apparitions and ghosts of departed persons are not the wandering souls of men, but the unquiet walks of Devils, prompting and suggesting us unto mischief, blood and villany."[12] Even those Protestant theorists who admitted the possibility of angelic visitation in the form of a ghost devoted almost all their attention to the dangers of demonic illusion. As disseminated to the general public, then, the Protestant view was virtually unanimous: any ghost that was not the hallucination of a sick mind was a demon masquerading as the spirit of a dead man in order to tempt the living.

The dominant view that all ghosts are demons is heard throughout Elizabethan literature. When Red Cross Knight first hears the piteous voice of Fradubio issuing from a tree, he considers two possibilities, both evil. It is

> [A] voyce of damned Ghost from *Limbo* lake,
> Or guilefull spright wandring in empty aire,
> Both which fraile men do often times mistake.
> (*The Faerie Queene*, I.ii.32)

The Protestant view is strikingly invoked by the chorus in Kyd's *Cornelia*, despite the play's pagan frame of reference. When Cornelia believes that she has been visited by Pompey's ghost, the Chorus chas-

---

[11] James I, *Daemonology*, p. 66. Cf. pp. 60–61.

[12] "Religio Medici," *The Works of Sir Thomas Browne*, ed. Geoffrey Keynes (London, 1928), I, 47. Others who believed all ghosts were devils include Smith (*The Sermons*, p. 261), Gifford (*A Discourse*, fol. C4ʳ), and Perkins ("A Discourse," *The Works*, III, 611). A touchstone in the controversy between Catholics and Protestants was the example of the appearance of the "ghost" of Samuel to Saul (I Samuel 28). Both the Geneva and the Bishops' bibles had a marginal note explaining that the "ghost" was really Satan (Richmond Noble, *Shakespeare's Biblical Knowledge*, New York, 1935, p. 203), and Protestants were unanimous in pronouncing the apparition an illusion of Satan. See "A Confutation of Unwritten Verities," *Miscellaneous Writings of Thomas Cranmer*, ed. for the Parker Society by the Rev. John Edmund Cox (Cambridge, Eng., 1846), p. 44; *Early Writings of John Hooper*, ed. for the Parker Society by the Rev. Samuel Carr (Cambridge, Eng., 1843), p. 326; Deacon and Walker, *Dialogical Discourses*, p. 126; and Perkins, *A Discourse*, pp. 626–28. The basic argument was that God has forbidden man to seek anything from the dead.

tises her for her "melancholie showes." After the soul is separated from the body,

> 'It eyther turneth to the Stygian Lake,
> 'Or staies for ever in th' Elisian fields....'

Therefore, Cornelia saw not "Pompeys spryte / But some false Daemon that beguild [her] sight" (III.i.128–47).[13] The belief that all ghosts were demonic was so familiar that it provided excellent opportunity for comedy. In *The Atheist's Tragedy,* Languebeau Snuffe is petrified by the unexpected entrance of Charlemont, whom he believed to be dead. A formulary Puritan, he shrieks, "Spirits are invisible. 'Tis the fiend i' the likeness of Charlemont. I will have no conversation with Satan," and rushes out in terror (III.ii.22–24).[14]

In only one instance in Elizabethan and Jacobean plays (and nowhere, so far as I have read, in popular literature) is there even a hint that a ghost may have returned from Purgatory. That play, of course, is *Hamlet.*

Although scholars have been quite accurate in defining the Protestant position, they have created serious confusion about Catholic beliefs. J. Dover Wilson and Lily Bess Campbell performed a valuable service in alerting us to the importance of Elizabethan ghost theories, but both of them drew misleading conclusions from incomplete evidence. In his edition of Lavater's *Of Ghostes and Spirites,* Wilson offers the following summary: "Most Catholics of Shakespeare's day believed in ghosts as spirits of the departed, allowed to return from Purgatory for some special purpose, which it was the duty of the pious to further if possible, that the soul might find rest. But for Protestants the matter was not so easy."[15] In *Shakespeare's Tragic Heroes,* Campbell draws similar conclusions: "Lavater ... argued ... against the Papists who believed that the spirits of the dead were released temporarily to return to earth.... Shakespeare has pictured a ghost from

---

13 Thomas Kyd, *Works,* ed. Frederick S. Boas (Oxford, 1901).

14 The same joke is found in *Every Woman in Her Humour.* Even a friar turns Protestant when he faces a man he had supposed dead. Knowing the "ghost" is a devil, he promptly proceeds to conjure it. See also the first jest in Richard Tarlton's *Newes Out of Purgatorie* (London, 1590), pp. 2–3.

15 Introduction, p. xvi. See also *What Happens in Hamlet,* 3d ed. (Cambridge, Eng., 1961), pp. 61–62.

Purgatory according to all the tests possible; a ghost which, especially since it appeared in the form and likeness of a parent, Hamlet must obey, failure in obedience being well reckoned as guilt."[16]

Although both writers leave the question open (Wilson by "most Catholics" and Campbell by the omission of a comma after "Papists"), both imply that the Catholic belief in Purgatorial spirits was in striking opposition to the Protestant belief in demonic illusion. Both imply that Catholics believed Purgatorial spirits might be permitted by the normal operation of divine law to return to earth for any purpose, and that obedience to any command was considered a religious obligation. Neither writer suggests the true Catholic position, as spelled out in the two works written in direct answer to Lavater: Le Loyer's *IIII Livres des Spectres* and Taillepied's *Psichologie ou traité de l'apparition des esprits.*

The matter was not easier for the Catholic than it was for the Protestant. On the contrary, his dilemma was greater, for he faced not three but four possibilities. He agreed that a ghost might be a hallucination, an angel, or a devil, but he also admitted the outside possibility that a ghost might be the true spirit of the departed. It cannot, however, be too strongly emphasized that such a visitation could take place only by divine intervention. Taillepied willingly accepts the Protestants' recurrent argument from Chrysostom that spirits cannot come back, but he interprets it from the Catholic point of view: Chrysostom actually meant "that Spirits do not come back at their own will or by their own power in the natural order of event; but, on extraordinary occasions if God so permits."[17] The visitation of a dead soul would indeed require a miracle, but the Catholic believed that "on extraordinary occasions" such a miracle might be granted.

Miracles, however, were considered extremely rare, and Catholics were warned that in most cases spirits professing to be dead souls were actually devils.[18] The Protestant and Catholic positions were thus much closer than is usually thought. Both sides in the debate cited

---

[16] Pp. 85–86, 126.

[17] Taillepied, *A Treatise of Ghosts*, p. 137.

[18] To my knowledge, Hankins is the only scholar who has noted that Catholics, as well as Protestants, believed most ghosts to be demons. See his discussion of Guazzo, in *The Character of Hamlet*, pp. 167–68. See also Le Loyer, *IIII Livres*, III, 167. Le Loyer's emphasis on demonic trickery is pervasive throughout his four-volume work. Portents in nature are the work of devils: troubling the air, stirring the winds, and making fire fall from on high (II,

II Corinthians 11:14 as their primary authority for warning that Satan can transform himself into an angel of light, that in all probability a given ghost is a "Satanicall imposture," "nothing else but an illusion and craft of the devil to make men believe lies."[19] For "the devil is a marvellous juggling deceiver, in taking on him divers forms and shapes," and the pious must be extremely wary.[20]

Throughout the period, popular literature echoes the basic Scriptural warning that "Satan is himself transformed into an angel of light"—that, in Hamlet's words, "the devil hath power / To assume a pleasing shape." It is directly invoked in Berowne's statement that "Devils soonest tempt, resembling spirits of light" (*Love's Labour's Lost*, IV.iii.257), and suggested in Juliet's cry on discovering that Romeo has killed Tybalt: "O serpent heart, hid with a flowering face!...fiend angelical!...Despised substance of divinest show!" (III.ii.73–77). We also find constant use of the specific belief that Satan masqueraded as souls of the departed to catch the souls of the living. For Satan cannot appear in his own nature, and just as "those that catch birdes imitate their voyces, so will hee imitate the voyces of Gods vengeance, to bring us like birds into the net of eternall damnation."[21]

Since these basic beliefs of both Protestants and Catholics were familiar to *Hamlet*'s audience, and since Shakespeare invites his audience to view the Ghost from a religious perspective, we are justified in asking a crucial question: how does one determine whether a ghost is a good spirit (whether angel or Purgatorial soul) or a demon? There was remarkable agreement among Protestants and Catholics on many points. All Christians were warned to be thoroughly suspicious of any supernatural visitation. Often repeated was I John 4:1: "Believe not every spirit, but try the spirits whether they are of God."

---

521). Tyrants and murderers who are pursued by the ghosts of their victims are actually being tormented by demonic agents of divine punishment, by *"les Diables executeurs de la vengeance Divine"* (II, 461–65). Le Loyer even agrees with the Protestants that the ghost of Samuel was a devil and he cites their argument: God has forbidden any conference between the living and the dead (IV, 269).

[19] Perkins, "Discourse," *The Works*, III, 611; Hooper, *Early Writings*, p. 326.

[20] Bullinger, *The Decades*, p. 354. See also Le Loyer, IV, 190–91: *"Car le Diable, fin & caut renard, ne les assault pas en armes pareilles & le glaive au poing, ains secretement & latentement sous ombre de bien.... Ce malin Esprit se transfigure aucunefois en Ange de lumiere a fin qu'il nuise d'avantage par la simulation de vertu...."*

[21] Nashe, "The Terrors of the Night," *Works*, I, 348.

If a spirit appeared as a lion or a dog or a toad, there was no problem: it was obviously a demon.[22] Even if it appeared as a man, and especially if it appeared as a loved one to whom one would instinctively give credence, it was probably a demon.[23] To distrust such an apparition was a sign of Christian prudence—not, as we have often read, a sign of lack of faith.[24]

On many of the actual tests, Protestants and Catholics were also agreed. First, when does the ghost appear? If at night, and especially at midnight—the dead hour—it is probably demonic. Although the Devil can appear at any time (except on Sunday), the Prince of Darkness has more power at night. He forms his body of the humors of the night, cloaking his evil plans in darkness.[25] If the ghost vanishes at daybreak, one should be especially suspicious, for the light of the sun chases away *"les estranges formes des songes, & les visions de la nuict,"* even as it dissipates dark shadows and illuminates the world.[26]

This warning provided perhaps the most widely known test of spirits. Thomas Nashe gives vivid expression to the belief that demonic visitations were limited to the time of darkness:

The divell is a speciall predominant Planet of the night, and . . . our creator for our punishment hath allotted it him as his peculiar segniorie and kingdome. . . . Like a cunning fowler, to this end he spreadeth his nets of temptation in the darke, that men might not see to avoyd them. . . . When hath the divell commonly first appeared unto anie man but in the night? . . . A generall principle it is, hee that doth ill hateth the light.[27]

Indeed, in the popular imagination it was almost axiomatic that "he that hateth the light doth ill," that any spirit shunning the light of day necessarily was evil. In *A Fig for Fortune,* Revenge vanishes at dawn and Elizian man concludes that she must have been a "sleight of Satan." In *A Midsummer Night's Dream,* Puck hails the approach of dawn:

---

[22] Taillepied, p. 163.

[23] The Devil often presents himself in the likeness of parents, warns Thomas Nashe, for he knows "that in these shapes . . . that wee are inclined to with a naturall kind of love, we will sooner harken to him than otherwise" (I, 348). See also Andrew Willet, *Hexapla in Exodum* (London, 1608), p. 81, and Le Loyer, IV, 297: the Devil takes a familiar form in order to capitalize on fellow human feeling.

[24] Le Loyer, III, 167; IV, 297.    [25] *Ibid.,* II, 515–19.    [26] *Ibid.,* IV, 337.

[27] "Terrors of the Night," *Works,* I, 346–47.

And yonder shines Aurora's harbinger,
At whose approach, ghosts, wandering here and there,
Troop home to churchyards: damned spirits all,
That in crossways and floods have burial,
Already to their wormy beds are gone;
For fear lest day should look their shames upon,
They wilfully themselves exile from light
And must for aye consort with black-brow'd night.

And Oberon responds: "But we are spirits of another sort" (III.ii.380–88). Of course these damned spirits are folk ghosts, since no responsible thinker believed damned souls could return from Hell, but the passage shows that Shakespeare was familiar with the popular belief that only hellish spirits were banished by the light of the sun.[28]

Where does the ghost appear? Although good and evil spirits can appear anywhere (demons are barred only from Heaven), devils have their favorite haunts: graveyards, scenes of horrible crimes, battlefields, gallows, prisons, ruined cities, old houses and castles, sites of buried treasure, and mines.[29] Above all, they seek deserted places, and one should be especially wary of a ghost who appears in any lonely place such as the desert or the woods or on a precipice.[30] The Devil is canny. He wants to get his victim alone, isolated from his fellow man: "For our nature is such, as in companies wee are not so soone mooved to anie such kinde of feare, as being solitare, which the Devill knowing well inough, hee will not therefore assaile us but when we are weake."[31] The association of devils and ghosts with desolated places such as graveyards and blasted heaths was widely

---

[28] The spirits to which Puck refers are souls of men who have taken their own lives. Some suicides were buried at crossroads with stakes through their hearts to prevent their return as vampires; some were tied in sacks and carried out to sea (Hankins, *The Character of Hamlet,* p. 226; Lavater, *Of Ghostes,* p. 80; Taillepied, *A Treatise of Ghosts,* p. 86). Shakespeare puts even these folk ghosts into a Christian context.

[29] Le Loyer, *IIII Livres,* II, 485–93; Taillepied, pp. 98–99; Lavater, pp. 73–74. A widespread belief in the period is noteworthy, though probably of no profound significance for *Hamlet.* Devils were thought to have a particular affinity for the Northern countries. James I singles out Lapland, Finland, and the northern isles as particularly subject to the abuse of incubi and succubi (*Daemonology,* p. 69); Le Loyer stresses the tyranny of Satan throughout the North, emphasizing the harassment in Denmark, where the Normans are tormented by the evil *Tervilles,* in Sweden and Iceland, where the people are especially tormented by devils feigning to be the ghosts of dead kinsmen and friends, and in Norway, where devils constantly appear (II, 495–96, and III, 62–63). The belief is reflected in Belleforest's treatment of Amleth's black magic.

[30] Le Loyer, IV, 301–2.

[31] James I, *Daemonology,* p. 58.

known; but the specific association of demons with precipices, found in Horatio's warning to Hamlet (I.iv.69–78) and in Gloucester's belief that a fiend had tempted him to the cliffs at Dover (*King Lear,* IV.vi.69–79), indicates Shakespeare's familiarity with more detailed demon lore.

To whom does the ghost appear? If to a man of healthy mind and stable faith, it may be either good or evil, for God permits the testing of the virtuous.[32] If, however, a ghost appears to any of the following, it is unquestionably demonic: the superstitious, the simple and credulous, innocent children, murderers and tyrants, demoniacs and magicians, and—above all—melancholics. The widespread belief that melancholy was "like a weapon taken into Sathans hand" is too familiar to require documentation here.[33] As Hamlet and his audience all knew, the Devil was "very potent with such spirits." Blinded by his humor and buffeted by passion, the melancholic was deluded by his senses, tricked by hallucinations, driven by terror and rage to despair or madness or heinous crimes. Moreover, the melancholic was not deluded solely by the fantasies of his unsound mind. Centuries of scholars—among them Johann Wier, Ficino, Agrippa, Guazzo, Le Loyer, Taillepied, du Laurens, and Burton—agreed that melancholics were particularly subject to visitations by Satan in the form of a ghost.

This evil Spirit goeth about seeking whom he may devour, and should he chance to find a man, already of a melancholic and Saturnian humour, who on account of some great losses, or haply because he deems his honour tarnished, the demon here has a fine field to his hand, and he will tempt the poor wretch to depths of misery and depression.[34]

In this significant statement by Taillepied, it should be noted that the "melancholy" making a man particularly prone to demonic temptations is not necessarily pathological. It may result from genuine grief, occasioned by a real loss. Nonetheless, a grief that becomes immoderate (*"une douleur demesurée"*), is Satan's most potent weapon.[35]

---

[32] *Ibid.,* p. 63; Le Loyer, IV, 191.

[33] Bright, *A Treatise of Melancholie,* p. 237 and *passim.* See also Le Loyer, *A Treatise,* fol. 131ᵛ, and Perkins, "Cases of Conscience," *The Works,* II, 46.

[34] Taillepied, p. 95. See the useful summary of Lawrence Babb, "Hamlet, Melancholy, and the Devil," *Modern Language Notes,* LIX (1944), 120–22.

[35] Le Loyer, II, 460; IV, 303–5.

in rage, the danger is compounded,
stitution of body" who are also "ready
tter" for Satan's service.[36]
hus far was absolute in itself. Good
at night, in deserted places, and even
Both Catholics and Protestants, how-
s of a ghost who appeared on a preci-
f he appeared to a melancholic who

nitive for both Protestants and Catho-
vas unquestionably demonic, even if it
Vestminster at high noon to Sir Thomas
ural citation was Galatians 1:8: "But
heaven, preach any other gospel unto
preached unto you, let him be accursed."
No matter how convincing a spirit might be in every other respect, if
it urged any action or made any statement that violated the teachings
of the Church, it was an agent of the Devil.[37]

It did not follow, however—and this point is repeatedly stressed by
both Protestant and Catholic writers—that a ghost proved it was a
spirit of grace solely by voicing Christian doctrine, for "the Devill is
alwayes readye to serve his own turne at a pynch."[38] "He may, it is not
impossible, for some dark design seem to applaud and exhort at first,
but he will very soon try to tempt men out of the right path and se-
duce them into error and sin."[39] But if demons assume the form of
ghosts only to damn men, "many will say, why then do they persuade
men unto good things, exhorte them unto vertue, and call them from
vice?"[40] Because the Devil is not a fool. He knows that "if he were to
show his horns at the first moment, we should be on our guard and
flee his wiles."[41] Shakespeare and his audience were fully aware that
a supernatural visitor was not trustworthy solely because it gave voice
to Christian precepts. In cautioning Bassanio not to misjudge Shylock, Antonio refers explicitly to one of Satan's most confusing tricks:

---

[36] Gifford, *A Discourse,* fol. I2ʳ. See also James I, *Daemonology,* pp. 8, 32, 35, and 43.
[37] Taillepied, pp. 66, 130; Lavater, pp. 198–99.
[38] Viret, *The Second Part of the Demoniacke Worlde,* fol. B3ʳ.
[39] Taillepied, p. 165.
[40] Lavater, p. 171.
[41] Taillepied, p. 165. See also Le Loyer, IV, 291.

> Mark you this, Bassanio,
> The devil can cite Scripture for his purpose. . . .
> O, what a goodly outside falsehood hath!
> (*Merchant of Venice,* I.iii.98–103)

In announcing his method, Iago is even more specific:

> Divinity of hell!
> When devils will their blackest sins put on,
> They do suggest at first with heavenly shows. . . .
> (*Othello,* II.iii.356–58)

In a vivid series of analogies, Taillepied expounds an extremely important corollary: a ghost does not prove itself to be a spirit of good by telling the truth.

Satan acts, I say, like a cunning gamester or tattmonger who when drawing in some rich gull loses a little money at first in order to enmesh his caravan and lure him until he is stripped of all. . . . In the same way does Satan feign to encourage us in the truth and speak seeming pious words. It is a snare to draw men by his birdlime flattery from the narrow path. He dares us with light as larks are dazzled and caught. Just as a merchant who wishes to sell of some commodity dresses it to the best advantage and deacons it devisedly, so Satan under show and colour of fairness and truth, envenoms and infects, the good with evil, for he has honey indeed in his mouth, but beware the serpent's fatal sting.[42]

Not only may a demonic apparition exhort us to virtue in order to gain authority; it also may tell us verifiable truths in order to gain credence.[43] Paradoxically, the "truth" that the Devil speaks is really not the truth at all, for he twists it to further his own ends. On the one hand, he may speak ambiguously, saying one thing but implying another, perhaps framing a negative in such a way that it could actually mean an affirmative.[44] On the other hand, he may state straightforward fact, but

he turneth the truth it selfe into lying, and maketh the trueth to bee no more trueth, when it once commeth out of his mouth. . . . For, Trueth, to

---

[42] Taillepied, p. 166.    [43] Lavater, p. 173.    [44] Le Loyer, II, 470–71; IV, 296.

speake properly, consisteth not in the bare woordes spoken, but in the meaning, for which cause they are uttered.... And therfore, when we are to
judge of the trueth, wee must not judge only according to the woords
which wee heare, nor yet take them by halfes, but receyve all the partes together, and so looke to what end and purpose they were spoken.[45]

As Macbeth learns too late, "these juggling fiends" may "palter with
us in a double sense" (V.viii.19–20). Banquo knows from the first
that truth itself may be the Devil's most insidious weapon. For

> often times to win us to our harm,
> The instruments of darkness tell us truths....
> (I.iii.123–24)

As references to Satanic imposture in *Love's Labour's Lost* and *Romeo and Juliet* make plain, these ideas were familiar to Shakespeare
throughout his career.

These two warnings cannot be emphasized too strongly because
they cast suspicion on two traditional assumptions about *Hamlet*. If
the Ghost is to be tested by Christian criteria, neither the fact that it
exhorts Hamlet to patience with Gertrude nor the fact that it tells the
truth about the murder necessarily proves that it is a "spirit of light."
To my knowledge, no study of ghost lore in relation to *Hamlet* has
even hinted that neither of these tests was considered valid by Lavater, Le Loyer, Taillepied, Viret, or any other Christian theorist. Agreement was unanimous that the Devil

often exhorts man to do the commandments of God; very often speaks the
truth; preaches virtue; dresses his ministers as ministers of Justice, making
night pass for day, death for life, despair for hope, apostasy for faith.... In
brief, the Devil intermingles the good with the evil, and the true with the
false.[46]

Agreement was unanimous that "therefore it behoveth us to be very
circumspect and warie."[47]

All of the tests and warnings mentioned thus far were common to
both Protestant and Catholic pneumatological treatises, and there is

---

[45] Viret, fols. B3ᵛ–4ʳ.    [46] Le Loyer, IV, 288.    [47] Lavater, pp. 200–201.

ample evidence that all of the tenets discussed above were familiar to Elizabethan laymen of both faiths as well as to Shakespeare himself. Since most scholars agree that the Ghost of Hamlet's father is a true Purgatorial spirit—many believing with Dover Wilson that "in fact he is the only Catholic in the whole of *Hamlet*"[48]—let us then turn to the method by which Catholics were to discern a ghost.

If confronted by a supernatural visitation, the wary Catholic was first to ask himself the questions that, as we have noted, Protestants were also to ask: when, where, and to whom does the spirit appear? Beyond these, he had several specific tests. First, how does the spirit respond to the invocation of God? At the moment we see a ghost, we must "fervently recommend ourselves to God": "If a Spirit appear, and we know not whether it be a good or an evil Spirit, call on JESUS, and ask Him if it be a good Spirit to grant us courage and understanding to hear what it may request us to do; or if it be an evil Spirit ask Him again to protect and shield us from the snare."[49] If spirits thus "conjured" "are from the Devil, their Prince, they will not be able to conceal themselves."[50] The form that the questioning takes is important. We are not to ask the ghost who it is or why it has come. We are only to charge it to speak, if it can, in the name of God. If it does not vanish, we must wait prayerfully and patiently for whatever it chooses to divulge. Indeed, Le Loyer warns that we must be especially suspicious of spirits who volunteer that they are the souls of the departed.[51] A good spirit cannot speak until he has been charged to do so in God's name. Once, twice, or even three times, we must say, *"If thou art of God, speak: if thou art not of God, be-gone."*[52]

What does the ghost look like? If an evil spirit takes the form of a

---

[48] Lavater, p. xxiii.       [49] Taillepied, pp. 169, 171.

[50] Le Loyer, IV, 301.       [51] *Ibid.*

[52] Taillepied, *A Treatise of Ghosts*, p. 168. Lavater's summary of Catholic beliefs seems to be wrong on this point. Believing, as a good Protestant, that it is blasphemous to ask questions of the dead, he attacks the Catholics for the questions that—according to him—they put to ghosts: "What mans soule he is? for what cause he is come, and what he doth desire? Whether he require any ayde by prayers and suffrages? Whether by Massing, or almes giving he may be released?" (*Of Ghostes*, p. 107). Neither Taillepied nor Le Loyer advises questioning a ghost at all. Le Loyer even goes so far as humbly but firmly to disagree with St. Thomas's view that one may in a spirit of pure devotion ask a departed soul to reveal his present state. To ask anything of the dead, Le Loyer believes, is to give evidence of doubt, presumption, and dangerous curiosity (*IIII Livres*, IV, 281–82). We are to ask nothing at all. We are merely to "conjure" the spirit in the name of God and then to await further developments.

man, rather than of "a lion, a bear, a black dog, a puddock or hop-toad, a serpent, a great grimalkin,"[53] it may be very difficult to detect. Both devils and angels appear luminous to men, but "the light of Demons is full of shadows," flickering like the fire of Hell, whereas angels are bathed in a steady, clear, and dazzling light like that of the sun. If the spirit is accompanied by sulphurous smoke, it is clearly evil.[54] If it is "all in white" and "of gracious aspect" (of "*aspect doux & aimable*"), it may be good.[55]

What is the tone of its voice? "It should be noted whether the voice is soft, agreeable, musical, sweetly-sounding, consolatory and sooth-ing; or else if it be rough, harsh, and loud," for the voice of a demon was said to be "*fort basse & gresle*" whereas the voice Paul heard on the road to Damascus spoke "*assez hautement.*"[56]

What is the spirit's purpose? "God, according to His Divine Will and as His inscrutable Providence directs, causes and permits Spirits to appear . . . in order to do His bidding and fulfill His command."[57] Since souls were released from Purgatory only to serve God's will, it followed that they could not return to further any temporal end, much less any purpose violating God's commandments. Most com-monly they returned to pray help in delivering them from their pains. Thus they "earnestly besought the living to have Masses said and dirges sung on their behalf, or to go on some pilgrimage for their deliverance." Even the popular belief that ghosts might return to re-veal hidden treasure found Christian sanction in the belief that they might need "to make restitution, to discharge obligations, to restore some goods or piece which may have been borrowed and not returned, or perchance filched and stolen." In addition to praying for aid, Pur-gatorial spirits might also appear to "aid and encheer" the living or to warn of impending calamity, although the latter function was nor-mally viewed as the province of angelic spirits.[58] Primarily the Purga-tory ghost appeared only to ask for masses, alms, fasts, pilgrimages, and, above all, prayers. Not one instance has ever been noted of a Purgatorial spirit's commanding revenge, either his own or God's.[59]

[53] Taillepied, p. 163.     [54] Le Loyer, IV, 290.
[55] Taillepied, p. 163; Le Loyer, IV, 290.     [56] Taillepied, p. 163; Le Loyer, II, 541.
[57] Taillepied, p. 119.
[58] *Ibid.*, pp. 140, 122–23. See also pp. 78–79, 117–18.
[59] In the many arguments that the ghost in *Hamlet* squares with Catholic theology, only one example of a "punitive ghost" has been suggested, that of a noble knight whose tale ap-

Clearly, then, if a ghost appeared to counsel anything other than actions conducive to the health of the soul, whether of the dead or of the living, it was a demonic imposture.

How does the spirit behave? "The words, gestures and look of the apparition are carefully to be remarked. Does the vision speak humbly, acknowledging sins and trespasses done, with tears and sad groans?" Such would be the behavior of a penitent spirit who acknowledges the justice of the pains he suffers in Purgatory. On the other hand, does it "vomit pride, threats, curses"?[60] By such actions an evil spirit, excluded from grace, will inevitably reveal its true nature. Does it accuse others of guilt? It is evil. The function of a Purgatory soul is not to find fault with another, not to complain of another's cruelty, but to lament its own sin, rehearse its own deserved misery, and pray for relief. Is it angry? It is evil. For in Purgatory, "no man can be angry."[61] Above all, as we have noted, we must "consider whether the apparition says or suggests anything contrary to the Word of God, to the Apostolic traditions, to the Catholic Faith; anything in fine contrary to faith and morals."[62]

What is the response of the living to a visitation? Good spirits at first inspire "a certain awe and reverential fear," but they "never depart without reassuring and comforting," without consoling and lifting the heart, without enflaming in men the love of things divine.[63] "In the case of evil Spirits it is quite the contrary. They flatter and cajole; then they lead to bad thoughts and wicked deeds and desires; and finally they exhibit their true colours, alarming and terrifying those who have seen them as they depart furiously."[64] Good spirits go with God, "who is the source of peace, of joy, and of tranquility."[65] Evil spirits cannot conceal the malice of Satan.

---

pears in *The Golden Legend*. After the knight's death in battle, his cousin fails to live up to a binding promise to give alms to the poor, and the soul of the knight appears to prophesy that devils will that day carry off the cousin's soul to Hell. The knight, however, is not seeking revenge, much less inciting someone to execute punishment. He merely prophesies the inevitable punishment of sin. (The example is offered by Monsignor I. J. Semper in *'Hamlet' without Tears*, Dubuque, Iowa, 1946, p. 227. For an effective argument that the example is irrelevant, see Robert H. West, *The Invisible World*, Athens, Ga., 1939, pp. 51–52.) If the many Catholic scholars working the field have been unable to discover any example of a Purgatory soul's commanding revenge, it is doubtful that one is to be found.

[60] Taillepied, p. 163.
[61] More, *The Supplication of Souls*, pp. 166, 168.
[62] Taillepied, p. 163.          [63] *Ibid.*; Le Loyer, IV, 291.
[64] Taillepied, p. 163.          [65] Le Loyer, IV, 290.

Several of these tests by which the Catholic was to discern whether or not a given spirit was a soul from Purgatory would also be meaningful to the Protestant. Both would beware of a spirit that vanished when charged to speak in the name of God, of a spirit that appeared in a light suggesting the flames of Hell, of a spirit that left behind the stench of sulphur, of a spirit that incited to vice, of a spirit moved by anger and malice. Those Protestants who believed that good spirits might take the form of the dead also agreed that God would effect such a miracle only to further His divine will, that the purpose and behavior of the ghost must accord with his divine mission. Moreover, most members of the predominantly Protestant audience probably would have been at least aware of many of those tests with which their church did not agree. Even skeptics who frankly doubted the appearance of ghosts of any type probably were familiar with ghost lore. Reginald Scot may have intended to destroy "the absurd opinions" of papists and witchmongers, but his *Discoverie of Witchcraft* actually provided a tantalizing summary of them. Thus many beliefs —for example, such specific Catholic tests as the warning that "a damned soule hath a verie heavie and sowre looke; but a saints soule hath a cheerefull and merrie countenance"—were available to all.[66] Catholic traditions were not easily destroyed, and they were given even wider currency by the heated debate over ghosts. For these reasons, the majority of *Hamlet's* original audience is likely to have been familiar with most, if not all, of the material we have considered in the present chapter.

Let us, then, join that audience and return to the play. Our first task —and Hamlet's—is to test that Ghost.

---

[66] Scot, *Discoverie*, p. 535.

# CHAPTER V

## Spirit of Health or Goblin Damned?

The study of Elizabethan ghost lore does not contradict our intuitive response to the first scene of *Hamlet*. It indicates that modern uneasiness may closely approximate the response of Shakespeare's audience. The play frankly invited both Protestants and Catholics to test the Ghost according to their religious beliefs and then presented them with recognizable warnings of danger.

No one in the first scene gives any indication of believing the Ghost to be the true soul of the dead King. The point of view is Protestant. Horatio, Marcellus, and Bernardo all consistently refer to the apparition as "it": not as the soul of the King himself, but as a spirit whose identity is in doubt. When Marcellus asks if this "thing" has appeared, his diction suggests not contemptuous levity but the cautious Protestant's awareness that the Ghost cannot be the actual King.[1] It is an unknown, the nature of which is still to be determined. Similarly, Horatio's "Stay, illusion" is not an echo of his earlier skepticism but the correct response of a wary Protestant. The Ghost is, indeed, an "illusion." The point at issue is what kind of illusion.

In its first minute on stage, the Ghost reveals that something is seriously wrong. What is the purpose of its first appearance? It merely enters and leaves. Little is established that could not be included in the second appearance. The usual explanation is that its first entrance

[1] Q₁ and F₁ give the line to Marcellus, Q₂ to Horatio. We need not give the line to Horatio on the grounds that Marcellus believes in ghosts and would not discount the apparition by calling it a "thing," whereas Horatio is skeptical of all ghosts until he sees one. Even after he has the witness of his own eyes, Horatio—like Marcellus and Bernardo—continues to treat the Ghost as "it," as a doubtful "thing." Either character could speak the given question, though I feel it better befits Marcellus. Horatio is mildly amused, quietly detached, for the first few moments. It is Marcellus who is eager for the latest news so that he can prove the apparition was not "all in his mind."

is a shrewd bit of theatrical trickery intended to catch the audience's attention. The episode does much more than that. It firmly establishes one point: this Ghost is forced to leave when Heaven is invoked. Horatio follows the warnings of religion. He charges the Ghost in the name of Heaven to identify itself, and it took no pious scholar to know that only demons would be "chased" by the invocation of God. The first episode reaches its climax as the Ghost is "offended" and stalks away, leaving Horatio pale and trembling.

A minor detail in this episode may also be a hint that this is a demon who usurps the form of the dead King. The Ghost "would be spoke to," and Horatio, as a scholar, is urged to question it. In my judgment, this fact has been faultily glossed. It is generally held that ghosts could not speak until they were spoken to, although the only corroborating evidence seems to be a remark about Samuel Johnson in the eighteenth century.[2] The Elizabethan belief appears to have been specifically related to the problem of identifying an evil spirit. A false spirit might speak first, in which case one should be even more cautious. The informed Christian would speak before being spoken to, conjuring the spirit in the name of God to reveal its nature: if good, by speaking; if bad, by leaving. In other words, the fact that "it would be spoke to" does not prove that Bernardo believes it is a true ghost. Moreover, the fact that a scholar is urged to address it may mean that Marcellus fears it is a demon. Since Francis Douce, editors have repeated his assertion that ghosts had to be addressed in Latin. On the contrary, the evidence most frequently cited indicates something quite different. In Fletcher's *The Night-Walker,* Coachman Toby says:

> Let's call the butler up, for he speaks Latine,
> And that will daunt the devil.
>
> (II.i)[3]

Exactly. Latin was the language used in the rite of exorcism. No writer claimed that good spirits must be so addressed. If Marcellus is appealing to Horatio to use Latin, he is fearful that the Ghost may be

---

[2] Tom Tyers, in describing Johnson, said, "Sir, you are like a ghost: you never speak till you are spoken to." *Boswell's Life of Johnson,* ed. George Birkbeck Hill, rev. L. F. Powell, Oxford, 1934, III, 307.

[3] *Works,* Vol. VII.

a demon.[4] More probably, however, Marcellus simply believes that a scholar is better equipped to address a doubtful spirit with safety. He is terrified, and with good reason.

The physical appearance of the Ghost may also suggest that it is suspect. As Catholics believed and Protestants had heard, Purgatory souls and good spirits both were "of sweet and amiable aspect," moved only by grace and charity. This ghost frowns as did the dead King once when he was angry with the Polacks. Moreover, Purgatory souls and good spirits are both spirits of peace. Many have noted the curious fact that the Ghost is in arms, bearing a truncheon as it moves with martial stalk. This is surely not the typical stage ghost described in the Induction to *A Warning for Fair Women* as "Lapt in some foul sheet or a leather pilch." It is conceivable that the costume is intended to lend awe, or to create a figure acceptable to a man of Hamlet's intelligence, or to portend some danger to the State. But it is also possible that Shakespeare's audience believed that armed spirits were demonic. Virgil had explained such apparitions as souls who still embraced the goods and appetites that had dominated them in life, but Le Loyer disagreed. Military garb proved that they were not souls but "devils who took the clothes and even the arms" of the men whose form they assumed.[5] I have found no indication that this belief was widespread, but it does suggest a possible association.

The second appearance of the Ghost reinforces the threat. Horatio, in an act of considerable courage, resolves to step into the path of the Ghost: "I'll cross it, though it blast me." The context makes it impossible that Shakespeare meant Horatio to make the sign of the cross. Horatio's point of view has been consistently Protestant, as shown by his repeated assumption that the Ghost is an "illusion," a spirit "usurping" the form of the dead King. Moreover, the stage direction in $Q_2$— "It spreads his armes"—probably refers to Horatio's movements in intercepting the Ghost's path. It does not describe the Catholic gesture, nor could it indicate any meaningful action by the Ghost. For three centuries, the direction apparently was assumed to mean that Horatio blocked the Ghost's path. Discussing Fechter's production of *Hamlet*

[4] My own feeling is that the audience would not have time to stop and make this connection. The scene goes too quickly and, of course, Horatio speaks English. S. A. Blackmore, S.J., *The Riddles of Hamlet* (Boston, 1917), p. 88.

[5] Le Loyer, *IIII Livres,* IV, 303–4.

in 1870, Kate Field expressed her delight at a new piece of business: "Heretofore Horatios have senselessly *crossed the Ghost's path,* as if such a step would stay its progress. Not so with Fechter, whose Horatio makes the sign of the cross, at which the Ghost stops, as a Catholic ghost should. Once interpreted thus, intelligence exclaims 'of course'; and yet Horatios have been crossing the stage for three hundred years!"[6] The witness of three centuries of stage tradition is not to be discounted.

Horatio's movement into the Ghost's path is, of course, not a senseless attempt to stop it. It is a determined challenge to a spirit that may be demonic, that may "blast" him with emanations of hellfire. Catholics believed the sign of the cross to be absolute protection against evil spirits, but Horatio realizes that his movement places him in danger. His courage is apparent when we note the Elizabethan belief that "crossing" the path of a specter made one subject to its malignant influence.[7] Modern directors too often have both Horatio and Hamlet cross themselves. To the Catholic, any spirit surviving such a test would necessarily be a spirit of grace, and it would hence be illogical for both Horatio and Hamlet to continue to doubt the Ghost even after it has withstood the most stringent Catholic test.[8]

A wise scholar, Horatio addresses the Ghost as both Protestants and Catholics advised. He does not question it. He charges it to speak, but only if it is a good spirit come upon some mission of grace. This time, it will be recalled, Horatio has not invoked Heaven, and the Ghost is about to speak when it is suddenly arrested by the crow of the cock. Modern editors who place the notation "Cock crows" in the middle of Horatio's speech create a misleading impression. In $Q_2$, the only version to indicate the sound effect, it appears opposite Horatio's last line. The Ghost is meant to react as suddenly to the voice of the cock as it did to Horatio's invocation of Heaven.

There can be little doubt that Shakespeare's audience was acquainted with the symbolic meaning of the cock. An ancient belief—found in traditional Jewish writings and later made specifically Christian

---

[6] Quoted by Arthur Colby Sprague in *Shakespeare and the Actors* (Cambridge, Mass., 1944), p. 132. Italics in the original.

[7] Blakeway noted this belief, citing a story in Lodge's *Illustrations of British History.* The Earl of Derby had supposedly been bewitched because a spirit had "twice crossed him swiftly." *Variorum Hamlet,* ed. Horace Howard Furness (New York, 1877), I, 21.

[8] Le Loyer, IV, 300.

by such writers as Prudentius and St. Ambrose—held that roving demons scattered in fear at cockcrow, and Le Loyer specially related the
belief to his discussion of demons appearing as dead souls.[9] The
Witches' Sabbath customarily began at midnight and lasted until
cockcrow, at which time Satan fled terrified. As the herald of the day,
the cock is the voice of light and thus of grace; in banishing night, he
banishes darkness and sin. Thus Christian tradition held that cocks
crowed all night at the Nativity and again at the Resurrection. More
specifically, the cock symbolized the voice of Christ when it called
Peter to repent, a belief reflected in the familiar weathervane cock on
church steeples.[10]

After Horatio and Marcellus comment on the Ghost's sudden dis-
appearance, even a modern audience should understand the significance of such a response to cockcrow. The Ghost "started like a guilty
thing / Upon a fearful summons," and Horatio is reminded that only
"extravagant and erring spirits" are banished by the herald of the sun.
Good spirits, as we noted earlier, can appear at any time. Marcellus
agrees and notes that evil spirits are dispelled during Advent by the
night-long crowing of the cock. Modern producers make a serious
mistake when they cut Marcellus's speech, for it does much more than
merely "give a religious background to the supernatural happen-
ings."[11] As H. D. F. Kitto notes, it gives "the logical and dynamic
centre of the whole play. We are in the presence of evil."[12]

The first scene thus serves several important functions. It establishes
that the Ghost is not a hallucination. It establishes that something is
rotten in the state of Denmark. It establishes suspense. It establishes
the Christian framework. But, above all, it establishes that the Ghost
is probably malignant. The first four purposes could have been served
by one appearance of the Ghost in a scene half the length, but the fifth

---

[9] *Ibid.*, II, 489. Cf. Le Loyer, *A Treatise*, fol. 32ᵛ.

[10] Montague Summers, *The History of Witchcraft and Demonology* (London, 1926), pp.
117–18; Christopher Devlin, *Hamlet's Divinity and Other Essays* (Carbondale, Ill., 1963), p.
31; Battenhouse, "The Ghost in Hamlet," pp. 180–81; Blackmore, *The Riddles of Hamlet*,
pp. 96–97. Catholic scholars believe that the cock-crown Hymn of St. Ambrose in the Liturgy
for Sunday Lauds finds clear echo in the play: "The herald of the morning sounds, and calls
out the sun ray. Wakened by him the day-star frees the sky from darkness: at his note the
troops of prowling outlaws (*Hoc omnis erronum cohors*) forsake their baleful course." Father
Devlin suggests that "extravagant and erring" looks like an etymological rendering of the
Latin words *erro, erronis*, meaning "a lawless vagabond" (p. 31).

[11] Wilson, *What Happens in Hamlet*, p. 67.

[12] H. D. F. Kitto, *Form and Meaning in Drama* (London, 1959), p. 255.

required that the audience recognize a suspicious pattern. Many members of the audience would probably have been alerted when the Ghost vanished at the invocation of Heaven, but some might have missed the full significance of such a swift action. When the Ghost vanishes a second time for an equally suspicious reason, the inference is unavoidable.

I do not mean to suggest that the Ghost is established as unquestionably demonic by the end of the first scene. It is an awe-inspiring figure of regal majesty whom a loving son will, understandably, be inclined to credit. When the Ghost and Hamlet meet, we will be seeing through Hamlet's eyes and might easily overlook hints of danger. In the first scene, however, we are not yet emotionally involved. While we are still fairly objective, Shakespeare plants several clear warnings that this "guilty thing" is a creature that must be tested with extreme caution, and tested by the teachings of the Church.

Of which church? Of both? Shakespeare wisely drew from both Catholic and Protestant beliefs in order to encourage the widest possible response. Though the characters are consistently Protestant in their viewpoint, nothing is said that would alienate the Catholic. He too believed in the need for discerning between good and evil spirits. Moreover, one small hint would allow the Catholic to consider the possibility that the Ghost might be a Purgatory soul: Horatio's request that it speak if anything may do it "ease." The suggestion that the living might ease the suffering of the dead is so subtle that it would pass a rigorous Anglican censor, but it suffices. When the Ghost next appeared, every member of Shakespeare's audience would probably be prepared to test it according to the beliefs of his own faith.[13]

13 Dover Wilson's analysis of the first scene has gained such widespread acceptance that it may be pertinent to note the objections raised by this study. He finds several different attitudes toward the Ghost expressed by the "four witnesses": Bernardo is the simple soldier, guided by superstition; Marcellus is the officer, vacillating between pre-Reformation superstition and Protestant belief; Hamlet is the student of the Protestant Lavater; Horatio enters a disciple of the skeptic Scot, but is converted to the position of Lavater (*What Happens in Hamlet*, pp. 66–75). As I read the evidence, all four characters respond in exactly the same manner. Until Horatio actually sees the Ghost, he quite sensibly suspects that it is a hallucination. Lavater and all knowledgeable Christians began with this assumption until they had proof to the contrary. Without the witness of his own eyes, even a plain soldier like Bernardo would probably have ridiculed such a report. Once Horatio has seen the Ghost, he, Marcellus, and Bernardo respond in exactly the same way. To all of them, the Ghost is a "thing," an "illusion," an "it" that is "like the dead King." Not one of them believes it is the dead King

## ACT I, SCENE II

As we eagerly await the expected report to "young Hamlet" (not "young *King* Hamlet"?... something is odd), we are surprised by the flourish of trumpets and the gaudy pageantry of a royal procession. From the cold, forbidding ramparts we have been suddenly transported to a lush court, jolted from a nightmare world of unknown terrors to the familiar world of sanity. But is this world so safe? We see first the reassuring figures of a confident King and his contented Queen, then his respectable councillors, including an elderly gentleman with a stylishly dressed young courtier—and then a discordant figure: a young man in rigid black.[14] As minor figures range themselves for the formal audience, he stands apart, a black exclamation point. Something is indeed wrong.

In Claudius's first words, we find reason for our uneasiness. The present King is the dead King's brother? If we had not realized it before, we now guess that the lone figure in mourning is the young Hamlet, logically the heir apparent. As the King launches into an expansive pronouncement on his wisdom in protecting the health of the State, we become increasingly aware that something is very rotten in Denmark. In what he agrees should be a time of mourning, Claudius has married his "sometime sister." His sister? In any age, the curious way in which Claudius almost flaunts the relationship would suggest incest. Moreover, the unctuous protestations of wisdom, discretion, and grief make us uneasy as we gradually realize what has taken place. "Mirth in funeral" together with "dirge in marriage"? And the court has "gone along" with this "affair"? Apparently it has not urged a necessary action but condoned something of which it would normally be expected to disapprove. At the very least, this marriage has been indecorous, and "the elaborate and frigid talk

---

himself. By the end of the scene, both Marcellus and Horatio believe the apparition is malignant, and nothing Bernardo says indicates a different view. Hamlet's response will be discussed in the ensuing pages. Here be it noted that his frame of reference is the same, even though he does not first assume the Ghost to be a hallucination. He has sufficient proof of its reality in the report of Horatio, a man whose judgment he can trust.

[14] The stage direction of Q₂ gives the director a useful hint: "*Enter Claudius, King of Denmarke, Gertrad the Queene, Counsaile: as Polonius, and his Sonne Laertes, Hamlet, Cum Alijs.*" The state is out of joint when the heir apparent sets himself apart from the ruling circle. Both Q₁ and F₁ follow proper precedence by putting Hamlet's entrance directly after that of Claudius and Gertrude. The direction in Q₂ seems closer to Shakespeare's intention.

about 'defeated joy' and the rest of it" begins to sound a bit phony.[15] As Granville-Barker notes, with an actor's sensitivity, "it all smack[s] too much of an apology."[16] We might go even further. It all smacks of dangerous arrogance. This man is convinced that he is the complete master of an obviously unhealthy situation.

Through all this, there is no word of the obvious heir, the character who has our keen interest in spite of, even because of, his silence.[17] Indeed, Claudius seems pointedly to be ignoring him as he turns to Laertes "and positively coos over him, caressing him with his name four times in nine lines."[18] When he finally deigns to recognize Hamlet, he greets his "cousin" and his "son" as a loved kinsman and heir, but the delayed recognition together with the emphasis on the dual relationship not only flouts propriety but also puts Hamlet in a position of dependence.

At last Hamlet speaks, and our sympathies go to him immediately. He is genuinely grief-stricken over his father's death and seems almost strangled by his loathing for Claudius. Apparently he has cause. Much recent criticism has argued that Hamlet's grief is shown to be unnatural by the kindly advice of Gertrude and Claudius. Their words of moral counsel are, of course, eminently proper, but the occasion of their sermons is highly suspect. We already know that Hamlet's father has died very recently, and that his death has been marked not by a respectful year of national mourning but by the joyful festivities of his widow's marriage. In this sleek, complacent court, only his son mourns, and for this he is roundly scolded as impious, peevish, and unnatural. Is this an "obstinate condolement" that "shows a will most incorrect to heaven"? The audience surely senses the irony of Claudius's patronizing pronouncements.[19] Moreover, is a formal court

---

[15] Kitto, p. 257. See his excellent analysis of Claudius's first speech. He notes the "first long and twisting sentence," the emphasis on "our sometime sister," and the fact that Claudius offers no reason for the hastiness of the marriage.

[16] Harley Granville-Barker, *Prefaces to Shakespeare* (Princeton, N.J., 1946), I, 50.

[17] The treatment of these first scenes makes it highly doubtful that the Elizabethan audience would promptly recognize Denmark as an elective monarchy and Claudius as the rightful king. Election is not mentioned until later. It seems probable that Elizabethans would automatically expect Hamlet to be the heir, be alerted by a brother's accession (especially under such odd circumstances), and thus suspect some sort of skulduggery. Had he wished, Shakespeare could easily have had Claudius mention the election.

[18] Wilson, *What Happens in Hamlet*, p. 31.

[19] Martin Holmes makes a perceptive observation. In chastising Hamlet, Claudius manages "to treat Hamlet's grief as unquestionably genuine but at the same time a little unbalanced

session the fit occasion for parental chastisement of such a private nature? Hamlet is being treated like a peevish child. He is, indeed, "too
much i' the sun."[20]

I have discussed the impressions created by the scene because they
indicate that the audience would have no reason to view Hamlet's first
soliloquy as the tortured writhings of an unbalanced neurotic who is
overreacting.[21] He is very young in these early scenes, perhaps only
eighteen. He has deeply loved his father and has believed his mother
an adoring wife. Suddenly his father dies and he is yanked home to
the funeral, where his mother too is grief-stricken. "And yet, within
a month...." In our own day, a young son would be stunned and
even society at large would be shocked. Elizabethans would have
been even more sympathetic to Hamlet's revulsion because they considered such a marriage incestuous.[22] Now, only two months later,
Hamlet is an outsider in court, pompously chastised in glib common-
places for being in mourning—when the whole court should be. He
is not allowed to escape to the sanctuary of the ivory tower. He must
sit, helpless, as this overripe, seemingly callous victor mouths maxims
and then walks out to drink "jocund health[s]." If Claudius is subtly
portrayed by a sensitive actor, the audience will fully sympathize with
Hamlet's wish that his "too too solid flesh would melt."[23]

---

and unsuitable to his dignity. It is all done in the kindest way, of course, but it is an excellent
chance for him to indicate that Hamlet is not the man to be put in charge of the country in
her present peril and he takes full advantage of it." *The Guns of Elsinore* (London, 1964),
pp. 68–69.

[20] Many interpretations of the line are possible. It may be a quibble suggesting that
Hamlet is "out of the house," and thus disinherited by Claudius. It may be an ironic taunt:
"I am too much in your 'royal' presence." I incline toward Beatrice's meaning when she says
that she is "sunburn'd," meaning that she is unmarried and thus unsheltered. Kitto (p. 259)
applies this interpretation to mean that Hamlet has lost his father and mother and is now
without the shelter of his family.

[21] For an able defense of Hamlet against T. S. Eliot's charge, see Joseph, *Conscience and
the King*, pp. 45–48. See also the delightful blast of Thomas M. Kettle: "Because, meshed
about with murder, adultery, usurpation, espionage, hypocrisy, and all other natural horrors,
reinforced by the still greater horror of the supernatural, because in these cheerful conditions
Hamlet is healthy-minded enough to grow 'thought-sick,' he is marked down as one 'unstable
as water.'" "A New Way of Misunderstanding *Hamlet*," *The Day's Burden* (New York,
1918), pp. 64–65.

[22] See Chapter 24 in Thomas Beard's *The Theatre of Gods Judgements* (1597), "Touching
Incestuous marriages" (pp. 327–30). Most of the chapter is a violent diatribe against a man's
marrying his brother's widow. Such marriages were illegal in England until 1917.

[23] Craig reads *sullied* for *solid*. This widely accepted emendation by Dover Wilson is, in
part, suggested on the grounds that Hamlet feels his own flesh to be defiled by Gertrude's
incest, but I find no supporting evidence in the soliloquy. As yet, Hamlet seems only shocked

But we have reason for new uneasiness. Is there not a hint that Hamlet's mind may become infected by the very evils that sicken him? His thoughts leap, twisting and turning; images explode. His father, a glorious Hyperion—this lecher uncle, a satyr. His devoted mother, an adoring wife? No! He is revolted by a sudden realization. She had never loved his father. Her apparent devotion had sprung not from love but sheer lust, a lust that "feeds" with compulsive hunger. His mind recoils, but then jerks back, driving on to the image he cannot expel: "O, most wicked speed, to post / With such dexterity to incestuous sheets!" The spitting sibilance punctuates his nausea.[24] As with Othello, Leontes, and Posthumus, Hamlet's mind is obsessed with obscene imaginings.

Is there not also a hint that Hamlet's grief may make him spiritually vulnerable? We need no Elizabethan treatise on mental pathology to tell us that he is melancholy, that he is in an emotional state that could lead to deep depression. He longs only for oblivion and is even led to consider suicide, the most heinous of Christian sins. There is also a related danger, one repeatedly stressed by Timothy Bright: "If choller have yeelded matter to this sharpe kind of melnncholie, then rage, revenge, and furie, possesse both hart and head, and the whole bodie is caried with that storme, contrarie to persuasion of reason."[25] Listless stupor, marked by brooding and an inability to act, was the least of the dangers Elizabethans attributed to the black humor. Bright's *Treatise of Melancholie* and other contemporary writings show that the melancholic might be particularly prone to violent action, and especially to revenge, if anger and frustration were added to his grief. Chapman's Byron, for example, is a "fiery man of action" who is suffering from "adust and melancholy choler" (*Byron's Con-*

---

by her indecency and repulsed by her grossness. There is no suggestion that he feels himself corrupted. The wider implications come later.

[24] Wilson analyzes the soliloquy in the light of the punctuation in $Q_2$, emphasizing that it is not a piece of declamatory rhetoric but a rush of meditation pointed almost entirely by commas. "His mind turns and turns upon itself in its effort to escape giving birth to the 'monster in his thought too hideous to be shown,' and at the exclamation 'Let me not thinke on't' he seems for a moment to batten it down beneath the hatches of consciousness. But the writhings begin again and the stream of images continues as uninterruptedly as before until there comes the second pause—this time in the middle of a sentence—and the dreadful thought is born at last, like a brood of hissing snakes." *The Manuscript of Shakespeare's "Hamlet"* (Cambridge, Eng., 1934), II, 200.

[25] Bright, *A Treatise of Melancholie*, pp. 111–12.

*spiracy*, II.ii.43), and no one could accuse Belleforest's barbaric Amleth of being irresolute, though he too is specifically called melancholy. As Shakespeare knew well, "melancholy is the nurse of frenzy" (*Taming of the Shrew*, Induction, ii.135).[26]
In Hamlet's first soliloquy, we sense his genuine grief, but we are even more painfully aware of his revulsion at his mother and his loathing for Claudius.[27] A potentially dangerous illness of mind and spirit attends him. At the moment, he can do nothing but hold his tongue, for there is nothing that could ease his agony. But we know that out there in the night some "thing" awaits him, apparently to divulge some terrible secret. What will happen when they meet? Even without the orientation of Shakespeare's audience, would we not be aware that Hamlet is in no condition for another shock? That in his state he is the last person who should have to face such a terrifying experience and the new burden that will probably result? Shakespeare's audience might have sensed an even greater danger: Hamlet's grief and loathing, together with his desire for suicide, have made him exactly the type of melancholic who is especially subject to the abuse of demons.

The average Elizabethan spectator might have missed these warnings during Hamlet's soliloquy, but in Horatio's ensuing report to Hamlet we are reminded of the Ghost's ambiguity. For the first time we see Hamlet at his best, as he rouses himself from distraction and warmly greets his old friend and the sentries. He is completely in control as Horatio cautiously suggests that he "thinks" he may have seen the dead King. There is no hysterical outburst, only rapt atten-

---

[26] For convincing cases against the assumption of Bradley and others that melancholy was considered a normal cause for inactivity, procrastination, and weakness, see Joseph, *Conscience*, pp. 26–30, and John W. Draper, *The "Hamlet" of Shakespeare's Audience* (Durham, N.C., 1938), pp. 173–82.

[27] It should be noted that Hamlet makes no mention in his soliloquy of Claudius's usurpation or of his frustrated hopes of the crown. His sole cause of grief is his father's death and his mother's hasty and incestuous remarriage. This fact casts doubt on the interpretations of those who see the political situation as crucial in understanding Hamlet's dilemma. Had Shakespeare intended to justify Hamlet's revenge on the grounds that he is the legitimate ruler empowered to execute traitors, would he not have given his audience some clue? At the beginning of the second scene the Elizabethan audience probably viewed Hamlet as the legal heir, but later in the play Hamlet's brief references to his being cheated of his right by election are much too ambiguous, suggesting, if anything, that he is not to be considered the rightful king. Belleforest's Amleth specifically justifies his revenge on the grounds that he is the legal ruler. Shakespeare omits any such implication. For discussion of this and other political issues, see Appendix C below, "The Relevance of Political Arguments to *Hamlet*," pp. 280–94.

tion, as Horatio describes the armed specter that has twice appeared "in the dead vast and middle of the night." Hamlet's response deserves close attention. He does not leap to a conclusion; he does not cry out; he does not immediately resolve to rush to the battlements and await his beloved father. He is very calm as he begins asking highly pertinent questions. Where did the Ghost appear? Did Horatio question "it"? Apparently Horatio's description of the terrifying armed figure of midnight has warned him to move warily. He too begins with the assumption that this "thing" must be tested. When Horatio pointedly says that it had "shrunk in haste away" at the crowing of the cock, Hamlet's brief response—" 'Tis very strange"— indicates his alertness and control. Thinking intently, he now asks even more crucial questions. The figure was fully armed, was it? The fact is significant; armor was not the conventional garb for ghosts. Does it make Hamlet think that the spirit really might be his father? Possibly, for Hamlet now shifts to the pronoun "he" in his questions. On the other hand, the armor may suggest to him a more ominous possibility, for he asks, "What, look'd he frowningly?" Horatio, for some unknown reason, belies his own observation by now reporting that it had "a countenance more in sorrow than in anger." The Ghost's aspect still concerns Hamlet: was it pale or red? "Nay, very pale." Is this an allusion to the belief that the flushed man is no threat but the pale man dangerously angry—like Revenge in *A Fig for Fortune*? The cool, brief questions continue, the mind darting.

To what conclusions do Horatio's answers lead him? "My father's spirit in arms! all is not well; / I doubt some foul play." There is no suggestion that Hamlet expects consolation from this ghost, that he expects a Purgatorial spirit—a humble, sorrowing, loving petitioner. Hamlet believes it to be a spirit—possibly good, but probably evil.

> If it assume my noble father's person,
> I'll speak to it, though hell itself should gape
> And bid me hold my peace.

He is aware of the danger, but he is determined to question the Ghost no matter what its nature, no matter what the consequences.

### ACT I, SCENE III

Laertes' leave-taking need detain us only briefly, for from this point on we shall focus on Hamlet himself. To be sure, everything in *Ham-*

*let* relates to its hero, but the materials encompassed by the present study primarily illuminate the nature of Hamlet's dilemma. I shall therefore limit myself to those elements that have been placed in new perspective.[28]

Following Horatio's report on the fearful apparition, we are again transported back to a familiar world, this time the world of domestic affection and platitudinous moralizing, of parental authority and vulnerable youth. In the advice of Laertes and peremptory command of Polonius to Ophelia, we learn an important fact about Hamlet. Since arriving home from Wittenberg, and thus since the death of his father, "he hath importuned [Ophelia] with love / In honorable fashion." We have no reason to doubt Ophelia's word or the witness of Laertes and Polonius, both of whom have noticed the recent attentions of the young prince. On the grounds that Shakespeare never misleads us in his exposition, Schücking argues that we are to believe Laertes: Hamlet has not really loved Ophelia.[29] It is true, as Schücking notes, that Shakespeare intends his audience to believe positive statements about offstage events, but only if it has been given no contradictory information. In this case, the audience has already seen Hamlet and knows him to be a sensitive man of deep feeling and genuine moral fervor. It is impossible that he should be the trifler Laertes assumes, that he should be indulging in a springtime frolic at this moment of grief. Even after the double shock of his father's death and his mother's betrayal, apparently Hamlet has still reached out to another. This fact lends significance to his forthcoming rejection of Ophelia and her eventual madness.

## ACT I, SCENE IV

At last the awaited moment approaches. We are on the platform. It is midnight. "The air bites shrewdly." Nervous conversation distracts the watchers from the one thing uppermost in their minds.[30] Suddenly, "Look, my lord, it comes!"

---

[28] On these grounds I touch only briefly on many important elements in Hamlet himself: his acute moral sensibility, his intense perception of experience, his incisive wit, etc. These I assume, for they have been delineated by generations of responsive critics.

[29] Levin L. Schücking, *Character Problems in Shakespeare's Plays* (Gloucester, Mass., 1959), pp. 67–71.

[30] I omit discussion of Hamlet's "mole of nature" speech because I find it irrelevant to the basic tragic issue, no matter how significant the idea it presents, and doubt that $F_1$ would cut a speech crucial to understanding the play. Hamlet muses on the fact that the smallest

In the first seconds of shock, Hamlet instinctively gasps out a prayer for divine protection—"Angels and ministers of grace defend us!"—the proper Protestant response. Again we note that he does not instinctively hail the spirit as the soul of his father. He assumes that it is either an angel come from Heaven on a mission of charity or a demon bearing the blasts of Hell. As yet there is no third possibility. The earlier fears of Horatio, Marcellus, and Hamlet himself are made explicit. And yet, despite his instinctive prayer for divine protection, Hamlet is so emotionally shattered that he immediately violates the warning Horatio had heeded. He does not beg the spirit to speak only if it has come on a mission of grace. He defies the powers of both Heaven and Hell as he cries out:

> Be thou a spirit of health or goblin damn'd,
> Bring with thee airs from heaven or blasts from hell,
> Be thy intents wicked or charitable,
> Thou comest in such a questionable shape
> That I will speak to thee.

He will dare damnation. All that matters is the familiar form of his beloved father. The shape is, indeed, "questionable." May we not have here a typical Shakespearean equivocation? The apparition is such as to invite questioning, but may it not also be "open to question," doubtful? Hamlet had so assumed until this very moment. He so assumes even as he determines to address the Ghost as if it were in fact his father. But then, in the rush of one agonized line .of mounting urgency—"King, father, royal Dane, O, answer me!"—he shifts to the impossible identification, against all that has so carefully been established.[31] So long as Hamlet is trapped by the stress of emotion, he will forget all doubts.

The curious speech in which he questions the Ghost may reflect the distracted state of his mind:

---

defect—even a birthmark, for which a man is not responsible—can blind society to his virtue. He is discussing reputation, not character. See Joseph, *Conscience and the King,* pp. 14–16, and Peter Alexander, *Hamlet: Father and Son* (Oxford, 1955), pp. 40–43. For a thoughtful refutation, see Hilton Landry, "The Leaven of Wickedness," in *Pacific Coast Studies in Shakespeare,* ed. Waldo F. McNeir and Thelma N. Greenfield (Eugene, Ore., 1966), pp. 122–23.

[31] Craig and F₁: *Dane:*. The commas of Q₂ seem more probable. The line is most effective if given as a four-part build, with a slight pause between each of the four elements as Hamlet becomes increasingly urgent in begging the silent figure to speak.

> What may this mean,
> That thou, dead corse, again in complete steel
> Revisit'st thus the glimpses of the moon,
> Making night hideous . . . ?

The suggestion that the Ghost is the actual corpse of Hamlet's father, that it has burst forth from the sepulcher, violates all Protestant and Catholic teaching of the period. The two faiths agreed that only the Devil could move an actual corpse. Of course many folktales told of ghosts rising from tombs. However, the explicitly Christian perspective established early in the play may make Hamlet's addressing the Ghost as "dead corse" significant, all the more so since folk revenants were inevitably dressed in their burial shrouds, as this ghost is not. Whether Hamlet's words are a sign of his distraction or one of the several ambiguities we shall shortly consider, Hamlet is undeniably aware that the night has been made "hideous." With all of these forewarnings, he nonetheless begs to hear the Ghost's commands: "What should we do?"

No matter how "courteous" the action of the Ghost in beckoning Hamlet to follow him apart, both Marcellus and Horatio urge him to disregard it. Hamlet thrusts off their fears. He is careless of his life, and as for his soul, "what can it do to that, / Being a thing immortal as itself?" A good deal, as Horatio knows, and he reminds Hamlet that usurping demons are known to haunt precipices. The apparition might "deprive [Hamlet's] sovereignty of reason / And draw [him] into madness." Hamlet does not even hear, and, as if hypnotized, he begins to follow the beckoning figure. Horatio and Marcellus make one last attempt by physically restraining him. At this, Hamlet bursts forth in violence. His "fate cries out" as he draws his sword against his friends:

> Unhand me, gentlemen.
> By heaven, I'll make a ghost of him that lets me!
> I say, away!

Horatio had just warned that the Ghost might trick Hamlet into madness and desperation, and his comment now has weight: "He waxes desperate with imagination."

To this point, what is our reaction? All three men are terrified and for carefully established reasons. The fears of even the rational Horatio have become so intense that he lays hands on his Prince in a futile attempt to save him. Even before hearing the Ghost, Hamlet's "sovereignty of reason" is threatened, the very danger we had feared during his first soliloquy. Remember, we do not yet know what the Ghost will say. If we could intervene at this moment, I submit that the response of all, Elizabethan and modern alike, would be the same: "Calm down! Don't follow it. If you do, for God's sake be suspicious of anything it says!"

## Act I, Scene v

Now, at last, the Ghost speaks. And now we face the first serious possibility that it may indeed be the departed soul of Hamlet's father, returned from Purgatory, where he is "doomed for a certain term" to "fast" in "sulphurous and tormenting flames" until his "foul crimes ... are burnt and purged away."[32] Very well, let us shift our perspective, as many in Shakespeare's audience may have done, and test it on its chosen grounds—test it, that is, by Catholic doctrine.

What is the mission of the Ghost? Even before it announces its identity, we are warned: it comes to command revenge. Its first long speech is skillfully adapted to its mission. It appeals to Hamlet's love and grief, relentlessly aggravating the son's anguish by describing the pains of Purgatory. Note that it does not state one specific fact, though literature abounded with useful details. It announces that it is forbidden to tell such secrets to mortal men, and then proceeds to create an even more horrifying impression than any description would. Of course Purgatory ghosts were under no such proscription. One of their purposes in returning was to make man understand the specific pains they were suffering, and thus their mission required

---

[32] Battenhouse suggests that the Ghost's description of its abode is not intended to suggest Purgatory. Citing Dante, he argues that Purgatory was envisioned as a place of angels and music and beauty, and thus that the Ghost's description of fire and horror is to be recognized as a picture of pagan hell ("The Ghost in Hamlet," pp. 185–89). I sympathize with Professor Battenhouse's awareness that the Ghost cannot possibly be a Christian spirit of grace, but the fact seems unavoidable that the Ghost uses details that would suggest Purgatory to the Elizabethan, even as they do to the modern. Sir Thomas More's description of Purgatory in the *Supplication of Souls* (p. 177) includes no songs of angels. It is a place of "sights unpleasant and loathsome," a place of tormenting flames surpassing in heat any fires known on earth. The Ghost's reference to "fasting" in fires until his "foul crimes" are "purged away," his reference to the final sacraments, and the familiar details of fire and pain make it certain that both Catholics and Protestants would have recognized that he was at least claiming to be a Purgatory soul.

them to give as much graphic detail as possible.[33] Why does this Ghost rely on the ghastly inference, the harrowing hint? It is skillfully arousing Hamlet's imagination, working entirely on his emotions. The speech builds to a compelling climax in "If thou didst ever thy dear father love—" What loving son could possibly remain calm? As Lady Macbeth knows, the most irresistible of human arguments is the question "Don't you love me?" With this preparation, it is no wonder that Hamlet leaps at the first word of murder:

> Haste me to know 't, that I, with wings as swift
> As meditation or the thoughts of love,
> May sweep to my revenge.

And the Ghost comments, "I find thee apt." That laconic observation is the first of several grim ironies in the Ghost's exhortation. Can Shakespeare have overlooked the clash of Hamlet's gentle metaphor with his violent meaning?[34] His mind is "out of joint," as he strains with passionate eagerness for confirmation of what he has already half suspected. He is, indeed, "apt," and at this moment, while Hamlet is taut, every sense alert, the Ghost plants an idea that later gives rise to the tragic dilemma:

> And duller shouldst thou be than the fat weed
> That roots itself in ease on Lethe wharf
> Wouldst thou not stir in this.

Its hearer is now ready, and now the Ghost reveals the identity of the murdering "serpent." Hamlet leaps: "O my prophetic soul! / My uncle!" It is clear that, like Macbeth, he had but awaited confirmation of an idea dictated by his own desires.

If we read the Ghost's long speech without preconceptions, we should be struck by its almost exclusive reliance on sensual imagery.

---

[33] More, *The Supplication of Souls,* pp. 171, 178–80. It is for this reason, More explains, that he speaks of the "head" and "hands" of disembodied souls. In order to make mortals realize the pains of suffering souls, he must explain in humanly understandable terms. One also wonders about the odd statement that the Ghost can walk only at night. True Purgatory spirits can appear at any time.

[34] "As so often in Shakespeare, the metaphors undo the logic and tell the truth over its head." Goddard, *The Meaning of Shakespeare,* p. 349.

Like Iago, it paints a series of obscene pictures and then insistently highlights the very images that Hamlet had tried to blot out in his early soliloquy: "that incestuous, that adulterate beast . . . shameful lust . . . lewdness . . . sate itself in a celestial bed . . . prey on garbage." Hamlet had known that for his own sanity he must not visualize that bed, but the Ghost rivets his eyes upon it. The culminating exhortation is not to purge the "royal throne of Denmark." It forces Hamlet again to peer into the horror that sickens him:

> Let not the royal bed of Denmark be
> A couch for luxury and damned incest.

Can this be a divine agent on a mission of health and consolation?

Moreover, if a pious son should immediately recognize that swift revenge was a "sacred duty," why does the Ghost find it necessary to present an extended, revolting description of the poisoning? Again its appeal is entirely to the senses. This Ghost is not appealing to Hamlet's love of virtue; it is not arousing his determination to serve the justice of God. It is doing everything possible to arouse nausea and loathing.

This Ghost cannot be a penitent soul from Purgatory. It says it is, but are we intended to believe it? It does, to be sure, speak of its agony at dying without the sacraments, but the reference serves as one more detail to intensify Hamlet's pain. Moreover, a subtle hint has been planted that is to bear terrible fruit in the Prayer Scene. The Ghost's attitude toward its suffering is also telling. Does it humbly confess its sins, acknowledging the justice of its punishment? On the contrary, it "groans" and "complains" of the agony resulting from its being unfairly deprived of final sacraments. For centuries editors have tried to give "O, horrible! O, horrible! most horrible!" to Hamlet on the grounds that the reaction ill befits a spirit of grace. So it does. A Purgatorial penitent would be a loving figure of consolation, but the Ghost that Shakespeare created dwells on the horror of its pains. The exclamation is a logical climax to the extended assault on Hamlet's emotions.

At that cry of horror, when Hamlet's agony is at a peak, the Ghost gives him the tragic burden: "If thou hast nature in thee. . . . Revenge. . . ." Nothing in the scene suggests that a divine minister is appealing to Hamlet's "nature" as a creature made in God's image whose role is to fulfill His commandments.[35] Nor does the usual explanation suffice—that the Ghost is appealing to Hamlet's "nature" as an obedient and loving son. Throughout the speech it has been appealing to Hamlet's "nature" as an instinctive creature of passions and appetites—"fallen nature," the theologian would say. Thus its challenge to Hamlet to prove his "nature" by committing murder is the same type of challenge heard in Lady Macbeth's "Are you a man?" That this is the issue as Hamlet himself is later to understand it will become clear in "To be or not to be." The Ghost, then, fails the test that every member of Shakespeare's audience undoubtedly would have recognized as the crucial one, a failure that scholars have been trying to rationalize for two centuries: its command violates Christian teaching.

Does the Ghost, in fact, pass any of the religious tests? Well, it appears as a man, not a hop-toad, and no one mentions that it smells of sulphur. On every other test, it fails. Is it humble? How is it conceivable, it asks, that Gertrude could "decline / Upon a wretch whose natural gifts were poor / To those of mine." (Characteristically, it draws our attention to the physical.) Is it in a charitable state? It is thoroughly vindictive, seething in its own hatred and aggravating Hamlet's loathing. Is its voice sweet, soft, musical, and soothing, or "terrible and full of reproach"? The actor who intones these lines with melodious grace is deaf to the meanings of words. Does it carefully refrain from charging others with sin? Its mission is to condemn Claudius. Does it beg Hamlet's prayers? It says "remember *me*."

Some critics have tried to explain these unsettling facts as further proof that the Ghost is from Purgatory on the grounds that his anger, vindictiveness, and sensuality merely indicate that he has not yet been sufficiently purged. This argument will not do. The purpose of Purgatory is not to reform a sinner but to erase the debt of punishment incurred by past sins that were repented before death. As Thomas More

---

[35] John F. Danby's discussion of the two meanings of "nature" is illuminating. On the one hand, "to follow nature" might mean to conform to one's role in the divine pattern ordained by God; on the other hand, it might mean to follow one's instincts. Danby clarifies the distinction by referring to the former as Hooker's sense of the word and to the latter as Hobbes's. (*Shakespeare's Doctrine of Nature*, London, 1949, pp. 15–53.) The Ghost's appeal has usually been interpreted in Hooker's sense: "If you have any filial feelings, obey your duty as a son." Since, however, "to follow nature" in this sense means to act by the dictates of disciplined reason, "to *have* nature" suggests that the word is used in Hobbes's sense. The Ghost seems to be appealing to something innate, something instinctive.

emphasizes, in Purgatory no soul can be angry, for all are in a state of grace.

But, it will be objected, the Ghost urges Christian forbearance for Gertrude. Admitted. But that is what we are warned the Devil will do: in order to disguise himself as an angel of light, he will, like Richard III, "clothe [his] naked villany" "with a piece of scripture" (I.iii.334–38). Catholics and Protestants both agreed that the mere repetition of Christian doctrine proved nothing. Both warned that we must be alert to the speaker's ultimate purpose. Let us note the context:

> If thou hast nature in thee, bear it not;
> Let not the royal bed of Denmark be
> A couch for luxury and damned incest.
> But, howsoever thou pursuest this act,
> Taint not thy mind, nor let thy soul contrive
> Against thy mother aught: leave her to heaven....

The lines are brutally ironic. "Taint not thy mind"? For over fifty lines, the Ghost has done everything possible to taint Hamlet's mind with lacerating grief, sexual nausea, hatred, and fury. It has just focused its appeal on the lewd picture that Hamlet knows can most corrupt him—and at this, it says, "Taint not thy mind"! One is reminded of Iago's consummate trickery: working Othello up to a screaming pitch and then remonstrating, "Tush, forget it. It probably means nothing."

And then: "leave her to heaven." The irony is surely the clue. Why Gertrude but not Claudius? The implication may not be immediately obvious when we see the play; we have been trapped along with Hamlet by our emotions. But if Shakespeare did not intend the irony, why did he so closely echo the familiar language of Christian exhortation—"leave them to heaven"?

Even though we have been caught up in the emotions of the scene, Hamlet's reaction when the Ghost vanishes should jolt us:

> O all you host of heaven! O earth! what else?
> And shall I couple hell? O, fie!

He is not merely adding a third power to his invocation of Heaven and earth. The word "couple" may here, as so often in Shakespeare, have a sexual connotation, reflecting the success of the Ghost's insidious method: shall Hamlet join himself to Hell? Even in his distraction, he again raises the dreadful possibility. But the moment of perspective is fleeting as the rush of emotion leads him to embrace the image of his father:

> Remember thee!
> Yea, from the table of my memory
> I'll wipe away all trivial fond records,
> All saws of books, all forms, all pressures past,
> That youth and observation copied there;
> And thy commandment all alone shall live
> Within the book and volume of my brain.

"Taint not thy mind"? He will wipe away all precepts, all codes, all that he has learned from books and experience. He does not say that he will erase all petty ideas in order to concentrate on his duty to his father. "Thy commandment *all alone* shall live / Within the book and volume of my brain." And that commandment is to exact revenge. So committed, he fixes his mind on his victim, furiously focusing on the image of the "smiling, damned villain."[36] When Horatio and Marcellus enter, he is hysterical with excitement.[37]

It may not be amiss to touch briefly on two counter-theories that have gained growing support during the last few years. Several critics have recognized that Shakespeare could not have intended a spirit of health, released from Purgatory by divine will, to corrupt his son by commanding blood revenge. Thus one theory has evolved that the Ghost commands Hamlet to bring Claudius to public justice, not to murder him. A related theory reads "Taint not thy mind" to mean that Hamlet, though he is to kill Claudius, is to do so in the spirit befitting a minister of God. Most of the critics holding these views believe that Hamlet fulfills the Ghost's demand, but several see Ham-

---

[36] The stage tradition that has Hamlet yank out his tables and frantically write down Claudius's villainy lest he forget it has always seemed unwise to me. The action strongly suggests that he has gone mad. The most effective interpretation I have seen was by a Hamlet who jabbed the picture into his brain with a rigid finger. This seems to me Shakespeare's meaning. Hamlet has said he will clear the "table of [his] memory" and put the Ghost's command in "the book and volume of [his] brain." The imagery indicates that the "tables" are not in his pocket but in his mind.

[37] The preceding analysis has been anticipated in certain respects by Murray, Knight, Siegel, and Goddard. It is most closely paralleled by L. C. Knights, *An Approach to "Hamlet"* (Stanford, Calif., 1961), pp. 45–46 and *passim,* and H. S. Wilson, *On the Design of Shakespearian Tragedy,* pp. 41–45.

let's tragedy as arising from the fact that he either misunderstands or disobeys the Ghost.[38] I can find no warrant in the play for believing that the Ghost is on a divine mission. Not once does the Ghost suggest that its command to revenge is the will of God. Not once does it suggest that its command—"Revenge his foul and most unnatural murder"—means anything other than what Hamlet takes it to mean: brutal, unqualified murder in direct retaliation. Any doubt is eliminated when Hamlet is told to pursue revenge in any way he chooses so long as he leaves Gertrude to Heaven. By implication, Claudius is not to be punished by Heaven. The Ghost treats Hamlet as if he were a private agent who is to act out of purely personal motives. "Remember me," says the Ghost, not "Cleanse Denmark in the name of God." Of course Hamlet may, in later scenes, qualify the command in his own mind. But in the first act, the Ghost is presented as malign.

The curious cellarage scene enforces this impression. We can probably never know exactly how Shakespeare's audience responded to the scene, much less exactly what Shakespeare intended. The repeated shifting of ground in order to swear suggests a specific convention, but a study of stage tradition helps little. The only direct echo occurs in a late comedy, which provides no guide to its meaning.[39] As Nevill Coghill has noted, however, three of Hamlet's lines, together with his actions and those of the Ghost, provide several clues.[40] The significant sequence is as follows:

> (The Ghost cries from under the stage.)
> Ah, ha, boy! say'st thou so? art thou there, truepenny?
> (Hamlet shifts ground; the Ghost shifts and cries again.)
> Hic et ubique? then we'll shift our ground.
> (Hamlet shifts; the Ghost shifts and cries again.)
> Well said, old mole! canst work i' the earth so fast?
> A worthy pioner! Once more remove, good friends.
> (Hamlet shifts.)

[38] These views have been fully developed by Bowers, Elliott, and Ribner.

[39] The echo occurs in Fletcher's *The Woman's Prize*, V.iii. In *Antonio's Revenge*, III.ii, the voices of the dead Andrugio and Feliche as well as that of the living Pandulpho echo Antonio's words "from above and beneath." The scene is a clear parallel but it does not include the device of shifting ground. Joseph Quincy Adams suggests that a clue may be found in the Chester *Processus Prophetarum*. Balaam, prevented by God from cursing the children of Israel, three times shifts his ground at the suggestion of Balak in an attempt to defy God's commandment. "Some Notes on Hamlet," *Modern Language Notes,* XXVIII (1913), 40.

[40] *Shakespeare's Professional Skills* (Cambridge, Eng., 1964), pp. 9–16. Throughout, Professor Coghill provides many insights arising from his intimate knowledge of the theater.

The clearest clue lies in the third line. We have noted that demons were believed to frequent mines, and Hamlet echoes this belief when he hails the "old mole" as a "worthy pioner" that works in the earth. That Hamlet is mockingly addressing an assumed demon seems likely when we find Toby Belch referring to the Devil as a "foul collier" (*Twelfth Night,* III.iv.130).

This clue illuminates the other two lines. When the voice first sounds below the stage, Hamlet is startled. Two readings of his question are possible. "Art *thou* there, truepenny?" would imply "So it's you who are down there." "Art thou *there?*" would imply "So that's where you are." Viewed in context, the line thus suggests, "So you *are* the Devil!" The Ghost is, of course, speaking from beneath the stage, the familiar abode in Elizabethan drama of demons, furies, and damned souls. Only a "goblin damn'd" speaks from the abyss of Hell. In *The Malcontent,* Malevole greets Mendoza with "Illo, ho ho ho, arte thou there old true penny?" (III.iii). It is significant that the line is a deliberate echo: Malevole is addressing a devilish villain. Although the OED defines "truepenny" as a trusty person, the word also seems to have been used as a term of scorn.[41] Hamlet's mocking tone, his almost taunting familiarity, could not be directed toward a spirit of health from Purgatory. Moreover, "hic et ubique" cannot refer to an "honest ghost," for only God and the Devil can be both here and everywhere at the same time. "*Then,*" Hamlet says, "we'll shift our ground." For obvious reasons, he must try to get away from the voice.

Whether or not this interpretation is accurate in all details, of one thing we can be sure: throughout the cellarage scene, the Ghost is acting like a devil. Scholars have been driven to fantastic lengths to explain this unavoidable fact. We read that Shakespeare is tricking his audience by stopping for a playful parody; the printer is tricking the reader by including a scene from the old "Ur-Hamlet"; the Ghost is tricking Hamlet; Hamlet is tricking the Ghost; Hamlet and the Ghost together are tricking the two amazed observers. The most popular explanation is the last: that Hamlet and the Ghost both pretend the voice is a devil to mislead Horatio and Marcellus. How could

---

[41] See *II Return from Parnassus* (London, 1606), fol. C3ᵛ (II.iv).

the audience be expected to know this? It is just as misled. And what motive could both Hamlet and a good Purgatorial spirit have for making Horatio and Marcellus think their Prince is in league with the Devil? "To terrify them into silence" is an inadequate answer. There is one logical explanation. Shakespeare made the Ghost act like a devil because he wanted his audience to notice that it acts like a devil.

It is true that Hamlet refers to St. Patrick, the "keeper of Purgatory," and that he tells Horatio "It is an honest ghost"; but can these two facts cancel all our other impressions? The oath by St. Patrick may suggest Hamlet's belief in the Ghost as a spirit from Purgatory, but it may just as well suggest that the Ghost has come to rid Denmark of a "serpent," even as St. Patrick had banished snakes from Ireland. And even though Hamlet does for the moment accept the Ghost as "honest," when he calms down he will be less sure.

Many readers, I would expect, have long been objecting, "But how is such an interpretation possible when it conflicts with our instinctive impression of the Ghost?" I believe that this interpretation is the only one that corresponds to our instinctive impressions—or would be, if we were free to react naturally, without the misleading preconceptions fostered by critical and theatrical tradition. We have already dealt with the faulty assumptions of scholarship, but let us now consider the Ghost as it usually appears on the stage. Of course, it may not appear at all. We may see nothing but a green light that fades in and out on cue. If it does appear, typically it is, in Robert Speaight's delightful phrase, "got up like the arch-Druid of Stonehenge."[42] Because of atmospheric lighting, costume, and makeup, we rarely detect any recognizable human features. Rarely do we see a vigorous, warlike figure of martial stalk and frowning aspect, much less a terrifying "thing" which reacts suddenly and suspiciously to Horatio's invocation of Heaven. When "offended," it usually turns sedately and moves with funereal dignity to the nearest exit. Rarely do we see a noticeable reaction to the crow of the cock, much less the threatening start of a guilty thing upon a fearful summons. In fact, Marcellus's speech on the significance of the Ghost's sudden exit is usually cut.

[42] "The Old Vic and Stratford-upon-Avon, 1960–61," *Shakespeare Quarterly*, XII (1961), 439.

The 1964 Gielgud-Burton production in New York was typical. The Ghost did not appear. It was a mere shadow on the backdrop, a disembodied voice filtered through an echo chamber. All the lines were exquisitely sung in the quavering tones of a dying saint. All of them, that is, except those that were too flagrantly sickening or obscene. These—the description of the poisoning and the picture of lust preying on garbage—were cut. In modern productions, are we ever really terrified or shocked by what the Ghost says and the way he says it? The actor is usually cast for his resonant voice and he knows it. Traditionally he chants the lines in mellifluous tones of melancholy tenderness—all the lines, including those of agony, pride, disgust, hatred, and urgency. Of course the actor is but following critical tradition, which emphasizes the Ghost's deep "glowing" love for Hamlet and his heartfelt compassion for Gertrude. But what is there in the play to justify this interpretation? One of the most striking facts about this supposed spirit of Hamlet's father is that he utters not one word of love for his son. The Ghost's appeal is directed to Hamlet's love for his father. Moreover, the command to leave Gertrude to Heaven is not framed in words of compassion, as it could have been. She is to be left to the thorns that will prick and sting her. The picture of Gertrude that we see through the Ghost's eyes is that of a hypocrite who has been led by lust to prey on garbage. Rarely, however, does a modern audience even hear the crucial lines, for the descriptions of the poisoning and the bed of filth are usually cut.

In my judgment, a production following Shakespeare's every clue would create the same response in us today as I have suggested it did in the original audience. If we heard the terrible human passions in the Ghost's voice and saw them in its face, if we were startled by its sudden recoil at Horatio's invocation of Heaven, if we were made aware of the significance of the cock—if, in short, we could once see the Ghost that Shakespeare created, would we not instinctively sense that we were in the presence of evil?

Throughout the preceding analysis, I have, of course, often viewed the action from a dispassionate perspective no audience can reach so long as it remains an audience. Although I have tried to maintain awareness of this fact, in emphasizing the Ghost's malignity I may have created a misconception. I am not suggesting that we are consciously aware of the Ghost's true nature or that we want Hamlet to ignore its terrible revelations. During a good production, we rarely make objective judgments. When Hamlet is onstage, we enter his world, seeing much as he sees, feeling much as he feels. But not completely. I have stressed the many warnings of evil to suggest that our response to the Ghost is too complicated to be accounted for solely by the fact that we identify with Hamlet.

The audience cannot meet the Ghost for the first time with Hamlet in the fourth scene. We have seen things that Hamlet does not see. The first Ghost Scene created a series of impressions that will necessarily color, if only slightly, our response to the second. And throughout the opening scene, the Ghost is consistently suspect. Later, however, ambiguities begin to appear. In the first scene, Horatio had said that the Ghost was frowning as "in an angry parle"; now, in the third, he tells Hamlet that it had "a countenance more in sorrow than in anger." In the fourth scene, the Ghost is addressed as a mouldering corpse from the grave, but it speaks as a suffering soul from Purgatory. It cries for revenge against Claudius, but pleads for forbearance with Gertrude. Each of these details can be harmonized into a consistent interpretation, but only by hindsight. In the theater, Shakespeare keeps shifting our point of view. Our response is further complicated by Hamlet's own shifting perspective. He defies damnation; he weeps for his dead father; he plays games with a devil; he affirms that the Ghost is "honest." We have been asked to test the Ghost, but we have not been allowed an easy answer.

Given the perspective of the entire play, we can discern a probability; but in the fleeting perspective of the dramatic moment, we find only questions. If we could unequivocally pronounce the Ghost a demon and its command a damnable temptation, the tragedy would be destroyed.[43] We cannot, and as a result are caught up in Hamlet's dilemma. The warnings have not made us pull back and condemn his vow to take revenge; they have made us aware of the intolerable alternatives he faces. He says he will go pray, but he will not be the man we want him to be if prayer is his only recourse. Somehow, in some way, we surely want him to act. To retreat into patience would be to acquiesce in the evil. But, as both Hamlet and the audience now know, to act may be to couple Hell.

---

[43] Although my study has challenged a few of Robert West's premises, it fully supports his conclusions on the dramatic function of the Ghost's ambiguity. See *Shakespeare and the Outer Mystery*, pp. 63–66.

# CHAPTER VI

## *To Be or Not To Be?*

### ACT II, SCENE I

Act II opens some two months later. When we last saw Hamlet, there was no doubt of his future course: he was wholly dedicated to his vow of vengeance and straining to act. What, then, has he been doing all this time? Are we to imagine that he has been endlessly brooding, sinking ever deeper into a slough of despond? The scholar may ask such questions in the quiet of his study, but I doubt that they even occur to an audience watching an exciting performance. Bradley felt called upon to correct the "popular theory" that Hamlet went rushing to Ophelia's closet immediately after seeing the Ghost, but the "popular theory" was instinctively right.

In Shakespeare's *Hamlet* as it is produced on the stage for which he wrote, there is no "problem of delay." Only when acts became separated by extended intermissions did delay theories evolve. As a perceptive actor who had given a dynamic portrayal of Hamlet on an Elizabethan stage once commented, "There is no time for Hamlet. Things happen too fast."[1] In the Globe Theatre, there was no interval between Hamlet's exit and the entrance of Polonius and Reynaldo. No member of Shakespeare's audience was aware of any act division. Moreover, it is doubtful that his audience was consciously aware that any time had elapsed before the entrance of Polonius. The suggestion that Laertes has been gone long enough to need money, and the fact that the Ambassadors have had time to visit Norway and

---

[1] Richard Risso, 1961 production at the Oregon Shakespearean Festival.

return, probably passed by unheeded.[2] Our only other clue, over an act later, is Ophelia's reference during the Play Scene to the passage of four months since the death of Hamlet's father. Surely no first-night spectator would detach himself from the dramatic action, recall Hamlet's earlier reference to an interval of less than two months, compare the conflicting figures, and think "Aha! Then Hamlet must have been brooding for two months."[3]

One of Stoll's most useful principles bears repeating: "On the stage only the positive counts; the negative—silence or reticence, mere omission—goes unnoticed."[4] For the first half of the play, the Hamlet that we see is busily, even energetically, active: greeting friends, taunting fools, struggling with moral issues, denouncing corruption, outwitting spies, planning a play, considering murder, lashing out at his mother, killing an eavesdropper—mourning, joking, shouting, singing, racing through the castle with every sense alert. With so much exciting activity going on, how could the audience cluck their tongues over this pallid melancholic who is paralyzed into inaction? If anything, the appearance of the Ghost has shocked Hamlet out of his lethargy, rather than into it.

It certainly would never occur to a first-night audience that Hamlet is waiting until he can expose Claudius publicly, or until he can expose Claudius without implicating Gertrude, or for any of the other reasons that scholars have proposed. Indeed, it would not occur to such an audience that he is waiting at all until he says he is and explains why. After the appearance of the Ghost, Hamlet and Claudius do not appear on stage together until the Play Scene. (Claudius appears twice, both times with his entourage.) The audience is much

---

[2] Charlton Lewis makes a pertinent comment explaining the assumption that Hamlet rushed from the battlements to Ophelia's closet: "This *seems* like an immediate sequel to the resolution taken in Act I. The things that suggest lapse of time are the affairs of other persons." *The Genesis of Hamlet* (New York, 1907), p. 18.

[3] Moreover, Ophelia's "twice two months" since the King's death is immediately undercut by Hamlet's echo: "die two months ago . . . ?"

[4] E. E. Stoll, *Hamlet,* University of Minnesota Studies in Language and Literature, No. 7 (Minneapolis, 1919), p. 41. A. J. A. Waldock applies this principle in noting that the interval before Act II "has really no dramatic existence. Delay does not exist in a drama simply because it is (as it were) embedded in it. The delay that exists in a drama is the delay that is displayed" (*"Hamlet": A Study in Critical Method,* Cambridge, Eng., 1931, pp. 80–81). As Bernard Grebanier insists, if the play were about Hamlet's delay, the element of time would be emphasized in the script. See his full argument in *The Heart of Hamlet* (New York, 1960), pp. 177–83.

too preoccupied to be wondering all this while where Hamlet is and why he does not rush into a royal council and stab the King on the spot.

If the Polonius-Reynaldo scene is not intended to indicate a lapse of time, what then is its purpose? In part, it supplies a necessary cushion between the exit of Hamlet and the entrance of Ophelia. On the Elizabethan stage, he would probably be leaving through one door as she entered through another, and her description of his grotesque appearance only seconds after we have seen him in mourning would defy credibility. As usual, however, Shakespeare put a requirement of his stage to good use. In the Ghost Scene, we have glimpsed the maelstrom that Hamlet is about to enter. The juxtaposition of supernatural horrors with details of notes and expense accounts and social activities jolts us back to reality. The events of the previous night seem unbelievable in this mundane world of gay young blades and clucking parents. The colloquy also serves to reinforce Laertes' role. He is to be absent from the stage for over an hour and the audience will need to remember him. Moreover, careful characterization of the father gives us some idea of what we may expect of the son. In *Every Man in His Humour,* Jonson gives the elder Knowell a delightful tirade on the younger generation and their delinquent parents. What, he sputters, can we expect when

> the first words
> We form their tongues with, are licentious jests:
> Can it call "whore"? cry "bastard"? O, then kiss it!
> A witty child! Can't swear? The father's darling!
> Give it two plums.
>
> (II.v.19–23)[5]

Polonius is just such a father. A little "drinking, fencing, swearing, quarrelling, drabbing"—these are but "the taints of liberty, / The flash and outbreak of a fiery mind, / A savageness in unreclaimed blood." If Laertes sows a few wild oats, Polonius will stand back and beam "That's my boy!" In the way of the world, the man who kicks over a few traces proves that he is "all man." The scene is as funny and

---

[5] C. F. Tucker Brooke and Nathaniel Burton Paradise, eds., *English Drama: 1580–1642* (Boston, 1933).

as applicable today as it was then, but it is no mere comic interlude. As we shall see, it is a satiric statement of the issue Hamlet is shortly to face.

In Ophelia's description of Hamlet's strange appearance in her closet, we hear that Hamlet has taken his first step. He has said that he would cut himself off from "all forms, all pressures," from all he has ever known. We have seen him reject the support of Horatio. Now, apparently, he has divorced himself from an even more intimate relationship. The ambiguity of Shakespeare's cryptic and contradictory references to the relationship between Hamlet and Ophelia can never be resolved to the satisfaction of everyone. But does a valid interpretation of the play require that we find "the truth"? May Shakespeare have been purposely ambiguous?[6] *Hamlet* is not a love story. Who first rejected whom is not crucial to the central dramatic issue. Polonius has ordered Ophelia to deny Hamlet access, and she says she has done so. Hamlet has said he would cut himself off from all normal ties, and Ophelia reports that he has, in effect, said good-bye to her, an implication that is confirmed by Hamlet's detached control at the opening of the Nunnery Scene. If we must inquire closely into Hamlet's motives—and I am not at all sure that we should, for the audience simply does not have time for conjectures—is it not possible that his distracted behavior in Ophelia's closet has several causes? Can he not be taking a last farewell both because she has rejected him and because he knows that he must now move alone?[7]

Ophelia's description of Hamlet's appearance in her closet does, however, raise an important question in the mind of the spectator. The "O that this too too solid flesh" soliloquy had warned that Hamlet was at the breaking point, and we have seen him behaving erratically. Now Ophelia's description suggests that he has, indeed, gone mad. But Hamlet has just said that he would put on an "antic disposition." Has his mind really slipped, or is he pretending? Our curiosity is aroused, and we wait expectantly for his next entrance.

---

[6] See Leo Kirschbaum, "Hamlet and Ophelia," *Philological Quarterly,* XXXV (1956), 376–93.

[7] One thing seems certain: we are not to believe that Hamlet is intentionally deceiving Ophelia, trying out his new "madman act" on her. Such a cold-blooded, heartless trick would make nonsense of his pain and shock in the Nunnery Scene and at her funeral. Hamlet has obviously loved Ophelia, though how deeply we cannot know. Any theory that Hamlet has seduced Ophelia would also make a mockery of his intense moral fervor. By such an implica-

## ACT II, SCENE II

As so often happens in this play, our expectations are frustrated. It is not Hamlet who enters but the King and Queen, greeting two young friends of their "too much changed son." Claudius seems so genuinely concerned about Hamlet's transformation, his motives in seeking the aid of Hamlet's own friends so free from suspicion, the entire situation so devoid of threat, that questions multiply. Can this efficient, ostensibly gracious King, respected by all, obviously adored by his wife, be the monster described by the Ghost? He may be a little too studied, a little too self-confident, perhaps a touch arrogant, but a lecher and a murderer? And this dignified Queen? Though she smacks a little of the middle-aged kitten, can she be a hypocrite and a wanton?[8] Can this relaxed court where such a tedious old fool as Polonius is granted patient if amused respect be such a hotbed of corruption? Surely the Ghost told the truth, and yet— What if Hamlet is in fact the madman everyone thinks he is? Suspense increases. He is coming. The audience half expects a ranting lunatic.

When Hamlet at last enters, he is quietly strolling, reading a book. The shock to the original audience must have been considerable.[9] This is no madman. Moreover, he is not even the mock-lunatic so popular on the Elizabethan stage. His clothes are as Ophelia described—his doublet unbraced, his stockings fouled and ungartered, sagging to his ankles—but he is playing no exhilarating game. Since we last saw him, Hamlet has become calm. Apparently he has been reading, thinking, gaining control. He is not, as we expected, on the attack. All he wants from Polonius is to be left alone with his thoughts.

At this point, let me state my position on the endless debate about Hamlet's "antic disposition." Hamlet is not mad. He never is. The

---

tion, Shakespeare would have thoroughly confused the character of Ophelia and the audience's response to her madness, not to mention the central dramatic issue of the play.

[8] There is something rather coy in her wholly unnecessary echo of the King's "Thanks, Rosencrantz and gentle Guildenstern." Reversing the names to apply "gentle" to Rosencrantz while giving priority to Guildenstern is a pretty little gesture out of key with the seriousness of the situation. It suggests that Gertrude is too conscious of the male ego and of her pleasant mission in life to flatter it.

[9] See Martin Holmes's sensitive analysis of the effect of Hamlet's delayed entrance: "The king and queen are perturbed, Ophelia has been terrified half out of her wits, Polonius had said in so many words that Hamlet 'raves,' and it would not be unjustifiable to expect the next stage-direction to be 'enter Hamlet, raving.' " *The Guns of Elsinore*, p. 87.

suggestion did not even arise until sentimental critics in the eighteenth century began to see Hamlet as a tender, virtuous soul unfit for this harsh world. To maintain such an interpretation, it was necessary to explain away certain unpleasant facts. Readers were instinctively appalled by Hamlet's hysteria and levity after the appearance of the Ghost, by his total indifference to the deaths of Polonius and Rosencrantz and Guildenstern, by his obscenity and brutality. Such actions were wholly inconsistent in a man of feeling. Since their hero could not be guilty, obviously he was not guilty by reason of insanity. By such simple logic, all indecorous behavior was dismissed as irrelevant to the "real" Hamlet. Contemporary accounts indicate that throughout the seventeenth and eighteenth centuries all the great Hamlets were unquestionably sane.[10]

If we want to know how Shakespeare and his audience conceived of real insanity, we can turn to Titus, Lear, and Ophelia. Each of them loses touch with reality. An even better test is provided by Edgar. Since Edgar completely submerges his own identity in order to counterfeit madness, his actions are good evidence of how Shakespeare's audience expected a real madman to behave. Edgar's imitation takes the form of totally incoherent raving and of complete disorientation. Hamlet, by contrast, never loses contact with reality. He always recognizes people (though he mockingly pretends not to do so); he always knows what he is doing. His speech is not even incoherent. The characters in the play are confused, but not the audience. We may be at a loss to explain some of Hamlet's cryptic lines, but no one has ever doubted that they all could be explained. To the alert Elizabethan, every ironic equivocation probably conveyed a rational meaning.[11]

[10] A century after the play's original production, James Drake had no doubt of Hamlet's sanity. Answering Jeremy Collier's attack on Ophelia, Drake argued that we must see the situation as it appears to her: "*Hamlet* by mistake kills her Father, and runs mad; or, which is all one to her, counterfeits madness so well, that she is cheated into a belief of the reality of it" (*The Antient and Modern Stages Survey'd*, London, 1699, p. 294). Aaron Hill also assumed that Hamlet was feigning. An ardent playgoer, Hill commended Wilks's performance as a mock-lunatic, thus indicating an assumption shared by actor and critic (*The Prompter*, No. 100, October 24, 1735). Lichtenberg's account in 1775 of Garrick's performance (*Variorum Hamlet*, II, 270) and Samuel Johnson's reference in 1765 to the "pretended madness of Hamlet" (*Johnson on Shakespeare*, ed. Walter Raleigh, Oxford, 1925, p. 196) indicate the same agreement between stage and study in the third quarter of the century. In the early nineteenth century Charles Kemble gave the first stage interpretation of Hamlet as insane.

[11] Harry Levin's analysis of Hamlet's shifts from verse to prose and back to verse offers good evidence for the argument that Hamlet consciously changes attitudes whenever he shifts to his assumed role. See *The Question of Hamlet* (Oxford, 1959), pp. 116–17.

It seems to me that Shakespeare insists on Hamlet's sanity throughout the play and that this fact is central to the tragic issue. Hamlet is unquestionably morbid at times, emotionally unbalanced at times, and even out of control for brief moments. But his erratic behavior cannot be compassionately dismissed as the symptom of a mental illness for which he is not responsible. The brief outbursts of hysteria are the inevitable results of the course he has consciously chosen to follow.

Why, then, does Shakespeare have Hamlet play the madman? It has long been noted that the pretense is not a device to allay suspicion, the conventional reason for feigning lunacy in other plays. Hamlet is in no danger from Claudius until he begins to act suspiciously. Many ingenious explanations have been offered: Hamlet knows that a harmless madman will have a better opportunity of trapping his victim unprotected; he knows that people speak unguardedly in the presence of madmen and children and hopes that Claudius may reveal himself; he intends by ironic double meaning to torture Claudius into public confession. Of course, there is no evidence for any of these theories, and I have no better to offer. The critic is fortunate; he can say when he doesn't know. But an actor must decide on his motivation. If I were directing the play, I would have Hamlet take his cue from Horatio's reaction to his hysterical levity: "These are but wild and whirling words, my lord." Hamlet realizes that the course he has chosen—acting alone and under intense emotional stress—is dangerous. Knowing himself, he realizes that he may act oddly and picks up the suggestion implicit in Horatio's puzzled response to his erratic behavior.

Hamlet's choice of words, "antic disposition," is significant. In Shakespeare's day, "antic" did not mean "mad." It was the usual epithet for Death and meant "grotesque," "ludicrous." The term is appropriate for the grinning skull and the tradition of Death laughing all to scorn, scoffing at the pretenses of puny man. May not this meaning be the operative one? Hamlet's hatred of Claudius and his scorn of pretense were ill-contained even before the Ghost appeared. He has good reason to expect that his loathing may break to the surface in the form most characteristic of him. In the ensuing scenes of pretended madness, his feigning always does, in fact, take the form of ironic mockery. Interestingly, most of his truly emotional outbursts, the moments when he approaches the breaking point, come when there is no suggestion of the mad role.[12]

Returning to the scene at hand, we see Hamlet's rational control in the very form of his "mad" exchange with Polonius and in the healthy warmth with which he greets his old companions, Rosencrantz and Guildenstern. For our purposes, we need pause at this point only to correct a faulty interpretation of Hamlet's comment that "there is nothing either good or bad, but thinking makes it so." The remark does not indicate philosophical relativism or personal moral despair. Hamlet is saying that appearance, not reality, depends on the eye of the beholder. Because three men seeing a high-altitude balloon in the setting sun may report seeing three different things (a planet, an airplane, a flying saucer), it does not follow that the balloon actually *is* three different things. To Rosencrantz and Guildenstern, Denmark is not a prison. To Hamlet, it is. There is no implication that good and evil do not exist.[13] Hamlet is tortured precisely because he is not a moral relativist. Lust, hypocrisy, dishonesty—these are absolute evils. He suffers not because there is no such thing as virtue but because reality fails to meet the exacting standards that he believes apply to all men.

His basic idealism is reflected in the apostrophe to man. Hamlet knows the earth to be a "goodly frame," the firmament a "majestical roof fretted with golden fire." He knows that man is a glorious "piece of work...noble in reason...infinite in faculty...like an angel... like a god!" However, because of the burden he bears, to him "the earth *seems*...a sterile promontory," to him "this brave o'erhanging firmament...*appears*...a foul and pestilent congregation of vapours." Even as he voices his own tortured view of the reality around him, he affirms his faith in the wonder of creation and the miracle of man. Hamlet is sickened by what some men are for the very reason that he is so acutely aware of what all men should and could be. Only by warping the lines can we make of him a spokesman for modern despair.

As if to emphasize that, despite the trial he is undergoing, Hamlet

---

[12] For example, his erratic behavior following the appearance of the Ghost, his hysteria following the Play Scene, and his frenzied outbursts in the Closet Scene. I would also add his behavior in the Nunnery Scene, though many might argue that he is feigning lunacy at that point.

[13] On this point, as on several others, Ulrici still seems remarkably clear-headed. See *Shakespeare's Dramatic Art,* trans. L. Dora Schmitz (London, 1876), I, 484.

is basically a healthy, vital young man who revels in worldly activities, Shakespeare now brings in the players and Hamlet is delighted. He has no apparent reason other than sheer enjoyment to ask for one speech he "chiefly loved," but the particular speech turns our minds once again to the dilemma Hamlet faces. The Player's Speech on Pyrrhus cannot be a burlesque. Hamlet, whose dramatic taste is scarcely that of a naïve groundling, finds it deeply moving. So does an audience when the speech is delivered by a capable actor who is trained in the "grand manner." The very features that have led many critics to consider the speech a travesty—the extended treatment of Pyrrhus and the violence of the description—may be clues to the speech's purpose. Although Hamlet's attention, and that of most critics, is focused on Hecuba's grief, the description of Pyrrhus's demonic savagery is three times as long, and in a good production should have much greater impact on the audience.

Significantly, Hamlet begins by misquoting: " 'The rugged Pyrrhus, like the Hyrcanian beast,'—it is not so:—it begins with Pyrrhus." Pyrrhus brings to his mind the tiger of Hyrcania, a familiar epitome of remorseless ferocity.[14] Hamlet thus identifies Pyrrhus with such utterly ruthless revengers as Queen Margaret, who, when she hands York the napkin stained with the blood of his own son, is branded as "more inhuman, more inexorable, / O, ten times more, than tigers of Hyrcania" (*3 Henry VI,* I.iv.155–56).[15] Hamlet's little slip reveals the light in which he instinctively sees Pyrrhus, and prepares the audience to respond properly. That the device succeeded is clear from an echo in *The Insatiate Countess* several years later:

> A player's passion I'll believe hereafter,
> And in a tragic scene weep for old Priam
> When fell-revenging Pyrrhus with supposed
> And artificial wounds mangles his breast....
> (I.i.121–24)

The story as told in the *Aeneid* (II.469–558) was familiar to the Elizabethan audience. After the death of Achilles, his son Pyrrhus went to Troy, where he avenged his father's death by killing Priam

---

14 The following analysis was prompted by Harry Levin's valuable contribution, "An Explication of the Player's Speech," *Kenyon Review,* XII (1950), 273–96 (reprinted in *The Question of Hamlet*). See also Arthur Johnston, "The Player's Speech in *Hamlet,*" *Shakespeare Quarterly,* XIII (1962), 21–30.

15 See also Macbeth's terrified response to the ghost of Banquo (III.iv.101).

at the altar of Zeus. His own eventual death at the altar in Delphi came to be viewed as Apollo's judgment on the murder of Priam. Thus, by tradition, Pyrrhus became the symbol of the remorseless and blasphemous revenger. Although Shakespeare seems to have used Ovid's *Metamorphoses* for the Hecuba material, he turned elsewhere for details about Pyrrhus: probably to *Dido, Queen of Carthage* by Marlowe and Nashe (II.i.213-88), possibly to the *Tale of Troy* by Peele (ll.440ff), and possibly to the *Aeneid*. His description goes far beyond anything in the three sources. In *Hamlet,* Pyrrhus does not meet Priam by chance in the course of a general attack. He alone "old grandsire Priam seeks," the detail perhaps inspired by Peele's comment that his father's angry ghost drove Pyrrhus to seek personal vengeance. He is not, as in the *Aeneid,* an exulting, triumphant figure whose bronze arms flash in the sunlight, nor is he merely Peele's savage butcher of grim, pale visage. His "sable arms" are as black as his purpose, black as his complexion. He does not merely drag Priam through blood (*Aeneid*) or wear a harness dripping with it (*Dido*); he is himself smeared in gore from head to foot. In appearance, he recalls the Furies in the dumb show preceding Act IV of *Gorboduc*: "there come from under the stage, as though out of hell, three Furies ..., clad in black garmentes sprinkled with bloud and flames."

In the Player's Speech, Pyrrhus too comes "as though out of hell," an implication for which Shakespeare alone is responsible. His sources treat Pyrrhus as a tyrannous butcher unrestrained by awe of the gods, but as a completely human figure. Shakespeare adds several striking details. We first see Pyrrhus as all black, then as all black but smeared with the red of gore. Then his appearance takes on a new horror as the image of hellfire is added:

> Now is he total gules; horridly trick'd
> With blood of fathers, mothers, daughters, sons,
> Baked and impasted with the parching streets,
> That lend a tyrannous and damned light
> To their lord's murder: roasted in wrath and fire,
> And thus o'er-sized with coagulate gore,
> With eyes like carbuncles, the hellish Pyrrhus
> Old grandsire Priam seeks.

Shakespeare picks up the hints of dripping blood from his sources and then adds the images of Satanic blasts and disease to create an inhuman monster. In the description of the encounter itself, he again goes beyond his sources to depict Pyrrhus as so maddened by fury that he loses control. Pyrrhus "in rage strikes wide." Although he misses Priam with his first stroke, the old man falls, and Pyrrhus is stunned into a moment of paralysis before renewing the attack with "aroused vengeance."

Most critics have analyzed the scene entirely in terms of Hamlet's identification with Hecuba's grief. Of the few who have linked Hamlet with Pyrrhus, most have felt that the two are similar only in that moment of inaction.[16] The speech is thus viewed as Hamlet's attempt to whip himself into action by picturing a figure wholly foreign to his own temperament, or as an attempt by Shakespeare to focus on Hamlet's inaction. Neither of these explanations, however, accounts for several clear parallels between Hamlet and Pyrrhus or for the emotional impact of the speech.

If Pyrrhus has any counterpart in the play at all, it must be Hamlet, and the emphasis on him as a revenger makes a parallel seem intended. Hamlet has a "suit of sables." He has been solicited by demonic power. He has already determined to dare the "blasts" of Hell. At a crucial moment later in the play, he will align himself with Satanic forces and bloody purpose. He is shortly to be so driven by passion that he too will "strike wide" when he kills Polonius instead of Claudius.[17] The situations are not exactly parallel (what, for example, is the exact counterpart in the play of Priam's premature fall?). Nonetheless, it seems clear that the Player's Speech serves as a comment on Hamlet.

Once we recognize this fact, we are faced with an important corollary. Throughout the speech, the audience's sympathies are entirely with Priam, the victim, not with the son who revenges the death of his father. In the ferocity of Pyrrhus, in his raging fury and diabolic resolution, we see exactly what Hamlet might become if he pursues the course upon which he has embarked. This, I suggest, may explain

---

16 For an exception, see Goddard, *The Meaning of Shakespeare,* pp. 362–63.

17 It is even possible that Shakespeare relied on his audience's knowledge that Priam was slain on the altar. That familiar detail may be echoed in the Prayer Scene and in Claudius's insidious advice to Laertes that not even a church should provide sanctuary against revenge. It is unwise to emphasize the possibility, however, since Shakespeare does not remind us of where Pyrrhus slew Priam.

Shakespeare's modification of the traditional description of Pyrrhus and his extended development of the parallel.[18] As Act I closed, Hamlet was hysterical, convinced of the Ghost's honesty, and resolved to act. Now, when we see him again, he appears calm: bitter and sardonic but objective about himself and apparently under control. What is he thinking? What will he do? It is at this point that our attention is focused on exactly what a continued determination to revenge could mean. For a few minutes, we are detached from the main action and enabled to consider the planned revenge objectively. Do we really want Hamlet to act like this?

Should not Hamlet himself be warned by the implications? Instead, he responds to Hecuba. In seeing the play, I have always been surprised by Hamlet's response. The violence of the Pyrrhus section seems much more compelling than the comparatively subdued description of Hecuba. For me, it is the ghastly image of Pyrrhus that remains in memory; for Hamlet, it is the grief-stricken Hecuba. If my response is valid, may it not put Hamlet's reaction in perspective? Driven by his own loss, Hamlet identifies with the grief of the victims rather than with the revenger, but does not see the irony. As so often, his passion has led him astray.

At last we are again alone with Hamlet as he lacerates himself for being a "rogue and peasant slave" who does nothing. Not until this moment is the audience made aware that Hamlet has had a choice in the matter. We had seen no evidence that he was delaying, but now he accuses himself of being a "dull and muddy-mettled rascal," and for the first time we wonder why he has not acted. Has he delayed, as he asks himself, because he is insensitive, because he has not been emotionally moved by the Ghost's revelation? What we have seen of Hamlet rules out this explanation. Has he delayed because he is a coward? Nothing in the Hamlet we have seen permits us to believe this. Why, then, these reproaches? What has restrained him when he had been so eager to act?

Hamlet does not give his explicit reason until the end of the soliloquy:

---

[18] Note the skillful division of the speech into three parts. Had the Player given the entire speech himself, the audience might have lost focus. Shakespeare wisely breaks it up, snapping us into renewed attention twice.

> The spirit that I have seen
> May be the devil: and the devil hath power
> To assume a pleasing shape; yea, and perhaps
> Out of my weakness and my melancholy,
> As he is very potent with such spirits,
> Abuses me to damn me: I'll have grounds
> More relative than this.

One can understand why so many readers have dismissed this sudden doubt of the Ghost as a rationalization by Hamlet for some hidden reluctance. If one assumes that the Ghost has been established as a "spirit of health" and that Hamlet is bound by both honor and piety to obey its command, Hamlet's hesitation seems a flagrant evasion of the obvious. If, however, the audience has been made increasingly aware that the Ghost may be a "goblin damn'd" and if it normally believes that private blood revenge endangers mind, body, and soul, Hamlet's doubt becomes the healthy recognition of a very real threat. He knows, and Shakespeare's audience knew, that melancholy is "the Divels baite," making a man dangerously prone to abuse by a demonic apparition in the form of a dead loved one. He knows, and Shakespeare's audience knew, that to follow the command of a suspect spirit might well lead to damnation. We now learn, then, that Hamlet's reason for inaction has been a thoroughly warranted concern over a real moral issue. We need no knowledge of Elizabethan beliefs to grasp the danger. We need only accept Hamlet's words on their own terms.

It seems to me that the moral issue is implicit throughout the entire soliloquy, and that it is so subtly treated only because Shakespeare felt no need to make it explicit. He could assume that his audience held a common body of attitudes about the morality of revenge and the danger of heeding ghosts. Moreover, he had made this specific ghost so suspicious and had so carefully prepared us to be concerned about Hamlet's emotional state by his early soliloquy, by his reaction to the Ghost, and by the image of the "hellish Pyrrhus" that further definition of the issue would belabor the obvious. I do not mean that Shakespeare consciously made the soliloquy subtle on these grounds; in my judgment, however, the need to make the moral issue explicit at this point simply would not have occurred to him.

But how can this interpretation fit Hamlet's self-reproaches for insensitivity and cowardice? Both charges, as we have seen, reflect the specific appeals of revenge that were recognized by writers of didactic treatises and imaginative literature.[19] Both charges, moreover, reveal the exact nature of the ethical dilemma facing Hamlet. The Ghost planted a potent hint:

> If thou didst ever thy dear father love—
>
> ... duller shouldst thou be than the fat weed
> That roots itself in ease on Lethe wharf,
> Wouldst thou not stir in this.
>
> If thou hast nature in thee. ...

Failure to act for any reason will give proof that Hamlet is insensitive, unnatural, unloving. The seed bears poisoned fruit in Hamlet's self-reproaches. If he can hesitate under such great provocation, surely he is less than human. As Alcibiades argued in *Timon of Athens* and Revenge in *A Fig for Fortune*, bearing is for asses. A man who is truly a man cannot be patient. If he has "nature" in him, he will strike where wrong is offered. From this point on in the play, the Ghost's gross image of the "fat weed" nodding stupidly by the river of forgetfulness will eat at Hamlet. Does his hesitation result merely from the lethargic passivity of "bestial oblivion"? Does it not, in fact, give proof that he is "pigeon-liver'd"? Almost certainly implicit in this second reproach is the ethical dilemma I have set forth in Part I above. It will be recalled that the charge of cowardice was widely recognized as the most powerful incitement to private revenge. Debates in *The Misfortunes of Arthur, Virtuous Octavia, Timon of Athens, The Maid's Tragedy,* and *The Revenge of Bussy D'Ambois,* as well as discussions by such men as La Primaudaye and Cornwallis, are all concerned with the dangerous temptation to view patience as mere cowardice. The specific diction of Hamlet's self-reproach defines the same issue. Who, he asks, tweaks him by the nose, gives him the lie in the throat? Who, that is, injures his honor in such a flagrant way that it must inevitably seem "faint-heartednesse and cowardlinesse ...

---

[19] See above, pp. 24–33.

not to render the like again"? Intellect may insist that patience is the "daughter of the vertue of Fortitude," but "nature" whispers that passive acquiescence to the laws of God and society is the rationalization of a timid weakling.[20] This worldly argument has been foreshadowed and our attitude toward it prepared by Polonius's assertion that "a savageness in unreclaimed blood" proves that a man is a "real man."[21]

Doubting his own motives, Hamlet whips himself into a furious outburst:

> bloody, bawdy villain!
> Remorseless, treacherous, lecherous, kindless villain!
> O, vengeance!

Suddenly he catches himself:

> Why, what an ass am I! This is most brave,
> That I, the son of a dear father murder'd
> Prompted to my revenge by heaven and hell,
> Must, like a whore, unpack my heart with words,
> And fall a-cursing, like a very drab,
> A scullion!
> Fie upon't! foh! About, my brain!

Reason has forced on him the ludicrousness of his rant. In abusing himself for not being a man, he has actually been acting like the basest of railing women. He is again in control, seeing, as did La Primaudaye, that "impatiencie and choler," rather than giving proof of masculine strength, actually "argue and accompany for the most part a weake and effeminate heart."[22]

By an act of will, Hamlet wrenches his mind from the detested image of Claudius and, calm once more, tells us of his plan to test the truth of the Ghost's charge. His doubt, though not stated until this

---

[20] La Primaudaye, *The French Academie*, p. 129. Hankins finds the same implications in Hamlet's reproaches. *The Character of Hamlet*, pp. 57–83.

[21] No Freudian implications are intended here.

[22] La Primaudaye, p. 129. Dover Wilson accepts the Q2 reading of "stallyon," arguing that Hamlet is referring to a male prostitute. *The Manuscript of Shakespeare's "Hamlet,"* I, 71. I find "scullion" much more apt. Hamlet is comparing himself to the lowest of kitchen slaveys. This is the term Falstaff applies to the Hostess (2 *Henry IV*, II.i.65), an appropriate epithet for a stupid woman who screams threats but is utterly harmless. Hamlet's objective awareness that his outburst is a sign of weakness makes the feminine connotation significant.

moment, has been implicit. Twice he has expressed his awareness that
he was prompted not only by Heaven but also by Hell. This spirit may
well be the Devil. We have seen a threat in the Ghost's behavior and
have seen that threat recognized by all: Marcellus, Bernardo, Horatio,
and Hamlet himself. We have seen a threat in Hamlet's melancholy
and in his tendency to hysteria. We have heard warnings again and
again of the potential dangers of Satanic influence. We have just
heard Hamlet torture himself with the possibility that his motives for
delay might be considered lethargic insensitivity and cowardice. At
the same time, we have also seen that Hamlet's reason does not yet
pander to his will. Whenever he is calm, he thinks clearly. All of these
facts suggest that Hamlet's detachment from the beginning of Act II,
indicated by his quiet reading and controlled irony, is to be attributed
to exactly the reason he gives. After that harrowing night on the platform, he has pulled himself together and realized the trap into which
he might be led. He will not act on what may be a demonic lie. The
play will give him proof.

But what if the Ghost's word does indeed prove true? Will that
necessarily mean that its command has divine authority and should
be followed?

> . . . oftentimes, to win us to our harm,
> The instruments of darkness tell us truths,
> Win us with honest trifles, to betray's
> In deepest consequence.

If we were pointedly reminded of this possibility, we would not be
ready to debate with Hamlet a far more profound dilemma.

## ACT III, SCENE I

The torrent of scholarship on Hamlet's most famous speech has all
but swamped the character of Hamlet himself, and anyone choosing
to add still more words to the deluge necessarily finds himself in a
state of panic. Unfortunately, however, any interpretation of the play
must come to terms with the soliloquy, and the present study makes
close analysis essential. I trust the reader will find that old arguments
are here put to a slightly new use and that the current investigation
has led, if not to any startling discoveries, at least to a fresh insight into
the soliloquy and its function in the play.

First, let us clear the field. The major question in "To be or not to be" cannot be suicide.[23] If it were, as many have noted, it would be dramatically irrelevant. Hamlet is no longer sunk in the depths of melancholy, as he was in his first soliloquy. He has been roused to action and has just discovered how to test the Ghost's word. When we last saw him, only five minutes before, he was anticipating the night's performance, and in only a few moments we shall see him eagerly instructing the players and excitedly telling Horatio of his plan. To have him enter at this point debating whether or not to kill himself would indeed be wholly inconsistent with both the character and the movement of the plot.

In answer to those who believe that this contradiction was exactly Shakespeare's point, one can point to an even more compelling argument: the imagery of the soliloquy. The metaphors all suggest that Hamlet's choice is between suffering the ills of this world and taking resolute action against them, not between enduring evil and evading it. "To take arms against a sea of troubles, / And by opposing end them" cannot logically be translated "To kill myself and thus escape from troubles." "To take arms against" troubles suggests the aggressive activity of battle; "by opposing end them" suggests that the troubles can in fact be destroyed. Similarly "enterprises of great pitch and moment" suggests worldly undertakings of great significance, momentous public actions of profound impact.[24] It cannot, by the very meaning of the words, refer to a private action of retreat.

A further objection to the suicide theory, one that may be even more significant in its implications, is the form of the question Hamlet puts to himself. He states his dilemma as "to be or not to be"—not as "to live or not to live." The issue, as he sees it, is not between mere temporal existence and non-existence, but between "being" and "non-being." In other words, he is struggling with a metaphysical issue: not the narrow personal question of whether he, an individual man, should kill himself, but the wider philosophical question of man's essence. It is the universal question heard in Job's "What is man?,"

---

[23] In this great debate, I am delighted to find myself on the side of Samuel Johnson, Tieck, Dowden, Murry, Kittredge, Charlton Lewis, Bertram Joseph, D. G. James, Hiram Haydn, Harry Levin, and Virgil Whitaker, among others.

[24] Sir Thomas Elyot uses the word "enterprise" to refer to the undertaking of "thynges dredefull, either for the publike weale or for wynning of perpetuall honour." *The Governour*, pp. 227–28.

suggested by Lear's "Is man no more than this?," and echoed by the trader in Conrad's *Lord Jim*: "How to be?"

Hamlet is facing the moral question that has too long been thought irrelevant to the play: whether or not he should effect private revenge. This fact has been obscured only because Shakespeare delves below the familiar platitudes. Hamlet does not ask the more obvious question: "Should I defy Heaven's injunction?" Instead he asks, "Can a man find his true self-identity by obeying an ethic of passivity?" To lesser playwrights the ethical issue had been obvious. Revenge was immoral and therefore their revengers openly choose to defy morality. Shakespeare creates in Hamlet a man who questions the familiar assumption. He does not ask, "Shall I or shall I not do an evil act?" but "Is this act truly evil?" The question is much more profound than that posed by Hieronimo or Titus.

But why should Hamlet raise the moral question at this particular point in the play? He is asking whether or not he should kill Claudius, although as yet he is not certain that Claudius is guilty. In the most comprehensive study yet made of the soliloquy, I. T. Richards argues that Hamlet is asking himself: "Whether Claudius is innocent or not, shall I kill him?"[25] This interpretation is unconvincing for several reasons. In the first place, such a debate would be based on grossly immoral premises. Can Hamlet possibly be asking himself whether or not he should kill a man who may be innocent? If so, his conclusion must be interpreted thus: "The conscience that warns me not to murder an innocent man makes me a coward, diverting me from great enterprises." Surely no one would suggest that his conscience could even debate such a matter. Moreover, is it reasonable for Hamlet to debate whether or not he should act without proof at the very moment when, for the first time, he has discovered a way to get that proof?

Hamlet faces a far more pertinent dilemma. Sometime before

---

[25] "The Meaning of Hamlet's Soliloquy," *PMLA*, XLVIII (1933), 741–66. The essay is an invaluable summary of scholarship as well as a thoughtful analysis in its own right. My own interpretation of the soliloquy differs with that of Richards only on the point considered above and on his insistence that suicide is never even suggested. Suicide is implied in the imagery of the middle section, but it seems to be mentioned only as a comparative example: "The fear of Hell that prevents man from committing suicide is the same thing that prevents him from taking arms against troubles." For a similar reading see Charlton Lewis, *The Genesis of Hamlet*, pp. 100–105.

the "Mousetrap," Hamlet must make his moral choice. After the Play Scene, events will move too rapidly, and the audience, as well as Hamlet, will be too excited to pause for objective deliberation on an abstract ethical issue. The ideal moment is now.[26] Hamlet knows that he will shortly have his answer. Until now he has not had to face the unavoidable moral question. If the Ghost's word is proved true, as he fully expects, what shall he do? He must decide now: "If Claudius is guilty, shall I kill him?" Claudius's aside confessing his guilt immediately before the soliloquy makes it almost certain that this is the question Shakespeare is posing. The confession is a device to warn the audience that Hamlet will not be debating the morality of killing an innocent man. Claudius has not been acting like a conventional villain, and the audience must not be misled.[27] Any doubt of his guilt would divert us from the real issue with which Hamlet is about to struggle: if Claudius is proved guilty (as we now know he is), should Hamlet kill him? Thus we are now prepared to face the full implications of the soliloquy.

> To be, or not to be: that is the question.

"To be"—what? To be a man, in the full metaphysical sense of "being" as it was understood by philosophers such as Plato and Aristotle.[28] "Being" is what a thing *is,* its essence, that which defines it. "Or not to be." There is no middle position. A thing is or it is not. The first line of the soliloquy, so often droned in a tone of meditative musing, should be spoken as an insistent, emphatic, even passionate demand. The whole moral question is focused in this challenge.

Now Hamlet defines this "being" and "non-being," and thus the choice facing him:

> Whether 'tis nobler in the mind to suffer
> The slings and arrows of outrageous fortune,
> Or to take arms against a sea of troubles,
> And by opposing end them?

[26] See D. G. James, *The Dream of Learning* (Oxford, 1951), p. 50.

[27] See Granville-Barker, *Prefaces to Shakespeare*, I, 219.

[28] The following discussion is based in large part on Etienne Gilson, *Being and Some Philosophers* (Toronto, 1949), and on Eugene F. Rice, *The Renaissance Idea of Wisdom* (Cambridge, Mass., 1958).

Is it truly nobler, Hamlet asks, to endure evil passively, as all the voices of Church and State and society have insisted, or does the true nobility of that which is man demand that he actively fight and conquer the evils that beset him? Can it really be "virtue" to sit back and leave it to Heaven? On one level, we are debating the morality of private revenge, but on another we are thrown headlong into the metaphysical dilemma of the Renaissance. In what does man find his "being"? To medieval theology, rooted in Augustine, man had no being in and of himself; man *is* only because he is created by God in His own image. Thus man defined himself in terms of what he believed; his proper function according to his "nature" was obedience to divine law. But in the fourteenth and fifteenth centuries new voices were raised, notably those of the Florentine humanists. Can man fulfill his given nature, can he attain true nobility, solely by withdrawal and contemplation? The focus of the attack was the statement, traditionally ascribed to Anaxagoras, that man was born to contemplate divine works. On the contrary, said Salutati and Alberti, among others: man is born to be useful to man. He fulfills his given nature by thinking, choosing, and acting usefully in the world.[29] The opposition of the two views is epitomized in the contrasting ideas of wisdom. To the medieval Augustinian mind, wisdom was metaphysical, attained by contemplation of the divine; to the Renaissance humanist, wisdom became ethical, developed in action in the affairs of the secular world.

In the sixteenth century, both traditions were vital. The medieval Augustinian ideal, static and contemplative, was reinvigorated by such men as Calvin and the Spanish mystics, while the Renaissance humanist ideal, dynamic and ethical, received impetus from such men as Bovillus and Pierre Charron. Of course both views were rooted in Christianity, but the humanists planted the seeds of rebellion. Sir Richard Barckley's unintended implication in his *Discourse of the Felicitie of Man* is typical. Felicity, he argues, resides not in pleasure, riches, glory, or position, or even in the moral virtue derived by philosophical contemplation. Man finds his chief felicity in active virtue, in plunging into life "by continuall fighting, like a man of warre." Barckley clearly means that one should fight the good fight against Satan, an aim with

---

[29] For a similar distinction between the two views, see Richard B. Sewall, *The Vision of Tragedy* (New Haven, Conn., 1959), p. 65.

which Augustine would be in complete accord, but his emphasis on action contains an implicit rationale for rebellion. "For hee deserveth not the name of a good man, that forbeareth to do evill, as though good were a privation, & a defect only from evill. . . . For good is not a defect, but an effect: not placed in idlenesse, but in doing."[30] Similarly, Milton was later to brand "a fugitive and cloistered virtue" as "a blank," a view that aligns him, somewhat curiously, with the pragmatic Bacon, who pronounced "that in this theatre of man's life it is reserved only for God and Angels to be lookers on."[31] The logical extension of this position is found in Hamlet's dilemma. If it is nobler to act than to contemplate, if it is nobler to use natural reason than passively to await divine revelation, can it really be nobler to assent to divine injunction when every instinct of man cries "No"?

If, moreover, the will is superior to the intellect, as Salutati and Charron asserted, then man's dignity depends on the freedom of that will. His very "being" depends on his exercising the freedom to choose. But can a man "be" if he retreats into passive resignation, if he refuses to struggle with issues, to make his free choices, and to act on his own initiative? The medieval mind, of course, would answer that man finds his self-identity, his "being," only in obedience to divine law. Those who "wittingly and willingly forsake goodnesse" cease "even to be at all. For they which leave the common end of all things which are, leave also being." Thus it follows that a man who refuses to follow the dictates of virtue "ceaseth to be a man, since he cannot be partaker of the Divine condition, [and] is turned into a beast."[32] By this view, the decision to surrender the will to God—for example, to obey the command against private vengeance—would not be ignoble retreat but the noblest act of which the free will is capable. It is this view that Hamlet challenges in the two great soliloquies of moral choice. On the one hand, the voice of conscience tells him that it is

---

[30] Pp. 599–600. See also the third dialogue in Petrarch's *Secret*. In a hypothetical debate with Augustine, Petrarch finally submits to the contemplative ideal but pleads that he must first straighten out his worldly affairs before he can devote himself to meditation. The irony is apparent. The dialogue reflects the Renaissance tension generated by the clash of the medieval and humanist positions.

[31] "Areopagitica," *The Works of John Milton,* ed. Frank Allen Patterson *et al.,* IV (New York, 1931), 311; Bacon, *The Works,* VI, 314.

[32] Boethius, *Five Bookes of Philosophicall Comfort* (London, 1609), fols. 94ʳ and 99ʳ. See also fols. 77ff.

nobler to endure than to act; on the other, the voice of instinct raises
an unsettling question, a question made more explicit later in the play:

> What is a man,
> If his chief good and market of his time
> Be but to sleep and feed? a beast, no more.
> Sure, he that made us with such large discourse,
> Looking before and after, gave us not
> That capability and god-like reason
> To fust in us unused.

Hamlet is trapped between two worlds. The moral code from
which he cannot escape is basically medieval, but his instincts are with
the Renaissance. Shocked from his unthinking acceptance of the commandments of Church and State, he is forced to find a new orientation. Can God have created man a thinking creature and yet have
ordered him not to use the very faculty that raises him above the animals? What is it, "to be"?[33]

Although the opening question of the soliloquy is concerned only
with the morality of taking aggressive action, the terms in which
Hamlet has phrased the alternative choices now suggest to Hamlet a
secondary consideration. In striking out at Claudius, it is highly probable that he himself would be killed. For the moment, moral consid-

---

[33] It is idle to speculate which view, the medieval or the Renaissance-humanist, determines
the form in which Hamlet puts his question. It may be that the parallel structure implies the
medieval premise: "to be" is "to suffer," whereas "not to be" is "to take arms." In this case,
Hamlet would be debating whether or not knowingly to embrace what conventional morality
would call "non-being." Two parallel Shakespearean passages are clearly based on this medieval equation. When Macbeth is first moved by the witches' prophecy, the thought of murder
"shakes so [his] single state of man" that "nothing is / But what is not" (I.iii.140–42).
Similarly, Brutus, at the climax of his struggle to decision, reveals the nightmare into which
his dilemma has led him: "Between the acting of a dreadful thing / And the first motion . . .
the state of man, / Like to a little kingdom, suffers then / The nature of an insurrection"
(II.i.63–69). Both statements reflect the medieval belief that evil is non-being, Macbeth's
being the more explicit of the two.

On the other hand, Hamlet's challenge to conventional morality may be inherent in the
question: "to be" is "to act," whereas "not to be" is "to suffer." (Shakespeare frequently uses
chiasmus, a figure of contrast by parallel structure in which the alternatives are repeated in
reverse order. See D. McElroy, "Rhetorical Patterns in 'Hamlet,'" *Notes & Queries*, n.s., VIII
[1961], 137, and Sister Miriam Joseph, *Shakespeare's Use of the Arts of Language*, New York,
1947, pp. 81–82.) In this case, Hamlet would be saying that every instinct cries out for a defiant refusal to permit evil to flourish; "to be a man" is to assert a man's individual judgment
and will. Although the movement of the soliloquy suggests the latter interpretation, either
would have meaning. The dilemma itself is clear.

erations are set aside. If he should die? Why death is but a sleep, nothing more. Surely a release from "the heart-ache and the thousand natural shocks / That flesh is heir to" would be "a consummation / Devoutly to be wish'd." Hamlet pauses, lingering over the image of the peace for which he longs: "To die, to sleep." But his mind cannot rest on the image of blessed oblivion. Forced by association to recall his own nightmares, he is jolted back again to the moral issue: the inevitable dreams to be endured in that sleep of death "must give us pause." For were there no threat of unknown terrors in Hell, what man would accept a code of patience? Beset by tyranny and injustice throughout his life, man retreats into passive resignation only because of the "dread of something after death." "There's the respect / That makes calamity of so long life," that makes evil so long endured. There's the respect that makes cowards of us all.

Hamlet does not fear the unknown after death because he doubts Christian doctrine about the afterlife. Why would a general fear of the unknown lead him to reject "enterprises of great pitch and moment"? More logically, despairing of an afterlife would lead him to crowd every moment with vital experience. The specific fear that Hamlet considers is related to some injunction against action. The threat of "dreams" that terrifies man into submission is thus the threat of Hell, the inevitable punishment awaiting the man who rebels against the divine law commanding patience.[34] An interesting echo in Massinger's *The Maid of Honour* (1632) supports this interpretation. The Duke of Urbin, facing inevitable defeat, would willingly, like Cato, tear out his bowels,

> But that religion, and the horrid dream
> To be suffered in the other world, denies it.
> (II.iv)[35]

To Massinger, the "dream" awaiting the man who defies God's law against suicide is obviously Hell.

---

[34] J. Middleton Murry makes an astute observation: "Some of the fundamental thinking of a Hamlet is remote from us. It charms and fascinates, but it does not horridly shake our dispositions. Dr. Johnson was far nearer to Hamlet, on this primitive religious side, than we are. He knew, and dreaded, that 'hunger of the imagination which preys upon life' " (*Shakespeare*, New York, 1936, p. 210). One regrets only his use of the word "primitive."

[35] *Plays of Philip Massinger*, ed. Arthur Symons for the Mermaid Series (London, 1887).

The same Christian orientation underlies Hamlet's much disputed reference to "The undiscover'd country from whose bourn / No traveller returns." The image was a popular commonplace, conveying not the slightest suggestion that the speaker doubted the existence of Heaven and Hell. Job refers to death as a land of darkness from whence he will not return. Cardan writes of a prophetic dream in which a man "travayleth in countries unknowen wythout hope of retourne." In arguing against the possibility of ghosts, Bullinger insists that "they which go a journey, chancing into unknown countries ... do not go astray [*non errare hic*] after death ... they cannot return of their own accord when they will return." La Primaudaye is also completely orthodox in noting that no one knows what becomes of men's souls after death, "or to what countrey they goe, because none ever returned from thence to bring any newes."[36] The image was thus a familiar Christian commonplace among the most devout, indicating merely the obvious fact that no dead man can return to life.

Despite the thesis of this study, I do not think that the image is intended to cast doubt on the Ghost at this point. It is true that the Protestants Bullinger and La Primaudaye both use it in passages denying the existence of ghosts, but the Catholics also used it in distinguishing between the pains of Purgatory, which were of limited duration, and the pains of Hell, which were eternal. A common gloss in Elizabethan Catholic books of devotion emphasized this distinction: for example, "the Hell of the damned, from whence is no returne."[37] Whether Hamlet's orientation is Protestant or Catholic at this point— whether he merely means that no man can return from death to life or that no damned soul can return from Hell—makes little difference. The entire soliloquy grapples with the problem faced only by a man who believes that Heaven and Hell do exist, who believes that after death a rebel against divine law will face inevitable and terrifying judgment.

Hamlet, unlike Macbeth, cannot "jump the life to come." In his moment of decision, Macbeth tries to shut his mind to the consequences. Hamlet cannot. Should he decide to act, he will knowingly

---

[36] Job 7:10, 10:20, 16:22; *Cardanus Comforte*, fol. D3ᵛ; Bullinger, *The Decades*, III, 402; La Primaudaye, *The French Academie*, p. 596. Note also the final speech of Mortimer in Marlowe's *Edward II*. Condemned to death, he travels "to discover countries yet unknown."

[37] A. C. Southern, *Elizabethan Recusant Prose: 1559–1582* (London, 1950), p. 255.

dare damnation. On the other hand, should he decide to do nothing, to obey God's command and leave Claudius to Heaven, would he not live a coward in his own esteem? Reflecting that it is only the fear of Hell which prevents man from either destroying evil by direct action or escaping from it by suicide, Hamlet arrives at his decision:

> Thus conscience does make cowards of us all;
> And thus the native hue of resolution
> Is sicklied o'er with the pale cast of thought,
> And enterprises of great pitch and moment
> With this regard their currents turn awry,
> And lose the name of action.

In the discussion of "O what a rogue and peasant slave am I," it was suggested that Hamlet's self-reproaches for cowardice indicated the moral nature of his dilemma, the charge of cowardice being considered by Shakespeare's contemporaries the most potent appeal of revenge. Hamlet's rebellion is now focused in exactly the same charge: "Thus conscience does make cowards of us all." The crux of the entire soliloquy lies in the word *conscience*. To Shakespeare and his contemporaries, the word rarely meant "consciousness," the usual editorial gloss. More commonly it meant the faculty that not only accused a man of past sin but also warned him against future sin. We find it used in this modern sense by Bright, Burton, Florio, Perkins, and Copley, to name but a few. Shakespeare himself often uses "conscience" to mean the internal lawgiver that judges the good or evil of a proposed action. Henry V asks if he can lay claim to France "with right and conscience" (I.ii.96). Launcelot Gobbo finds conscience "hanging about the neck of [his] heart," counseling him not to run away (*Merchant of Venice*, II.ii.1–33). Timon's fair-weather friends refuse to give him aid because "policy sits above conscience" (III.ii. 94).[38] There is only one reason for not understanding the word in its modern sense: the belief that Hamlet never considers the possibility that revenge is immoral. Once suspend that assumption, and the final lines of the soliloquy can mean only one thing: that the inner voice of judgment, by warning us that a proposed action is damnable, pre-

---

[38] See also *Titus Andronicus*, V.i.74–75, *Richard III*, I.iv.137–42 and V.iii.308–10, *Othello*, I.ii.3 and III.iii.201–4, *Hamlet*, V.ii.307.

vents us from undertaking great enterprises and thus makes us cowards.[39]

That this concept defines Hamlet's challenge to accepted morality seems certain when we consider certain parallels in the other plays. In *Richard III*, the equation of conscience with cowardice is the ironic rationalization of a hired killer. When the second murderer finds conscience at his elbow warning him not to kill Clarence, a pointed reference to the promised gold reminds him that conscience "makes man a coward ... 'tis a blushing shamefast spirit that mutinies in a man's bosom; it fills one full of obstacles" (I.iv.137–42). Richard III, following his fearful night before the battle of Bosworth, cries

> Let not our babbling dreams affright our souls:
> Conscience is but a word that cowards use,
> Devis'd at first to keep the strong in awe.
>                                   (V.iii.308–10)

In *Richard II*, the Duchess of Gloucester uses a more subtle argument but the same logic in trying to break Gaunt's determination to leave vengeance to God:

> Call it not patience, Gaunt; it is despair:
> In suffering thus thy brother to be slaughter'd,
> Thou showest the naked pathway to thy life,
> Teaching stern murder how to butcher thee:
> That which in mean men we intitle patience
> Is pale cold cowardice in noble breasts.
>                                   (I.ii.29–34)

"Fell, revenging Clifford" would agree, as would Alcibiades, that "patience is for poltroons" (*3 Henry VI*, I.i.62).

So too would Lady Macbeth and Troilus. In the arguments of both, we find significant parallels to the argument Hamlet cannot resist. To Lady Macbeth, moral considerations are for cowards. Does Macbeth dare to "be a man"? That is her question. When Macbeth first broke the enterprise, then he was a man, but now, when he hesitates,

---

[39] C. S. Lewis is certain that in context the word conscience here "means nothing more or less than 'fear of Hell'" (*Studies in Words*, Cambridge, Eng., 1960, pp. 205–8). See also Bertram Joseph, *Conscience and the King*, pp. 108–10.

she sees him as a timorous, sottish beast. In his last attempt to withstand her many taunts, Macbeth gives what is surely to be recognized as the valid argument: the "courage" that leads a man to defy reason and moral law is not courage at all. He who dares do so is no longer a "man" in the true sense. To Macbeth, man can "be" only to the extent that his reason controls his will. To Lady Macbeth, man can "be" only to the extent that his will dominates his reason. Her definition is clear in her challenge:

> Art thou afeard
> To be the same in thine own act and valour
> As thou art in desire? Wouldst thou have that
> Which thou esteem'st the ornament of life,
> And live a coward in thine own esteem...?
>
> (I.vii.39–43)

To her, the man who fails to act upon his instinctive hungers, the man who is deterred by the warnings of conscience, is a coward. One of the curiosities of Shakespearean criticism is the number of readers who have agreed with her.

The great debate of the Trojans in *Troilus and Cressida* is more obviously pertinent since the question is whether or not to take revenge, and the ethical issues are exactly the same. Hector argues that to spill blood over a worthless cause is irrational. When Helenus joins in defense of reason, Troilus explodes:

> You are for dreams and slumbers, brother priest;
> You fur your gloves with reason...
> And reason flies the object of all harm....
>       Nay, if we talk of reason,
> Let's shut our gates and sleep: manhood and honour
> Should have hare-hearts, would they but fat their thoughts
> With this cramm'd reason: reason and respect
> Make livers pale and lustihood deject.
>
> (II.ii.37–50)

To Troilus, "manhood" means following instinct, acting in the teeth of any principle rather than be thought a coward. Hector digs below the surface and challenges Troilus on his basic premise:

> But value dwells not in particular will ...
> And the will dotes that is attributive
> To what infectiously itself affects,
> Without some image of the affected merit.
>
> (II.ii.53–60)

To Hector, value dwells in universal principles ("images of merit") derived by reason. When an individual man sophistically erects a code to justify following his own instinctive desires, reason panders will.

The striking parallels between *Hamlet* and *Troilus and Cressida* suggest confirmation for the preceding analysis of Hamlet's dilemma. To Troilus, the man who resigns himself to patience falls into the sleep of the sated glutton, his brain fattened, not nourished, by reason; the Ghost's most insidious image had pictured the patient man as "duller than the fat weed" that nods by the river of forgetfulness. To Troilus, "reason and respect / Make livers pale and lustihood deject"; to Hamlet, the "respect" that is conscience makes cowards of us all by infecting "the native hue of resolution" with "the pale cast of thought." Hamlet is not saying, as Coleridge believed, that too much thought prevents man from taking any action at all. He is agreeing with Troilus that the thoughts prompted by conscience prevent a man from following his own instincts. As Clemen notes, " 'Native hue of resolution' suggests that Shakespeare viewed resolution as an innate human quality, not as a moral virtue to be consciously striven after."[40] It is the instinctive nature of man to want to act. It is his reason that restrains him. Which shall Hamlet follow in order "to be"?[41]

Hamlet's tragic dilemma has arisen not because he instinctively shrinks from action. Quite the contrary. Every instinct in him cries out to act; every instinct rebels against a metaphysic that defines man in terms of obedience to imposed law, in terms of surrender of his will,

[40] Wolfgang Clemen, *The Development of Shakespeare's Imagery* (Cambridge, Mass., 1951), p. 112.

[41] Could Hamlet freely obey his "nature," he might easily join with that arch-villain Selimus, who derides religious commands as "onely bug-beares to keepe the world in fear, / And make men quietly a yoake to beare." The comparison may seem farfetched, but Hamlet and Selimus both ask the same unsettling question that has faced Christianity throughout the ages: "Why should we seeke to make that soule a slave, / To which dame Nature so large freedome gave?" *Selimus,* ed. W. Bang for the Malone Society (1908), ll. 336–37 and 352–53.

in terms of passivity and resignation. The Ghost's challenge has fallen on receptive ears: "If thou hast nature in thee...." The resolution of the soliloquy on the word "action," Hamlet's rejection of coward conscience, and his actions following the Play Scene all indicate that he has accepted the challenge. He has decided to act.

Paradoxically, from this point on, it matters little whether the Ghost came from Heaven or from Hell. What matters to Hamlet is not the source of the command, but its very nature. In the soliloquy he grants that Heaven's law demands patience; thus, by implication, the command to act can come only from Hell. But Hamlet does not rest content with this easy answer. He digs below the surface to challenge the validity of divine law.

The Ghost, then, is not a mere demonic tempter, blinding Hamlet, tricking him into pursuing an obviously evil course. On the contrary, in one sense it opens Hamlet's eyes—shattering all conventional ethical assumptions, forcing him to define his own code, to determine for himself his own course. In "To be or not to be," as we fight through the dilemma with Hamlet, we suspend all easy ethical assumptions. We too will be pulled into the maelstrom.

# CHAPTER VII

## Heaven's Scourge or Minister?

### ACT III, SCENE I (cont.)

In Hamlet's treatment of Ophelia in the Nunnery Scene, we see the first ominous results of his decision to reject coward conscience. Following "To be or not to be," he is a different man from the controlled, detached thinker of Act II. He has freed himself from the "pale cast of thought" and now embarks on a course of impulsive and violent action. The transition comes as the sight of Ophelia, apparently at prayer, suddenly interrupts his train of thought.

The explosive energy with which he has hurled aside the rule of conscience in the final lines of the soliloquy now leads Hamlet to check himself before speaking to this child who has no reality in the world of horrors he has entered:

> Soft you now!
> The fair Ophelia! Nymph in thy orisons
> Be all my sins remember'd.

Hamlet is not being ironic, using deliberately affected language and referring sardonically to his sins. There is detachment, yes, a sense of nostalgia for the fairy-tale world of innocence that Ophelia represents to him, a world he has left forever. In his polite but withdrawn response to her awkward inquiry after his health—"I humbly thank you; well, well, well"—there is a suggestion that he will pass on and leave Ophelia untouched by the illness he knows attends him. Suddenly, however, he lashes out and mortally infects her with the filth corrupting his own imaginings. Why?

From the beginning of *Hamlet* criticism, readers have been so appalled by Hamlet's savagery and obscenity with Ophelia that they have refused to accept the Nunnery Scene on its own terms. Hamlet's behavior is "inexcusable," "incomprehensible." The critics' dilemma is epitomized by Arthur Quiller-Couch: "My instinct all through prompts me to say, 'Yes, yes, you are driven. But for God's sake, need you speak to this child as to a strumpet? O man, leave *her,* at least, alone!'"[1] Convincing himself that instinct was not to be trusted, Quiller-Couch sought for some explanation that would relieve Hamlet of guilt, finding it, he thought, in the fact that the girl in Belleforest is a courtesan, and concluding that Shakespeare had been too careless to revise the scene when he changed the character of Ophelia. Some dismiss Hamlet's behavior as irrelevant both to the play and to Hamlet himself on the grounds that Shakespeare merely followed traditional treatments of the melancholic; others excuse it on the grounds that Hamlet knows Ophelia has taken a new lover, that she is, indeed, all that he accuses her of being. The majority rely on the explanation that Hamlet knows he is being overheard; in their view his behavior is an act put on for the eavesdroppers. All of these explanations are significant: they indicate widespread recognition that Hamlet's violence and brutality cannot reflect the "real" feelings of the tender, sensitive, hesitant hero of tradition. Indeed, they cannot. But if we have no reason to doubt that Hamlet's actions reveal his true state of mind, should we not question the tradition rather than our feelings? The present study suggests that, with Quiller-Couch, we should follow instinct, and instinct cries out that Ophelia does not deserve such treatment.[2]

There is no need to seek beyond the lines for an explanation of Hamlet's sudden change in tone. Uneasily, regretfully, Ophelia offers to return his lover's tokens. Hamlet is not taken aback. Her action might have been expected, for she had refused to see him, but now such trifles seem to him a mere nothing: "I never gave you aught." He is probably continuing a controlled exit when Ophelia, stung by what she takes to be a literal denial, follows him insistently: He did!

---

[1] *Shakespeare's Workmanship* (London, 1919), p. 209.
[2] The same instinctive response has been shared by critics since the beginning of *Hamlet* criticism. See below, pp. 244–48.

He knows he did. She urges him to remember how sweet those days had been, but suddenly she catches herself. Recalling her father's command, she forces herself to obey, stiffly holding out the pathetic gifts and, in a manner totally foreign to her, parroting one of her father's many maxims:

> Take these again; for to the noble mind
> Rich gifts wax poor when givers prove unkind.
> There my lord.

Hamlet jerks around: "Ha, ha! are you honest?" The foolish little platitude warns him that something is wrong. By putting all the blame for their estrangement on him and by her stilted manner, she reveals that she is playing a role. This simple bit of dishonesty, no matter how well-intentioned on Ophelia's part, suffices to trigger Hamlet's fury. At first, he expresses only sardonic awareness that yet another illusion has been shattered. Even this charming bit of seeming innocence is not what she appears to be. Nothing is what it once seemed. His mother had once seemed an adoring wife, but he has come to view her seeming love as compulsive animal hunger. He had once thought he loved Ophelia, but he has come to scorn the devotions of his blind youth as lying games that hide mere lust. "Virtue cannot so inoculate our old stock but we shall relish of it": in the endless struggle between reason and the old Adam, he has come to believe, the man who bets on reason has laid his odds on the weaker side. "We are arrant knaves, all." He too. He is "proud, revengeful, and ambitious," as he admits. Hamlet's acknowledgment of his own guilt should not be dismissed as an ironic assertion to mislead eavesdroppers. The same self-knowledge lay behind his earlier appeal that Ophelia remember his sins in her prayers. His first charge that Ophelia retire to a nunnery seems sincere.

But the tone changes rapidly. Before he asks where her father is and Ophelia answers with her innocuous lie, "At home, my lord," he is fairly temperate, speaking with brutal but hardheaded honesty. Now he shifts into a frenzied diatribe, three times taking leave of her only to rush back and renew the assault. Does he suddenly infer from her manner that Polonius is eavesdropping? Possibly, but the director is wise to avoid any such implication. If Hamlet sees a movement of the arras or is suddenly reminded that he heard Polonius planning just such a trap, his responding with a deliberate shift into maniacal nonsense throws the scene out of focus. The audience inevitably turns its attention to the arras hiding the eavesdroppers. The point of the scene, I am convinced, should be Hamlet's changing attitude toward Ophelia and her stunned reaction.[3] Moreover, if Hamlet were consciously directing all of his remarks to eavesdroppers, the scene would be out of character. A man capable of such convincing lunacy would delight in rushing over, pulling aside the arras, and making the most of his victims' embarrassment. And if his remarks were all intentional, why would he alert Claudius by shouting that he intends murder?[4]

The simplest explanation is the most convincing. Once Hamlet has been forced to consider Ophelia as a fallible woman, his mind swiftly associates her with Gertrude. As the associations flood in and his disgust and rage mount, he becomes progressively more reckless, unintentionally revealing not only the sex nausea that is poisoning his mind, but even his plan. The first—the obscene imaginings that Ophelia only vaguely glimpses—will eventually drive her to madness.[5] The second—the warning to Claudius—will contribute to Hamlet's own death. Neither does Hamlet intend. He is not pretending madness; he has lost control.

[3] In "Hamlet and Ophelia," *Proceedings of the British Academy*, XLIX (1953), 135–51, Harold Jenkins agrees that Hamlet's behavior is wholly explained by his tainted view of Ophelia. His interesting contribution is the argument that Hamlet's diatribe is directed entirely against marriage, that Hamlet is trying to convince Ophelia, for her own protection, that love is impossible in such a corrupt world. The argument is provocative, though it does not account for Hamlet's shift in tone and his sudden violence.

[4] Kitto, *Form and Meaning*, pp. 280–81. I find an argument by Helen Gardner all but conclusive. In "Lawful Espials" (*Modern Language Review*, XXXIII, 1938, 345–55), she presents a detailed analysis of the conventions pertaining to eavesdropping in the plays of Shakespeare and his contemporaries. By convention, the audience knew that a victim of eavesdropping was unaware that he was overheard. Therefore, whenever he did become aware, the playwright was careful to make him comment on the fact. "Only direct statement from Hamlet himself can suspend these conventions" (p. 353). If Shakespeare intended Hamlet to know that Polonius and Claudius were behind the arras, it would be the only instance in which he violated the convention.

[5] Despite well-reasoned objections, the traditional assumption that Hamlet shifts his definition of "nunnery" to mean "bawdy-house" is probably correct. In *Der bestrafte Brudermord*, which is obviously related in some way to Shakespeare's play, Hamlet is explicit: "Go to a nunnery, but not to a Nunnery where two pairs of slippers lie at the bedside" (*Variorum Hamlet*, II, 128). The same meaning seems implicit in Hamlet's references to bawdry, wantonness, and painted women.

The Nunnery Scene, then, is the direct result of Hamlet's decision in "To be or not to be." By defying the injunctions of reason and by choosing to surrender himself to "the native hue of resolution," he has necessarily surrendered himself to instinct and to passion. Although his sole aim has been to destroy evil, ironically his chosen course has led him to foster further evil. The tragic cycle has begun.

By any other interpretation of the Nunnery Scene, Shakespeare's treatment of Ophelia seems inexplicable. If Hamlet's behavior is just a clever pretense at madness for which he should be applauded, not condemned, why did Shakespeare make Ophelia so sympathetic?[6] He makes her innocent of any conspiracy; he treats her apparent betrayal of Hamlet as the result of her filial obedience and of her desire to help the man she loves. Even those who judge her compliance most harshly must admit that the audience shares Ophelia's pain in this scene. Significantly, when our sympathy for her is at its height, she has a soliloquy that has been accepted, at least in part, as Shakespeare's judgment. Before the Ghost came to Elsinore, Hamlet had been "the expectancy and rose of the fair state." Is she to be considered entirely mistaken, then, when she says that this "noble mind is here o'er-thrown . . . blasted with ecstasy"? I do not mean that Hamlet has gone mad in the clinical sense. He has, however, lost rational control. The word "blasted" may be significant. The image of "blown youth" now "blasted" may suggest not merely a flower, but also the demonic "blasts" that both Horatio and Hamlet had feared might emanate from the Ghost. Whether or not Shakespeare intended a specific echo, Hamlet's raving and brutality in the Nunnery Scene reflect precisely that "taint" which the Ghost had fostered so carefully.

## ACT III, SCENE II

Between the Nunnery and the Play scenes, Shakespeare interposes another moment of quiet, as Hamlet advises the players on decorum in acting, applauds Horatio for his balance of judgment and passion, and restates his doubts of the Ghost. The relaxation of tension is another example of a technique Shakespeare uses throughout the play: a scene of gripping emotion is immediately followed by a period of calm, which in turn is followed by another scene of high tension.

---

[6] Among many excellent defenses of Ophelia, those of Bradley (*Shakespearean Tragedy*, pp. 160–65) and Granville-Barker (*Prefaces*, I, 212–16) remain among the best.

I doubt that this technique can be explained as a result of Shake-speare's belief in periodic respites for his audience. In each case, the audience is abruptly shifted from one orientation to another, jerked out of emotional involvement with the characters and into detached objectivity. We have noted several such shifts. The first Ghost Scene is immediately followed by the calm discussion of one way in which a Christian detects a malignant spirit. Following the ensuing court scene, we are thrust into Hamlet's agony, only to be snapped out again by a mundane bit of domesticity. Suddenly we are back in Hamlet's hell, confronting the Ghost, being driven to hysteria by the terrifying abyss he sees opening—but then we are pulled back to the real world of petty men who approve the "taints of liberty" as "the flash and outbreak of a fiery mind." Hamlet's first explicit question-ing both of the morality of revenge and of the nature of the Ghost is immediately preceded by the Player's Speech on "hellish Pyrrhus," an epitome of revenge. In each case, a scene in which we emotionally identify with Hamlet's point of view is both preceded and followed by a scene that pulls us away from the situation and forces us to see it in different perspective.

Such a period of objectivity occurs immediately before the Play Scene. Hamlet's speeches to the players and to Horatio both focus on a recurrent theme, a theme that has been developed in Polonius's fool-ish words to Reynaldo, in the Player's Speech, and in Hamlet's behav-ior in the Nunnery Scene. We have just seen him helplessly caught up in a tempest of passion. Now, having regained control, he advises the players, the men who are to "hold the mirror up to nature," that they must beget temperance. Brandes is one of the very few to have seen that the speech to the players has direct bearing on the tragic issue in *Hamlet*. In the first half of the speech, Hamlet warns against the dangers of overacting. In the second half, he begins warning against excessive tameness, and one expects the subject of underplaying to receive equal treatment. He immediately returns, however, to the dangers of uncontrolled rant. As Brandes notes, "It is not the dan-ger of tameness, but of violence, that is uppermost in Shakespeare's mind."[7] It is also uppermost in Hamlet's mind in those moments when he is able to see clearly.

---

[7] *William Shakespeare* (New York, 1936), p. 388.

The same concern is reflected in Hamlet's speech praising Horatio. In this calm and lucid moment, just before both he and the audience are caught up in a whirlwind of passion, Hamlet shows that he knows himself well:

> ... blest are those
> Whose blood and judgement are so well commeddled,
> That they are not a pipe for fortune's finger
> To sound what stop she please. Give me that man
> That is not passion's slave ...

Hamlet is not commending the man who withdraws into Stoic indifference. Horatio is a man who, in suffering all, suffers nothing; that is, he feels the agonies of the human condition, but his instinct and his judgment function in such harmony that passion is the servant of reason, not the master. Such a man is Hamlet's ideal: a man who is guided by the principle that it is "nobler in the mind to suffer." Hamlet knows himself to be "passion's slave."

In the same speech we are again reminded, and for the last time, of Hamlet's doubts about the Ghost.[8] The issue now seems clear to him: if Claudius is not trapped into revealing his guilt,

> It is a damned ghost that we have seen,
> And my imaginations are as foul
> As Vulcan's stithy.

There is no hint that a damned ghost might have told the truth. In light of all that has happened, should we be trapped into this faulty dilemma along with Hamlet? For the moment, we must be. The ethical premise of this study would be strengthened if Horatio countered with the warning that the instruments of darkness can tell us truths in order to betray us, but the play would be seriously weakened. The Ghost's behavior and the effects of its challenge on Hamlet's mind have long since been established as implicit warnings. An explicit statement of the warning would complicate our response in the en-

---

[8] We need not concern ourselves here with the fact that Horatio now knows all about the Ghost. In Act I, Shakespeare wanted Hamlet to isolate himself. Now he wants to give Hamlet a confidant and the audience a norm. Contradictory, yes, but no audience ever notices.

suing climactic scenes. For the moment, our only question must be how Claudius will react to the Mousetrap. From the beginning of the Play Scene to the departure for England, we will be swept along with Hamlet. Only when our judgment is no longer passion's slave will we, and Hamlet, be able to view the events in true perspective.

Our enforced period of objectivity is abruptly ended as the royal entourage sweeps in and settles down for the evening's diversion. Despite his rational approval of temperance, stated so calmly and compellingly only moments before to both Horatio and the players, Hamlet's emotions progressively master him. Tense with anticipation, he takes grim delight in his pretense of lunacy, ill concealing his loathing of Claudius, openly insulting Gertrude, turning his scorn for the court into a mocking game. His bawdy banter with Ophelia cannot be dismissed as appropriate teasing for a sophisticated Renaissance court. Even if it is socially acceptable, it too clearly reveals Hamlet's obsession, the "taint" that has infected him. He treats Ophelia as a mere sexual object. Whether it was a damned ghost or not, Hamlet's imaginations are "as foul as Vulcan's stithy." As the play progresses, the images of the murderous brother and the faithless Queen increasingly agitate him until he is spitting innuendos and insults. His rage at the actor portraying Lucianus is fully understandable without recourse to ingenious theories. All of his behavior reflects his mounting excitement. He is straining at the leash, almost frenzied in his eagerness to get to the crucial moment in "The Murder of Gonzago." Unable to wait for the mousetrap to spring in its own good time, he lashes out at the actor, all but screaming "Get on with it!" Finally he himself leaps in to stab the implications into Claudius's conscience.[9]

---

[9] Hamlet's curious reference to the murderer Lucianus as "nephew to the king," rather than "brother," lends support to this interpretation. Dover Wilson's theory that Hamlet is intentionally confusing the court, hiding Claudius's crime in order to protect Gertrude, overlooks two objections (*What Happens in Hamlet,* pp. 164–74). If Hamlet is so concerned with protecting Gertrude's reputation, why does he publicly insult her? Moreover, why would Hamlet want the court to believe that the forthcoming killing of Claudius is an unprovoked act of treachery by an ambitious and villainous nephew? There is too much evidence in the play that he wants the truth known, that he cares about his reputation. By referring to the play-murderer as the King's "nephew," he blinds the court to the truth, confirming Claudius's later assertion that his nephew is a threat to the State. There seems no logical reason why he should thus divert attention and place his own plans in jeopardy. The increasing rashness of his outburst, however, makes it probable that the error is a slip of the tongue, again revealing the turbulence of Hamlet's emotions. His hatred of Claudius is so intense that he is led subconsciously to identify himself with the murderer.

When Claudius at last falls into the trap, Hamlet explodes in a triumphantly manic fit of song. In his hysterical abandon we sense that he is now freed of all restraints. Wildly exultant, he is itching to act. It is possible that Shakespeare has once again suggested the perspective from which we are to view this decision. The long speech of the Player King, an abstract discussion of the relation of passion to action, oddly interrupts a scene of mounting tension and has often seemed irrelevant. I find much of it to be amplification beyond the needs of the play, but one passage may be directly relevant:

> What to ourselves in passion we propose,
> The passion ending, doth the purpose lose.
> The violence of either grief or joy
> Their own enactures with themselves destroy.

A common interpretation is that man must act immediately on a decision because "purpose is but the slave to memory"; therefore, if Hamlet delays he will lose the incentive to act. Shakespeare, however, is discussing only certain decisions: those made in the heat of passion. A purpose prompted by emotion will wither as the emotion dies, because the purpose has not been confirmed by reason. Shakespeare's implication may be illuminated by two passages in *The French Academie*. In a discussion of rashness, La Primaudaye defines the prudent man's method of reacting to injury:

[We] ought to doe nothing in choler. For that unreasonable part of the soule beeing mooved, foreseeth nothing wisely, but beeing driven forward with a contentious desire, suffereth it selfe to bee carried hither and thither, as if it were drunken. Also wee must take great heede, that wee doe not alwaies put in execution whatsoever wee have a minde unto, but onely that which moderate reason commaundeth us.[10]

In a discussion of fortitude, La Primaudaye similarly treats the relation of passion and reason to choice:

This vertue standeth not in neede either of choler, rancor, ambition, pride, or of any other evill passion, whereby to bring to passe brave and glorious effects, but is rather an utter enemie unto them, because it proceedeth from

---

[10] La Primaudaye, pp. 157–58.

a mature and ripe consideration and election of reason, which causeth a man boldly to put in execution whatsoever hee knoweth to belong to duty and honesty.[11]

Although the Player King is discussing the failure to act whereas La Primaudaye is discussing unjustified action, the basic premise seems to be the same: whatever is proposed in passion is "of violent birth, but poor validity." Only a choice that is maturely considered and ratified by reason can lead to virtuous action.

Hamlet's decision has been proposed in passion, and following the Play Scene, when he is at last alone, the terrible violence of that passion is laid bare. The theory that Hamlet instinctively shrinks from a dread command for which he is ill-fitted is belied by his obvious jubilation at having proof of Claudius's guilt, and by the ferocious eagerness with which he now allies himself with the powers of Hell:

> 'Tis now the very witching time of night,
> When churchyards yawn and hell itself breathes out
> Contagion to this world: now could I drink hot blood,
> And do such bitter business as the day
> Would quake to look on.

The speech is appalling in its implications. As noted in Chapter II, the night speech, a familiar convention on the Elizabethan stage, was traditionally a sign of fiendish villainy, a speech in which a murderer either invoked night to aid him or hailed night—the time of black thoughts, of screeching owls, ravens, and open graves—as congenial to his purpose. The night that Hamlet welcomes is even more ghastly than most in its explicit association with Hell, the demonic practices of witchcraft, and the blasts of contagion.

We cannot lightly dismiss Hamlet's grisly avowal that now he could "drink hot blood." To the Elizabethan audience, the statement would inevitably have suggested one of the most degenerate practices of the Black Mass. In the line signaling the surrender of his will to Hell, Faustus vows to build an altar to Beelzebub "and offer lukewarm blood of newborn babes." The inhuman ferocity of many stage villains is epitomized precisely by their gleeful thirst for the blood of

---

[11] *Ibid.*, p. 110.

their victims. Thus Edricus in *Edmond Ironside* desires "to Drinke kinge Edmmund['s] blood" (l. 1990).[12] Thus Piero in *Antonio's Revenge* exults over the corpse of his murdered enemy: "I have been nurs'd in blood, and still have suck'd / The steam of reeking gore" (II.i.19–20). Thus D'Amville, the villain-protagonist of *The Atheist's Tragedy,* signals his descent into lunacy by vowing:

> I could now commit a murder, were
> It but to drink the fresh warm blood of him
> I murder'd.
>
> (IV.iii.240–42)

If we accept the speech on its own terms, we find Hamlet's thirst for blood a terrifying indication of his state of mind. The thought of murder does not appall him. It excites him to a state of inhuman frenzy.[13]

Recalling the command to attend on his mother, Hamlet now attempts to check his emotions, for he recognizes a very real danger. If he does not contain this storm of destructive rage, he may impulsively kill her. His alliance with the witching time of night, his thirst for blood, and his determination to give vent to his feelings in words but not in action—all indicate unmistakably that his thoughts at this moment are murderous. Why, then, does he go to Gertrude instead of immediately seeking Claudius? The usual explanation is that he shrinks from the dreadful duty and welcomes an opportunity to delay; but the violence of the soliloquy, together with Hamlet's well-founded fears of his own instincts, indicates his passionate eagerness to sweep to his revenge. For the moment, however, he can do nothing. Rosencrantz and Guildenstern have announced that the King is "in his retirement." What would we have Hamlet do? Go roaring to the King's private chamber, the door of which would, of course, be conveniently open and unguarded? Shakespeare has established that Claudius is out of the way for the night, and the normal assumption would be that he is inaccessible. Had Shakespeare intended Hamlet to be procrastinating when he calls for the recorders or when he willingly heeds his mother's command, he could easily have told us so. Horatio could have asked, "Seek you the King tonight?" and Hamlet

---

12 Ed. Eleanore Boswell for the Malone Society, 1927.
13 See Siegel, *Shakespearean Tragedy,* pp. 105–6.

have evaded the question with "Ay, anon, anon. But first let us have some music." The scene contains no such hint. On the contrary, all that has preceded and all that follows confirms that the soliloquy is to be taken at face value. It reveals that Hamlet's thoughts are homicidal and also that he views his forthcoming act as essentially evil, as a deed wholly alien to the light of day, befitting the dark and the demonic. The soliloquy unmistakably harks back to the Ghost scenes.[14]

## ACT III, SCENE III

The Prayer Scene provides one of the most profoundly moving moments of the play. Claudius is himself a tragic figure, not the greasy, vulture-eyed villain pictured by those who bolster Hamlet's virtue by blackening his opponents. He is a strong and self-willed but sensitive man, whose passions have led him to choose evil but who has never deluded himself into calling that evil good. He has an active conscience that cannot be silenced. He is far closer to Macbeth than to Iago or Richard III.[15]

Perhaps no character is more compelling on stage than the contrite sinner struggling to repent, a fact that medieval dramatists put to good use in their treatments of Mary Magdalene. No situation so clearly unites a dramatic character with his audience by a bond of shared humanity. No matter what his religious or cultural heritage, every man but the amoral freak tries and fails, feels the pangs of guilt and regret, and struggles to shape himself anew to that image of good toward which he strives.

Shakespeare dramatizes this struggle in Christian terms, using specific points of doctrine his audience would recognize. One by one, Claudius mounts three of the four steps comprising what was known as the "ladder of repentance": contrition, confession, faith, and amendment.[16] His prayer is not motivated by fear of detection. His conscience has led him to true contrition: loathing of his sin because it is an offense to God, because "it smells to heaven." Moreover, it has led him

---

[14] Kitto, *Form and Meaning*, p. 313.

[15] H. S. Wilson, *On the Design of Shakespearian Tragedy*, p. 47.

[16] Homily of Repentance, *Certaine Sermons*, II, 264. Catholics differed only in eliminating faith as a specific step, arguing that faith necessarily precedes a movement to repent. Claudius's prayer would be as familiar in doctrine and as emotionally gripping to a Catholic as to a Protestant.

to confession: acknowledgment before God that he knows the full horror of his sin. Compelled by the inexorable witness of conscience to see his past action in its true nature and be revolted by it, he nonetheless cannot bring himself to surrender the motives which led him to that action and which still dominate him. He is trapped. Claudius is in a state of human torment, not of theological despair. He has absolute faith: even if his sin were greater than the crime first cursed of God, the gracious rain of divine mercy could wash the blood from his hand. The fault of the murder itself is past and easily repented. If his "strong intent," his genuine longing to find peace, can but defeat his "stronger guilt"—the sins of ambition and lust that still corrupt him—forgiveness, he knows, awaits. He has but to choose by an act of will.

But can he make that choice? The tortured outcries reveal the intense agony of a man paralyzed between the longing of soul and the solicitation of appetite: "O limed soul, that, struggling to be free, / Art more engaged!" Ironically, Claudius knows that this movement to repent has necessarily enslaved him even more to his sin. He has honestly diagnosed the cancer that is destroying him, but has consciously refused the only medicine that could heal him. Because he has brought all the evil out into the open but has deliberately rejected grace, he is doubly damned.[17] Even at this moment, however, he decides to make one final attempt and retires to pray. "All may be well." The line is a masterly stroke. The impotence of his will, his half-hope, half-rejection—all are pointed in this indefinite half-promise. It is the final summation of his "limed soul," and at the same time it serves a brilliant dramatic function. It leaves the audience in a state of suspense throughout Hamlet's hesitation. Will Claudius be able to take that final step? There is little doubt, but there is still some. Irony and suspense are both maintained until his final lines before retiring:

---

[17] Two lines of Claudius's soliloquy have been thought to be illogical:

Try what repentance can: what can it not?
Yet what can it when one can not repent?

Warburton dismissed this as redundant nonsense and emended the second line to read "when one can *but* repent" (i.e., feel contrition but refuse to make restitution), a confusion indicating the rapidly changing meaning of "repentance." The lines present a tight contrast between the abstract power of repentance to change man and the inability of the sinner to take the specific action required of him. As Claudius knows, the mercy of God to the penitent is without measure. "What can it not?" But he also knows that he cannot "repent" because he cannot take the final step of amendment. Mere sorrow for sin cannot be called repentance.

My words fly up, my thoughts remain below:
Words without thoughts never to heaven go.

With a rush of irony, the audience now realizes that Hamlet's moment was ideal for the total revenge he intended: death at the very moment Claudius was rejecting the call of grace and thus willfully choosing damnation.

Another ironic implication may underlie the Prayer Scene. Since dramatic characters have no life beyond the text of the play, speculation about "what might have happened under different circumstances" should normally be avoided. Nonetheless, may this question be pertinent: What if Claudius had been left to Heaven? By now it is apparent that Heaven is doing a very good job. Even before he realizes that Hamlet is a threat, Claudius has revealed in his aside that he is tortured by conscience, that his will is not totally perverted. In the Prayer Scene we see even more vividly that his conscience is a remorseless judge. Even after he knowingly chooses damnation and embarks on a course of full villainy, his "soul is full of discord and dismay." He never becomes so completely hardened that he can enjoy evil itself or revel in the fruits of his crime. If he had been left to his burning conscience, if he had not been driven by fear for his life to wade still further into blood—might there not have been hope for such a man?[18]

I have dealt rather extensively with the religious issues in Claudius's speech in order to justify two important premises that will be crucial in interpreting Hamlet's ensuing soliloquy. First, no matter how we have seen Claudius previously, we sympathize with him in the Prayer Scene.[19] He is a human being in torment, facing his own question of "being." Only a bigoted Pharisee swelling with more spiritual sins than Claudius would sit back smugly and crow, "It serves him right." Second, the profound and moving presentation of Christian doctrine in the speech makes it inconceivable that Shakespeare in-

[18] I find no suggestion that Claudius plans Hamlet's death before the Closet Scene. Following the play-within-a-play, he tells Rosencrantz and Guildenstern that he "will forthwith dispatch" their commission. Had Shakespeare intended his attempt to repent as the hypocritical act of a man who has just ordered a murder, he could well have had Claudius inform us of his true intent in an aside. It is only after the Prayer Scene, when he rejects the call of grace, and after the Closet Scene, when he recognizes the killing of Polonius as an abortive attempt on his own life, that Claudius makes his plan.

[19] G. L. Kittredge, *Sixteen Plays of Shakespeare* (Boston, 1946), pp. 967–68.

tended his audience simply to forget its religious values when Hamlet enters. He has pointedly insisted that the world of *Hamlet* is a Christian world in which the redeeming values are self-knowledge, forgiveness, and mercy, a world in which eternal salvation is man's ultimate goal. Would Shakespeare have devoted such attention to Claudius's moral struggle if he wanted us to approve without question of Hamlet's ensuing actions?

Picture the scene. His stubborn knees at last bent, Claudius is kneeling in prayer. Hamlet runs in, on his way to Gertrude's chamber. He stops short, pulls his sword, sneaks up behind the bent figure, raises his arm— Is it possible that any normally sensitive, decent man could genuinely want him to strike? Stab a defenseless man? In the back? While he is praying? If we forget all we have heard about pagan ethics and Elizabethan revenge codes and dramatic conventions, does not the voice of instinct cry "No"?

Unexpectedly, Hamlet stays his hand, but his reason is frightful. A terrible hint had been planted by the Ghost: Hamlet's father had been cut off in a state of sin. Would it then be "revenge" to kill Claudius while he is praying? If, perchance, he is repenting, his soul would go to Heaven.

> No!
> Up, sword; and know thou a more horrid hent:
> When he is drunk asleep, or in his rage,
> Or in the incestuous pleasure of his bed;
> At gaming, swearing, or about some act
> That has no relish of salvation in 't;
> Then trip him, that his heels may kick at heaven,
> And that his soul may be as damn'd and black
> As hell, whereto it goes.

As Granville-Barker wrote, perhaps with more significance than he intended, "Into such a devil's labyrinth is [Hamlet] led!"[20]

In what is perhaps the most sensible and temperate assessment of traditional *Hamlet* criticism yet written, A. J. A. Waldock noted that this speech "is really a test passage of great importance." He insisted, moreover, that its meaning is obvious and that "it is something of a

[20] *Prefaces,* I, 249.

responsibility to refuse obvious meanings in a Shakespearean play."[21] Curiously, however, the obvious meaning—Hamlet's descent to the most savage malice of which a Christian can conceive—has been almost unanimously refused.[22] For over two centuries critics have been personally appalled by Hamlet's expressed reason for refusing to kill Claudius at prayer. The speech is "too horrible to be read or to be uttered"; it expresses "one of the most revolting sentiments in all Shakespeare . . . in language hardly equalled for repulsiveness"; the words are "frightful," the idea "fiendish."[23] Almost to a man, however, critics believe that the speech could not possibly reflect Hamlet's real sentiments and that their personal revulsion is therefore invalid. Seeking for some logical explanation, they have generally divided into two camps. Many have argued that Hamlet's vicious reason is so inconsistent with his character that it cannot be his real reason. Actually he finds undercover tactics abhorrent, or he realizes a public occasion would be more fitting, or he shrinks from killing a defenseless man, or he really does not want to act at all. There is, however, an obvious objection to any theory that Hamlet is rationalizing. Rationalization is a process of attributing morally acceptable motives to unacceptable desires or actions. If Hamlet's real motive were as commendable as the desire for public justice or the refusal to stab a defenseless man in the back, why would he need to conceal the motive from himself? More important, why would Shakespeare conceal it from the audience? If Hamlet's motive is not commendable, if he is temporizing out of weakness, why did not Shakespeare offer a rationalization that sounds virtuous? Hamlet could easily hesitate on the grounds that Claudius may be repenting and hence may confess publicly. The audience might then sense the contradiction between his stated thirst for blood and his hesitation and realize that he is rationalizing. In the play as Shakespeare wrote it, however, there is no contradiction between Hamlet's expressed motives and his actions.

21 *"Hamlet,"* p. 40. For his discussion of the Prayer Scene, see pp. 37–43.

22 Exceptions include *ibid.,* p. 39; G. Wilson Knight, *The Wheel of Fire,* 4th rev. ed. (London, 1956), p. 36; Granville-Barker, *Prefaces,* I, 220, 249; Hankins, *The Character of Hamlet,* pp. 188–91; and Kitto, *Form and Meaning,* pp. 313–14.

23 Raleigh, *Johnson on Shakespeare,* p. 193; J. Q. Adams, ed., *Hamlet* (New York, 1929), p. 275; Blackmore, *The Riddles of Hamlet,* p. 326.

A second group of critics accept Hamlet's reason, although they agree it is abhorrent to the modern mind. They assert, however, that he is merely voicing a conventional sentiment of the Elizabethan stage and that we should therefore suspend moral judgment. The speech, it is argued, does not reflect a vicious state of mind but a dutiful attempt to heed an ethic of revenge that Shakespeare's audience never questioned, a code that made the damnation of one's victim a moral requisite to a perfect revenge. Thus Hamlet is not to blame. In spite of his own moral sensibilities, he is courageously trying to effect equal justice by a device long approved in the theater.

Outside the theater, the voices of Elizabethan morality were, of course, unanimous. Their attitude is implicit in recurrent assertions that we must pray for the salvation of our enemies, that private revenge is a blasphemous usurpation of God's prerogative. Gentillet explicitly attacks the fiendish "Italianate" practice of "immortal vengeance," whereby the villains of Machiavelli's nation "seeke in slaying the bodie to damne the Soule."[24] Despite this evidence, many believe that audiences were trained to accept a pagan revenge code in the theater and thus to accord the dramatic convention of "immortal vengeance" full moral approval.

But does the drama of the period support this assumption? To my knowledge, no one has ever studied the convention in its dramatic context. Plays have been named, characters listed, and lines quoted, but no attempt has been made to determine audience response. What kinds of characters either desire or plan to kill their victims in a way that will ensure their damnation? What was the audience's moral attitude? Where did its sympathies lie? The answers to these questions constitute an astounding contradiction of the widespread belief that the revenger who sets out to damn his victim is merely fulfilling an ethical obligation.

In twenty-six works of both dramatic and non-dramatic literature written between 1585 and 1642, we find the convention reflected in twenty-three characters who either desire or act upon the desire to damn their victims, and in three characters who reject any such mo-

---

[24] *Against Machiavell*, p. 178. Fredson Bowers has insisted repeatedly that the convention reflects the code of the Italianate villain, not the approved morality of a hero. See, for example, *Elizabethan Revenge Tragedy*, pp. 51–52, and "Dramatic Structure and Criticism: Plot in *Hamlet*," *Shakespeare Quarterly*, XV (1964), 212–13.

tive. In only three instances is there any possibility that the convention received either the moral approval or the sympathy of the audience. Of these three, one occurs in *Antonio's Revenge*, a play so contradictory in its appeals that the modern reader cannot know where the audience's sympathies lay; one is found in the wish, but not the actions, of the virtuous Iden of 2 *Henry VI*, who regrets that his sword could not have killed the soul as well as the body of a traitor. We have, then, only one clear example of an ostensibly virtuous hero who acts upon the desire to damn his enemy—Perolet in *Four Plays* (1608)—and even this example is doubtful because of the confused ethics so typical of Beaumont and Fletcher.

Of the remaining twenty-three examples, not one could be offered in support of the traditional view. In all twenty-three cases, even the mere desire to damn another soul for eternity was unquestionably viewed by the audience as morally reprehensible and emotionally horrifying. In some cases, a basically good man refuses to send an unprepared soul to Hell, a sentiment arousing obvious sympathy. In some cases, a virtuous man momentarily wishes that he could damn a sinner but is immediately castigated for even entertaining such a thought. In most cases—eighteen in all—the character who merely considers the idea is unmistakably evil. Typical is Cutwolfe in *The Unfortunate Traveller,* the character most often cited as "proof" that Hamlet is but following an accepted convention. In the eyes of Nashe and his readers, Cutwolfe is a loathsome cutthroat whose method of revenge exemplifies the fiendish practices of the depraved Italians. Among the other seventeen characters who exemplify the convention, we find Spanish monsters, corrupt voluptuaries, presumptuous traitors, vindictive whores, and, of course, Machiavellian villains.[25] Hamlet is in very curious company.

The foregoing summary is not an attempt to argue that we can understand Hamlet's actions only if we are scholars of Renaissance stage traditions. On the contrary, it is intended to suggest that our spontaneous reactions are right, but that we have been led by scholars to mistrust them. Once we eliminate the faulty assumption that immortal vengeance was a convention unquestioned in Shakespeare's day, we are free to recognize that his audience was undoubtedly as

[25] For a detailed analysis of the evidence, see Appendix B, pp. 265–79.

morally revolted by Hamlet's malevolence in the Prayer Scene as the modern reader is. Our intuitions are valid.

Let us, then, return to our intuitive response. Hamlet states his reason for hesitating to kill Claudius, and nothing suggests that we should doubt him. The sentiment is wholly consistent with what has preceded and what will follow. At the end of the Play Scene, he had been violent and bloodthirsty, eagerly allying himself with the forces of Hell; now he viciously determines to be the agent of Claudius's damnation; shortly, in the Closet Scene, he will still be violent and murderous. Moreover, he will do exactly what he said he would do: strike out the minute he believes Claudius to be trapped in an act "that has no relish of salvation in 't." His stated motive is confirmed by his actions.[26] Once we accept the soliloquy as a true expression of Hamlet's state of mind, we see the Prayer Scene as the inevitable culmination of all that has preceded, the terrible fulfillment of the many warnings so carefully planted. It matters little whether we recall the Ghost at this point. No reminders are necessary to make us realize that Hamlet at this moment is the servant of malign forces.[27]

Once we accept the soliloquy at face value, we also see that Hamlet, at least at this point in the play, is closely allied to many of the villain-revengers in Elizabethan and Jacobean drama. Echoing many familiar conventions, he has defied patience, hailed the black night as congenial to his purpose, aligned himself with Hell, expressed a thirst for blood, and descended into savagery. Even more significant, he is following the pattern that we have found in several of Shakespeare's plays. The surrender to revenge is accompanied by a rejection of "all forms, all pressures past," and of all natural ties; it is followed by a surrender

---

[26] It has rarely been noted that Hamlet's desire to damn Claudius goes far beyond a mere desire to effect a revenge equal to the crime. If he conceives of his father's unprepared spirit as being in Purgatory, the Prayer Scene would provide the perfect opportunity for exacting an eye for an eye. If killed while repenting, Claudius would still have a considerable debt to be settled in Purgatory. But pains equal to those of his father would not satisfy Hamlet. He wants to damn Claudius irrevocably to Hell.

[27] G. Wilson Knight has been widely berated for asking a highly pertinent question. With Claudius kneeling in prayer, fighting to submit his will to God while Hamlet is deciding to take God's judgment into his own hands, "Which, then, at this moment in the play, is nearer the Kingdom of Heaven?" *Wheel of Fire*, p. 36. Knight's perceptive comments on this scene have probably been dismissed because, in an attempt to emphasize Hamlet's guilt, he felt compelled to mitigate that of Claudius. Claudius is undeniably guilty of murder and lechery and various other sins. We do not need to make of him a noble man, a man of compassion and integrity with but one small fault, to see Hamlet's vindictiveness in its true light.

to instinct with a resulting loss of rational control. Any interpretation of *Hamlet* must stand or fall on the play itself, but other plays by both Shakespeare and his contemporaries would seem to confirm the view that Hamlet has set his foot on a path that can lead only to barbarism, destruction, and Hell.

## ACT III, SCENE IV–ACT IV, SCENE I

The Closet Scene offers further evidence of Hamlet's progressive descent into evil. Finally embarked on his course, exhilarated at the perfection of his plan—conceived only seconds before in the Prayer Scene—eagerly awaiting the opportunity that may come at any moment, he enters the chamber in a mood that Gertrude immediately recognizes as murderous. At first, she is merely indignant and adopts the role of scolding parent, but the violence under his sardonic taunts suddenly warns her that she is not safe alone. As she moves to the door to seek help, he drops all pretense and seizes her roughly, revealing the rage that is seething within him. Gertrude has good reason to believe that he is about to kill her and cries out in terror. It seems highly probable that, in accordance with stage tradition, he brutally thrusts her into a chair. Perhaps he forces her down with his hands on her shoulders, his violence suggesting that he is about to strangle her. Perhaps he has his hand on his sword or even begins to draw it.[28] Although he does not consciously intend to murder Gertrude, her fears are not groundless. At the end of the Play Scene, Hamlet faced the possibility that he might kill her on impulse. One senses at this moment that he might indeed, were he not suddenly offered another outlet for his fury.

Hearing a muffled cry behind the arras, Hamlet lunges with his sword. There seems no reason to doubt that he believes he is stabbing the King. He had announced his intent to strike at just such a moment, and his shout is the triumphant pronouncement of a victor: "How now! a rat? Dead, for a ducat, dead!" Even so easily has the vermin been exterminated. Hamlet does not immediately rush over to discover the identity of the eavesdropper. He assumes he knows, and his attention rapidly turns to Gertrude. Apparently he has al-

---

[28] Hankins, *The Character of Hamlet*, p. 22. My own preference is to have Hamlet lower the sword in the Prayer Scene, not replace it, and then rush into the closet with the forgotten sword trailing in his hand. Once Gertrude senses his true emotional state, the sword becomes immediately ominous, especially if it moves suddenly as he raises his hands to stop her.

ready started his arraignment of her when, without any sign of curiosity, he lifts the arras and discovers his error.[29]

Although Hamlet contemptuously dismisses the murder of Polonius as an unfortunate but trivial mistake, we should not. From that moment he is doomed.[30] According to both Elizabethan and modern law, his intent, his "malice forethought," makes him as guilty of first-degree murder as if his victim had actually been Claudius. Not until this moment is Hamlet morally, legally, and dramatically under sentence of death. The fatal thrust through the arras marks the turning point, for not until then does Claudius realize the immediate threat to his life and change his plan of counterattack from self-defense to murder. The ensuing horrors—the madness and death of Ophelia, the revenge of Laertes, the intrigue that engulfs Laertes, Gertrude, Claudius, and Hamlet himself—all become inevitable not when Hamlet spares Claudius at prayer, but when he tries to kill him.

Many have suggested that Hamlet's fault at this point is a mere error in judgment, a rash imprudence leading him to kill the wrong man. But Polonius is basically innocent, a well-meaning though officious old fool, whose foibles merit laughter, not execution. Eavesdropping is scarcely a capital crime or proof of corruption, nor does Hamlet suggest that it is. He treats Polonius in death as he had in life: as a foolish child who, as usual, has been "too busy."[31] The unintentional slaughter of an innocent is bad enough, but Hamlet's guilt goes much further. What if the eavesdropper had, in fact, been Claudius? Even if the operating code in *Hamlet* were frankly pagan, would we applaud the hugger-mugger of an unthinking thrust at a hidden villain who does not even know what struck him? Of course Hamlet

[29] Many have argued that Hamlet cannot believe the eavesdropper to be Claudius because he has just left him in another room. If the play is produced on a modern proscenium stage with realistic settings, this interpretation might occur to the audience, though I doubt it. Surely the idea would not have occurred to Shakespeare's audience. The Elizabethan stage is completely unlocalized. A spectator never pauses to consider what room is where or how long adjoining corridors may be. The action is too swift to allow him to consider anything but what is specifically mentioned or enacted. Hamlet wanted to catch Claudius in just such a place. He assumes the eavesdropper is Claudius. Claudius believes that Hamlet assumed it was he. The spectator is given no reason to doubt it.

[30] For parallel arguments that the murder of Polonius is the turning point of the play, see Bowers, "Hamlet as Minister and Scourge," *PMLA*, LXX (1955), 740–49, and Bernard Grebanier, *The Heart of Hamlet*, pp. 190–91.

[31] See Schücking's defense of Polonius against those who would make of him a nasty, corrupt old man. *Character Problems in Shakesepare*, pp. 99–103.

becomes even more guilty if, as the present study suggests, Shakespeare has continually reinforced a Christian orientation. Hamlet's fault is not merely the rashness that leads him to kill the wrong man; it is the uncontrolled fury that leads him to kill at all.[32]

Now, turning from the corpse of Polonius with no sign of regret, Hamlet begins the castigation of his mother, castigation, we might note, for a sin considerably less than premeditated murder. Shakespeare has been held at fault in the Closet Scene for making Hamlet's emotion exceed what the facts warrant and for including dramatically irrelevant discussions of Renaissance psychology. It is quite true that the intensity of Hamlet's tirade goes far beyond Gertrude's guilt and that his indictment of her sin, together with his profound statements on reason, will, habit, and repentance, has no effect on her whatsoever. The fault, however, lies with Hamlet, not Shakespeare.

Many Christian commentators who see Hamlet as the divinely appointed minister of God's punishment view his shending of Gertrude as priest-like, as an attempt to shock her into self-knowledge and repentance. Hamlet cannot be thus absolved. A priest does not talk to a sinner as Hamlet talks to Gertrude. There is no compassion, no mercy in his tone, no suggestion that he is but waiting to hear the voluntary words of confession that will indicate his charges have struck home. On the contrary, he does not want to hear his mother speak at all. He drowns her in words, barely heeding her strangled cries.

To be sure, he passionately affirms the most thoughtful tenets of Renaissance religion and psychology. Here lies the root of the problem: he affirms them "passionately." Hamlet's "moral fervor" is often commended, but is morality a matter to be approached with fervor? Ethical principles to Hamlet are not rational concepts to be adopted after judicious consideration; they are passionate beliefs to be embraced with absolute devotion. The beliefs themselves are good. In fact, they are the very principles that infuse the entire play: the

---

[32] The strongest argument against the present discussion of Polonius's death is well stated by Robert Ornstein: "The murder of Polonius does not disturb us because it does not disturb Hamlet; it is not near our conscience because it is not near his" ("Historical Criticism and the Interpretation of Shakespeare," *Shakespeare Quarterly*, X, 1959, 4). Although I agree that any interpretation must conform to the audience's reaction, I am not at all sure that either the Elizabethan or the modern spectator has wholly identified with Hamlet at this moment. Even if he has, it seems to me that later, when he is returned to objectivity by the parallel of Laertes or after the play is over, he will see the sudden, savage thrust and Hamlet's reaction in true perspective.

Devil (whether symbolically or literally) cozens man by appealing to the senses; man blinds his judgment until his reason becomes the corrupt servant of his will; he descends step by step, led by the monster habit, until he has lost "all quantity of choice" and becomes passion's slave, the helpless prey of sensual appetite and mere instinct. If these principles are valid, should Hamlet be so blind to the implications they hold for him? Is it not terribly ironic that Hamlet, having himself just slain Polonius, should rage at the Queen for letting her blood master her judgment?[33]

It appears to me that Shakespeare includes such a detailed exposition of ethics in order to underline the clash between Hamlet's expressed ideals and his behavior. Hamlet does not excoriate Gertrude in words befitting a man of rational discipline, much less a minister of God whose only purpose is the salvation of his hearer. The obscene imaginings, apparent in Hamlet's opening soliloquy and aggravated by the Ghost, spew forth. He holds up to Gertrude a mirror in which she sees lust preying on garbage, not an image of forgiveness, or grace, or the true "nature" that she should follow. He does not appeal to love or hope or contrition; he rubs her nose in her own filth—or, rather, the filth he sees in her. One can understand why Freudians have had a field day with Hamlet. He is fascinated by the very images that nauseate him. Again and again he returns to the same picture: Gertrude wallowing in incestuous sheets, being pawed by a sweating beast.

"Taint not thy mind," the Ghost had said. The Closet Scene reveals the full irony of its command. The Ghost had couched an apparent exhortation to virtue entirely in sensual terms, and now Hamlet does the same. The clash between seeming motive and actual method in both cases is too striking to be accidental. How does Hamlet try to convince his mother that her behavior has violated rational principles? By picturing it as sensually revolting, not as ethically corrupt. "Look here, upon this picture, and on this," he insists: "Look on these two men as physical objects of sexual desire." Once having loved a man of Jove's visage, Hyperion's curls, Mars's eyes—a man of god-like form—how could she suffer the embraces of "a mildew'd ear"? It

---

[33] Goddard views this irony as crucial to our understanding of the Closet Scene. "It is not by chance that a looking glass is the central symbol throughout this scene." *The Meaning of Shakespeare,* p. 371.

may be fairly objected that Hamlet sees his father's physical beauty as a sign of his inward grace, but my point here is that he pictures Gertrude's sin entirely in terms of his own nausea at her carnal desire for the man he loathes, of his own disgust that a middle-aged woman should still feel sexual hunger at all (a reaction suggesting that, in Shakespeare's mind, Hamlet is still the very young man of the opening scenes). He charges her with being aesthetically, not spiritually, blind. What devil cozened her, dulling her senses of sight, touch, hearing, and smell? How can she tolerate the caresses of such a slimy creature? In sum, he charges her not with violating the laws of God but with sensual grossness. He does, of course, follow his arraignment with the ethical abstractions noted earlier, but is the arraignment itself phrased in a way that will lead Gertrude to a rational conviction and choice? Would a divine agent use such an appeal?[34]

Nonetheless, Gertrude's cries of anguish indicate that his words have moved her beyond mere terror to the first conviction of sin, and it seems likely that she will repent. At that moment the Ghost enters.

The final appearance of the Ghost presents an insoluble problem. Every theory about its purpose is faced with some contradiction, but rather than refute the most popular, I should like to propose a new one. Although it, too, will be met with valid objections, I offer it in the belief that it explains one important fact: the fact that despite her recognition of guilt just before the Ghost enters, Gertrude does not repent. We can all agree that the Ghost's appearance indicates that Hamlet is doing something the Ghost believes he should not be doing. What, then, is he doing? If we can judge from Gertrude's response, his words are beginning to pierce through her complacency. For the first time, she sees the "black and grained spots" tainting her own soul, and we sense that if Hamlet would but pause to heed her, if she had but a moment of calm, she might speak her first words of true repentance. At that precise moment, her beloved son has a hallucination, or so she thinks. "Alas, he's mad!" It is a cry of pain, but also a gasp of relief. Gertrude is off the hook. Immediately she reverts to her

---

[34] L. C. Knights is, in my judgment, one of the few who have faced squarely the implications of Hamlet's "fascinated insistence on lust." He finds that throughout the Closet Scene "runs the impure streak of the indulgence of an obsessive passion.... Hamlet, in short, is fascinated by what he condemns." See *Explorations* (London, 1958), p. 69, and *An Approach to Hamlet*, p. 65; see also Waldock, "*Hamlet*," p. 58.

old self, acting the role of compassionate mother tending her sick son, speaking matronly words of counsel. The fleeting moment of proffered grace is gone.[35]

Gertrude's ensuing behavior gives no hint that she has repented in any way. When Claudius enters shortly, she turns to him with relief, greeting him as "mine own lord," betraying not the slightest constraint. With the exception of a little white lie to protect her lunatic son, she tells the truth exactly as she sees it.[36] Throughout the rest of the play, she remains loyal to Claudius, even fiercely protective when he is threatened by Laertes. Gertrude, then, has done exactly as Hamlet feared: she has laid to her soul the "flattering unction" that "not [her] trespass but [his] madness speaks."

No matter what the Ghost may be, the one direct result of its appearance in the Closet Scene is to forestall Gertrude's repentance by convincing her that Hamlet is mad. May not the immediate result be a clue to the purpose?[37] Several details seem to confirm this possibility, the most significant being the Ghost's command that Hamlet "step between" Gertrude and her "fighting soul." The line is usually interpreted to mean "Comfort your mother," but the diction conveys an exact meaning that has not been noted. "To step between" is defined in the OED as "to come between . . . by way of severance, interruption, or interception." The phrase is used in this sense in Helena's vow that "deadly divorce" shall "step between" her and Bertram if her tale is not true (*All's Well*, V.iii.319). The Ghost may well mean

---

[35] Her later cry of anguish—"O Hamlet, thou hast cleft my heart in twain"—does not seem to me an intentional allusion to the theological commonplace that contrition rends the heart. The cry suggests, I think, her genuine pain at what has happened to her son rather than a confession of personal guilt. Cf. Hankins, *The Character of Hamlet*, p. 209, and Grebanier, *The Heart of Hamlet*, pp. 272–73.

[36] Her insistence that Hamlet wept repentant tears over the body befits Gertrude's sentimental character. Finding that Claudius interprets the killing as a direct threat to himself, a threat that must be dealt with as "a foul disease," she offers the pathetic excuse in a belated attempt to mitigate the impression she has just given. See Kittredge, *Sixteen Plays*, p. 1081.

[37] Many have recognized that the Ghost forestalls Gertrude's repentance and thus her reconciliation with Hamlet. See, for example, Maurice Baudin, "The Role of the Ghost in Hamlet," *Modern Language Notes*, XXXVII (1922), 185–86; W. J. Lawrence, *Shakespeare's Workshop* (Oxford, 1928), pp. 130–36; M. M. Mahood, *Shakespeare's Word Play* (London, 1957), p. 125; Grebanier, *The Heart of Hamlet*, pp. 272–73; Hankins, *The Character of Hamlet*, p. 193. To this extent, the theory proposed above is not new. Most who believe that the Ghost thwarts Gertrude's repentance believe, however, that it did not intend to do so: that, ironically, in striving to save the Queen, it actually destroys her. I am suggesting that the Ghost's appearance is as malign in purpose as in result.

exactly what he says: Hamlet is to cut Gertrude off from her fighting conscience.[38]

Many have noted the puzzling fact that Hamlet accuses himself of being "lapsed in passion" and that the Ghost has come to whet the revenger's "almost blunted purpose," although Hamlet has at last been acting with unequaled passion and directly to his purpose. Recall the speech of the Player King:

> What to ourselves in passion we propose,
> The passion ending, doth the purpose lose.
> The violence of either grief or joy
> Their own enactures with themselves destroy.

The same might be said of the violence of fury. Is it not possible that Hamlet will expend all his pent-up anger in chastising Gertrude? Hamlet knows that he has "lapsed" into an outburst of passion, not that his passion has cooled; the Ghost sees the outburst as a dangerous sign that he may be diverted from his purpose of revenge on Claudius. It does, indeed, seem possible—if the speculation be permitted—that had the Ghost not appeared and had Hamlet and Gertrude continued in the direction each was going, Gertrude would have repented, mother and son would have been reconciled, and Hamlet would have been drained of his rage. Moreover, had Gertrude joined Hamlet in loathing both Claudius and her own sin, Hamlet would have been freed of the obsession that is his main motive for revenge. All this is prevented by the Ghost's appearance.

And why does the Ghost not appear to Gertrude? The usual explanation, that the loving husband wants to spare his wife this added horror, will not withstand close scrutiny. Nor will the closely related theory that the Ghost appears to prevent Hamlet from telling Gertrude that her present husband is a murderer. Both theories assume that it is charitable to mislead Gertrude, to permit her to believe a lie. It is, indeed, easier on her, for it frees her from the necessity of facing her own guilt and that of the man to whom she has given herself. If the Ghost did show himself to Gertrude, she would know that Hamlet is sane, she would learn the truth about Claudius, and she would

---

[38] May it also be significant that Hamlet mentions "how pale" the Ghost "glares," two features that were thought to indicate a malignant spirit?

have to face herself honestly. Of course she would be put through torture, but out of such painful self-knowledge comes salvation. Would
a merciful spirit of grace want to convince her that her beloved son is
a lunatic whose words can be dismissed as mere raving? And which
would show the greater love: to warn her that she is living with a
murderer, or to let her go on blindly trusting Claudius until that mis-
placed trust causes her own death? The sole hint of compassion
in the Ghost is the puzzling reference to the "piteous action" that
Hamlet fears may distract him, which is the major objection to the
present interpretation and one for which I can find no answer.[39] All
the other evidence—the timing of the Ghost's entrance, its words, and
its effect on both Gertrude and Hamlet—indicates that its appearance
has served only one purpose: not to lead Gertrude to Heaven but to
leave her to Hell.[40]

Many believe that the moments immediately following the Ghost's
exit mark the turning point of the play: that Hamlet's rage has passed,
that he repents the death of Polonius, and that he forgives Gertrude—
in short, that he undergoes a change of heart. The interpretation does
indeed seem warranted when we first consider Hamlet's immediate
response to the Ghost. He is calm and objective, a figure of complete

[39] According to Dover Wilson, the "piteous action" indicates that the Ghost is holding out
his hands in supplication to Gertrude, begging her to see him, but suddenly he realizes in
horror that she is blinded by her state of sin and exits in shame (*What Happens in Hamlet*,
p. 255). The explanation is unconvincing. The Ghost knows well enough Gertrude's state of
soul. It would come as no shock to him.

[40] An alternative theory has considerable merit: that Shakespeare intended this final appearance of the Ghost to be, as Gertrude believes, a hallucination. This appearance is clearly
different. The Ghost is not in armor but "in his habit as he lived." He does not appear to all
who are present, only to Hamlet (and, of course, the audience). Had Shakespeare meant that
Gertrude could not see a spirit of grace because she is a sinner, he could have had Hamlet say
so, but Hamlet is frantic in his attempts to make her see. He has no idea why it appears only
to him. As F. M. Salter notes, "When Shakespeare is thus at pains to emphasize a difference,
there must be some artistic purpose involved." "Shakespeare's Interpretation of Hamlet,"
*Transactions of the Royal Society of Canada*, Sect. 2, Ser. 3, XLII (1948), 182.

This, then, may be a different Ghost—a reflection, in fact, of Hamlet's own state of mind.
Here, in his mother's private chamber, Hamlet may now visualize his father as he had often
seen him, probably, as Q₁ indicates, in his nightclothes. (Lawrence refutes the theory on the
grounds that a coinage of the brain would again be in armor, whereas Hamlet is surprised by
the change of garb [*Shakespeare's Workshop*, p. 128]. On the contrary, Hamlet mentions the
garments only as the Ghost leaves, and then only in a last desperate attempt to force Gertrude
to see it.) The effect on Gertrude and on Hamlet is the same whether the Ghost is a hallucination or the malignant spirit proposed above. The determination not to be diverted from revenge has the same result whether it is the incitement of a personified demonic force or of
Hamlet's own mind. For, of course, the Ghost in Act I had been in a sense an embodiment
of Hamlet's own desires, even though it actually appears on stage. See Richard G. Moulton,
*The Moral System of Shakespeare* (New York, 1903), pp. 299–302.

sanity and compassion, as he urges Gertrude not to dismiss his words as madness and begs her to repent "for love of grace" and confess herself to Heaven. Were he to exit when he first bids her goodnight, we might well believe that he is now acting as a willing minister of God. Immediately, however, we see that he is still a slave to the same corroding obsession. As he reaches the door to exit, he stops abruptly and turns to her again: "but go not to mine uncle's bed." Four times he bids her goodnight, three times returning to protest, to plead, to excoriate, his words mounting once again to a frenzy.[41]

Hamlet says that he repents the killing of Polonius, but are we to accept his words in their religious sense or as a simple expression of regret? In the same speech he both attributes all to the will of Heaven and warns that "worse" is yet to follow. He sees himself as guilty of no more than an unfortunate error. The words so often cited as an indication that he forgives Gertrude actually suggest something quite different. Yes, he will beg blessing of her, but only, he adds, when she is "desirous to be bless'd," only when she repents and again becomes a worthy mother. He begs forgiveness for his brutal castigation, but his words are an ironic taunt: in the corruption of such evil days, the "virtue" that wishes to reform "vice" must stoop to insinuating itself into vice's good favor. In all charity, we can only call his attitude self-righteous. While reading the play we often forget that the corpse of Polonius is in full view throughout the Closet Scene. Sitting in the theater, ever aware of the crumpled body at Hamlet's feet as he continues to berate Gertrude and protest his own virtue, how do we react to his assertion that he has been chosen by Heaven to be its "scourge and minister"?

In a thoughtful paper, Fredson Bowers proposed an interpretation that is rapidly gaining support.[42] At this moment, he argues, Hamlet recognizes that he deserves the punishment of Heaven for attempting to take his revenge in private. Since the divine command was to effect public justice, not private revenge, Heaven has punished him by making him kill the wrong man. From this point on, according to Bowers, Hamlet becomes a public rather than a private revenger, a "minister" rather than a "scourge."

The two terms are so contradictory that they are irreconcilable. The

---

[41] Note the parallel of Hamlet's behavior in the Nunnery Scene. Repeatedly he takes his leave of Ophelia only to return and renew the attack.
[42] "Hamlet as Minister and Scourge."

concept of "the scourge of God" was used to explain the paradox that
Divine Providence operates even when evil appears to triumph. "God
punisheth sinne with sinne."[43] Even the carnage of war is an indication of God's justice, for, as Henry V tells his soldiers, "war is his
beadle, war is his vengeance" (IV.i.178). In the same way, God may
choose an evil man as his agent of punishment, using "the wicked
against the wicked, for the good of his, without good to themselves."[44]
The fact that a murderous tyrant, for example, was carrying out the
will of God in punishing a sinful nation did not exonerate him, as a
metaphor popular from the twelfth to the seventeenth centuries made
clear: just as a good father burns the rod after chastening his erring
son, even so God consigns his scourge to eternal fire after it has served
its function.[45] Most simply, God elects as his scourge only a sinner
who already deserves damnation.

A minister of God, by contrast, was conceived to be a divine agent
not only in his punitive function but also in his motives and method.
Such a man might be a severe but compassionate judge, who may
sentence a criminal to death but seeks only to save the condemned
man's soul, warn other sinners, and restore order. A "hanging judge,"
motivated by personal vindictiveness, would be considered a scourge,
not a minister. In his defense of dueling, Saviolo, it will be recalled,
insists that single combat is a legitimate means of punishing evil only
if the challenger is free of any personal motive: "For I ought in all
particular injuries present unto mine eyes, not the persons either of-
fending or offended, but rather fall into consideration how much
that offense displeaseth almightie God." Even in a case so extreme as
murder, the challenger must not engage in combat because he wants
to kill his opponent. He must act, "as it were, the minister to execute
God devine pleasure": putting himself at the disposal of Providence,
he must leave the outcome to God.[46]

So long as Hamlet loathes Claudius, so long as he desires to kill, so
long as he consciously intends still further "knavery," it is doubtful
that Shakespeare's audience could consider him the minister of divine

---

[43] Beard, *The Theatre of Gods Judgements*, p. 207. See Battenhouse's analysis of Tamburlaine as a "scourge," *Marlowe's "Tamburlaine"* (Nashville, Tenn., 1941), pp. 13–15,
108–13.

[44] George Moore, *A Demonstration of God in his workes* (London, 1587), p. 118.

[45] George Whetstone, *The English Myrror* (London, 1586), p. 114.

[46] *Vicentio Saviolo his Practise*, fols. Y4$^v$ and Z1$^v$.

justice. Granted, Hamlet pronounces himself Heaven's minister, but the context makes this a terribly ironic presumption. Earlier he had recognized that he was prompted by both Heaven and Hell: he knew, that is, that God in His justice demanded the punishment of Claudius, but also that his own personal motives were evil in origin. Just before entering Gertrude's closet, he had in fact "coupled Hell" in his soliloquies both before and after Claudius's speech. He does not say that he has been Heaven's scourge but now will become its minister. He says he is both.

Even were Hamlet to exit after this curious speech, there would be ample evidence that he is acting as a scourge, pursuing a course that, although it ultimately will effect the will of Providence, is nonetheless evil in motive and method. But more is to follow. Again he is moving to exit, and again he is stopped in his tracks by his obsession. Gertrude's anguished wail—"What shall I do?"—triggers another onslaught.[47] This time Hamlet's lewd picture of Gertrude in bed, being teased into compliance by the "reechy kisses" and wandering fingers of the naked King, far surpasses any of his previous imaginings in lascivious detail and loathing revulsion.[48] His bitterness has not been purged. If anything, Hamlet's mind is more tainted now than it was before this last appearance of the Ghost. Spitting out his virulence on Claudius—this toad, this bat, this tomcat!—he rises to a state of hysteria, incoherently raving, or so it seems, about an ape creeping into a basket and Gertrude breaking her neck.[49] His emotions are so uncontrolled and his words so grotesque and erratic that to Gertrude they prove he is insane. Her stunned protestation that she will conceal his

[47] Gertrude's cry seems not a direct question to Hamlet but a wail of helplessness. See Baudin, "The Role of the Ghost," p. 186.

[48] Where Qq read "Let the blowt king tempt you again to bed" and Ff read "the blunt king," modern editions accept Warburton's emendation of "bloat." May not Shakespeare have known the sixteenth-century Scotch word *blowt,* meaning "naked"? If so, the Qq reading seems far more fitting in context.

[49] By diligent study, a scholar can reconstruct an apparent fable behind this seeming gibberish. According to Kittredge, "an ape finds a basket full of birds on the housetop and opens it. The birds fly away. The ape gets into the basket and jumps out in an attempt to fly, but falls from the roof and breaks his neck" (*Sixteen Plays,* p. 1079). Nonetheless, neither Gertrude nor a first-night audience can make any sense out of it. Since there is no suggestion that Hamlet is feigning madness at this point, it seems apparent that he has lost control. See Brents Stirling, *Unity in Shakespearian Tragedy* (New York, 1956), pp. 90–94. Stirling, in fact, presents strong arguments that we are to believe Gertrude, that Hamlet does indeed slip into "ecstasy."

words probably does not indicate an intention to help in his plot. If
her life depended on it, Gertrude could never repeat what he has said.
Indeed, even if she understood every word, and of course she could
not, what woman would repeat the humiliating and disgusting obscenities to anyone, let alone the very man against whom they were
directed? Least of all if she loved her mad son, wanted to protect him,
and believed he was not responsible for his actions.

Hamlet's return to calm in the final moments of the Closet Scene
does not, as it has in previous scenes, indicate a return to objectivity.
He has controlled his rage not by subjecting it to reason but by chan-
neling it into hardened malice. Having learned (though we cannot
guess how) that Rosencrantz and Guildenstern are to escort him to
England, he determines to trust them as "adders fang'd," and eagerly
awaits the "sweet" satisfaction of somehow turning their assumed
treachery against them and "blow[ing] them at the moon"—in fact,
of killing them. He is even more resolved in his deadly purpose, now
extending his murderous intent beyond Claudius to include two men
who, so far as we yet know, are completely innocent. Though Hamlet
assumes they are guilty, even he recognizes that his intention signifies
a commitment to evil: Rosencrantz and Guildenstern will "marshal
[him] to knavery."

His state of cold resolution is also indicated by his attitude toward
Polonius. There is no suggestion of remorse, of compassion, or even
of decent respect in his callous indifference not only to the memory
of the man he has slaughtered but to the corpse itself. "I'll lug the
guts into the neighbour room." Alive or dead, Polonius is a mere
thing to be brushed aside like an annoying gnat. The line, of course,
is horribly comic. In this grotesque bit of sardonic brutality and in his
eagerness for further knavery, Hamlet is now acting much like the
medieval Vice.[50]

[50] Hamlets who take their clue from Gertrude's white lie and exit sobbing over the corpse
have been seriously misled either by sentimental interpretations or by a comment of Schücking.
Applying his principle that eyewitness accounts of offstage events are to be believed, Schücking
argued that we are to believe Gertrude when she says that Hamlet weeps (*Character Problems,*
pp. 225–26). As he himself notes, however, such accounts are to be believed only if the audience does not have knowledge to the contrary, and in this case we do. We have seen Hamlet's
attitude toward the corpse and it was anything but tearful. Moreover, there is no possibility
that Gertrude is reporting some offstage event that we have not witnessed. As all texts indicate, only Hamlet exits at the end of the Closet Scene. There is no break between the third
and fourth acts. Claudius enters immediately. Thus it is impossible that Gertrude has seen

## ACT IV, SCENES II–III

Our impression of Hamlet at the end of the Closet Scene is confirmed by his behavior after hiding the body. He is having a thoroughly delightful time: reveling in the license of his feigned lunacy, slashing Rosencrantz and Guildenstern with his spiteful malice, rendering them helpless by his air of innocuous idiocy, suddenly darting from them to race through the castle in a childish game of hide and seek. The grotesque nonsense continues as he is brought before Claudius. Polonius is to Hamlet now no more than a potential stench in the nostrils as he makes appalling jokes about worms and maggots and cannibalism feeding on putrefaction. His tone is scarcely that of a soul purged of anger as he hurls one last sneering taunt at "mother" Claudius and exits. Although he will suffer himself to be shipped off to England (what choice does he have?), it is clear that his passion and purpose have by no means abated.

This fact, I believe, makes Claudius's soliloquy particularly significant to the audience. Earlier we had learned that Rosencrantz and Guildenstern were to escort Hamlet and that Claudius would shortly prepare their "commission." In the Closet Scene, Hamlet had announced his determination to kill them on mere suspicion, although as yet the audience had no knowledge that either the trip itself or their role is murderous in intent. Now, as Claudius dispatches the two young men, he indicates that he has not yet given them the "seal'd" orders. It seems clear that Rosencrantz and Guildenstern are now and will continue to be ignorant of the commission's true content. Had Shakespeare intended otherwise, he could easily have so indicated. Stoll's basic principle cannot be repeated too often: in interpreting a Shakespearean play, we should consider only what the audience actually sees and hears. The audience hears that the commission is sealed, immediately hears Rosencrantz and Guildenstern ordered out of the royal presence and sees them exit, and then hears Claudius, now alone on the stage, reveal his treacherous plans. When we see the play on the stage, the obvious implication is that Claudius

---

Hamlet in tears at some time between the acts. (Even Q₂ indicates that action is continuous, despite the stage direction opening IV.i: *Enter King, and Queene, with Rosencrans and Guyldensterne.* The editor is merely following the classical principle that all characters in a given scene are listed among those who "enter," even if they are already on stage. At the end of the Closet Scene, the only stage direction is *Exit,* referring to Hamlet alone.)

can voice his intentions only to himself, and thus that Rosencrantz and Guildenstern know nothing of his plot.[51] Hamlet has sworn to "blow them at the moon." Before he finally faces the one man who is guilty, will he kill two more innocents?

[51] Stage directions are incomplete in $Q_2$ and $F_1$. Neither indicates an exit for Rosencrantz and Guildenstern; both indicate merely *"Exit,"* not *"Exeunt,"* when Hamlet leaves and again when Claudius completes his soliloquy. Even so, it seems clear that Rosencrantz and Guildenstern exit when Claudius commands them, for the third time, to make haste. His repeated insistence on speed suggests that his hearers are not responding as he wishes, perhaps standing in baffled silence, stunned by all that has happened, perhaps waiting for further instructions. The final curt command, "pray you make haste," suggests a tone of exasperation that would require immediate compliance. Their exit is also indicated by Claudius's immediate shift in tone and point of view. There are no hearers present as he turns his thoughts inward to address his intentions to England. (In $Q_1$ Hamlet and the Lords *exeunt* together, after which Gertrude is dismissed. Claudius is alone for the soliloquy.)

# CHAPTER VIII

# The Mirror Up to Hamlet

## ACT IV, SCENE IV

Hamlet's pause while en route to England to debate, once again, the moral issue presents a serious problem. Was the soliloquy ever included in productions during Shakespeare's day? It does not appear in $Q_1$ or $F_1$, nor do we find any sign in these versions that something has been cut. Fortinbras sends a captain to beg safe passage through Danish territory and exits. Hamlet does not appear. $Q_2$ provides our only text for Hamlet's soliloquy and the brief introductory dialogue with the Captain. Even there, however, we have good reason to doubt that Shakespeare included the sequence in his final stage version.

Apparently Hamlet is on a casual saunter through his domain, accompanied by his friends and the usual attendants, when he sees the troops of Fortinbras. After a quiet colloquy with the Captain, Rosencrantz asks if it falls within the royal pleasure to move on. It does not, and Hamlet sends his compliant entourage ahead while he pauses to meditate. Although theoretically Hamlet is being conveyed "with haste" out of Denmark, we find no mention of his destination, no sense of urgency, no suggestion that he is a dangerous lunatic under close guard.

At this point in the play, the soliloquy is as irrelevant as the situation. It serves the same function and debates the same issue as "To be or not to be." We are back in the third act. At the opening of "How all occasions do inform against me," Hamlet has not yet made his final decision between the warnings of conscience and the demands of "honor." He still has the "means" to effect his revenge; he is still reproaching himself for cowardly inaction. By the close of the soliloquy he has determined to reject all thoughts but those of murder.

The Hamlet we have just seen leaving the Danish court with defiant scorn had long since been confirmed in bloody thoughts, had long since cast off coward conscience. Moreover, the audience knows that Hamlet is being forcibly conveyed to England and thus, at least temporarily, has lost the means to do anything at all. For these reasons, it seems possible that Shakespeare originally intended the entire scene for earlier in the play (probably before the mousetrap), that he realized it was redundant, tentatively shifted it to its present position, but ultimately cut it for the stage version. Whatever the explanation, the soliloquy clearly makes neither logical nor dramatic sense in Shakespeare's final version of the play.

It represents, in short, one of many loose ends in *Hamlet*. The play is full of inconsistencies that defy the logic of the plot. Characters must be told things they already know; they already know things they have not yet been told. Horatio's shifting role, Hamlet's shifting age, divergent accounts of Ophelia's death—such curiosities can never be "interpreted" according to what happens in the play; they can only be "explained" by speculating about Shakespeare's method of writing it. Such inattention to details should come as no surprise to us, for we find it throughout the Shakespearean canon, from the careless errors in apprentice plays such as *King John* to the notorious loose ends in mature works such as *Macbeth* and, especially, *King Lear*. Many problems can be easily explained as the result of Shakespeare's attention to dramatic impact and thematic purpose in preference to factual accuracy; many can be explained by studying how Shakespeare used a specific source. Almost none present problems crucial to interpretation.[1] "How all occasions" is a case in point. The only detail in it that conflicts with the present interpretation, Hamlet's statement that he still has the means to effect his revenge, also conflicts with the facts of the plot. In all other respects, the soliloquy not only harmonizes with but lends additional support to the preceding analysis.

If, as $F_1$ suggests, Shakespeare cut the passage for the final stage version, he was wise. The issues have long been defined, and Hamlet's thoughts were sufficiently bloody when he taunted "mother" Claudius and left for England. A pause while Hamlet asks the same

---

[1] The final dialogue between Hamlet and Horatio does, however, present such a problem. See below, pp. 227–30.

question and gets the same answer would slow the dramatic momentum. Nonetheless, we are fortunate in having the soliloquy. "To be or not to be" and "How all occasions" exactly parallel each other in the issues debated and the decision reached, and the interpretation of one can be checked against that of the other. Such a comparison confirms the analysis of Hamlet's dilemma presented in Chapter VI.

> What is a man,
> If his chief good and market of his time
> Be but to sleep and feed? a beast, no more.
> Sure, he that made us with such large discourse,
> Looking before and after, gave us not
> That capability and god-like reason
> To fust in us unused. Now, whether it be
> Bestial oblivion, or some craven scruple
> Of thinking too precisely on the event,
> A thought which, quarter'd, hath but one part wisdom
> And ever three parts coward, I do not know
> Why yet I live to say 'This thing's to do.'

"What is a man?"—what is it "to be"? Is it to do no more than sleep and feed, to retreat into the bestial oblivion some men call "resignation"? Is it to do no more than passively assent to the nay-saying of fearful conscience, to let our God-given power of reason surrender its right to choose and act? In His infinite wisdom, is it conceivable that God gave man such large discourse and yet commanded him not to use it? If reason's proper function is merely to think precisely on the probable consequences of an action and to reject what is forbidden solely out of fear of punishment, is not God's "reason" but the craven excuse of a coward?[2]

The second half of the soliloquy, Hamlet's comparison of himself with Fortinbras, is usually interpreted as a thematic statement by Shakespeare: as a clue that Fortinbras is a moral exemplar against which Hamlet is to be judged. In the light of the moral issues defined

---

[2] Compare the analysis of Arthur Sewell: "Hamlet is here persuading himself that, whatever evil and whatever death be the consequence of action, man's reason is god-like and should not grow stale through lack of use. To address ourselves to the world in action may involve us in evil; but not so to address ourselves is to be less than a man" (*Character and Society in Shakespeare*, Oxford, 1951, p. 59). Sewell, however, would probably not agree that the evil into which action precipitates man has any theological referent.

in the soliloquy and of Shakespeare's treatment of Fortinbras both in this scene and throughout the play, should we be as blind as Hamlet to the contradictions in his reasoning? He knows Fortinbras to be "puff'd" with "divine ambition" (the divinity of which the context makes ironic). He knows that the current campaign against Poland has no justification. Twenty thousand men are being led to their death, and for what? For a worthless patch of ground, an eggshell, a straw. For "no profit but the name." In the first part of the scene, Hamlet instinctively sees the campaign as an abscess; the band of marauders whom Fortinbras had gathered were an "imposthume" that would destroy Norway if their lawlessness exploded within her borders. The only rationalization for the campaign, then, is expediency: to drain the poison off into Poland before it "breaks inward."

Nowhere in prior references to Fortinbras or in Hamlet's comments on the campaign do we find even the name, no matter how hollow, of honor. Curiously, however, in the middle of the soliloquy, Hamlet begins to twist this example, an example that he fully recognizes to be "gross as earth," until it exhorts him. Yet in Hamlet's very approval of Fortinbras, there lies an implicit condemnation. This "delicate and tender prince" is like a spoiled and heedless child, contemptuously "making mouths" at the consequences of his actions. Conscience quite obviously has not succeeded in making a coward of Fortinbras, and his example puts Hamlet to "shame." Why? Because he sees

> The imminent death of twenty thousand men,
> That, for a fantasy and trick of fame,
> Go to their graves like beds, fight for a plot
> Whereon the numbers cannot try the cause,
> Which is not tomb enough and continent
> To hide the slain.

Incited by the prospect of meaningless carnage over a worthless cause, Hamlet is "shamed" into resolution.

Can Shakespeare intend the audience to view Fortinbras as a moral norm? Is an undertaking "for a fantasy and trick of fame" to be equated with an "enterprise of great pitch and moment"? Shakespeare is never one to dismiss the butchery of war casually, least of all when the cause is tainted. The parallel between Fortinbras and Troilus is instructive: both will "find quarrel in a straw when honour's at the stake."[3] Is this "rightly to be great"? If so, then Hotspur is the epitome of virtue. In the abstract, Hamlet's definition of honor sounds commendable, but the example that exhorts him shows that he is not defining honor at all, but rationalizing his instinctive admiration for a man who can act on his own initiative without restraint, for a man, moreover, in whom the "taints of liberty"—violence, capriciousness, rashness, defiance—are to be commended as "the flash and outbreak of a fiery mind." Polonius would have admired Fortinbras on exactly the same grounds. Hamlet has come a long way from the man who held up Horatio as his ideal.[4]

References to Fortinbras early in the play have prepared the audience to see him objectively at this point as well as through Hamlet's eyes. Horatio presented a clear picture of him in the opening scene. Although the elder Fortinbras had forfeited his lands to Hamlet's father by a compact "well ratified by law and heraldry," young Fortinbras had "shark'd up a list of lawless resolutes" and set out to recapture his inheritance illegally. In Horatio's eyes, Fortinbras is a brash and inexperienced young hothead. Drawing to himself a band of desperados itching for a fight, he has defied the law, betrayed his father's words, and set out on a completely spurious campaign. Further information confirms Horatio's estimate. Knowing that his invalid uncle, the reigning monarch, would disapprove, Fortinbras had been acting on his own and in secret. Learning of the plot, the uncle immediately commanded his wayward nephew to desist and was so pleased at Fortinbras's prompt obedience that he gave the good boy a plum: an annual income and a commission to use the same renegades in a campaign against the Polacks. With these facts in mind, the audience should have little trouble viewing both Fortinbras and the Polish campaign in their true light. This rash young Prince has been diverted to a pointless campaign in Poland primarily to keep him and his army of marauders out of trouble. He is without question a man of action, but the completely amoral man of action: "strong in arm" but weak in right reason, "exposing all that is mortal

---

[3] It may be worth noting that, in her madness, Ophelia "spurns enviously at straws."

[4] Cf. Knights, *An Approach to Hamlet,* p. 83, and G. K. Hunter, "The Heroism of Hamlet," *Stratford-upon-Avon Studies* 5 (1963), pp. 95–96.

and unsure / To all that fortune, death and danger dare." For a brittle
eggshell, Fortinbras will dare defeat, death, and damnation. Can we
possibly want Hamlet to follow his example?

Now Hamlet is to vanish from the stage for over half an hour, the
fact primarily responsible for the lull often noted in the fourth act. If
the conclusions of this study are valid, the lull is essential for the audience. Shakespeare has made Hamlet such a compelling figure that
most of us have undoubtedly been trapped into identifying with him.
In the period since his decision in "To be or not to be," events have
moved at whirlwind speed, and, despite the many warnings to be
found in the play, only a saint with the perspective of Aquinas and
the objectivity of Socrates could fail to be caught up in the emotional
maelstrom. Our instincts, too, are on the side of action. Our instincts,
too, are on the side of the rebel who refuses to tolerate injustice. When
we learn, moreover, that Hamlet is being led to his death by the most
underhanded treachery, we may embrace the cause of the underdog
so thoroughly that we lose all perspective.

The five hundred lines intervening between Hamlet's departure
for England and his reappearance in the graveyard seem designed to
jolt us back into objectivity. In the scenes involving Ophelia and
Laertes, Gertrude and Claudius, there is no character with whom we
identify. Hamlet has our emotional allegiance and thus we stand
outside the action. Throughout the play, Shakespeare has given us
brief periods in which to regain perspective, but each time he has immediately pulled us back into Hamlet's struggle. This time he forces
on us a full half hour during which we cannot be misled into seeing
through Hamlet's eyes.

### Act IV, Scene v

To what purpose, then, do we pause for two extended episodes
exhibiting Ophelia's madness? They are, of course, unnecessary to the
plot itself. The death of Polonius provides Laertes with sufficient motive for his revenge, and Shakespeare could easily have killed Ophelia
without adding the mad scenes. For these reasons, some have suggested that Shakespeare was sidetracked by his own virtuosity, that
Ophelia's madness is "a beautiful dramatic luxury" that could be cut

without changing the dramatic issue.[5] If the play's basic premise is that Hamlet is morally obligated to take revenge, this view is convincing, for then Ophelia is merely an unfortunate victim of an arrow that missed its mark. If, however, the basic premise is that Hamlet should not take revenge, her madness and ensuing death are frightful consequences of a course that should never have been initiated.

Although we had suffered for Ophelia in the Nunnery Scene, we have long forgotten her, and our sympathies are with the absent Hamlet as she now enters. We are, or should be, shocked into a new perspective. Hamlet's earlier diatribe and rash thrust through the arras have taken a terrible toll. There is nothing grotesque in Ophelia's madness, nothing that would alienate an audience. She is completely pathetic, painfully vulnerable. The confused terrors that have driven her to lunacy are laid bare. And those terrors were planted by Hamlet. We can understand her grief for her father and her baffled pain at being rejected by her lover. But why these bawdy songs? The images are those that Hamlet created in her mind. Ophelia senses that, in some horrible way, lust and her father's death are connected. Hamlet had given her reason to think so. As she sees the awful sequence of events, Hamlet had gone mad for her love, had revealed the cause of that madness in the filth spewed forth in the Nunnery Scene and in the lewd jokes at her expense before the play, and immediately thereafter had killed her father. Ophelia has been crushed by forces that she could not possibly understand. And Hamlet is to blame. He has tainted more minds than his own. That the audience is meant to focus on Ophelia's madness alone, without any distractions, seems clear from the fact that she enters twice. Her mad entrance could have been delayed until the arrival of Laertes, but then our attention is diverted by a new plot consideration, a new threat against Hamlet. In Ophelia's first appearance, our attention is undivided. The plot stands still as Shakespeare provides a parenthesis of dramatic commentary on what has preceded.

Once he has shocked us out of identifying with Hamlet and begun to show us the consequences of his past actions, Shakespeare proceeds to suggest in an unmistakable parallel the implications of the course Hamlet has chosen, a course, we have every reason to believe, that he

---

[5] Schücking, *Character Problems*, p. 172.

is still determined to follow. As a result of his decision, Hamlet
may become a Laertes.[6] The parallels between the two young men
are so striking and our emotional reactions so obvious that it is surprising to find that the function of Laertes in this scene can be mis-
interpreted.[7] Laertes can be viewed as a norm, against whom Hamlet
is to be judged and found wanting, only if we are determined to prove
that the basic ethic of the play is a condemnation of thinking precisely
on the event. Laertes, moreover, can be considered an admirable young
man only if we forcibly suppress our instinctive reactions. Whenever
I see the play, I wonder at those who, in the calm of the study, hail
this rash and dangerous hothead as "a blast of fresh air" who has the
loyalty and courage to act as we want Hamlet to act.[8]

Laertes is not a whiff of fresh air. He is a hurricane. He rushes into
the palace in an uncontrolled rage, roaring for blood, having no
idea whom he seeks but ready, "swoopstake," to smash all in his way.
He defies his sovereign King, his conscience, and his God:

> To hell, allegiance! vows, to the blackest devil!
> Conscience and grace, to the profoundest pit!
> I dare damnation. To this point I stand,
> That both the worlds I give to negligence,
> Let come what comes; only I'll be revenged
> Most throughly for my father.

This is one of the most dreadful speeches in all Shakespeare, matched
in its total surrender to malignant fury only by the terrible curses of
Lear.

Do we really want Hamlet to act this way? In point of fact, he has
said exactly the same things. The parallels are too close to be mere
coincidence. Laertes' assertion that patience would proclaim him a
bastard to his father echoes the Ghost's appeal to Hamlet's "nature."
Both swear to forget all forms, all vows, all allegiances, and to devote
themselves wholly to revenge. Both reject conscience. Both determine
to dare damnation. Both openly align themselves with Hell and the

[6] For a parallel discussion of Laertes' function in the play, see Vyvyan, *Shakespearean Ethic,*
pp. 49–52.

[7] See, for example, J. Dover Wilson, *What Happens in Hamlet,* pp. 271 and 275, and
Adams, *Hamlet,* p. 306.

[8] Knight, *Wheel of Fire,* p. 40.

demonic. The only difference is that Laertes compresses all of these desperate resolutions into one furious minute, and expresses them so violently that we cannot miss their implications, especially because this time the virulence is directed against our hero. Throughout the past three acts, Hamlet has said no less. Even if we have been trapped before by our emotions, we may now begin to see him in a new light.

The plot material in the three episodes involving Laertes—his return, his reaction to Ophelia's madness, and his acquiescence in the King's plot against Hamlet—could all have been handled in one scene of perhaps five minutes. But Shakespeare does not let us off that easily. He makes us watch Laertes in three different situations, in each emphasizing again and again the relevance of his example to Hamlet. In Laertes' moving response to Ophelia, we see that he is not a complete reprobate whose example can be dismissed. Like Hamlet, he has genuine cause for his grief. Like Hamlet, he has genuine cause for his fury. Like Hamlet, he wins our sympathy in his passion for revenge. In fact, we are almost trapped again as Laertes weeps for his sister. We will not be able to consider him merely a malicious threat against Hamlet. We must see him, too, as a suffering human being. Thus the parallel of Laertes has even more meaning in the ensuing scene of intrigue with Claudius.

### ACT IV, SCENE VII

The scene opens in complete calm as quietly, slowly, the parallel is enforced. The colloquy is too long for its dramatic function, but the slow pace seems designed to ensure our objectivity. A letter arrives from Hamlet, indicating by its insolent tone that he, too, has arrived in Denmark roaring for blood. He will shortly arrive in Laertes' mood. Will he act like Laertes? Now we stand back and watch exactly to what the "sickness in [Laertes'] blood" will lead him.

It leads Laertes to become mere putty in the King's hands. Determined to act on his own initiative in the name of honor, he is so blinded by rage that he becomes a mere pawn in another man's plot. Claudius appeals to him as did the Ghost to Hamlet. Did Laertes really love his father? Beneath that appearance of filial devotion is there a "heart"? In other words, does Laertes have "nature" in him? Having planted a challenge that few men could withstand, least of all a man already distracted by grief and rage, Claudius launches into an extremely revealing argument:

> There lives within the very flame of love
> A kind of wick or snuff that will abate it;
> And nothing is at a like goodness still;
> For goodness, growing to a plurisy
> Dies in his own too much: that we would do,
> We should do when we would: for this 'would' changes
> And hath abatements and delays as many
> As there are tongues, are hands, are accidents:
> And then this 'should' is like a spendthrift sigh,
> That hurts by easing. But, to the quick o' the ulcer;
> Hamlet comes back: what would you undertake,
> To show yourself your father's son in deed
> More than in words?

Laertes reveals the extent of his willingness:

> To cut his throat i' the church.

Claudius finds him apt:

> No place, indeed, should murder sanctuarize,
> Revenge should have no bounds.

One is stunned to find some of the greatest of Shakespearean scholars interpreting Claudius's speech as the moral of the entire play.[9] By this argument, a villain incites his pawn to a rage that would embrace the most blasphemous murder. Claudius's statement that no place "should murder sanctuarize" not only means that no murderer (in this case, Hamlet) should be able to find protection from just punishment even in church. It also means that not even a church should provide sanctuary against murder, for "revenge should have no bounds." Can these words possibly express Shakespeare's considered moral judgment?

---

[9] Gervinus found Claudius's speech "more calculated for Hamlet" than for Laertes (*Shakespeare Commentaries*, trans. F. E. Bennett, rev. ed., 1883, p. 557). Bradley apparently agreed. Because the words are "not in character" for Claudius, they "are all the more important as showing what was in Shakespeare's mind at the time" (*Shakespearean Tragedy*, p. 91). To J. Dover Wilson, the speech contains "the whole moral of *Hamlet*." *What Happens in Hamlet*, p. 265.

What, actually, is Claudius's argument? Most simply, that if we would do something, we should do it immediately lest our determination weaken. Claudius is not speaking of what we *should* do in the line of duty but of what we *would* do, of what we choose to do. In other words, "Kill Hamlet while you are moved to revenge by grief and rage, or you may delay so long that you lose the impetus to do it." Basically Claudius is saying exactly the same thing that the Player King said, but to a different purpose:

> What to ourselves in passion we propose,
> The passion ending, doth the purpose lose.

Claudius perverts this truth about human nature into an ethical principle, but the witness of the entire play denounces that principle as false. He is arguing that man should be the "slave of passion," instinctively responsive to its demands. Yet all of the characters in the play who have been moved by passion to act—Claudius, Gertrude, Fortinbras, Laertes, and Hamlet himself—all would have done well to "think precisely on the event." More specifically, the play suggests that tragedy would have been averted if both Hamlet and Laertes had not chosen to act on a proposal "of violent birth but poor validity," but had waited until the passion had subsided and, with it, the purpose.

We cannot possibly accept the King's argument or Laertes' violence as moral guides to the play when we see their results. Claudius' suggestion of a duel with Laertes' foil unbated is bad enough, but at least it leaves Hamlet a chance. Laertes, however, is led to a more abhorrent plan: poisoning his unbated sword. He has lost all pretense to honor. If we idealize him into a figure of noble daring, we are deaf to the implications of his speeches at the end of the play. He knows that he has been trapped by his own treachery, a plan on which he had embarked in defiance of conscience. The "savageness in unreclaimed blood" that Polonius had so complacently approved ultimately destroys Laertes. Will it destroy Hamlet?

Laertes, then, does provide a standard against which we judge Hamlet, but he is not a moral exemplar whom we wish our hero to emulate. He allows us to evaluate objectively the course that we have every reason to believe Hamlet is still pursuing. Laertes is Hamlet; Hamlet might be when he next appears.

# CHAPTER IX

## The Readiness Is All

### ACT V, SCENE I

When we next see Hamlet, he is a changed man. In defiance of every probability established thus far in the play, he has apparently checked his own descent into Hell. It is not a barbaric young revenger, consumed by rage and confirmed in murderous thoughts, who appears in the graveyard, but a mature man of poise and serenity. This sudden reversal of direction in a tragedy is curious: it is as if Macbeth were to repent in the fifth act. In some wholly inexplicable way, Hamlet seems to have come to terms with himself.

When did the change take place? No hypothetical reconstruction of offstage events during his absence can provide an answer. Has Hamlet simply undergone a therapeutic sea voyage? Or later, when we hear of his miraculous escape, are we to understand that the intervention of "divinity" somehow changed his purpose? Apparently not, for his letter to Claudius indicates that he has landed in Denmark as bitter in mood and thus as bloody in thought as when he had departed. Has something happened between his landing and his meeting with Horatio? Shakespeare offers no clue. Nonetheless, when Hamlet enters the graveyard, his fury is spent. The present study suggests that the change in Hamlet is symbolized in the Graveyard Scene. I say "symbolized" rather than "enacted" for we do not see the change take place. Hamlet does not enter the graveyard in rage and leave in peace; if anything, as many will object, the opposite seems true. Even so, I am convinced that the Graveyard Scene represents the turning point in Hamlet himself.[1]

The audience is prepared for Hamlet's new orientation by the open-

---

[1] See a parallel discussion in an essay by Maynard Mack that is noteworthy for its fresh insights and sensitivity: "The World of *Hamlet*," *Yale Review*, XLI (1952), 520–23. See also the perceptive comments of H. S. Wilson, *Design of Shakespearian Tragedy*, pp. 37ff.

ing colloquy between the two gravediggers. Although the episode has almost universally been considered mere comic relief, in fact it serves four important functions. First, it reminds us again that the world of *Hamlet* is a Christian world. The primary concern of even these two clowns is the issue of salvation. In their comments on Ophelia's burial rights, on the difference between voluntary and involuntary action, and on the gallows that do well to those that do ill, we are reminded that man's ultimate responsibility is to divine law, and that judgment awaits. Second, the gravediggers' parody of legal distinctions emphasizes the basis on which that final judgment will be made. If a man willingly goes to the water and drowns himself, he is guilty of sin, but if the water comes to the man, he is not. Guilt is determined by whether or not an act is voluntary. Is this not a comic statement pointing to the resolution of the play? If Hamlet goes to Claudius, he will be guilty of premeditated murder. As we shall note shortly, Shakespeare seems to do everything possible to indicate that the final killing is thrust upon him. Third, our attention is riveted on death, not only by the preparations for Ophelia's funeral but also by the grotesque riddles. The gravemaker maintains Adam's profession; he builds stronger than even the gallows-maker; his houses last until Doomsday. Death was and is and ever shall be. To this, the body must come.

The fourth function of the scene is the reestablishment of perspective. Just as we see Hamlet and Horatio enter, the first gravedigger sends his companion to fetch a stoup of liquor and begins lustily singing of his lost youth and love. This time we are not immediately thrust back into a state of tension when Hamlet appears. Somehow the question of his revenge seems unimportant. We are concerned with the immediate moment: with the idiotic nonsense of a witty old rascal and a country bumpkin, with an open grave, with the painful reminder that life is fleeting, and with a skull that is suddenly clunked unceremoniously onstage. We are, in other words, made aware of the ultimate insignificance of even the most agonizing struggles of any single human being, for death will come, but life will go on. Of course the scene is comic in its effect, but in the very act of laughing we gain perspective.[2]

[2] The Porter in *Macbeth* serves a function similar to that of the gravediggers. In his drunken meanderings, he not only provides grotesque comment on the inevitability of Hell and damnation for sinners; he also reminds us that somewhere, outside the maelstrom engulfing the principals, there is a normal world going on unconcerned.

Now Hamlet speaks, and we hear a new tone.[3] In the shadow of the grave, his disposition is positively sunny. So, for the moment, is that of the audience. In the theater, one is struck by the fact that the Graveyard Scene is a breathing time of complete relaxation and pleasure. The threat of Claudius and Laertes is forgotten. Hamlet's fury is forgotten. For the first time in the play we are completely free to laugh without bitterness and to enjoy our hero without reservations. And, curiously, we are free because we, together with Hamlet, are looking at death. There is no hint of morbidity in Hamlet's tone.[4] There is wry and affectionate humor in his "Alas, poor Yorick," as he demonstrates by immediately turning to Horatio and recalling the delightful games of his youth. An actor who plays Hamlet as plunged into deep mourning makes lugubrious nonsense of Yorick's infinite jest. Moreover, Hamlet's sudden disgust at the smell is not morbid. Putrefaction does smell—that is simply a fact. We are still free to smile, though probably not to laugh, as Hamlet puts down the skull in revulsion and muses that even Alexander might eventually serve only to stop a bung-hole. His tone is one of detached, bemused irony, not agonized despair.

The philosophy underlying the graveyard meditations has been called cynical, nihilistic, and fatalistic, the philosophy of a man driven by despair and obsessed with death. If this is true of Hamlet's philosophy, then it is also true of Christianity. The modern agnostic may dismiss the Christian preoccupations with death and the grave as morbid and life-denying, but he should not assume that Shakespeare's audience shared this view. Renaissance man would have been startled to hear that meditating on death is a sign of an unhealthy mind. Although many have noted that the scene reflects the traditions of *de contemptu mundi* and *memento mori*, little attention has been paid to their implications in interpreting the play. Shakespeare's audience considered meditating on death a spiritual exercise, even as devout Christians do today. The only difference lies in the more brutal real-

---

[3] As Granville-Barker noted with his alert eye for staging, Hamlet is changed in appearance. He has shed his garments of mock-madness but should not return to his sable suit of mourning. A wise director will have him appear with his "sea-gown" still "scarf'd" about him. *Prefaces to Shakespeare*, I, 232–34.

[4] "The so-called 'graveyard imagination' of the Romantics, by saturating Hamlet in this scene with self-centered gloom, spoiled the chief dramatic contrast: the opposition of the hero's light mood to the deathliness of his environment." G. R. Elliott, *Scourge and Minister*, p. 161.

ism with which the Elizabethan faced the unavoidable facts. Beginning with the Dance of Death at the end of the fourteenth century, the skeleton became the accepted Christian symbol of death, and by the Elizabethan period the skull had become an extremely popular symbol for everything from tomb monuments to jewelry. Falstaff indicates its purpose in his joke about Bardolph's red face: "I make as good use of it as many a man doth of a Death's-head or a memento mori: I never see thy face but I think upon hell-fire" (*1 Henry IV*, III.iii.32–35). When Doll asks why he does not begin to patch up his old body for Heaven, he begs her to forgo that unpleasant subject: "Peace, good Doll! do not speak like a death's-head; do not bid me remember mine end" (*2 Henry IV*, II.iv.255–60).

The skull was to remind man not of the futility of life but of the inevitability and the meaning of death. The emblematic tradition fused with the meditative tradition to make of the skull a sermon-in-little: "Remember, man, the day of your death is coming and with it your day of judgment. Since you know not the appointed day, keep your soul ever in readiness. Look on death and know that the things of this world are transitory. Your life on earth is but a parenthesis in a vast eternity. Your body is for worms; your soul is for God." Meditating on maggots and bones and putrefaction was an exercise of faith. Its aim was to instill disgust for that which would rot into corruption, and thus to turn man's eyes to the eternal.[5] In many paintings of Magdalene and St. Francis, the skull is an emblem signifying the spiritual joy man attains when he learns to live daily with the knowledge of his own death.[6] Shall we call Mary Queen of Scots morbid because she had a watch in the form of a death's-head? Every time she lowered the jaw to read the hands, she was to be reminded of the end to which each fleeting minute was drawing her.

The Graveyard Scene is further illuminated by an extremely interesting parallel pointed out by Louis B. Martz in the meditations of Luis de Granada.[7] Although Martz was interested primarily in noting Shakespeare's relation to the meditative tradition, it seems to me quite

---

[5] When Hamlet speaks of "my Lady Worm," he seems to be echoing Job 17:14: "I have said to corruption, Thou art my father: to the worm, Thou art my mother, and my sister." Hankins, *The Character of Hamlet*, p. 185.

[6] For example, see Bellini's *St. Francis in Ecstasy* and Titian's *The Penitent Magdalene*. Note also *The Temptation of St. Anthony* by David Teniers, the Younger.

[7] *The Poetry of Meditation* (New Haven, Conn., 1954), pp. 137–38.

likely that *Of Prayer and Meditation*, translated into English in five editions by 1602, had a direct influence on *Hamlet*. A series of passages is of such interest that I shall quote rather extensively, indicating possible parallels.

The meditation for Wednesday night is on the hour of death: a consideration of "How filthie and lothsome the bodie is after it is dead: And of the buryinge of it in the grave."[8]

[The man meditating on death] considereth and waygheth with himselfe, that the lodginge which they will prepare for him in the earth, shalbe strait, and narrowe, that it shalbe also obscure, stinkinge, full of wormes, maggottes, bones and dead mens skulles, and withall so horrible, that it shalbe verie ircksome to them that be alive onely to looke upon it.... He seeth that his bodie which he was wont to make so much of, his bellie which he esteimed for his God, his mowth for whose delightes the lande and sea coulde scarselie serve, and his fleash for which golde and silke was wont to be woven with great curiositie, and a soft bed prepared to laie it in, must now be laide in such a filthie and miserable donghill, where it shalbe troden upon, & eaten with fowle wormes, and maggottes, and within fewe daies be of as owglie a forme, as a dead Carrion that lyeth in the feildes, insomuch that the waiefaringe man will stoppe his nose, and ronne awaie in great hast to avoid the stinkinge savour of it.

Of course Shakespeare needed no source to suggest the "convention of politic worms" partaking of supper on Polonius, or the stench of a rotting corpse, or the fact that "your fat king and your lean beggar" are all equal to hungry maggots. What this particular passage does show is that Shakespeare's satirical treatment of the most gruesome detail was in perfect harmony with the spirit and aims of devout Christians.[9] The tradition of meditation required that man use all of his senses in order to fully experience what death would actually be: he must feel the hard ground and narrow box, see the bones and worms and maggots, smell the decaying flesh.

As we read further in the meditation, we hear many specific echoes, both in the rhetorical form and in the specific images:

---

[8] Quotations are from the Douay edition of 1612, fols. 201$^\text{v}$–222$^\text{r}$.

[9] This fact should not be misconstrued to exonerate Hamlet for his malicious jokes about the corpse of Polonius. Luis would be the first to condemn him. At the end of the Closet Scene, Hamlet is not meditating on the meaning of his own death; he is sardonically dismissing the death of the man he has killed.

Consider, in what case the bodie is, after the soule is departed out of it. What thinge is more esteemed than the bodie of a prince whiles he is a live? And what thinge is more contemptible, and more vyle, than the verie same bodie when it is dead? Where is then that former pryncely maiestie become? Where is that royall behaviour, and glorious magnificence? Where is that highe authoritie, and soveraintie? Where is that terrour, and feare, at the beholdinge of his presence? Where is that cappinge, and kneelinge, and speakinge unto him with such reverence, aud subjection? ["Where be his quiddities now, his quillets . . . ?"] How quicklie is all this gaye pompe utterly overthrowen, and come to nothinge, as if it had bene but a mere dreame, or a plaie on a stage, that is dispatched in an howre?

Then out of hande the wyndinge sheete is provided, and brought forrh, which is the richest jewell he maie take with him out of this lyfe. . . .

Then doe they make a hole in the earthe of seven or eight foote longe, (and no longer though it be for Alexander the great, whom the whole world coulde not holde) and with that finalle rowme onelie must his bodie be contente. ["The very conveyances of his lands will hardly be in this box; and must the inheritor himself have no more, ha?"] There they appoint him his howse for ever. There he taketh up his perpetuall lodginge untill the last daye of generall Judgment ["the houses that he makes last till doomsday"], in companie with other dead bodies: There the wormes crawle out to geve him his interteinement: To be short, there they let him downe in a poore white sheete, his face beinge covered with a napkin, and his handes and feete fast bownde: which trewlie needeth not, for he is then sure enough for breakinge out of prison, neither shall he be able to defende himselfe against anie man. There the earthe receyveth him into her lappe: There the bones of dead men kisse, and welcome him: There the dust of his auncesters embraceth him, and invite him to that table, and howse, which is appointed for all men livinge. . . . Why shoulde a man desire and gape after so manie thinges for this present lyfe, being so shorte as it is, seinge so litle will content him at the howre of his death?

Then the grave maker taketh the spade, and pykeaxe into his hande ["a pick-axe, and a spade, a spade"], and beginneth to tumble downe bones upon bones, and to tread downe the earth verie harde upon him. ["Did these bones cost no more the breeding, but to play at loggats with 'em?"] Insomuch that the fairest face in all the worlde, the best trimmed, and most charily kepte from wynde, and sonne, shall lye there, and be stamped upon by the rude grave maker, who will not sticke to laie him on the face, and rappe him on the sculle, yea and to batter downe his eies and nose flatte to his face, that they maie lye well and even with the earth. ["How the knave jowls it to the ground." Though that skull might once have been a courtier, it is now "chapless, and knocked about the mazzard with a sexton's spade."] And the fyne dapperde gentleman who whiles he lived might in no wise abide the wynde to blowe upon him, no nor so much as a little haire or moote to falle upon his garmentes, but in all hast it must be brusshed of with great curiositie, here they laie and hurle upon him a donghill of filthines, and dirte.... Is this that Jezabell? Is this that amiable face, which I knewe so faire, and livelie? Are these those eies, that were so cleare, and brighte to beholde? Is this that pleasaunt rowlinge tongue, that talked so eloquently, and made such goodlie discourses? ["Here hung those lips.... Where be your gibes now? your gambols? your songs?"] Is this that fyne and neate bodie, that was so trimlie pollished, and adorned? Is this the ende of the maiestie of Princes scepters, and roiall crownes? Is this the ende of the glorie of the worlde?

...And such is the great chaunge and alteration in worldlie affaires that it maie so come to passe, as a time maie happen, when some buildings maie be made neare unto thy grave, (be it never so gaie, and sumptuous,) and that they maie digge for some earthe out of the same to make morter for a walle, and so shall thy seelie bodie (beinge now changed into earth) become afterwardes an earthen walle, although it be at this present the most noble bodie and most delicately cherished of all bodies in the worlde. And how manie bodies of Kinges and Emperors trowest thou have come already to this promotion. ["Alexander died, Alexander was buried, Alexander returneth into dust; the dust is earth; of earth we make loam.... Imperious Caesar, dead and turn'd to clay" might "patch a wall."]

To Luis, as well as to Hamlet, Alexander looked and smelled even so when he returned to the dust from whence he came. Luis too felt his gorge rise. To just such an end is his meditation directed. Surely no one would suggest that Luis de Granada was a despairing nihilist; yet we note in him the same grisly humor, the same attention to revolting sights and smells, the same insistence that man's body is destined merely to stop a bung-hole. That is his point: the total worthlessness of the physical, the vanity of temporal concerns. As he warns repeatedly, "Because ye knowe not the howre (sayeth our Saviour) watche ye, and be alwaies in a readines."[10] Meditating on the death of the body is but a preparation for meditating on the more important truth: the eternal life of the soul. It seems clear that Shakespeare de-

---

[10] *Ibid.*, fol. 183ʳ. For further discussion of this passage, see below, p. 233.

rived his materials for the Graveyard Scene from the same Christian tradition.

As Montaigne said, "to Philosophise is to learne how to die," and he applauded the practice of placing graveyards next to churches as a constant reminder of death.[11] The graveyard in *Hamlet* serves the same function. In an excellent article on "Hamlet's Quintessence of Dust," Raymond H. Reno notes the recurrent echoes of "dust," "dirt," and "earth" throughout the play.[12] The cluster of images crystallizes in Hamlet's echo of the familiar funeral service: "Alexander return-eth to dust." Gertrude had charged her son not to seek for his noble father in the dust, but that is precisely where Hamlet must eventually find all of his answers. As many thoughtful readers have noted, the whole play is about coming to terms with death.[13] Hamlet's new poise in the final act is not, however, mere fatalistic composure in the face of an overpowering mystery. It is the composure of a man who has at last seen death, his own and that of all mankind, in true perspective. Gertrude had said:

> Thou know'st 'tis common. All that lives must die,
> Passing through nature to eternity.

The fatalist accepts only the first fact: the inevitable annihilation of the physical. On the basis of the Graveyard Scene alone, a reader who does not recognize the Christian symbols might assume that Hamlet goes no further. As we shall shortly note, however, the next scene makes it clear that he has come to see death, and thus life, in the context of eternity.

Hamlet's new poise is disturbed only momentarily during Ophelia's funeral. I join with those who doubt that Shakespeare intended Hamlet to leap into the grave, even though Burbage probably did so. As Granville-Barker suggests, Burbage must have been carried away, for the action is contradicted by the lines.[14] Laertes is the aggressor,

---

[11] *Essays,* I, 64.

[12] *Shakespeare Quarterly,* XII (1961), 107–13.

[13] For example, see C. S. Lewis, "Hamlet: The Prince or the Poem?" *Proceedings of the British Academy,* XXVIII (London, 1942), 148–51, and Ornstein, *Moral Vision of Jacobean Tragedy,* pp. 237–40.

[14] *Prefaces,* I, 139n. An elegy on the death of Burbage says "oft have I seene him, leap into the Grave," indicating that the direction in Q1 accurately reflects contemporary stage business. For the context, see *Shakespeare Allusion Book,* originally compiled by C. M. Ingleby *et al.,* rev. John Munro (London, 1932), I, 272.

probably leaping out of the grave to grab Hamlet by the throat. Hamlet's lines indicate strong restraint. He answers Laertes' "The devil take thy soul!" with the calm "Thou pray'st not well" and begs his assailant not to provoke him into an outburst. Moreover, the only line on which Hamlet could leap into the grave is "This is I, / Hamlet the Dane." The statement is an insistence on self-identity, an assertion of the unconquerable spirit heard in "I am Duchess of Malfi still," in Lear's "Ay, every inch a king," in Hermione's "The Emperor of Russia was my father," in Coriolanus's "I / Flutter'd your Volscians in Corioli: / Alone I did it." In *Hamlet,* I take the statement to be Hamlet's conscious assertion not only of his royal dignity but also of his sanity. The power of the assertion is destroyed by a grotesque jump down to Laertes' level in the trap.[15] The line requires a positive movement, with Hamlet stepping forward to declare himself.

Although Laertes' rant and physical assault temporarily shatter his calm, Hamlet's outburst does not indicate that he has reverted to his former mood. For the first time, perhaps, his emotion does not exceed the facts as we see them. Extreme provocation coupled with his shock at Ophelia's death is surely sufficient to account for a momentary release of emotion. Moreover, we are shortly to see him regret his lack of restraint. Even before his exit from the funeral, he regains control, asking Laertes the cause of his violence. "But it is no matter." From the aspect of eternity, even agonizing human squabbles are of passing concern.

## ACT V, SCENE II

In Hamlet's dialogue with Horatio, there are several contradictory details that seriously challenge the interpretation of *Hamlet* advanced in the present study. Although I believe that they are far outweighed by counter-evidence, I must grant them close attention and leave the verdict to the reader.

The report on the dispatching of Rosencrantz and Guildenstern reminds us of the Hamlet who departed for England. His malice has led him far beyond the needs of self-protection. In blowing his two old friends at the moon, he has acted exactly as he vowed he would act. He has, moreover, accomplished the same fate he intended for Claudius by damning his assumed enemies to Hell. There is no de-

---

[15] Inevitably one hears a stifled "Oof!" from the audience, and often a snort of laughter. It is all too apparent that someone must have landed on Ophelia's stomach.

fense for his desire that they be immediately executed in England, "not shriving-time allow'd." It is often argued that Hamlet must make certain that they do not tell the King of England the truth. What truth? They do not know it. Or, it is argued, Hamlet must be sure that they do not escape execution. But why must he? Or, it is argued, he is not to be blamed because he does not know they are innocent. It would be as logical to justify Othello's killing of Desdemona on the same grounds. Rosencrantz and Guildenstern are not the slimy weaklings critics have often made of them. As Gertrude tells us, they have been Hamlet's two closest friends, a fact confirmed by his genuine delight when they first enter. They believe they are helping their sick friend and serving their lawful ruler by protecting the State. Had they knowingly set out to trap Hamlet, they certainly would not have been speechless when Hamlet asked if they were sent for. Corrupt spies would have planned a lie to cover the truth. And are we to see their acceptance of Claudius's absolute authority as a sign of corruption? How would we feel if these same lines about the "cease of majesty" had been addressed to Henry V? Of course Rosencrantz and Guildenstern are not very perceptive, but, given the circumstances, would we have seen through Claudius?

Horatio does not applaud the justice of the device with a resounding "E'en so they deserved." All we hear is a cool, "So Guildenstern and Rosencrantz go to't." He is not dismissing their deaths casually, as Hamlet's response makes clear.[16] Sensing a tone of criticism, Hamlet seeks to justify himself:

> Why, man, they did make love to this employment;
> They are not near my conscience; their defeat
> Does by their own insinuation grow:
> 'Tis dangerous when the baser nature comes
> Between the pass and fell incensed points
> Of mighty opposites.

There is something curious about this justification. In the Closet Scene, Hamlet implied that Rosencrantz and Guildenstern knew of

---

[16] Many have sensed a tone of reproach or at least uneasiness in Horatio's response. See, for example, Gervinus, *Shakespeare Commentaries*, p. 578; Murry, *Shakespeare*, pp. 217–18; Schücking, *Character Problems*, p. 32, and *The Meaning of Hamlet*, p. 164; Knight, *Wheel of Fire*, p. 26; and Hankins, *The Character of Hamlet*, p. 73.

the plot. A similar statement in this scene would probably justify his trick in the minds of the audience. But Hamlet shifts his defense to other grounds: his imagery suggests two passive observers caught between mighty opponents in a duel.[17] He dismisses the two courtiers as "baser natures" whose toadying has led them blindly to their deaths. Is Hamlet trying to rationalize his doubts?

Thus far one might argue that the dispatching of Rosencrantz and Guildenstern shows just how far Hamlet's bloody thoughts had driven him before he entered the graveyard. The argument will not hold. In the first place, Hamlet's conviction that "heaven [was] ordinant" in providing him the means for the killing implies that he believes divine will favored the revenge.[18] Moreover, the obvious satisfaction with which he now reports his trick seems to indicate that he has not been purged in any way.

Similar problems arise as, seizing on Horatio's reference to the villainy of Claudius, Hamlet demands:

> Does it not, thinks't thee, stand me now upon— ...
> ... is't not perfect conscience,
> To quit him with this arm? and is't not to be damn'd
> To let this canker of our nature come
> In further evil?

Once again we are thrust back into the ethical dilemma, the urgent questions suggesting that the matter is again unsettled in Hamlet's own mind. Further, the broken phrasing suggests the old fury against the man who had whored his mother, the old vindictive purpose.

Horatio does not answer but instead warns that Claudius will shortly receive word from England. Surprisingly, Hamlet does not vow immediate action. The time, he knows, will be short, but

> the interim is mine;
> And a man's life's no more than to say "One."
> But I am very sorry, good Horatio,

---

[17] Nigel Alexander, "Critical Disagreement about Oedipus and Hamlet," *Shakespeare Survey*, XX (1967), 36–39.

[18] A related line—"There's a divinity that shapes our ends"—makes no such implication, though it is often cited as proof that God is on the side of the revenger. Hamlet is praising the "rashness" that made him rise from his cabin and discover the true contents of the commission. He attributes to Providence only the impulse that saved his life.

> That to Laertes I forgot myself;
> For, by the image of my cause, I see
> The portraiture of his: I'll court his favours.

The words may be ambiguous, but the restraint is apparent. Both context and tone imply that he does not mean to use the brief time to strike down Claudius. At this moment he turns his attention to his own rashness toward Laertes. The vow to forget all forms and pressures, to devote himself wholly to revenge, has at last been broken. He is thinking now not of murder but of reconciliation with a man he has hurt, not of the injury to himself but of one he has inflicted on another.

In this speech we hear again the tone of the Hamlet who emerged from the graveyard, and from this point to the catastrophe he will remain consistent. How, then, can we account for the contradictory details in the brief colloquy just ended? Only, perhaps, by classing them among the many loose ends in *Hamlet* that have led several critics to believe that Shakespeare did not finish polishing the play. The "loose ends" in this particular scene, however, are not incidental to the main action but crucial to interpretation, and thus the theory of incomplete revision can satisfy no one. I can offer no better.[19] The contradictions in the colloquy are undeniably disturbing, but I find them to be minor in light of the play as a whole.

The dominant impression by the time of Osric's entrance is that Hamlet is a far different man from the raging youth who left for England. He reveals his new self-knowledge by seeing himself in Laertes. In this moment of insight, Shakespeare underlines the parallel established in Act IV—but at the same time ends it. We are reminded of the treachery on which Laertes has embarked, and at the same time are shown that Hamlet has turned his course.

---

[19] Or, rather, I can as yet offer no explanation that deserves serious consideration. Many inconsistencies might be explained if we could agree on the genesis of *Hamlet*, since loose ends in other plays can often be traced to Shakespeare's source. Thus far, my investigation strongly suggests that *Der bestrafte Brudermord* derives from the "Ur-Hamlet," not from Shakespeare's play; that $Q_1$ derives in some way from Shakespeare's first version (and thus elements common to *Brudermord* and $Q_1$ may have appeared in the "Ur-Hamlet"); that $Q_2$-$F_1$ represent revision for clearly definable reasons; and that inconsistencies in $Q_2$-$F_1$ result from Shakespeare's incomplete articulation of his revision with his first version. (My conclusions are almost identical with those of Virgil Whitaker in *Shakespeare's Use of Learning* [San Marino, Calif., 1953], pp. 251–65, 329–45. For related arguments, see Charlton Lewis, *The Genesis of Hamlet*, pp. 100–105; and Hardin Craig, *A New Look at Shakespeare's*

Perhaps in no scene in the play is Hamlet more delightful than in his encounter with Osric. Here at last we see the "rose of the fair state, the glass of fashion"—that is, we see Hamlet as he was before his mind became infected with horrors. Here is wit without bitterness, satire without malice. Hamlet does not want to wound this water-fly, only to play with him. To Osric, he is the epitome of princely graciousness. To the audience, he is a marvelous tease. The episode should not be cut as an irrelevant bit of comic relief. The leisurely parenthesis of relaxed fun conveys Hamlet's new serenity and poise in a way that the Graveyard Scene could not. For a brief moment, death is far away.[20]

Suddenly it is very close as Hamlet is summoned for the duel and is surprised by a feeling of uneasiness. But, as he said to Laertes, "it is no matter." Now we learn why even the fear of death no longer touches him:

We defy augury: there's a special providence in the fall of a sparrow. If it be now, 'tis not to come; if it be not to come, it will be now; if it be not now, yet it will come: the readiness is all: since no man has aught of what he leaves, what is 't to leave betimes? Let be.

Let be what shall be. In this assent, Hamlet has found his "being."

---

*Quartos* [Stanford, Calif., 1961], pp. 75–83.)

G. I. Duthie's detailed refutation of this theory of the genesis of the play in *The 'Bad'-Quarto of Hamlet* (Cambridge, 1941) relies on verbal parallels too loose to meet the stringent tests of currrent scholarship and overlooks the possibility that abridgement may account for many of the missing lines in $Q_1$. Duthie's own theory—that $Q_1$ is based on memorial reconstruction of Shakespeare's final version—fails to account for structural improvements in $Q_2$–$F_1$. Faced with structural anomalies common to $Q_1$ and *Brudermord*, Duthie grants their probable derivation from the "Ur-Hamlet," and even admits that the Nunnery Scene in $Q_1$ might be derived from "a previous stage version of the $Q_2$ text" (p. 273). Such survivals he can attribute only to the ingenuity or the faulty memory of the reporter. Moreover, the theory of memorial reconstruction itself has been challenged by Albert B. Weiner in his introduction to *Hamlet: The First Quarto* (Great Neck, N.Y., 1962). Unfortunately, Weiner's unscholarly editing of the text and his superficial argument that $Q_1$ is a legitimate abridgement of $Q_2$ made on foul papers have diverted attention from what I find to be a convincing refutation of the reporter theory.

My early findings suggest three distinct steps in the development of *Hamlet*—from the "Ur-Hamlet" and Belleforest to Shakespeare's first version to his final revision—each step a clear progression toward the dramatic concept analyzed in the present study. They also suggest that further study of the problems involved in the final revision may explain many of the troublesome "loose ends." I hope to pursue the investigation.

[20] See Elliott, *Scourge and Minister*, pp. 185–87.

It is matter for considerable wonder that anyone has been able to read these lines as a statement of classic despair or Stoic fatalism, as sheer fatigue or mere defeat. Hamlet's tone is wholly serene and confident, wholly contented, and his words clearly place his new orientation in the context of Christian faith. The references to "a special providence," "the fall of a sparrow," and "readiness" would have been immediately recognized by the Elizabethans. It is inconceivable that Shakespeare would have used the familiar language of Christian doctrine and specific references to a familiar Biblical passage had he intended his audience to think Hamlet was embracing pagan fatalism. To argue otherwise is to assume that Shakespeare did not know the meaning of his own words.

The speech admits of only one translation: "God's will be done. Amen." In it, Hamlet surrenders his will to Divine Providence: more specifically, to the "special providence" that is ordained for each individual. There is a divinity that shapes the end not only for the universal order of nature ("general Providence"), but also for each living creature. The New Testament passage that Hamlet echoes is a divine promise:

And fear not them which kill the body, but are not able to kill the soul: but rather fear him which is able to destroy both soul and body in hell.

Are not two sparrows sold for a farthing? and one of them shall not fall on the ground without your Father.

But the very hairs of your head are all numbered.

Fear ye not therefore, ye are of more value than many sparrows.[21]

In his infinite love, God has ordained a plan for every man. Man cannot know that plan. He can only, by an act of faith, lay hold of the promise that God knows the plan to be good. And the plan includes his own death.[22]

---

[21] Matthew 10:28–31. See also Luke 12:4-7. For further discussion of the source and its significance, see J. V. Cunningham, "Woe or Wonder," *Tradition and Poetic Structure* (Denver, Col., 1960), pp. 135–41, and Bertram Joseph, *Conscience and the King*, pp. 138–42.

[22] Much has been made of late of the negative connotations in the word "fall" and of the threat of death in the verse immediately preceding the sparrow passage. On such grounds, many have argued that the passage reveals Hamlet's awareness of the threat of death and thus that it refutes any theory of his redemption. Of course Hamlet's speech indicates his recognition that he may be killed. As the Gospel makes clear, God does not promise to protect man from the death of the body. Quite the opposite. It is decreed that man must "fall." Would anyone argue that Hamlet is a redeemed Christian if he were to say, "I do not fear

The speech thus indicates that Hamlet is resigned to death, but his is not a resignation of despair. The speech is a statement of affirmation. As the Biblical context of the sparrow passage indicates, man has no reason to fear the death of the body. The only terror is the death of the soul. Since, therefore, the hour of death is hidden from him, man must keep his soul prepared to pass through nature to eternity: "the readiness is all." As Luke says in a verse immediately following the sparrow passage, "Be ye therefore ready also: for the Son of man cometh at an hour when ye think not."

Hamlet's speech and its relation to the graveyard meditation is again illuminated by the meditation of Luis de Granada. Earlier we noted a passage that now bears quoting in full. Immediately preceding his meditation on graveyards and corpses and worms, Luis indicates the end to which his thoughts are directed:

Because ye knowe not the howre (sayeth our Saviour) watche ye, and be alwaies in a readines. As if he had sayed in expresse wordes: because ye knowe not the howre, watche everie howre: because ye knowe not the moneth, watche everie moneth: and because yee knowe not the yeare, be still in a readines everie yeare. For although ye knowe not certainly what yeare he will call you, yet most certaine it is, that a yeare shall come in which untowredlie he will call you.[23]

Set this passage beside the following:

If it be now, 'tis not to come; if it be not to come, it will be now; if it be not now, yet it will come: the readiness is all.

Although the parallels suggest direct influence, Shakespeare's specific source matters little, if, indeed, he had one. The concept of "readiness" was a Christian commonplace echoed in countless homiletic works. A passage from Thomas Wilson's *The Arte of Rhetorique* shows the layman's understanding of the term. In a sample oration on the death of the two young sons of Suffolk, Wilson compares man to an apple. Some apples ripen in summer, whereas some remain green until winter. Even so can the mourners comfort themselves

---

the forthcoming duel because I know God will not let me be killed?" Many recent discussions seem based on this argument. To a Christian, such an idea would be at best naïve, at worst presumptuous. It would scarcely indicate that Hamlet is "ready" to meet his Maker.

[23] *Of Prayer and Meditation,* fol. 183$^r$.

that the "ripenesse for vertue" of the two young men had been brought "even to perfection." "Therefore being both now ripe, they were most readie for God."[24] The same understanding of the two terms underlies Edgar's echo of Hamlet in "Ripeness is all" (*King Lear*, V.ii.11). The evidence thus suggests that Hamlet has become not so much resigned to the inevitable as reconciled to the eternal. When we read nihilism into his graveyard meditation and pagan despair into his resignation, are we not using Hamlet as a mirror for modern anxieties?

If my reading of the play is correct, we are to believe at this point that Hamlet has rejected his intention of usurping God's function. Many have been puzzled that his tone is so confident when he has no plan of action, but that appears to be exactly Shakespeare's point.[25] Hamlet now rests serene in the faith that Providence has a plan. God may decree that he shall be the instrument to punish Claudius. Or He may not. "It is no matter." The point is not that nothing matters to Hamlet anymore; the point is that "the slings and arrows of outrageous fortune," "the thousand natural shocks that flesh is heir to"—these no longer matter when one's eye is on eternity. Hamlet is now ready to become the willing minister of Heaven. He has put himself at the disposal of God to use as, in His knowledge, He shall see fit.

Before we turn to the catastrophe of the play, perhaps this is the most appropriate moment to reconsider a work discussed in Part I.[26] Anthonie Copley's *A Fig for Fortune* offers so many striking parallels to *Hamlet* that a summary of its argument amounts to a summary of Hamlet's development. It will be recalled that Copley's "Elizian man" is led by his horse, Melancholie, to an encounter first with suicide and then with Revenge. Melancholie next carries him on a terrifying ride until "Rages ryotize" abates and his steed faints

[24] London, 1560, pp. 83–84. See also Elyot's discussion of virtue as "maturitie." "Maturum in latyn maye be enterpretid ripe or redy, as fruite whan it is ripe, it is at the very poynte to be gathered and eaten" (*The Governour*, I, 98). To be sure, the concept of "readiness" is found in Stoic literature, but much of Shakespearean criticism seems based on a faulty dilemma: the assumption that the presence of a Stoic commonplace proves a non-Christian orientation. Stoics defied augury; therefore it follows that Hamlet's resignation is pagan. Stoics believe in being "ready" for death; therefore Hamlet's resignation is classic despair. By such logic, Augustine can be made into a pagan.
[25] See Bowers, "Hamlet as Minister and Scourge," p. 748.
[26] See above, pp. 28–34.

and vanishes. Thereupon, Elizian man is conducted to a hermit who kneels in meditation before

> a Death's-head full of wormes,
> The picture of a Grave, and an Hower-glasse,
> *A* map of Doomsday, and *H*ell in fearfull formes
> And Heaven figur'd all in *S*aintlie sollace.[27]

In an extended speech on *de contemptu mundi* themes, the hermit exhorts Elizian man to scorn the agonies of this world and seek the glories of the next, to think upon his death:

> Time and thy grave did first salute thy Nature
> Even in her infancie and cradle-Rightes
> Inviting it to dustie Deaths defeature,
> *A*nd therewithall thy Fortunes fierce despights:
> > Death is the gulfe of all: and then I say
> > Thou art as good as *Caesar* in his clay.

> Death is the drearie Dad, and dust the Dame
> Of all flesh-frailtie, woe or majestie;
> All sinkes to earth that surgeth from the same,
> Nature and Fortune must together die:
> > Only faire Vertue skales eternitie
> > Above Earths all-abating tyrannie.[28]

Now Elizian man begins to feel the wonders of God's grace. Loathing his former mood, he vows "to be a beast no more," but gladly to be crucified with Christ.[29] An Angel then arms him with, among other things, a shield engraved with Christ's Passion in the center, surrounded with a circle of death's-heads, and Elizian man wends his way homeward.

Hamlet too is led by melancholy first to consider and reject suicide and then to be prompted to revenge by a demonic spirit that cannot endure the light of day. He too is led into a riot of rage. He too is transformed when he meditates on "dusty Death." He too finds a new orientation in the serene assurance that nothing matters but that which passes through nature to eternity. He too turns his back on the hell of his own making. He too is ready to return to the land of

---

[27] Copley, p. 22.    [28] *Ibid.*, p. 49.    [29] *Ibid.*, p. 52.

the living because he has looked on death. It is not my intention to urge a specific source for *Hamlet* but rather to note the common tradition in which Shakespeare and Copley worked. The two works are remarkably parallel in the development of the plot, the discussion of moral issues, and the use of Christian symbols. Surely no one could argue that Copley's figure of Revenge is an agent of the divine, that the hermit's exhortations to patience are the voice of cowardice, or that Elizian man returns home a defeated, exhausted fatalist. Elizian man and Hamlet both fight their way through "the devil's labyrinth" of melancholy, despair, and revenge; both emerge into the light when they look upon the skull.

Many critics have charged Hamlet with moral dereliction because he kills Claudius only when he is finally rushed into it precipitately by an avalanche of catastrophic events. Hamlet, they note, is merely striking back at Claudius in instinctive retaliation for his own and Gertrude's death, not consciously fulfilling his vow of revenge. Quite true. But should we condemn him for failing to commit premeditated murder?

Shakespeare does everything in his power to make Hamlet's killing of both Laertes and Claudius as sympathetic as possible.[30] Hamlet's behavior before the duel reflects his new-won poise. There is no trace of the old bitterness, no suggestion of suppressed malice. He is warm and gracious, and even civil to Claudius. More than that, he reaches out with genuine humility to Laertes, trying to effect a reconciliation by admitting, before all, for the first time in the play, that he has done wrong, and begging for forgiveness. His apology, however, includes a curious disclaimer. "What I have done," he says, "I here proclaim was madness." Is he lying, offering his nonexistent madness as a defense?

> Was't Hamlet wrong'd Laertes? Never Hamlet:
> If Hamlet from himself be ta'en away,
> And when he's not himself does wrong Laertes,
> Then Hamlet does it not, Hamlet denies it.
> Who does it then? His madness. . . .

---

[30] The point has been amply demonstrated by Fredson Bowers in "The Death of Hamlet," *Studies in the English Renaissance Drama in Memory of Karl Julius Holzknecht,* ed. Josephine W. Bennett, Oscar Cargill, and Vernon Hall, Jr. (New York, 1959), pp. 28–42.

The apology somehow has the ring of honesty, and it seems inconceivable that Hamlet would lie, especially at this moment. The apparent disclaimer of responsibility may, in fact, be Hamlet's acknowledgment of error. In Romans 7:14-17, Paul makes a similar kind of statement:

> For we know that the law is spiritual: but I am carnal, sold under sin.
> For that which I do I allow not; for what I would, that do I not; but what I hate, that do I.
> If then I do that which I would not, I consent unto the law that it is good.
> Now then it is no more I that do it, but sin that dwelleth in me.

Just as Paul's statement is a confession, not a disclaimer, of sin, may Hamlet's apology convey his new self-knowledge: an admission that he now sees his former course as sheer "madness," though not in the clinical sense? By totally abandoning his reason to his passion, he has been led to do an evil he would not rationally have chosen to do.[31] Granted, few in the audience would catch such a subtle allusion to Paul's intricate argument, but there is little room for doubt either that the apology is sincere or that the audience so accepts it. Hamlet reaches out to his "brother," forgetting his own injury, and in that moment we sense again that he is transformed. There is nothing on his mind but the desire to restore human ties and to pass the breathing time of day with a pleasant bout. The revenger died in the graveyard.

Would we prefer it otherwise? As Shakespeare presents the final killing of Claudius, Hamlet is guilty of manslaughter, not premeditated murder. He would undoubtedly have received a royal pardon in the Elizabethan courts and even today would be treated with leniency. In a swift succession of terrible revelations, he realizes that his life is threatened, sees his mother die, hears that he himself is dying, and learns that the King is to blame for all. He administers the deathblow instinctively. He could do so under no more sympathetic circumstances.[32] Of course, he is no saint. He is enraged and

---

[31] For a parallel discussion of Hamlet's apology in the light of the Pauline argument, though a contrasting interpretation of the term "madness," see Roger L. Cox, "Hamlet's *Hamartia*: Aristotle or St. Paul?" *Yale Review*, LV (1966), 347-64.

[32] Hamlet is even more blameless in the death of Laertes. We have no reason to believe that he exchanges swords with the express purpose of killing Laertes. The exchange seems an instinctive reaction of self-defense.

savage as he forces the poisoned drink between the King's lips.[33] He is still a terribly human being who has had his new armor of patience all but ripped from him. But no matter how violent he is in these awful moments, the fact remains that, in the gravedigger's metaphor, Hamlet did not go to the water. The water came to him.

And, for Hamlet, the rest is silence. I find no sign of despair in his dying words, no suggestion that nothing matters any more. His violent interference with Horatio's attempt at suicide shows his hunger to have his story told aright. It matters to Hamlet that the world should not think too ill of him. "The rest is silence" carries no weighty implication that man's life is meaningless or that there is no afterlife. It means, simply, "I die."[34] Had he but time—but he does not. The very simplicity of Hamlet's final words makes his death profoundly moving. Comparison with $Q_1$ illuminates the power of the standard text. There, Hamlet's dying line is the conventional tag for a hero who dies in a state of grace: "Farewel *Horatio*, heaven receive my soule." There, too, Hamlet has no time to tell his story, but one brief line suffices to absolve him of all guilt in the eyes of the audience. In $Q_2$ Hamlet has considerably more time to speak, but he makes no such presumption. He does not ask for forgiveness. He asks only that his story be told, honestly. He leaves the judgment to others and passes to silence. Time is suspended. Action on stage is frozen. In this play, perhaps the noisiest of Shakespeare's tragedies, the shock of silence stuns.[35] We do not think. We only feel. And the silence is broken as Horatio assures us that flights of angels will sing Hamlet to his rest.

Gunnar Boklund speaks movingly of this moment. "The feeling of waste, that something precious and irreplaceable has been lost when Hamlet dies, is strong and essential. The feeling of relief, that death

---

[33] If he does. I am drawn to Capell's explanation that "Drink off this potion" is figurative as Hamlet strikes the second time. In the theater, I find the thrust of this climactic moment weakened if Hamlet, after his first stroke, must turn away from Claudius to get the cup. Moreover, probability is seriously strained when Hamlet violently empties the contents down Claudius's throat—only to have Horatio announce a few moments later that some liquor remains. Claudius dies immediately when the "potion" is administered, suggesting that he is killed by a second and mortal wound, rather than by poison. See Kittredge, *Sixteen Plays*, p. 1105.

[34] As Noble has pointed out, the association of death with silence is found throughout the Bible. *Shakespeare's Biblical Knowledge*, p. 209.

[35] See Maurice Charney, *Style in "Hamlet"* (Princeton, N.J., 1969), pp. 17–21, 177–86.

comes as a liberator to Hamlet, is equally strong and equally essential. The feeling of victory, that, to his own satisfaction, Hamlet has triumphed over himself, is problematic and will always make the impact of the ending disturbing. Further I do not believe that Shakespeare goes, and further we need not go.... We should have charity and self-knowledge enough to let flights of angels sing Hamlet to his rest."[36] If we were to judge Hamlet in the final moments of his life, we would be uneasy. But Shakespeare does not ask us to judge. All great literature, wrote Yeats, is "Forgiveness of Sin."[37]

There can be no doubt, however, that we are forced to see the tragic cycle in its full horror. Even Fortinbras, not a man to flinch at the sight of death, is stunned at the bloody burden of the stage: "This quarry cries on havoc." In the language of sport, the phrase suggested the wanton slaughter of game by an inexperienced or reckless hunter; in warfare, it suggested the ruthless and pointless pillaging of the helpless. The same connotations are conveyed by Antony's prophecy that Caesar's spirit, ranging for revenge, shall join with Ate to "Cry 'Havoc.'" The comment implies that Hamlet's revenge has led him to wanton and meaningless slaughter. He may have ultimately won the battle within himself, but he dies with the blood of eight men on his hands, five of them innocent victims, helpless bystanders who were pointlessly struck down because they came between two mighty opposites. Hamlet's revenge has led to the destruction of two entire families and to the abandonment of the State to a foreign adventurer.

I, for one, see no hope for Denmark in the fact that Fortinbras is now at the helm. His past actions give little assurance that he will be a temperate and judicious ruler who seeks only peace and stability. The manner of his final entrance is in itself matter for alarm. When he had marched through Denmark previously, he had been granted "quiet pass," a condition he was careful to fulfill when he commanded his forces to "go softly on." Now, returning from Poland, flushed with victory, he reenters Denmark like a conquering hero. Hamlet is startled by the "warlike noise" of the volley with which Fortinbras greets the ambassadors from England. He is acting not like a privileged guest in Denmark but like its sovereign. Un-

---

[36] "Judgment in *Hamlet*," in *Essays in Shakespeare*, ed. Gerald W. Chapman (Princeton, 1965), p. 137.

[37] *Ideas of Good and Evil*, 3d ed. (London, 1907), p. 153.

announced, he marches into the royal court with his military train, to the accompaniment of drums. Even before he hears that he has Hamlet's dying voice, he orders a council of the nobles and announces that he claims his "rights." According to early exposition in the play, he has no rights.[34] The implication seems unmistakable that Denmark too has been a helpless victim of the general havoc. Order has been restored, but not by a figure representing the rule of reason and integrity. A strong man has taken over.[38]

Horatio's final evaluation is unequivocal. When he fulfills Hamlet's request and tells the true story, of what will he speak?

> Of carnal, bloody, and unnatural acts,
> Of accidental judgments, casual slaughters,
> Of deaths put on by cunning and forced cause,
> And, in this upshot, purposes mistook
> Fall'n on the inventors' heads.

There is no word here of righteous revenge, of just punishment of the wicked, of a divine command. There is no suggestion that Horatio attributes everything to the necessary workings of Providence. His is a statement of awful chaos. Horatio has been Hamlet's dear friend and moral exemplar. His word is to be heeded. And in Horatio's eyes, Hamlet has somehow been granted salvation—but in spite of, not because of, his revenge. He has fought his way out of Hell.

---

[38] The critical commonplace that Shakespeare always reestablishes order at the end of his tragedies seems to me to merit reconsideration. Order of a sort is always established, but is the audience necessarily to rejoice that the commonwealth has been healed? I find no reassurance in the triumph of the bloodlessly efficient Octavius in *Julius Caesar* and *Antony and Cleopatra*, of Aufidius in *Coriolanus,* or of Fortinbras in *Hamlet.* Even when health is clearly restored, as in *Othello* and *King Lear,* does the audience give a thought to the future of the State? All of our attention is on the dead. On the basis of *Romeo and Juliet* and *Macbeth,* too often, in my judgment, we have forced a positive meaning into the closing lines of the tragedies. See Ornstein, *Moral Vision,* p. 275.

# CHAPTER X

# Conclusion

Throughout the preceding discussion, the reader has undoubtedly been aware of a major objection. How can any theory be valid when it conflicts with almost four centuries of stage tradition and dramatic criticism? Despite changing tastes and shifting interpretations, the history of *Hamlet* on the stage and in the study indicates almost unanimous agreement on one basic assumption: that Hamlet is morally obligated to obey the Ghost. It may well be, as many have suggested, that we today are so imbued with traditional attitudes toward the play that we can no longer trust our first impressions, but surely the reactions of actors, critics, and audiences closer to Shakespeare's day must be heeded.

The objection is so obvious and based on such valid principles that it deserves careful attention. The witness of four centuries cannot be ignored. If it were true that Hamlet's revenge has always been accorded moral approval, the theory detailed here would be pointless. It has found support, however, in the curious fact that both stage and study have tenaciously maintained the traditional assumption in defiance of intuitive reactions. From the Restoration to the present day, we find widespread agreement, both tacit and expressed, that something is seriously wrong.

Since actual production should be the ultimate test of any theory, let us first consider the history of *Hamlet* on the stage.[1] At first glance

[1] Throughout the following discussion, I am indebted to P. S. Conklin, *A History of 'Hamlet' Criticism: 1601–1821* (New York, 1947), G. C. D. Odell, *Shakespeare from Betterton to Irving*, 2 vols. (New York, 1920), and Arthur Colby Sprague, *Shakespeare and the Actors.*

it would appear that the interpretation of Shakespeare's own company was handed down through Davenant to Betterton and then on to such famous Hamlets as Wilks, Garrick, Kemble, Kean, Irving, Forbes-Robertson, Barrymore, Evans, Olivier, and Gielgud.[2] However, a good case can be made for the proposition that Shakespeare's play vanished from the stage in 1642. The modern stage tradition of *Hamlet* began in the Restoration. Records for the period before 1642 are unfortunately meager, but the dominant impression of Hamlet conveyed by several allusions is of a counterfeit madman, acting like Bedlam let loose. In these early allusions, we find no suggestion of the heroic figure who appeared on the Restoration stage. Elizabethan and Jacobean audiences apparently were most struck by Hamlet's zany behavior.[3]

The Restoration Hamlet seems to have been an entirely different character. From accounts of Betterton's performance, we gather that audiences were most struck by Hamlet's robust energy. Even at the age of seventy, Betterton drew cheers for his performance of "a young man of great expectation, vivacity, and enterprise."[4] Hamlet was still active, but to Restoration audiences his violence apparently suggested the admirable determination of a heroic avenger. When we study the Restoration stage abridgments, we can understand the reason for this change in response.[5] The standard Restoration quartos cut all passages casting doubt on the nature of the Ghost and on the validity of Hamlet's revenge. Davenant's version, used into the eighteenth century, ruthlessly cut the verse and such significant passages as the scene between Polonius and Reynaldo, the Player King's speech, Hamlet's self-reproaches for insensitivity and cowardice, the speech to the Players exhorting to moderation, and Hamlet's determination to send

[2] The evidence for the continuity of acting tradition is a statement by John Downes in *Roscius Anglicanus* (London, 1708), p. 21. He notes that Betterton was trained in the role by Davenant and that Davenant had seen Taylor act it before the Revolution. Although Davenant apparently claimed that Taylor had been taught by Shakespeare himself, Taylor did not join Shakespeare's company until 1619, three years after his supposed tutor's death.

[3] Note especially the allusions in Dekker's *Dead Terme* and *Lanthorne and Candle-light* and in Scolaker's *Diaphantus in Love,* as well as several parodies of "mad Hamlet." *Shakespeare Allusion Book,* I, 185, 156, 133.

[4] *The Tatler* No. 71, *British Essayists,* ed. A. Chalmers (Boston, 1855), II, 219.

[5] See Odell, *Betterton to Irving,* I, 25; Hazelton Spencer, *Shakespeare Improved: The Restoration Versions in Quarto and on the Stage* (Cambridge, Mass., 1927), *passim*; and J. G. McManaway, "The Two Earliest Prompt Books of *Hamlet,*" *Papers of the Bibliographical Society of America,* XLIII (1949), 288–320.

Claudius to Hell. Basically, the Restoration Hamlet was an energetic, justified revenger, but only severe cutting made this interpretation possible. Although it has often been said that the "problem of Hamlet" did not arise until the latter half of the eighteenth century, stage tradition thus indicates that it is rooted in the Restoration.[6] Betterton's audiences did not see Shakespeare's play. They saw a "heroic tragedy." The audience that found Almanzor a noble figure of daring and enterprise adapted Hamlet to fit its ideal, and its ideal required changing the basic premise of the play.[7] To the Restoration, the noble Dane was resolutely performing his duty.

The entire history of *Hamlet* on the stage reveals the same problem. For three hundred years, directors and actors have cut and rewritten the script to fit their own interpretations. Garrick's virtuoso conception of a volatile, heroic prince led him to completely rewrite the fifth act: cutting the melancholy nonsense of the Graveyard Scene, erasing the Laertes parallel by omitting the plotting scenes and making Laertes a noble figure, changing the catastrophe so that our stalwart hero kills Claudius in a fair fight and Horatio restores order to the kingdom. Hamlet could do no wrong. Of course, Horatio's evaluation of the tragic cycle was cut, as it still is in most productions today. Shakespeare's script was similarly mangled in early productions of *Hamlet* in France and Germany.[8] If Hamlet is guiltless, why is he killed? And why should the innocent Ophelia suffer? And why does the Queen have to die? Obviously, Shakespeare did not understand poetic justice, but men such as J. F. Ducis in France and Franz Heufeld were glad to correct his errors. Thus in Ducis's 1769 version there is no Ghost, Gertrude is made a murderess who commits suicide, and Hamlet manfully besieges the palace, kills the usurper, and is rewarded with the hand of Ophelia. This is the version that held the French stage for over forty years, the version made famous by Talma.

---

[6] See Lawlor, "The Tragic Conflict in *Hamlet*," p. 113.

[7] Many small details had to be changed as well. In Davenant's revision of 1676, for example, Hamlet's stockings are "loose," not "fouled." That we are the inheritors of Davenant, not Shakespeare, is clear in the many modern Hamlets who refuse to condescend further than to take off their doublets when Hamlet adopts the mad role.

[8] See Richard Flatter, *Hamlet's Father* (New Haven, Conn., 1949), pp. 4–5, 34–36, and 161–62, and F. W. Meisnet, "Wieland's Translation of Shakespeare," *Modern Language Review*, IX (1914), 12–40.

Heufeld's adaptation reflects the same logic. Hamlet is ordered to revenge, he does, and that is that. He survives and no innocents suffer. And this version was dominant in Germany for half a century.

The significant point to be noted in the revisions by Garrick, Ducis, and Heufeld is their tacit agreement that something is wrong with Shakespeare's play if its basic premise is that Hamlet is morally obligated to kill Claudius. We shudder at their solutions to the problem, but their intuitions spoke true.

Of course, not all productions were based on such brutally mutilated scripts, but no attempt was made to produce Shakespeare's full play until F. R. Benson's six-hour version of the Folio at the Lyceum in 1900. Given the elaborate staging of the eighteenth and nineteenth centuries, some cuts clearly had to be made, but the material consistently eliminated from the Restoration to the present day indicates a long history of uneasiness with the Hamlet that Shakespeare created. As sentimentalism took hold on the stage, more passages had to be cut. Even Betterton had felt obliged to omit the three lines in which Hamlet wants to trip Claudius's heels and send him to Hell; but by the end of the eighteenth century the entire speech had to be eliminated, thereby making nonsense of the plot. John Philip Kemble's Hamlet of "sepulchral melancholy" naturally required that he omit Hamlet's hysteria during the Ghost Scenes and after the Play Scene. Bell's acting edition of 1773 accommodated the insistence on a pensive, genteel man of feeling by cutting still another section: all of Hamlet's grotesque comments in the cellarage scene.

By the middle of the nineteenth century, Hamlet became so emasculated and sentimental that he was wholly unrelated to Shakespeare's conception. Consider Henry Irving's famous portrayal of a passionate lover. In addition to many of the standard cuts, he slashed the end of the fourth act to omit everything after the appearance of the Ghost: Hamlet's violence, the bestowing of Polonius, the callousness over the corpse, the mad interlude with Rosencrantz and Guildenstern, and the shipping of Hamlet to England. Characteristically, he ended the play with "The rest is silence." In our own time, Olivier's cinematic portrait of the melancholy Dane required that he cut all doubts of the Ghost, together with most of the Ghost's suspicious behavior (including his first appearance, his most prideful and sensual lines, and the cellarage scene), the Player's Speech on Pyrrhus, Hamlet's self-reproaches and frenzied outburst at the close of the Closet Scene, the parallel scenes of Laertes' fury, the characters of Fortinbras and of Rosencrantz and Guildenstern, and Horatio's evaluation.

The evolving stage tradition is reflected not only in the increasing cuts but also in the changing acting conventions. Of special interest is the evolving interpretation of the Ghost and of Hamlet's reaction to it. Throughout the Restoration and most of the eighteenth century, the Ghost was treated as a terrifying figure. Betterton and Garrick were both noted for making the specter as fearful to the audience as it was to Hamlet. We are particularly fortunate in having several detailed accounts of Garrick's famous interpretation.[9] At the appearance of the Ghost, Garrick froze, petrified with fear. "So expressive of horror is his mien," wrote G. C. Lichtenberg, "that a shudder seized me again and again even before he began to speak." Garrick spoke with a breathless voice that trembled with terror. Violently breaking from his friends "with a quickness which makes one shudder" and drawing his sword to force them back, he turned and slowly followed the Ghost, extending his sword in front of him to keep a cautious interval. It is small wonder that Partridge in *Tom Jones* thinks the little man foolhardy for following such a forbidding figure. During a performance of *Hamlet* by Garrick he remarks, significantly, to Tom, "I'd follow the devil as soon. Nay, perhaps it is the devil—for they say he can put on what likeness he pleases." By the end of the Ghost scenes, Partridge has no doubts: "Ay, you may draw your sword; what signifies a sword against the power of the devil?" Apparently Garrick's production presented a thoroughly ominous Ghost. Arthur Murphy's prologue to *The Apprentice* indicates that in the latter half of the eighteenth century the Ghost was still traditionally treated as a threatening figure. In the prologue, Murphy satirizes the stagestruck youths who meet at the "spouting club," apparently to mimic their favorite actors:

---

[9] For comments on Betterton's portrayal, see Colley Cibber's *Apology* (London, 1740), pp. 84–85. For accounts of Garrick's reaction to the Ghost, see, among others, G. C. Lichtenberg, as quoted in *Variorum Hamlet*, II, 269–72; Thomas Davies, *Memoirs of the Life of David Garrick, Esq.*, 4th ed. (London, 1784), I, 63; Henry Fielding, *Tom Jones* (London, 1749), Book XVI, Chap. V; and Percy Fitzgerald, *The Life of David Garrick*, 2d ed. (London, 1899), p. 255.

There Hamlet's Ghost stalks forth with doubl'd fist;
Cries out with hollow voice—*List, list, O list,*
And frightens Denmark's prince—a young Tobacconist.[10]

This description accurately fits Shakespeare's angry spirit of martial stalk and terrifying aspect.

By the early nineteenth century, however, Shakespeare's Ghost had vanished. Two small changes in acting convention may signal its demise. In the Newcastle promptbook, used at Chester in 1785, George Frederick Cooke deleted *"Ghost beneath"* in the cellarage scene and noted his objection to the old tradition of having the Ghost sink through the trap.[11] The rapidly evolving figure of majestic dignity obviously could not speak from the bowels of the earth. Shortly thereafter, John Philip Kemble instituted the now-accepted business of kneeling before the honored spirit of his beloved father.[12] The questionable spirit that had so terrified Betterton and Garrick became transmuted by sentimentalism into an unquestioned spirit of health who aroused not horror but reverence. As a result, the Ghost became a pompous bore. In both Germany and London, as Tieck noted in 1824, the Ghost spoke its part "as if it were a cold-blooded lecture," using a "slow, dull, monotonous recitation, accompanied by hardly a gesture."[13] Of course, as Tieck objected, the scene dragged. It usually drags today and for much the same reasons. Modern productions of the Ghost scenes owe far more to Kemble and Fechter than they do to Garrick and Betterton and Shakespeare.[14]

Thus the stage history of *Hamlet* supports, rather than refutes, the conclusions of the present study. The traditional view that the Ghost's command is to be obeyed has, indeed, held the stage since the Restoration, but this view has been made possible only by changing stage business, by modifying the interpretation of the Ghost, and, above all, by cutting contradictory lines and scenes.

The history of *Hamlet* criticism reveals exactly the same uneasiness.

10 Quoted in Conklin, *A History of "Hamlet" Criticism,* p. 32.
11 M. St. Clare Byrne, "The Earliest 'Hamlet' Prompt Book in an English Library," *Theatre Notebook,* XV (1960), 29.
12 Noted in Boaden's *Life of John Philip Kemble,* quoted in the *Variorum Hamlet,* II, 249.
13 *Ibid.,* II, 287.
14 Fechter was the first to have Horatio react to the Ghost by making the sign of the cross. See above, pp. 120–21.

Often the passages that critics have found puzzling or offensive are precisely those passages cut in performance. It has recently been argued that centuries of critics have accused Hamlet only of delay in killing Claudius, and thus that Hamlet's moral obligation to revenge cannot be questioned. On the contrary, centuries of critics have accused him of the very things that I have argued cannot be ignored.

In the first extended criticism of the play, the uneasiness is apparent. The anonymous author of *Some Remarks on the Tragedy of Hamlet* ... (1736), possibly Sir Thomas Hanmer, was offended by many features: Hamlet's levity following the Ghost Scene, the "want of decency" in his conduct during the Play Scene, his cruelty to Ophelia, his "jocose and trivial" behavior after killing Polonius, the shocking form of Ophelia's madness, and, above all, Hamlet's reason for refusing to kill the King at prayer. Since this is our earliest record of an emotional response to the Prayer Scene, it bears close attention.

HAMLET's Speech upon seeing the King at Prayers, has always given me great offence. There is something so very Bloody in it, so inhuman, so unworthy of a Hero, that I wish our poet had omitted it. To desire to destroy a Man's Soul, to make him eternally miserable, by cutting him off from all hopes of Repentance; this surely, in a Christian Prince, is such a Piece of Revenge, as no Tenderness for any Parent can justify. To put the Usurper to Death, to deprive him of the Fruits of his vile Crime, and to rescue the Throne of *Denmark* from Pollution, was highly requisite; But there our young Prince's Desires should have stop'd, nor should he have wished to pursue the Criminal in the other World, but rather have hoped for his Conversion, before his putting him to Death; for even with his Repentance, there was at least Purgatory for him to pass through, as we find even in a virtuous Prince, the Father of *Hamlet*.[15]

The author of *Some Remarks* fully believes that Hamlet is morally obligated to revenge, but he cannot ignore his instinctive revulsion at his hero's behavior. The faults, therefore, must be those of Shakespeare, not of Hamlet. As a playwright, Shakespeare showed a distinct want of decorum.

Samuel Johnson's brief notes on *Hamlet* in his *Preface to Shakespeare* (1765) reflect the same uncomfortable suspicion that something is wrong. Why does the Ghost demand a revenge that is ef-

---

[15] *Some Remarks*, pp. 39, 44, and 41.

fected only by the death of Hamlet and of the innocent Ophelia? And why, if Hamlet is obliged to act, does he become a passive instrument in the last part of the play? And why does he feign madness? There seems no cause. Moreover, by such a course, Hamlet is led to treat Ophelia with useless and wanton cruelty. Above all, Johnson shuddered at Hamlet's soliloquy in the Prayer Scene. This speech, "in which *Hamlet,* represented as a virtuous character, is not content with taking blood for blood, but contrives damnation for the man that he would punish, is too horrible to be read or to be uttered." In light of these many failings, Johnson found Hamlet's defense to Laertes thoroughly unworthy: "it is unsuitable to the character of a good or a brave man, to shelter himself in falsehood."[16]

One of the most thorough indictments of Hamlet in the eighteenth century is found in *The Dramatic Censor* (1770) of Francis Gentleman. Again, however, the "virtuous character" of Hamlet is absolved, as all faults are laid to Shakespeare. "We are to lament that the hero, who is intended as amiable, should be such an apparent heap of inconsistency." Though of philosophical bent, this attractive young Prince is given the contradictory trait of impetuosity and made to do shocking things. Gentleman found many passages thoroughly offensive: Hamlet's blasphemous determination to question the Ghost though Hell itself should gape; his frenzy and levity in the cellarage scene; his "diabolical" sentiments in the Prayer Scene ("more suitable to an assassin of the basest kind, than a virtuous prince and a feeling man"); his totally unwarranted killing of "an innocent inoffensive old man"; his complete lack of "common humanity," as evidenced by his indifference to the death of Polonius and his "making himself the vindictive minister of heaven, in arraigning providence, for influencing punishment where no guilt has appeared"; his despicable dispatching of Rosencrantz and Guildenstern ("we lament such low chicanery in a character of dignity"); and his "mean prevarication" to Laertes. Of special interest is Gentleman's objection to the Ghost: "his stimulation to revenge furnishes a very gross idea of immortality, which should be freed from the passions and remembrances of day."[17]

Curiously, however, Gentleman did not pursue his many criticisms to their logical conclusion: that Shakespeare intended the Ghost's

---

16 Raleigh, ed., *Johnson on Shakespeare*, pp. 193, 195.
17 *Dramatic Censor*, I, 16–33.

command to be suspect and Hamlet's "diabolical" sentiments and actions to be every bit as disturbing as Gentleman sensed they were.

George Steevens was apparently the first critic of note to broach that unthinkable conclusion. "Hamlet cannot be said to have pursued his ends by very warrantable means; and if the poet, when he sacrificed him at last, meant to have enforced such a moral, it is not the worst that can be deduced from the play."[18] Although many have cited Steevens as the first to voice a negative view of Hamlet, he was merely the first to suggest that the blame for Hamlet's violence and obscenity and barbaric savagery might be attributed to the character himself, and not to a careless playwright of unenlightened Gothic tastes.

As one reads eighteenth-century *Hamlet* criticism, one becomes increasingly aware of a curious effect of the moral revolution that had taken place since Shakespeare's day. The eighteenth century loved Hamlet for what he said, though it could not tolerate what he did. In the "beauties criticism," again and again we find reference to the "virtuous" Prince, the "good Mr. Hamlet," the reflective speaker of admirable aphorisms, the exquisite sufferer of delicate sensibility. In an age when heightened sensibility was itself considered a sign of virtue, Hamlet's intense feelings and moral pronouncements inevitably blinded readers to the significance of his acts.[19]

Hamlet's behavior, however, could not be completely ignored, and as Shakespeare idolatry increased, it became less and less possible to assume that such a genius did not know what he was writing. Suddenly, in the last half of the century, two related theories were born that have remained popular into our own day. Both effectively relieved Hamlet of any moral guilt. The greatest stumbling block to the concept of Hamlet as a tender, delicate man of feeling was his reason for sparing Claudius at prayer. That problem was easily eliminated. Obviously, said William Richardson, Hamlet does not state his real reasons, for "there is nothing in the whole character of Hamlet that justifies such savage enormity." Clearly, Hamlet stayed his hand out of virtuous principles.[20] Others could not so easily blind them-

---

[18] *The Plays of William Shakespeare* (1778 ed.), quoted in the *Variorum Hamlet*, II, 147.

[19] One wonders how Shakespeare would have reacted to Steele's determination to undergo a moral experience by retiring to his closet to be melancholy, or to Mackenzie's ecstatic reference to the "majesty of Melancholy" in which the playwright had wrapped his hero. *The Mirror*, No. 99, 1780.

[20] *A Philosophical Analysis of Some of Shakespeare's Remarkable Characters*, 2d ed. (1784), quoted in Conklin, *"Hamlet" Criticism*, p. 73.

selves to the many moments in the play in which Hamlet shows himself capable of such savagery, and so a second theory was born. As
Dr. Akenside put it, "the conduct of Hamlet was every way unnatural
and indefensible, unless he were to be regarded as a young man whose
intellects were in some degree impaired by his own misfortunes."[21]
Thus was Hamlet relieved of all moral responsibility as latent insanity
became the solution to every puzzle. The more irrational and violent
Hamlet became, the more he was to be pitied. His pure soul remained
untouched.

Romantic criticism of *Hamlet* is too familiar to warrant discussion
here. For our purposes, we need note only the general agreement of
Coleridge, Lamb, and Hazlitt that their Hamlet could not be acted
on the stage. Given the style of acting and the emphasis on stage
spectacle in the early nineteenth century, they doubtless had good
reason for disliking contemporary productions. Even so, their insistence that Hamlet could be known only in the closet is revealing: their
vision of a pensive, retiring scholar could not stand the test of performance, even the sentimental performances of contemporary actors.

Charles Lamb states most clearly a view implicit in the writings of
both Coleridge and Hazlitt. In the theater, he was deeply offended
by "temporary deformities" in Hamlet: for example, by the "vulgar
scorn at Polonius which utterly degrades his gentility, and which no
explanation can render palatable" and by the "soreness of mind" that
leads him to treat Ophelia with such "asperity." "These tokens of an
unhinged mind ... we *forgive afterwards,* and explain by the whole
of his character, but *at the time* they are harsh and unpleasant." Only
in the closet, after long study, could the reader ignore those passages
contradicting what Lamb frankly calls a "dream." His Hamlet was
destroyed when "brought down . . . to the standard of flesh and
blood."[22] Lamb had similar difficulties with Macbeth, Richard III, and
Iago.[23] He was not objecting to specific interpretations as faulty, but
admitting that his interpretations could not be realized even by good
actors. If Macbeth was acted well, he instinctively sensed a "painful

---

[21] Quoted by Steevens in the 1778 edition of the plays; reprinted in *Variorum Hamlet,*
II, 147.

[22] "On the Tragedies of Shakespeare, Considered with reference to their fitness for Stage
Representation," *Shakespeare Criticism, A Selection: 1623–1840,* ed. D. Nichol Smith, World's
Classics (London, 1958), pp. 190, 192.

[23] *Ibid.,* pp. 203–4.

anxiety about the act," but in the closet he could ignore the act and concentrate with "delight" on the "sublime images." Similarly, in the closet he could overlook the crimes of Richard III and see only "the lofty genius, the man of vast capacity—the profound, the witty, accomplished Richard." In the theater, Lamb was forced to view Richard and Macbeth and Hamlet with horror. In the theater, he could not forgive them.

Lamb was not alone. Coleridge too found his visions of Shakespeare's plays consistently violated on the stage. The same attitude underlies Hazlitt's criticism of the "determined inveteracy of purpose" with which Kemble acted the role and the "splenetic and rash" Hamlet of Kean, marked by a "severity, approaching to virulence." Indeed, Hamlet "seems hardly capable of being acted."[24] Hazlitt was, of course, quite right. Given the play as Shakespeare wrote it, no actor could portray the Hamlet envisioned by the Romantics: the reflective thinker of pensive sadness, free from all taints of violence or cruelty, shrinking from action.

The Romantic critics thus felt exactly the same uneasiness we have noted throughout the Restoration and eighteenth century: an instinctive condemnation of Hamlet that could be quelled only by ignoring or cutting or rationalizing certain speeches and scenes. Further evidence from the early nineteenth century to the present day would merely bear out the same point. Millions of words have been written to explain away the same stumbling blocks: Hamlet's treatment of Ophelia, his killing of innocents, his tainted mind, his soliloquy in the Prayer Scene, and the patently un-Christian nature of the Ghost's command. The fact that we still feel these features of the play require explanation indicates that we too sense something wrong in the traditional assumptions. Instinctively, we are aware that someone or something must be at fault. Responsibility for the command to revenge and Hamlet's ensuing course has been variously attributed to the degraded taste of Shakespeare's audience, Elizabethan dramatic conventions, the excessive villainy of the other characters, and the play's barbaric source. The present study leads to a far more obvious explanation for our uneasiness: the command to murder is as malign as we sense it to be, and Hamlet himself is responsible for his descent into savagery.

---

[24] "Characters of Shakespeare's Plays," in Smith, ed., *Shakespeare Criticism*, p. 291.

May not the peculiar power of the play be based to a large extent on our ability to sympathize with Hamlet and yet judge him for the course he pursues? And is this not exactly our response to Shakespeare's other great tragic figures? It has been harder to admit our intuitive judgment of Hamlet because his tragic choice commands not merely our sympathy but our admiration. In the first place, his situation is much closer to our own than that of Macbeth or Antony or Lear. All men hunger for revenge. The defiant refusal to submit to injury, the desire to assert one's identity by retaliation, the gnawing ache to assault injustice by giving measure for measure—these are reflected in our daily response to even the mildest of insults. In the serious drama from the beginning of time, the dilemma of the revenger has been one of the universal problems of man writ large.

An even more important reason for our sympathy is the motivation that drives Hamlet. Macbeth, Lear, and Antony obviously violate moral law, and for selfish ends. We suffer with them but for human reasons, for the agony they bring on themselves. Hamlet's motivation is far more complex and, to a great extent, we identify with him for solid moral reasons. In large part his course to the fifth act is the result of his moral sensitivity, his unflinching discernment of evil and his determination that it shall not thrive. We admire his hatred of corruption and his vision of what man could and should be. Even as he is engulfed by the evil against which he takes arms, we sense that he would have been a lesser man had he refused the challenge.

At this point, the reader may object that my discussion of *Hamlet*'s universal appeal contradicts my earlier insistence on the play's Christian perspective. Throughout the preceding pages, it may have seemed that I was forcing *Hamlet* into a straitjacket of Christian morality, thereby seriously restricting its meaning and impact. This has been far from my intention. Paradoxical as it may seem, I believe that we can understand *Hamlet*'s unrivaled power to move emotions and stimulate thought only when we grant the basic Christian perspective in which the action is placed. To do so requires no knowledge of religious doctrine, no scholarly investigation into Elizabethan theories about ghosts or the meditations of Luis de Granada or archaic meanings of "conscience." Shakespeare gives us everything we need to know.[25] In short, we must take the play on its own terms. Only

---

[25] In the very few instances in which ideas or symbols might convey a different meaning to a modern reader, context and tone provide sufficient clues to understanding. The graveyard meditation and the "readiness is all" speech are probably cases in point.

when we cease searching for explanations outside it, whether in pagan codes or obsolete theatrical conventions, can we respond directly to the play itself.

Once we do so, we sense that the Ghost is ominous, we sense that Hamlet's early surrender to rage can lead only to chaos and destruction but that his later serenity is somehow his salvation—in short, we sense that the desire to inflict private punishment can lead only to evil. The social compact is largely based on the belief that man can fulfill his special potential only when there is social order, that the unrestrained private will leads inevitably to anarchy, and that man must willingly assent to certain fiats of authority. The consensus of civilized man, therefore, is that discipline of emotions, obedience to established law, and love (or, at least, respect) for one's fellow man are moral goods, whereas surrender to emotions, defiance of law, and hatred of (or, at least, indifference to) one's fellow man are moral ills. By granting the Christian perspective of *Hamlet*, we thus do not narrow the ethical base of the play; we broaden it. Christian ideas and symbols become merely familiar signs by which we recognize the basic view of man held throughout the civilized world.

At the same time, we recognize a major reason for *Hamlet*'s enduring appeal. In Hamlet's dilemma, we find the dilemma of civilized man, a dilemma that becomes more profound as civilization becomes progressively restrictive. In our own day, the dilemma looms large. Caught in an age of increasing frustration, hemmed in by civil law and social codes, lost in the mass, many have raised Hamlet's questions. What is man if his chief good be but passive resignation to a will other than his own? The law not only delays but winks; corruption thrives; the establishment condones dishonesty, injustice, and brutality in the name of order. When is obedience merely a euphemism for cowardice? In the modern world, many have argued that man can find his "being" only by trusting his instincts and obeying his own private moral code—only by defying, or at least ignoring, the dictates of civil and social law. Their challenge is epitomized in the thesis of Gertrude Stein's play cryptically entitled *Yes Is for a Very Young Man*.

Hamlet arrives at the opposite conclusion. In the first part of the play, a very young man defiantly shouts "No," but he is transformed in the fifth act when he finds his being in "Yes." It is for this reason, perhaps, that several readers have sensed what they call a "tragic

retreat" in the play. Hamlet does, indeed, retreat from rebellion, a fact
that a modern reader may regret. But does Shakespeare invite us to
view Hamlet's retreat as a weakness? In one sense, Hamlet is medieval
man teetering on the brink of the modern world. He defiantly asserts
his own being against all limitation, but he ultimately accepts limitation as the only means of freeing himself to find that being. Some
today may find his retreat from defiance a step backward, but such
a reading seems clearly at odds with the play. Hamlet does not sink
into passive resignation; he rises to affirmative reconciliation. He has
not abandoned his search for being. His search has ended in the serene
knowledge that "the readiness is all."

Theories of tragedy are many, but common to almost all is a basic
pattern that fits *Hamlet*. Man in some way hurls himself against the
barricades that confine him, whether of family or society or universal
order or faith. In some way he defies the established code—challenges
it, questions it, tests it—and is ultimately shattered by it. In the
struggle, we see his greatness, but we know that he must go down.
In the truly great tragedies, the tragic hero at his fall in some way
attains a new awareness of the mystery of life and of his own role in
that mystery. Thus the tragic self stands at the end inviolate in a new
dignity. This applies no less to Hamlet than to Oedipus and King Lear.

For my part, this long study has led for the first time to an awareness that many strikingly diverse and even contradictory views of
*Hamlet* can be illuminating. The Christian may find the fundamental
question the play raises to be "How can man be saved?" The existen-
tialist, "What is man's essence?" Are not both right? The Freudian
may view Hamlet's problem as one of sexual obsession; the Nietz-
schean, as a conflict between the Dionysian motive of instinct, the
barbarizing principle that leads to chaos, and the Apollonian motive
of reconciliation, the civilizing principle that leads to order. Is there
not truth in both views? From Aristotle's familiar definition of the
tragic hero to Murray Krieger's discussion of the "tragic visionary"—
the ethical man who undergoes a cosmic shock, finds his ethical assumptions inadequate, and either yields in resignation to the demands
of ethical absolutes or "surge[s] toward the demoniac"—every sensitive analysis of the tragic experience can lend new insight.[26] And,

---

[26] Krieger, *The Tragic Vision* (New York, 1960), pp. 11–14. See also the highly pertinent
discussion by Sewall in *The Vision of Tragedy,* especially in the introductory chapter and the
analysis of Faustus.

curiously enough, it can do so because of, not in spite of, our recognition that the orientation of *Hamlet* is explicitly Christian. Only when we grant that the world of *Hamlet* is not an ethical never-never land, governed by some artificial theatrical code at variance with the code of daily life, can we grant that Shakespeare probably intended his audience to respond naturally.

Is it not likely, then, that the best way to approach *Hamlet* today is to forget all one has ever heard about Elizabethan codes and counter-codes, about dramatic sources and theatrical conventions—to respond as naturally as one would to a modern play? Our attitude toward revenge is almost the same as the Elizabethan attitude, and it is doubtful that human nature has changed. If we recognize that our intuitions have always been valid, that, despite our sympathy for Hamlet's agony, the savage course on which he embarks is designed to appall us, we find the tragic issue to be rooted in an ethical dilemma that is universal.

# Appendixes

# The Relevance of Religious Tests
## to the Stage Ghost, 1560–1610

A survey of ghosts on the Elizabethan and Jacobean stage makes it apparent that Shakespeare was not merely revitalizing a familiar convention in *Hamlet*. The spirit that visits Elsinore is like no other in the drama of the English Renaissance. Its nature is in question, and both Hamlet and the audience are called upon to test it according to Christian doctrine. Since the present study finds Shakespeare's departure from convention highly significant, it may be useful to summarize the functions served by stage ghosts in the drama of his contemporaries, paying particular attention to the religious perspective in which they may be placed.

In the extant drama produced between 1560 and 1610, twenty-six plays include fifty-one ghosts. Of these, one-third are wholly irrelevant to revenge: they appear as voices of comfort, most often in dreams (as in Posthumus's dream of the Leonati family in *Cymbeline* and Ferdinand's vision of Isabella in *The White Devil*); they are evoked by acts of black magic (as in *Alphonsus, King of Arragon* and *The Divils Charter*); they serve as devices of exposition (as in the prologues to *Grim the Collier* and *The Divils Charter*); they are even comic characters (as in *The Old Wives' Tale*). In none of these cases is the nature of the ghost at issue in the play or of concern to the scholar.

Among the thirty-six ghosts appearing in revenge plays or serving a similar function in other genres, over one-third are outside the action of the play itself, appearing as prologue or chorus or both. Typical of this group are Gorlois, who cries for general revenge in the prologue to *The Misfortunes of Arthur* and then appears at the end to pronounce the moral and proclaim his satisfaction; Clarence, who merely introduces *The True Tragedy of Richard III* by crying *"Vendicta"* for his own murder; and Corineus, who appears in the fifth act of *Locrine* to serve as the spectator to the working out of divine vengeance in the denouement. Among this group, the theological debate about ghosts again seems irrelevant. These ghosts are the sons of Seneca, announcing that they come from "Pluto's pits" (Gorlois) or Hades (Andrea in *1 Jeronimo*), or even Elysium (although the only example noted is Andrea in *The Spanish Tragedy*). For the most part they are mere presenters, establishing the playwright's theme of the inevitability of nemesis.

The second most common function of revenge ghosts is to appear to a sinner, voicing his own pangs of conscience and prophesying inevitable retribution. Again, such ghosts are identified as pagan, if they are identified at all. The only play in which they function in anything like a Christian framework is *Richard III,* and there they defy religious analysis. According to accepted belief, spirits that tortured the guilty were demons whereas spirits that comforted the blessed were angels, but the voices of Richard's eleven victims serve both functions, appearing to both Richard and Richmond. Obviously no member of Shakespeare's audience was expected to apply religious tests.

These two functions—serving as prologue and chorus or as the voice of conscience and nemesis—account for forty-six of the fifty-one ghosts under consideration. Not one is related to the issues that Shakespeare raises in *Hamlet*. Not one comes from Purgatory; not one from Heaven; not one from the Christian Hell. If these ghosts are given any place of origin, it is Pluto's kingdom. Indeed, most playwrights seem to go out of their way to avoid arousing any Christian associations by relying on a Senecan convention that is totally divorced from the real life and beliefs of their audiences. It is possible, nonetheless, that in these ghosts we find a few hints of contemporary theories. Several of the most voluble in their hunger for revenge are treated as malign. Gorlois raves for revenge in language customarily reserved for fiendish villains, calling for all the chaos fury can invent, hoping that all victims may be destroyed before they have time to repent. He serves as the voice of virtue in the epilogue, but there he is an entirely different character. Similarly, Albanact, in his screaming pursuit of the defeated Humber in *Locrine,* acts like a devil in a morality play: snatching food from his victim's hands, hounding the starving Humber to despair and suicide. However, the treatment of even these malign spirits offers no hint that they are to be viewed as devils, much less that they are to be judged in Christian terms.

Only five plays remain to be considered, and they reveal some significant facts. Except for the voices that torment Richard III, only four ghosts in the entire period are placed even vaguely in Christian perspective: those in *Hamlet, Bussy D'Ambois, The Atheist's Tragedy,* and *The Revenge of Bussy D'Ambois.* In *The Atheist's Tragedy,* the ghost of Montferrers is Christian only to the extent that his message is Christian. His place of origin is not mentioned; he is not characterized. His role is sketchy, serving only to expound Christian patience to Charlemont and to announce impending doom to D'Amville. If he did not reveal secret information, he could be considered the voice of conscience in both cases. The Umbra of Bussy in *The Revenge of Bussy D'Ambois* is a contradictory figure. Although he exhorts Clermont to do the justice of God, thus arousing a Christian response in the audience, Chapman clearly considers him a pagan ghost. Umbra Bussy has risen "up from the chaos of eternal night" (V.i.1); he warns Tamyra that the air in which his form appears will "blast" (V.ii.49); and he announces that the ghosts who dance around the corpse of Montsurry are celebrating "with dances dire and of infernal hate" (V.iii.56–57). Moreover, he argues to the audience that Christianity is unnecessary if one has a concept of the universal. All in all, Umbra Bussy is a compound of many elements, serving Chapman's immediate purpose in any given scene. Even more confused is Umbra Friar in *Bussy D'Ambois.* Here Chapman created the most curious ghost of the entire period. In the denouement, Umbra Friar begins to act like a Christian spirit of good: calling on Bussy to forgive his murderers, pronouncing the apotheosis of the hero, and trying to effect a virtuous reconciliation between Montsurry and Tamyra. The Catholic setting and Chapman's obvious use of Christian symbols might seem to indicate that we have here a true Purgatorial spirit, but the Friar's role defies all logic. Alive, he has been an apologist for adultery, a pander, and a worker of black magic who invoked the Prince of Darkness. As a ghost, he begins to function as a Christian only after Bussy has been fatally wounded. Dead as well as alive, he is plot-ridden. As a ghost, he gives Bussy a wholly useless warning and leaves. Then he gives Tamyra another vague warning, protesting that he cannot appear to Bussy because his "power is limited" (V.iii.21). No clear concept can be discerned beneath the many contradictions.

Even though these three ghosts have little in common, two similarities are of interest. First, Christian elements in these ghosts are largely incidental. In no case does the playwright intend his audience to test the ghost against its religious beliefs about supernatural visitations. The ghost of Montferrers might seem to be an exception, but even his nature is not defined. He appears to be a returned soul, yet there is no suggestion that he is from the other world, much less from Purgatory. He appears to be a voice of divine counsel, yet he visits a sinner, a function relegated by religious theorists to devils. Tourneur was uninterested in what he was, only in what he said. *Hamlet* alone forces the audience to ponder the exact identity of a ghost.

The placing of all three ghosts in a Christian context lends considerable significance to a second point of similarity: not one of them counsels action opposed to Christian teaching. Montsurry warns that revenge must be left to God, and Umbra Friar urges Christian forgiveness and reconciliation. It is true that Umbra Bussy commands Clermont to take revenge on Montsurry, but he is a good Stoic philosopher, exhorting that the deed be one of justice, befitting eternity. Actually, then, he is a restraining influence, and Clermont's "revenge" does indeed take a laudable Christian form as he effects the regeneration of his enemy.

Only two ghosts in the half century under consideration appear to a protagonist to command blood revenge: Andrugio in *Antonio's Revenge* and the Ghost in *Hamlet*. This is, perhaps, the most surprising fact to emerge from a survey of sixteenth- and seventeenth-century stage ghosts. Almost all studies of the revenge play imply that the Senecan ghost who appeared to further his vengeance by inciting a revenger was a conventional figure. If we can judge from the extant plays, he was not.[1] It seems likely that the "Ur-Hamlet" introduced him; Marston's *Antonio's Revenge* capitalized upon him; Shakespeare's *Hamlet* refined him; and that was that. Nor did this type of

[1] Although Caesar's Ghost appears to Antony and Octavian in *Caesar's Revenge* (c. 1592–96), he does not institute a revenge action. The two men have already vowed the destruction of Caesar's assassins. When they are momentarily diverted by ambitious rivalry, Caesar's Ghost appears to shame them into reuniting in his memory. Although he is seen by both characters, dramatically he serves as the voice of conscience. With Brutus, he functions as the voice of both conscience and Nemesis.

revenge ghost reappear in the years between 1610 and the closing of the theaters.[2]

Whether *Antonio's Revenge* was written in imitation of Shakespeare's *Hamlet* or whether both were based independently on the "Ur-Hamlet," comparison of the two ghosts would undoubtedly prove useful if we could discern Marston's purpose. Unfortunately, we cannot. The ghost of Andrugio is as ambiguous as the play itself. Of only one thing can we be sure: he is not a Christian spirit in any sense. He has risen from his coffin and cannot touch the banks of rest until his murder is revenged—both strictly pagan ideas. Beyond that, all is chaos. He is a spirit of malevolence, passionately vindictive, who urges his son to the most barbaric revenge:

> Invent some stratagem of vengeance
> Which, but to think on, may like lightning glide
> With horror through thy breast.
> (III.i.48–50)

When Antonio wavers in his determination to kill Julio, a scene in which, as I suggested in Chapter II (pp. 59–60), the audience's sympathies are with the little boy, it is the voice of the ghost crying for revenge that hardens Antonio's heart. A spectator to Antonio's ghastly torture and murder of Piero, he sits above the stage exulting:

> Blest be thy hand. I taste the joys of heaven,
> Viewing my son triumph in his black blood.
> (V.iii.67–68)

The fantastic invoking of Heaven to bless the spilling of black blood typifies the character's ambiguity. Despite the demonic function and language of the ghost, he is treated as a divine agent: calling down the

---

[2] Two plays might seem to conflict with this assertion. In the closet scene of *II Iron Age* (1613), when Clitemnestra swears that she and Egistus are innocent, Orestes invokes the powers of heaven or hell to give him a sign. The ghost of Agamemnon appears, indicates his wounds, and then points to Clitemnestra and the dead Egistus. He is merely a "testate" to the fact, not a spirit exhorting revenge. Similarly, the ghost of the Lady in *The Second Maiden's Tragedy* (1611) does not appear to command revenge, although summaries often list her as a typical revenge ghost. She appears to urge Govianus, her bereaved lover, to retrieve her corpse from the Tyrant, who has hidden it. Her sole concern, and that of Govianus, is that her body should be freed from the Tyrant's loathsome caresses and that it should have proper burial. The playwright even attempts to clear Govianus of any revenge taint in his eventual poisoning of the Tyrant, by having him pray to Heaven to keep him from rage. He kills the villain almost unwillingly, acting only to give his loved one peace.

blessings of peace on his wife and son, hailing the justice of Heaven in effecting "the scourge of murder and impiety" (V.i.25), apparently viewing Antonio as the minister of God. What Andrugio's ghost may be, however, is a question only for scholars. Nothing in the play suggests that its nature was at issue. Neither Antonio nor the audience would have any reason to doubt that the ghost is the spirit of Andrugio.

From this brief survey, perhaps only one conclusion emerges that is of real importance. The Ghost in Shakespeare's *Hamlet* is not merely the "traditional revenge ghost" modified by the addition of Christian concepts. It is radically different from any ghost that preceded or followed it in the drama of the English Renaissance. In the extant plays, it is the only ghost to alert both the characters and the audience to the necessity of identifying exactly what it is, and of doing so by established Christian tests.

# The Convention of Immortal Vengeance, 1585–1642

Scholars have long been aware that Hamlet's stated desire to kill Claudius in a way that will damn his soul eternally reflects a convention familiar to the Elizabethan and Jacobean audiences. From Steevens and Malone to Kittredge and Stoll, parallels in both dramatic and non-dramatic literature have been cited, and still more can be added to the growing list. The convention was obviously popular. What conclusions can we derive from this mass of evidence?

Agreement has been almost unanimous. No matter how much the modern spectator is offended by such vicious vindictiveness, Shakespeare's audience, it is contended, viewed Hamlet's reason for not killing Claudius at prayer as "right and proper" for a revenge play, as an "acceptable convention" that "no Elizabethan would have thought of questioning." Thus the desire to damn Claudius is in no way to suggest savagery or blasphemy on Hamlet's part. "Such behavior was in accord with the prevailing ethics of revenge," an approved code requiring "above all that the victim, after exquisite torments of body and mind, should go straight to Hell, there to remain in everlasting torment." In sum, "Hamlet is not to blame . . . ; he is trying to do the thing properly."[1]

But does the evidence warrant this assumption? Although the familiar parallels are named again and again, little attention has been paid to the context in which they appear. We have learned almost nothing when we discover that, in addition to Hamlet, some twenty-

---

[1] Stoll, *Hamlet*, p. 51; Waldock, *"Hamlet": A Study*, p. 42; Wilson, *What Happens in Hamlet*, p. 245; Adams, *Hamlet*, p. 276; Harrison, *Shakespeare's Tragedies*, p. 90; Hardin Craig, *An Interpretation of Shakespeare* (New York, 1948), pp. 189–90.

three characters desire or plan or actually effect the damnation of their victims. We have proved that a convention existed, but as yet we know nothing of the audience's attitude toward that convention. What kind of character expresses such sentiments? What is the context? And what of those characters who explicitly refuse to damn their victims? These questions have never been asked.

The answers are so startling and the implications so significant in interpreting both the Prayer Scene and the entire play of *Hamlet* that it seems wise to present the evidence in full detail. A mere summary might suggest that only extreme cases have been cited or that evidence supporting the traditional assumption has been dismissed as atypical. In the following discussion I shall cover every parallel that has been offered previously, in addition to several discovered during the present investigation.

Some of the parallels most frequently cited are actually irrelevant. The most flagrant example is Pistol's frustrated yelp at Fluellen: "Die and be damn'd! and figo for thy friendship!" (*Henry V*, III.vi.60). The expression is a meaningless outburst of impotent rage, not a conscious statement that Pistol himself intends to ensure Fluellen's eternal damnation. Even if the line were pertinent, surely no one would suggest that Pistol represents the moral norm. Equally misleading are several citations of the familiar vow "I will send thy black soul to hell." In *The Spanish Tragedy*, Bel-Imperia vows that she herself will send the villains' souls to Hell if Hieronimo is remiss in his revenge; in *2 Henry VI*, Warwick swears that if Suffolk were not guilty of murder and thus under sentence of death, he would take it on himself to send the "blood-sucker" to Hell; in *Richard II*, Aumerle casts down his gage as a pledge that he will send Bagot to Hell by defeating him in combat; and in *1 Jeronimo*, Horatio, stunned at the revelation of Lorenzo's murderous plot against Andrea, swears that if his father had not been present, he would have stabbed the villain on the spot and sent his soul to damnation. In all four cases, the speaker means only that the villain in question is so evil that his death would necessarily send him to Hell. Thus none of the four exemplifies the specific convention used in *Hamlet*.[2]

---

[2] The final chorus in *The Spanish Tragedy* has also been offered as evidence, but it is even more obviously unrelated to the specific convention under discussion. Revenge and the Ghost

The convention is operative, however, in some twenty-three characters who wish to predetermine God's judgment on their enemies by controlling the actual conditions of death. Two of the best-known examples are found in non-dramatic works, though they were probably instrumental in popularizing the dramatic convention. The first appears in Edward Daunce's *A Briefe Discourse of the Spanish State* (1590), a description of the depraved character and conduct of the Spaniards. In it, he cites the example of a fiendish monster who threatened to kill his enemy unless he forswore God. Of course the terrified victim did, whereupon the villain cried, "nowe will I kill thy bodie and soule, and at that instant thrust him through with his Rapier."[3] Daunce may have provided Thomas Nashe with a source for an incident in *The Unfortunate Traveller*. The book culminates in the story of Cutwolfe, whose fiendish revenge and ghastly torture and execution so revolt Jack Wilton that he reforms on the spot and rushes out of the "*Sodom* of *Italy*" back to the land of Gloriana and virtue.[4] In an "insulting oration" of confession, Cutwolfe glories in the exquisite perfection of his revenge for his murdered brother. He has pursued his enemy, Esdras, for twenty months, often seeing him, but waiting for the perfect opportunity. Finally trapping his cowering victim, Cutwolfe exults, "I have promist the divell thy soule within this houre." Esdras frantically begs for mutilation, not death, so that he may have time to repent:

A lingring death maye availe my soule, but it is the illest of ills that can befortune my bodie. For my soules health I beg my bodies torment: bee not thou a divell to torment my soule, and send me to eternall damnation.... Thy brothers bodie only I pearst unadvisedly, his soule meant I no harme to at all: my bodie & soule both shalt thou cast awaie quite, if thou doest at this instant what thou maist. Spare me, spare me, I beseech thee; by thy own soules salvation I desire thee, seeke not my souls utter perdition: in destroying me, thou destroyest thy selfe and me.

But Cutwolfe defies damnation:

---

of Don Andrea describe the future punishments of the villains in Hades, but of course they take no active role in the play at all, much less in the villains' deaths. They serve a choral function at the end, merely pointing the "moral": villains will suffer eternal torments.

[3] Daunce, *A Briefe Discourse*, p. 24.

[4] Nashe, II, 319–27.

Though I knew God would never have mercy upon me except I had mercie on thee, yet of thee no mercy would I have. Revenge in our tragedies is continually raised from hell: of hell doe I esteeme better than heaven, if it afford me revenge. There is no heaven but revenge.

Seeing the utter depravity of his foe and faced with instant death, Esdras hysterically offers to do anything to save his life: cut his kindred's throats, burn children in their beds, "sweare and forsweare, renounce my baptisme." At this, Cutwolfe suddenly gets an idea:

With my selfe I devised how to plague him double for his base minde: my thoughtes traveled in quest of some notable newe Italionisme, whose murderous platforme might not onely extend on his bodie, but his soul also.

He finds the perfect device, offering Esdras his life if he will renounce and curse God, sign a pact with the Devil, and pray that God will never have mercy on him. Esdras eagerly complies, whereupon Cutwolfe promptly shoots him in the mouth so "that he might never speak after, or repent him."

We recall with amazement the frequent citation of Nashe's *Unfortunate Traveller* as proof that Hamlet is but following an "accepted" code of revenge. Jack Wilton is stunned into virtue, and even the Italians are outraged. Just as Daunce used revenge by damnation to indicate the enormities of which the Spanish were capable, so Nashe is using a device he knows will represent the most Satanic acts of an Italianate villain. Apparently the same judgment held firm into the Stuart period. Heywood's *Gynaikeion* (1629) tells of a "gentleman of Mediolanum" who made his enemy renounce the Savior in hope of life but then slew the apostate in the very act of blaspheming. The example appears in a discussion of witches, and Heywood uses it to show, by comparison, the treacherous method of the Devil. To Daunce, Nashe, and Heywood, such behavior was clearly demonic.

The convention bore the same connotation when it entered the theater. In *Alphonsus, Emperor of Germany* (1594-97), the Spanish villain, Alexander, commits the most monstrous of his many crimes when he tricks Alphonsus into forswearing God before killing him with the triumphant shout: "Die and be damn'd! Now am I satisfied!" (V.i.324). Even though Alphonsus undeniably deserves damnation, there is no possibility that the audience approved of Alexander's method of "immortal vengeance." He is branded a loathsome Judas and condemned to be hanged on a "Jewish gallows."

In no other extant play does a character again use this specific trick, but reactions to two characters who consider using it indicate the same moral attitude. In *The Dutch Courtezan* (1603-4), the ludicrous vintner Master Mulligrub rages against the coney-catching Cocledemoy, envisioning all the horrible fates he would like to visit on the knave: perhaps driving him to despair and killing him before he can sing any psalm, perhaps hiring "some sectary" to make him a heretic before he dies. Similarly Lodovico in *The White Devil* (1611-12) imagines with vicious glee the most Italianate revenges he can recall: he will poison Brachiano with his own prayer book or rosary, he will catch his victim just as he has sworn himself to Hell. Mulligrub is a comic fool, Lodovico an unrelieved villain. Neither earns a drop of sympathy.

More commonly the conventional way of ensuring a victim's damnation is either to kill a sinful man before he has time to pray or to kill him in one of the specific situations that Hamlet envisions:

> When he is drunk asleep, or in his rage,
> Or in the incestuous pleasure of his bed;
> At gaming, swearing, or about some act
> That has no relish of salvation in 't;
> Then trip him, that his heels may kick at heaven,
> And that his soul may be as damn'd and black
> As hell, whereto it goes.

Of course Hamlet does not mean that the simple act of drinking or gaming automatically condemns a man to Hell, a confusion of which he has been accused. His point is that although Claudius may now be repenting, he must not be allowed to persevere in a state of grace. The surest guarantee will be to kill him when his thoughts cannot possibly be turned to Heaven, to "trip him"—that is, to kill him instantly, allowing no time for last-minute repentance—in some new act that "has no relish of salvation in 't." This is the thinking behind the many characters who desire to kill their victims when they are drinking or are engaged in an act of lust or when for some reason—the deathblow will be too swift or their mouths will be stopped—they will be unable to pray.

In this specific form, the convention appears in seventeen plays written between 1585 and 1642. In nine plays, a character merely desires or plans to ensure the eternal damnation of his victim; in eight, a character takes specific action to carry out such a plan. Hamlet falls in the second group. He does more than merely desire the damnation of Claudius: he changes his course of action in order to fulfill that desire. Even the first group, however, will help us determine what kinds of characters entertained such a wish and how the audience reacted to them. In eight of the nine plays in the first group, the temptation or intention or mere wish to effect the damnation of a human soul is unmistakably judged as evil. The idea may be the insidious suggestion of a malignant tempter. In a scene in *The Dumb Knight* (1607-8) that echoes *Othello,* Epire "begrudgingly" tells the King that his wife is unfaithful, incites his pawn to the height of frenzy, and then makes a clearly diabolical suggestion:

> And you shall take them, as they clip each other,
> Even in their height of sin, then damn them both,
> And let them sink before they ask God pardon
> That your revenge may stretch unto their souls.
>                                        (III.i)[5]

In *'Tis Pity She's a Whore* (1633), the Spanish villain Vasques urges Soranzo to kill Giovanni while he is in bed with Annabella so that his enemy may "post to hell in the very act of his damnation" (V.iv).[6] The idea may be part of the extravagant rhetoric of villains. As Isabella in *The Insatiate Countess* (c. 1610) is led to execution, she glories that Sago, her tool, has effected her revenge against Massino, regretting only that Sago had not killed her defamer when he was drunk or in an act of lust. When the Cardinal begs her to have charity, she scornfully gives him her purse for the poor. In *The Tragedy of Thierry and Theodoret* (1607-21), the degenerate Brunhalt, accurately branded a whore by her virtuous son, begins to plan his murder with this vicious outburst:

---

[5] Dodsley, Vol. X.
[6] *The Best Plays of John Ford,* ed. Havelock Ellis for the Mermaid Series (London, 1888).

Throw all the mischiefs on him that thy self,
Or woman worse than thou art, have invented,
And kill him drunk, or doubtfull [i.e., in a state of despair].

(I.i)[7]

In *Match Me in London* (1630), Gazetto, a rejected suitor turned revenger, threatens the heroine with several terrors, culminating in the threat to make her swear falsely and then kill her, making her soul reel to Hell. In *Revenge for Honour* (1637-41), the adulteress Caropia, in revenge for the death of her lover (whose death she herself had inadvertently caused), stabs her husband and taunts the dying man with the wish that she might with the same blow kill his eternity. All of these characters except Gazetto are totally depraved, and our attitude even toward Gazetto's threat is unequivocal. Although he is reconciled by the end of the play, he is equally to be condemned for even considering a device of what he gloatingly calls "hot Spanish vengeance."

In light of the six villains just considered, it is surprising to find three unmistakably sympathetic characters expressing a wish to damn their enemies. However, before assuming that we thus have three instances in which the convention was morally approved, we should note the context. In *The Gentleman Usher* (c. 1602), Strozza, the noble confidant of our young hero, wants to kill Medici before the villain has time to confess and thus be forgiven. Strozza has been established as the voice of reason in the play, a man of "spirit prophetic," and now he says that Heaven forbids that Medici should repent. Thus far, one might think that his wish reflects a religious duty that the audience is intended to accept. Immediately, however, the hero pleads that Strozza be not uncharitable, that he allow time for confession. At the command of the Duke, Strozza relents, and we now see that his threat has been a trick to terrorize Medici into confession. In itself, the desire to damn has been judged reprehensible.[8] In *The Cardinal*

---

[7] Beaumont and Fletcher, *Works*, Vol. X.

[8] I do not wish to leave the impression that the play is basically Christian in its ethics. The denouement is morally chaotic. Medici is spared out of Christian charity, but then, when he does repent and confess, all the "virtuous" characters loathe him even more. Their reason is indicative of Chapman's often twisted ideas about "noblesse": in Medici's confession they learn that he has only pretended to be of noble birth, a crime all find to be much worse than attempted murder. He is beaten out of court in a state of despair.

(1641), the brave Don Hernando swears that if he were to kill the corrupt Cardinal, he would allow no time for prayer. He is not stating a specific intention, merely venting his fury in words. Even so, his companions immediately judge the sentiment appalling, and Hernando prays that God will forgive him for his lack of charity. In both instances, the convention is seen in Christian perspective and soundly condemned.

The third virtuous character who expresses a desire to damn an enemy is Iden in *2 Henry VI*. He has just killed the rebel Cade in fair fight, and the sympathies of the audience are with him as he soliloquizes over the dead body:

> Die, damned wretch, the curse of her that bare thee;
> And as I thrust thy body in with my sword,
> So wish I, I might thrust thy soul to hell.
> (IV.x.83–85)

In the nine works considered thus far, this is the only expression of such sentiments to be greeted with anything but horror. Iden undoubtedly is to receive both the sympathy and the moral admiration of his audience, but how much weight should we give to this one example when we consider the eight that contradict it? Moreover, there is a vast difference between wishing that one could effect the impossible and taking action in full expectation of success. Hamlet goes beyond the mere expression of a futile wish.

Let us, then, turn to that group of characters directly relevant to Hamlet: those who not only express an intention to predetermine God's judgment but act upon that intention. The earliest example that I have discovered is Absolon in *David and Bethsabe* (c. 1587). In revenge for the rape of his sister Thamar, Absolon kills Ammon while the unsuspecting brother is drinking and cries in triumph: "Die with thy draught perish and die accurst" (l. 790). The line is not mere rhetorical extravagance. Earlier, Absolon had sworn that "Ammon shall beare his violence to hell" and had planned "to worke false Ammon an ungracious end" (ll. 364, 376). That neither of these statements means simply "I will kill him" becomes clear in Adonia's report of the murder to David. Absolon had ordered his men not to attack until "Ammons heart / Is merry and secure" (ll. 904–5). In the

Bible, Absalom merely orders his men to wait until the victim is "merry" and thus unsuspecting (II Samuel 13). Peele's addition of drinking, together with Absolon's intention to send Ammon to Hell by devising a grace-less end, suggests that Absolon's specific means of exacting revenge is significant. If so, the example is instructive. Doubtless there is some sympathy for Absolon, but our moral judgment of him is clear: he is a "Rebell to nature, hate to heaven and earth" (l. 1579), an arrogant, presumptuous sinner who revels in his self-appointed role as the licensed favorite of God.

There may be some doubt that Absolon consciously chooses to damn his victim, or that the audience is horrified at his desire to damn a man guilty of incest and rape, but there can be no doubt about either the intentions or the audience's judgment of three villains. In *The Revenger's Tragedy* (1606–7), Lussurioso is brought before what he supposes to be the unconscious figure of his enemy, "Piato." Believing his victim to be sleeping off a drunken stupor, Lussurioso is about to kill him when Vindici, delighting in the success of his trickery, offers a mock objection to killing a drunken man. Lussurioso finds this the best time of all—"let him reel to hell" (V.i.49)—and commands his supposed henchman to strike. The moment is one of the most ghastly in the play, for the audience knows that the "sleeping Piato" is really a corpse and, what is worse, the corpse of Lussurioso's own father. A vague echo may be found in *The Honest Lawyer* (1616). Bromley, a wealthy but avaricious villain, is the legal heir of Sager's lands, but he is unwilling to wait for the old man's death. Unexpectedly finding Sager asleep, Bromley is about to kill him but suddenly hesitates. What if Sager has recently sinned? If so, to murder him asleep and thus unprepared would make his soul as well as his body "sink." But the chidings of conscience are not strong enough to make Bromley reject the chance fate has offered, and he strikes. For our purposes, it matters little that the "body" of Sager is really a dummy left in Bromley's path as a test. Nor does it matter that he had not originally intended to effect Sager's damnation. His speech makes the audience aware that he knows the terrible implications of his choice but chooses to buy his luxury at the cost of another human soul.

Neither can there be any doubt about the audience's reaction to the Duke of Averne in *The Captives* (1624). When the faithful Duchess tells her husband that a lusty friar has been making advances, the

Duke responds with such rage that he frightens her. She pleads for pity, begging that he shame the friar but not kill him. The Duke refuses to listen and, forcing her to arrange a rendezvous with the friar, kills his trapped victim in a burst of fury: "Strangle him / With all his sinnes about him. 'Twere not elce / A revendge woorthe my fury" (III.ii.71–73).[9] Immediately his conscience is horrified, specifically by the sin of preying upon a human soul. By the end of the play he amply repents, but nothing suggests that the audience is to sympathize with either his uncontrolled thirst for revenge or his method of effecting it.

The same judgment is indicated in *The Pilgrim* (1621), even though the proposal to damn is made by a heroine. This play provides the clearest example of the need to analyze context. Alinda, in disguise, is cleverly talking the villain, Roderigo, out of murdering the hero, a noble pilgrim who is obviously in a state of grace:

> Is that revenge,
> To slight your cause, and Saint your enemy,
> Clap the Doves wings of downy peace unto him,
> And let him soar to Heaven, whilst you are sighing?
> Is this revenge?

Wait, she pleads, until he is unprepared:

> When he appears a subject fit for anger,
> And fit for you, his pious Armour off,
> His hopes no higher than your sword may reach at,
> Then strike, and then ye know revenge; then take it.
> (II.ii)[10]

The trick succeeds. Alinda makes the proposal not because she approves of it, but because she knows that only the most malignant motive could persuade Roderigo. Both the villain and the convention stand condemned.

A similar judgment of the convention itself seems to underlie the murder scene in *The Maid's Tragedy* (1609–11), although it is difficult to determine Fletcher's exact intentions. It is true that Evadne's

[9] Ed. Alexander Corbin Judson (New Haven, Conn., 1921).
[10] Beaumont and Fletcher, *Works*, Vol. V.

murder of her royal lover is presented as proof of her repentance, but the killing itself is treated as vindictive and sadistic. Entering the King's bedchamber, Evadne pauses before killing him, and in a soliloquy places her coming deed in the familiar tradition of villainy. She knows that her purpose is "black," even as the horrible night; she knows that she is being led (ironically, she says by "conscience") to "things dismal, as the depth of Hell."[11] Although she says that she will awaken the King to arouse his conscience before she kills him, the context implies that she actually wants to damn him. To kill him asleep would be to "rock him to another world," and such a vengeance would be too tame. Instead she will arouse him and catalog his evils:

> I'le shake his sins like furies, till I waken
> His evil Angel, his sick Conscience:
> And then I'le strike him dead.

When the King awakens, she does, indeed, say that she wants him to repent, but her indictment is actually a means of torture. She shuts off his strangled cries with a torrent of words and kills him before he has a chance to speak at all, much less to express contrition or pray. By strict Christian standards, Evadne's stated purpose is merely a rationalization for her vituperative cataloging of the King's sins. It is never wise, however, to theorize about Fletcher's intentions on the basis of ethics. Too often, in defiance of logic, he has his characters express approved Christian sentiments solely to arouse a favorable emotional response. The present scene may be a case in point. He may intend Evadne's expression of Christian charity to soften her obvious evil. Her struggle would have little emotional impact on the audience if her actions too flagrantly fit the stereotype of villainy. No matter what Fletcher's intentions, however, we may assume that the audience approved of Evadne's expressed intention not to kill an unprepared soul but condemned the savagery of the murder itself.[12]

---

[11] *Ibid*. Quotations are from Act V.

[12] The killing is not swift punishment by one who now hates the evil that before she loved; it is a sadistic, slow death. She binds the King to the bed while he is helpless in his sleep and then proceeds to curse him, placing all blame on him for her fall (in violation of the facts as we have seen them), and then stabs him repeatedly—not to kill but to torture.

Only two plays in which characters succeed in damning their victims are even remotely ambiguous in their use of the convention. The confusions in *Antonio's Revenge* make it difficult to determine the audience's attitude toward Antonio's murder of Piero. As the conspirators bind Piero, Antonio plucks out his victim's tongue and cries: "Murder and torture; no prayers, no entreats" (V.v.63). The audience probably supplied the conventional reason, especially since Antonio, just before striking the deathblow, reminds Piero of the Hell to which he is damned. Antonio has gone to the most barbaric lengths to make certain that his victim cannot pray and thus be saved.[13] As noted earlier (pp. 57–62), I am convinced that Marston's audience followed Antonio's course with a horror approaching nausea. Since, however, the final scene apparently exonerates him, let us set aside this example. *Antonio's Revenge* is so ambiguous that it can prove nothing.

I find the same to be true of Fletcher's *The Triumph of Death* (1608), although the reader may disagree. The ostensibly virtuous Gabriella, disgraced when her corrupt husband, Lavall, casts her off, tricks him into an assignation with the sister of her ex-lover, Perolet. Drugging Lavall's wine, she plans to wait until he is helpless and then taunt him with his treachery. At this point, Perolet, also posited as virtuous, comes to her aid, hears the evil husband making obscene addresses to his sister, and enthusiastically joins Gabriella in a plan to kill the lecher. But how shall they do it? Gabriella would wait until Lavall wakes from his drugged sleep and then bind and torture him. Perolet has a better idea:

> Take him dead drunk now without repentance,
> His leachery inseam'd upon him.[14]

And Perolet strikes. There is no hint that he is anything but the noble defender of innocence. Gabriella, even though she seems to us to become a demonic fiend in her trickery and vindictive fury, is for-

---

[13] No one but Hamlet ever considers the fact that salvation does not depend on whether or not the sinner actually prays aloud. As Hamlet knows, the prayer of a true penitent need not even be completed. It suffices that the will has turned to God. Because an audience cannot read minds, dramatic convention required oral prayer for salvation.

[14] In *Four Plays*, Beaumont and Fletcher, *Works*, X, 335.

given by the Duke, who appears to justify her actions. The fact that Perolet is killed in the struggle with Lavall and Gabriella takes her own life may suggest implicit judgment of them, but the play closes with a pat moral about the dangers of a life of sensual indulgence—a condemnation of Lavall that says nothing about the method used to punish him. One might offer the many cases considered earlier as proof that Fletcher knowingly used the convention to show how revenge could corrupt the virtuous, but such an argument would probably be begging the question. Apparently Perolet is a virtuous hero, even in his attempt to predetermine God's judgment. If so, he is the only such hero in the entire extant drama of the English Renaissance.

To my knowledge, the drama to 1642 includes no further examples of the convention.[15] Three plays, however, remain to be considered: plays in which a character refuses to kill an unprepared sinner. The most obvious example is that of Frankford in *A Woman Killed with Kindness* (1603). Finding Anne in bed with her lover, Wendoll, Frankford stays his hand and rushes out of the bedchamber. He would have killed them on the spot,

> But that I would not damn two precious souls
> Bought with my Saviour's blood, and send them laden
> With all their scarlet sins upon their backs
> Unto a fearful Judgement.[16]
>
> (xiii.44–47)

Frankford wants to save their souls, not damn them. In effect, he leaves both to Heaven, trusting to conscience to effect his "revenge." Later we see Wendoll tortured by conscience and hear Frankford's patience approved by all as the means of bringing Anne to true repentance.

---

[15] One other parallel to the Prayer Scene might be cited, but it is actually irrelevant to the specific convention. In *The Jealous Lovers* (1632), Tyndarus, jealous over the supposed faithlessness of his beloved, the virtuous Evadne, is about to kill her but delays in order to kill her in bed with her imagined lover. His intention is not to damn her soul but merely to kill more sin at one blow by killing two sinners. It is possible that the audience would assume the convention, but the playwright does not so intend. Tyndarus is later exonerated on the grounds that his jealousy was nature's way of warning him against incest, Evadne being his sister.

[16] Ed. R. W. Van Fossen, Revels Plays (Cambridge, Mass., 1961).

Two similar examples are from Shakespeare. In Othello's terrible calm before he murders Desdemona, convinced that he is doing an act of justice, at last he is free to reveal the depth of love that he still feels for her. Thus, he tells her to pray.

> I would not kill thy unprepared spirit;
> No; heaven forfend! I would not kill thy soul.
>                    (V.ii.31–32)

Part of our pain results from our feeling that even now if he but retained this mood of compassion and love and if he went slowly, he would never strike. Part of the horror of the sudden, savage throttling results from the fact that she has inadvertently rearoused his fury so that he denies her the last moment for prayer that she begs. A brief passage in *Measure for Measure* is also pertinent. The Duke delays the execution of Barnardine because the criminal, though unfit to live, is

> A creature unprepared, unmeet for death;
> And to transport him in the mind he is
> Were damnable.
>                    (IV.iii.71–73)

Although the question of revenge is not involved and although the situation is comic, it shows that such motives are associated with the virtuous.

Oddly, these three parallels have not been noted in discussions of moral attitudes toward Hamlet in the Prayer Scene. They should be. In each case, the explicit refusal to kill a sinner in such a way as to damn him arouses the moral approval and sympathy of the audience. Even though they are not placed in exactly analogous situations, both Malevole in *The Malcontent* and Clermont in *The Revenge of Bussy D'Ambois* evoke a similar response when they effect the regeneration of their enemies.[17]

---

[17] For discussion of Malevole, see above, p. 67. In *The Revenge of Bussy D'Ambois* (c. 1610), the ghost of Bussy commands Clermont to effect justice on Montsurry but without, it is emphasized, lowering himself to the level of a villain. Clermont amply fulfills the command. Our Senecal hero challenges the craven Montsurry to open combat and shames the ignoble fool into sudden courage by his "noblesse." Thus miraculously converted to virtue, Montsurry falls in fair fight and dies a penitent Christian, freeing his opponent of any possible revenge taint. Clermont prays that the "worthy soul" may find rest in Heaven.

We have now considered a total of twenty-three plays and three non-dramatic works, each of which in some way is related to Hamlet's stated reason for refusing to kill Claudius. In light of the accepted belief that Hamlet's intention to damn Claudius for all eternity merely reflects a moral code unquestioned in the theater, the evidence is surprising. The extant drama to 1642 yields only one example of a virtuous man intentionally damning his victim, and that example is open to question. Even if we could be certain that the Jacobean audience accorded Perolet its full approval, surely no one would suggest that Fletcher provides a reliable guide to the ethical norms of Shakespeare's audience. In addition there is one virtuous man (Iden) who wishes that he had been able to damn his victim. These two are the only examples that might support the traditional assumption.

When we eliminate *Antonio's Revenge* from consideration because of its ambiguity, we are left with twenty-three examples, out of a total of twenty-six, which unmistakably indicate that the device of "immortal vengeance" was morally revolting to Shakespeare's audience, even as it is today. Three characters refuse to kill an unprepared soul and thereby gain the audience's sympathy. Two virtuous characters express a desire to do so and are promptly condemned for their lack of charity. Three-quarters of the characters we have considered, eighteen in all, are unmistakably evil, most of them demonic villains, unnatural monsters whose ruthless desire to subject their enemies to eternal torment was obviously viewed by the audience as a sign of their total depravity. In the light of this evidence, traditional criticism of the Prayer Scene and thus of Hamlet himself appears to have been based on a faulty assumption.

# The Relevance of Political Arguments to 'Hamlet'

It has often been suggested that the situation in which Hamlet finds himself posits a political duty that would have taken precedence in the Elizabethan period over the injunction against private revenge. Whereas some have argued that the Tudor doctrine of passive obedience underlies the play, others have argued the wide currency in the sixteenth century of a belief that even a private citizen might assassinate a tyrant. Still others have posited an Elizabethan belief that a legitimate heir would be duty-bound to depose a usurper. Each of these positions can be supported by documented evidence, and the unwary reader may be convinced by one or two pertinent quotations that Hamlet's political duty is clear.

Unfortunately, however, even the briefest foray into Elizabethan politics makes it apparent that Hamlet's "political duty" can never be really clear.[1] It is possible to single out several different armies involved in the battles over the English and Scottish crowns and to discuss the positions of their major champions, but the arguments advanced to support these positions are often ambiguous and contradictory. For example, that solid figure of the Establishment Richard Hooker can be—and has been—cited to prove both Hamlet's political duty to depose Claudius as a usurper, and his political duty to obey Claudius as a crowned king.

---

[1] The following discussion is based in large part on R. W. Carlyle and A. J. Carlyle, *A History of Mediaeval Political Theory in the West*, Vol. VI: *Political Theory from 1300 to 1600* (Edinburgh, 1936); John Neville Figgis, *The Divine Right of Kings*, 2d ed. (Cambridge, 1914); Charles Howard McIlwain's introduction to *The Political Works of James I* (Cambridge, Mass., 1918); and F. J. Shirley, *Richard Hooker and Contemporary Political Ideas* (London, 1949). Christopher Morris provides an excellent summary for the student in *Political Thought in England, Tyndale to Hooker* (Home University Library; London, 1953), but his book is of limited use to the scholar because he provides no documentation.

The purpose of this brief discussion is, then, not to suggest what the "average Elizabethan" thought about the political issues of his day, for we cannot know. It is, rather, to suggest the need of extreme caution in applying political arguments to *Hamlet*.

The problem is epitomized when we attempt to answer what should be the simplest of questions: did the members of Shakespeare's audience regard their own monarchy as elective or hereditary? With a settled answer to that question, some critics have suggested, we might at least conjecture about their expectations in the opening scenes of *Hamlet*. But no firm answer is possible. In the early years of her reign, Elizabeth faced a serious threat from Mary Stuart. If she claimed the throne by hereditary right, she was on very shaky ground indeed. Mary's champions had primogeniture on their side if they could argue, as they did, that Catherine of Aragon's divorce was invalid. Elizabeth needed a defense far stronger than the validity of her father's legal maneuvers, and her government hit on an absolute argument. The monarchy was not hereditary but elective. Moreover, "the possession of the crowne purgeth all defects, and maketh good the actes of him that is in authoritie."[2] And that was that. This argument underlies the countless demands, too well known to document here, for absolute obedience, even to a bloody tyrant. By an act of Parliament it was made high treason to question Parliament's right to alter the succession and thus illegal to argue for the law of primogeniture. Obviously, then, we find no such arguments throughout Elizabeth's reign.

There is, however, good evidence that sentiment clung tenaciously to a belief that the English monarchy was, in fact, hereditary. Following the death of Mary Queen of Scots in 1587, and the relieved recognition that her Protestant son James would be an acceptable heir, we find the "treasonous" argument an open assumption in works of the most orthodox spokesmen. In 1585, Bishop Bilson exhibits no uneasiness in flatly asserting that Elizabeth succeeded, not by election, but by inheritance. He states emphatically that "the greatest kingdomes of the West partes, as Fraunce, England, Spaine, Scotland and others have always gone by succession since they were divided from the Empire, and never by election."[3] In the last decade of the century,

---

[2] [Sir John Hayward], *An Answer to ... Dolman* (London, 1603), fol. K3ᵛ.
[3] *The True Difference Between Christian Subjection and Unchristian Rebellion* (Oxford, 1585), pp. 518, 515.

Richard Hooker's position is equally explicit: "in this realm . . . princes . . . are not made heads of the people by force of voluntary election, but born the sovereign lords."[4] To be sure, Hooker's theory of monarchy posited a social contract between people and sovereign, but at some undefined period in the past. The people had made their choice and from that time on, the English monarchy was hereditary.

By the time of *Hamlet,* what did the audience believe? At the end of the sixteenth century there was obviously strong sentiment in favor of an orderly succession of the crown to the next in blood. In spite of two acts of Parliament excluding his house from succession, James was welcomed to the throne.[5] Of course it is quite possible that some members of the audience, and perhaps all, had mixed beliefs and emotions. We can never determine their expectations with certainty.

The problem is far more complicated when we turn to the major political question often asked in regard to *Hamlet*: did the members of Shakespeare's audience believe that the killing or even the deposition of a crowned king was ever justifiable? On this question we find a plethora of relevant evidence in treatises published not only in Scotland and on the Continent but in England; again, however, we are faced with contradictions, with positions shifting according to the political situation at a given moment. The Establishment reasserted its absolute position throughout Elizabeth's reign: unquestioning obedience under any circumstances. Nonetheless, it was trapped into contradiction by the pressure of events. When Mary Queen of Scots was expelled by her Protestant subjects in 1568, orthodox spokesmen like the eminently respectable Bishop Jewel were forced to justify the deposition of even a *de jure* monarch.[6] At exactly the same time, ironically, the Northern Rebellion of 1569–70 compelled the Church to formulate its most vehement attack on disobedience and rebellion in the Homily of 1571. Faced with a similar challenge to orthodoxy by the revolts of the Protestants against the Catholics on the Continent, the conservative Bishop Bilson argued in 1585 for tyrannicide (though, as we shall note, his argument did not apply to England).

---

[4] *Laws of Ecclesiastical Polity,* V.lxxx.11; *The Works,* ed. John Keble, 3d ed., 3 vols. (Oxford, 1845), II, 507.

[5] See Figgis, *Divine Right,* p. 88.

[6] In *The Defence of the Apology,* 1570. In the following discussion, I do not offer quotations from Jewel because I find both his argument and his rhetoric tangled. Morris is surely right in asserting that Jewel argues against rebellion by private authority, but the argument is in the form of a dialogue and it seems dangerous to cite rhetorical questions as assertions.

The contradiction seems striking when we find Hooker saying that a legitimate heir may dispossess a crowned usurper, and at the same time insisting that "All 'powers are of God' ... either instituting or permitting them," and that such power must be obeyed.[7]

The same contradictions are found in both the writings and the actions of the radical factions. During the 1550's the Marian exiles saw both Scotland and England suffering under the religious persecution of Catholic queens and argued vehemently for the people's right to rebel. When Elizabeth came to the throne and they returned home, they understandably fell silent, and not only for fear of legal reprisal. Until the seventeenth century, the Puritans accepted the system and worked for reform within it. So long as they could hope for change, they affirmed the rule of obedience. The Catholics were far more obviously contradictory. While Mary Stuart lived, they argued for hereditary right and followed Bellarmine's counsel that subjects must never rebel. As late as 1584, William Allen (later Cardinal) was proposing only that the Church had the right to intervene, and then only if religion was endangered. With the death of Mary, however, the Jesuits did a direct about-face: denying that James's blood right gave him any claim to the throne, and calling on the English people to depose and execute Elizabeth as a traitor, a usurper, and an infidel.

Even a brief survey of all the chaotic evidence makes one thing immediately clear: the need for extreme caution in any attempt to determine the "average Elizabethan's" attitude on passive obedience. The critic who seeks to ascertain the political assumptions underlying *Hamlet* must give equal attention to all the available evidence, not just to that supporting one view. He must also return to the primary sources. Often scholars paraphrase in language determined by the position they seek to establish. Thus one reads that a certain document asserts the duty of every private man to "take vengeance on" or "kill" a tyrant, when the actual word is "resist"; that another document argues the duty of a legal heir to "kill" a usurper, when the actual words are "may dispossess." Moreover, every statement must be returned to its context. In isolation, a quoted passage may say "a private man has the right to kill a usurper," but in context we may find that right severely limited by a series of conditions—"if," for ex-

---

[7] Supposed fragment of a sermon on civil disobedience, *Works,* III, 458. The reference is to Romans 13:1.

ample, "the usurper has not yet been crowned," or "if he has been legally sentenced to death by the commonwealth." Such conditions often make the quoted passage irrelevant to *Hamlet*. The political issue in the play (if indeed there is one) is the right of a legitimate heir or private man to assassinate, on his own authority, a crowned usurper. For the moment let us grant that morally, if not legally, Claudius might be so viewed. Whether the Danish monarchy is to be considered elective or hereditary, Claudius has actually gained the throne by regicide.

Let us maintain focus on this specific political issue and return to the heated controversy over tyrannicide raging throughout the last half of the sixteenth century. Arguments for tyrannicide are clearly relevant to *Hamlet* because a usurper was, by definition, a tyrant. In the fourteenth century, Bartolus had distinguished between two types of tyrant: the tyrant *absque titulo* is the illegal ruler who has seized power in defiance of law, the usurper; the tyrant *exercitio* is the rightful ruler who wields power tyrannically, the oppressor. Most sixteenth-century definitions of the tyrant maintain this distinction, but add a significant differentia. Sir Thomas Smith's contrast between the tyrant and the true king contains a typical definition. The "tyrant by entrie" has seized the throne "against the will of the people"; the "tyrant by administration" may be a legitimate "king by entrie," but he rules "without the advise and consent of the people."[8]

This new criterion—the will of the people—figures prominently in almost every sixteenth-century defense of tyrannicide. The usual argument is that kings derive their authority from the consent of the governed; prince and commonwealth consent to a mutual contract. If the king breaks the contract by wielding power to serve his own private ends rather than the general welfare, the people may withdraw their consent. Thus a tyrant is commonly defined according to whether or not the people do, in fact, grant that consent. This criterion is crucial when we turn to discussions of the tyrant *absque titulo*. Scholars often state that during the Renaissance many people believed a usurper might be slain by anyone. Such a belief is, in fact, rarely expressed in extant documents of the sixteenth century, and it is carefully qualified in the examples I have noted. Three of the most

---

[8] *De Republica Anglorum* (London, 1583), I.7.

radical polemicists—the unknown author of the *Vindiciae contra Tyrannos* (1579), George Buchanan (*De Jure Regni apud Scotos,* 1578) and Mariana (*De Rege et Regis Institutione,* 1599)—all agree that if the people accept a usurper, he is no longer to be defined as a "tyrant." The *Vindiciae's* basic premise is that a man is not king until he receives the crown and the scepter from the hands of the people. Once he has been crowned, however, and the people swear obedience, he is the legal king and the private citizen must obey. Even "the meanest private person" may, it is true, lawfully kill a tyrant *absque titulo* in defense of his country. This, however, "is to be understood of a tyranny not yet firmly rooted, to wit, whilst a tyrant conspires, machinates, and lays his plots and practices." Once a usurper is made legal possessor of the state by the people's consent, the private man may not resist.[9]

The same principle of consent is explicit in Mariana's often quoted argument that a usurper might be slain by anyone and by any means except slow poison. We must note the care with which he defines *usurper.* "Both philosophers and theologians agree, that the Prince who seizes the State with force and arms, and with no legal right, no public, civic approval, may be killed by anyone."[10] If, however, he holds his power by consent of the people, he must be tolerated. On the basis of his administration, he may later be judged a tyrant *exercitio,* but the fact that he entered by force or fraud is insufficient grounds for punishment.

George Buchanan's position is the same. A usurper whose authority is accepted is no longer a tyrant *absque titulo.* In fact, adds Buchanan, such usurpers may govern well and gain the approbation of the people. They are still dangerous, but "it may be best to endure a

9 III, pp. 192–93. Page references are to Harold Laski's edition of the 1689 translation, *A Defense of Liberty Against Tyrants* (London, 1924). In support of the argument that any-one might kill a tyrant openly or secretly, W. A. Armstrong cites *Of Wisdome* by Pierre Charron, translated by Sampson Lennard in 1612. Charron's point, however, is exactly the same as one found in the *Vindiciae.* Anyone may "resist," "stay," and "hinder" an invader in his attempt to seize power, but once a tyrant *absque titulo* is "installed and acknowledged" he must be obeyed (III.10, p. 414). A tyrant *exercitio* may lawfully be resisted, but never by his own subjects. "It is honorable for a stranger, yea, it is most noble and heroicall in a prince by warlike means to defend a people unjustlie oppressed," but subjects may never move against their sovereign (p. 493). Cf. Armstrong's discussion in "The Elizabethan Conception of the Tyrant," *Review of English Studies,* XXII (1946), 166.

10 *De Rege,* I.6, p. 147. Page references are to George Albert Moore's translation, *The King and the Education of the King* (Washington, D.C., 1948).

tyranny of this sort if it is not possible to get rid of it without public calamity."[11] I have found no argument that a successful usurper was under automatic sentence of death solely because of the means by which he gained the crown. The test is whether or not the people assent to his rule.

But what of the tyrant *exercitio,* the legal king whose rule is so manifestly in defiance of law that the people have withdrawn their consent? In only one instance (to be discussed) do we find any suggestion that a private man might act on his own authority. The tyrant may be expelled only in accordance with the known will of the people, defined variously as the commonwealth, the nobility, "the greater part," men of "graver sort," etc.

Calvin's argument in the *Institutes* is echoed throughout the century. Under no circumstances may the private man rebel against his king; but if the people have appointed magistrates to restrain their rulers, such as the ephors in Sparta or the assembly of the three estates in some modern kingdoms, then those magistrates may take legal action. In other words, wherever it is legal to depose a king, it is legal. The Elizabethan Establishment embraced this argument with relief when it was trapped by the need to justify Protestant rebellions on the Continent but to condemn rebellion at home. Bishop Bilson thus argues that deposition by constitutionally established authority of the commonwealth is legal elsewhere, but never in a hereditary monarchy, never in England.[12]

Calvin's argument is remarkably similar to that of even the most passionate Monarchomachs. The vast majority restricted the right of action to legally appointed representatives of the people, and outlined a legal procedure to be checked, at every step, by public voice. Typical

---

[11] *De Jure,* ch. 29, p. 93. Page references are to Charles Flinn Arrowood's translation, *The Powers of the Crown in Scotland* (Austin, 1948). See also Chapter 49, p. 146.

[12] Pp. 513–21. John Sibly cites Bilson's justification of the execution of Athaliah as evidence for a code of extralegal revenge on a usurper by an individual ("The Duty of Revenge in Tudor and Stuart Drama," *Review of English Literature* VIII [July, 1967], 52–53). Sibly, however, fails to note Bilson's many arguments: Jehoiada acted not as a private individual but as a "Prince of his Tribe," whose duty it was to pacify the realm. Moreover, he did not act alone. He called together "forces both of the Priestes and people; proclaimed the right heire that was in his custodie [he had saved the child from being killed by the usurper]; annointed and crowned him King." No action was taken until "the rightfull inheritour of the Scepter [was] first proclaimed and Crowned by the Consent of his whole Realme." The procedure was legal. Bilson is absolute in his injunction against private action, and the issue of "revenge" is wholly irrelevant. For Bilson's full discussion, see *The True Difference,* pp. 329–30.

is the position of the *Vindiciae contra Tyrannos,* the most influential
of the Huguenot tracts written in the 1570's. When a king violates the
laws of God, the people are guilty of his crime if they do not resist,
but the form of resistance is carefully defined. The king must be publicly judged a tyrant *exercitio* by officers of the kingdom, inferior magistrates such as the peers or the assembly of the estates. If the tyrant
does not submit to legal deposition, the officers of the kingdom may
publicly renounce him and even call the people to arms. But what if
the principal officers either conspire with the tyrant or are "lulled in
a dull and drowsy dream of security"? The private man is absolutely
helpless. God did not put the sword into his hands. He can act only
"if all the principal officers of state, or divers of them, or but one"
have the courage to move against the tyrant and command the people's support.[13] The tyranny must be manifest, and action can be instituted only by those magistrates such as constables or marshals who
are entrusted with the protection of the entire kingdom. Governors
of a single part of the kingdom may expel the tyranny from their
own areas of jurisdiction, but they may not act against the life or
crown of the tyrant without command by the principal officers. The
*Vindiciae,* though radical for its day, is scarcely democratic in persuasion. So long as the aristocracy supports a tyrant, the private man
has recourse only to the bended knee and the humble heart.

In the heat of the battle at the end of the century, one might expect
the Jesuits to encourage in their polemical treatises, as they did in
action, the right of the individual to rebel. In their writings, however, they are remarkably restrained. Robert Parsons was probably
behind most of the plots against Elizabeth's life, but in *A Conference about the Next Succession to the Crown of England* (1594) he
absolutely prohibits assassination. "Whatsoever a Princes title be, if
once he be setled in the crowne, and admitted by the commonwealth
... every man is bound to setle his conscience to obey the same, in al
that lawfully he may commaunde, and this without examination of
his title, or interest." Although the individual may not act, the whole
body of the commonwealth retains the power to restrain and even
dispossess a king "uppon due & waighty considerations."[14] Parsons
does not require specific constitutional authorization for such an

---

13 III, pp. 205, 211. Moreover, the officers must act not "as private men and subjects, but
as the representative body of the people, yea, and as the sovereignty itself" (III, p. 199).
14 Pp. 34, 36.

action, but otherwise he is in agreement with Calvin, Bilson, and the Huguenots: a king may be judged and punished only by public authority.

Among the treatises whose arguments might have been known to Elizabethans, I have found only three even suggesting that an individual might have the right to take upon himself the punishment of a tyrant *exercitio*. Again the carefully defined conditions are so significant that we should consider each argument in detail.

Mariana's position is perhaps the most extreme to be found in the period, but even he urges great caution, "lest evil pile on evil, and crime [be] avenged with crime." Ideally, a national assembly should convene, determine its judgment, and admonish the king. If he refuses to amend, the assembly may rescind his power, a step that will necessarily entail war to drive the tyrant out. In the worst extremity, the assembly can proscribe him as a public enemy and pass sentence of death. Under these clearly defined conditions of open war, anyone may execute the public sentence. Should the tyranny be so absolute that public assembly is impossible, the individual may be permitted to act—but, Mariana emphasizes, never on his judgment alone. "For we do not leave this to the decision of any individual, or even to the judgment of many, unless the voice of the people publicly takes part, and learned and serious men are associated with the deliberation."[15] The will of the people must, in some way, be made manifest.

Because George Buchanan is defending the deposition of Mary, his attention is focused on defending legal deposition. He touches only briefly on possible courses of action if the king will not willingly submit to open trial, and his comments are puzzling. In such a case, the king is to be treated like a common criminal. He is a public enemy, whom any man has the right to destroy: for "anyone may slay a thief by night, and may slay him by day in self-defense." Buchanan insists, against obvious objections, that his argument could never grant license to evil men. He would never sanction an attack on a ruler who has been accepted by the people, no matter how he acquired his power. But then, it seems to me, he frankly hedges: "Moreover, I am discussing what may legally be done or ought to be done in a case of this sort; I do not advise what ought to be undertaken in a particular

[15] *De Rege*, I.6, pp. 147, 148. Mariana even pauses to condemn the "idle talk" of Jean Petit who had argued in the early fifteenth century that anyone has the right to kill a tyrant (p. 150).

case."[16] It is possible that a reader of the words might infer license for private decision and action, but the inference would be, I think, dangerous. Throughout, Buchanan has insisted on the absolute supremacy of law, on the need for lawyers to interpret that law, on obeying the will of the people, on the danger of relying on the judgment of a single man.[17] His whole argument tends to Mariana's opinion: under conditions of total oppression, the individual may act, but only if he has sure knowledge that he is carrying out the public's wishes.

In all the evidence, I have thus far found only one writer who suggests that a private man might assassinate a tyrant solely on his own authority: Bishop John Ponet, leader of the Marian exiles in Strasbourg. Close study of Ponet's full discussion in *A Shorte Treatise of Politike Power* (1556) reveals, however, many important conditions. In the *Treatise* Ponet's primary emphasis is on the usual argument that deposition and execution must be effected "by the body of the hole congregacion or common wealthe," acting through the nobility. The private individual must never undertake punishment except under four circumstances. The first three present no problem. Every man has the duty to act immediately if the tyrant is caught in the act of betraying his country, if he is about to murder an innocent, or if he is in bed with a man's own wife or daughter. Surely no one but an Amintor, a devout believer in divine right, could object. The fourth, however, might offer astounding license to a fanatic. "What if," Ponet asks, "the nobilitie, and those that be called to common Counselles . . . will not or dare not execute their autoritie?" What if, perhaps, they join with the prince to "conspire the subversion or alteracion of their contrey and people"? The private man's first recourse must be to "complayne to som minister of the worde of God" who has power to excommunicate. If that fails, if all public authority demands obedience, the private man must endure—unless he has "some special inwarde commaundement or surely proved mocion of God." Ponet must explain the case of Ehud in Judges 3:12–28. No, Ehud did not seek the counsel of the people; he could not risk betrayal. Scripture clearly commends his murder of the king of the Moabites; but scripture also clearly points out that Ehud, "(being a private per-

---

[16] *De Jure*, ch. 47, pp. 141–42; ch. 49, p. 146.
[17] See chapters 20, 21, and 43.

sone) was stered up only by the spirite of God."[18] No one but a religious fanatic could accept Ponet's last resort as warrant for assassination. The commandment, we note, must be "surely proved."

A pertinent refutation of this argument is found in the *Vindiciae*.
It is quite true, the author admits, that the Scriptures tell of cases in
which God chose private men to destroy tyrants. But in such cases
God's command was confirmed by "miraculous testimonies," and, he
argues as a good Protestant, the age of miracles is past. Certainly anything is within God's power, and He might, conceivably, perform a
miracle, but "where God Almighty does not speak with His own
mouth, nor extraordinarily by His prophets, it is there that we ought
to be exceedingly cautious, and to stand upon our guard." A man who
flatters himself he is inspired by God should take heed "lest he make
not a God to himself of his own fancy, and sacrifice to his own intentions."[19] Was the learned author of the *Vindiciae* answering Ponet
directly in his comprehensive survey of every conceivable argument?
Or does his discussion indicate a view sufficiently widespread to demand refutation? We cannot know.

We have, of course, ample evidence that some Elizabethans did believe in divine warrant. In 1570, the bull of Pius V excommunicating
Elizabeth convinced some Catholics that it would be a religious duty
to assassinate her as a tyrant and an infidel. The immediate result was
Ridolfi's Plot of 1571. In 1580 the Jesuit missions were instituted,
Robert Parsons landed in England disguised as a captain, and plots
multiplied. The several plots against Elizabeth are, however, no proof
that even among the most fanatical Catholics there were many who
believed assassination justifiable. In 1580 Humphrey Ely, an English
Catholic lawyer, said that some nobles were uneasy: they needed
assurance from the highest authority that assassination would not, in
fact, be a sin. The Papal Nuncio in Spain gave them that assurance,
and a letter from Galli, Cardinal of Como, confirmed that anyone
dispatching Elizabeth from this world would in fact do a deed of
merit. When the letter was revealed in 1585, loyal English Catholics
were genuinely horrified.[20] By the turn of the century, William Wat-

---

[18] Pp. 106, 117, 111–12, 123. Winthrop S. Hudson includes a facsimile reprint in *John
Ponet: Advocate of Limited Monarchy* (Chicago, 1942).

[19] III, p. 212; II, p. 112.

[20] The revelation of the letter gave playwrights material for a new convention to signify
papist villainy. In *The Troublesome Reign of King John* (published 1591), an abbot absolves

son probably spoke for a majority of the Catholics in England when he branded Parsons as a "pestilent traitor," whose "Jesuiticall Hispanized faction of falsehood, hypocrisie, sedition and treason" was devoted solely to Spanish conquest.[21]

By the time of *Hamlet,* then, I can discover nothing to suggest widespread belief that an individual—whether a private citizen or an officer of the kingdom—had the right to kill either a tyrant *absque titulo* or a tyrant *exercitio* on his own authority. There was certainly a body of solid and even respectable opinion that the people as a whole had the right to depose a tyrant, but even the most passionate revolutionaries insisted on specified legal procedures requiring consultation with and consent of the commonwealth at every step.

Might the case be different for a legitimate heir? Some have argued that the Elizabethan audience would have assumed the monarchy in *Hamlet* to be hereditary, despite the references to election. If so, we should consider any available evidence. Unfortunately, however, none of the political crises of the period involved a prince in Hamlet's particular situation, and all the surviving political polemics were directed to immediate issues. Elizabeth's blood right was questionable; Mary Stuart's religion entailed a foreign threat. In contrast, Hamlet is a first-born son, and his religion presents no problem. In a hereditary monarchy his right would be incontestable. Had Parliament bypassed a Hamlet in establishing the succession, the ensuing controversy would have been highly pertinent to the play. Politically, Hamlet is in a unique situation, a situation that may well make irrelevant all the arguments we have considered about the rights and duties of "principal officers" and "private men."

In the course of my research in the period, I have encountered only one statement that might be relevant to Hamlet's situation: Hooker's comment that in hereditary kingdoms "the death of the predecessor" automatically puts "the successor by blood in seisin." Even though a usurper has been crowned by the people, "the inheritor by blood may dispossess him."[22] It is difficult to know how much weight we should

---

a monk in advance for the projected murder of John, because the "deed is meritorious." In *The Massacre at Paris* (1593), Marlowe gives the same words to a friar who plans to kill the king in order to wipe out the record of his many sins.

[21] Watson's Epistle preceding *Important Considerations,* 1601. Watson violently denounces the Jesuit plots and swears that he and other secular priests in England will never be traitors, "no, if the Popes Holinesse should charge us to obey in this sense, to advance an enimie to the English Crowne."

[22] Laws, VIII. ii. 9; *Works,* III, 349.

attach to this one statement, especially when we find Buchanan, Mariana, and the author of the *Vindiciae*—all fervent champions of rebellion—insisting that the people's consent makes a usurper a lawful king who must be obeyed. Of course, these three men all place the right of the people above the right of primogeniture, and their opinion may be counter to popular assumptions in England. The ease with which Hooker makes his assertion—he feels no need to qualify or explain—may indicate that we should accept his statement as evidence of widespread Elizabethan sentiment. If we do, however, we should pay close attention to his exact words. "May dispossess" in no way suggests "obligation to eliminate by any means." Hooker might be cited to support Hamlet's political right to take open action, but not to argue his political duty to assassinate Claudius.

On the basis of this brief survey, I have, in fact, found no clue at all to Hamlet's "political duty," or to any historical political assumptions that are crucial to our understanding of the play. The survey has, on the contrary, led me to the conclusion that certain political arguments are probably irrelevant to Hamlet.[23]

The evidence suggests, moreover, that we cannot determine the political assumptions underlying *Hamlet* by reference to *Macbeth* and *Richard III*, two plays in which the killing of a king is clearly approved. In both plays the act meets widely accepted criteria. In both, the king is publicly branded a tyrant: in *Macbeth* the words "tyrant" and "tyranny" toll throughout. In both, the commonwealth has withdrawn its consent, a fact made clear by the consultation of nobles and their invitation to a legitimate contender to lead the rebellion. In both, rebellion is open and the tyrant is killed in fair combat. In both, the motive of the rebels is solely the purgation of the kingdom, and we are reminded again and again that God is on their side. None of these conditions obtains in *Hamlet*.

After comparing the facts in *Hamlet* with political arguments, we can safely conclude, I think, that Shakespeare did not consciously set out to justify Hamlet on political grounds. It is clear that the court has crowned Claudius with full assent: in the first Court Scene, Clau-

---

[23] The political controversies of the sixteenth century are far too complicated for any but the qualified historian to untangle, and there may be significant evidence of which I am not yet aware. In addition, it is quite possible that men believed in and privately discussed arguments that they would not commit to print, even on the Continent. My conclusions are thus highly tentative.

dius pointedly notes that he has not acted against the will of the "better wisdoms" of the state. They have "freely gone / With this affair along," and he thanks them for their support. If political considerations were relevant, the installation of Claudius with consent might indicate that he is not to be classed as a tyrant *absque titulo,* no matter how he obtained the crown. Similarly, it might be significant that Hamlet never considers appealing to the nobility. He does not "consult" with Horatio as a representative Dane but merely informs a personal friend of his plan.

More significant might be the fact that Shakespeare almost seems to go out of his way to avoid labeling Claudius a "tyrant." If Hamlet regards himself as the legitimate heir, he would have solid reason to consider Claudius a tyrant *absque titulo.* Even if the kingdom is elective and Claudius is the rightful king, the second half of the play suggests the reign of a tyrant *exercitio.* The rumblings of the people, the English plot against Hamlet, the final perfidy of the duel—all of these bespeak the wielding of power to further a ruler's own ends, not to serve the people. To have Hamlet brand Claudius a tyrant from the beginning would be natural; to have someone at the end of the play so judge him would seem inevitable. But neither occurs. The only "tyrant" in the play is Pyrrhus.

This fact is thrown into relief when we note that in Belleforest the king is insistently branded as a tyrant, a usurper, and a traitor. When we further consider the fact that the monarchy is even more clearly elective in *Hamlet* than in Belleforest and that Hamlet speaks only of his frustrated hopes, never of his violated rights, any argument that Hamlet has a clear political duty to kill Claudius, or even to depose him, becomes highly suspect.[24]

All this, however, is not to say that Shakespeare consciously set out to preclude a political justification for Hamlet's actions. Explicit definition of the monarchy as elective comes late in the play. In the first scenes, I find it probable that Shakespeare's audience would assume, as we do, that the son should succeed the father.[25] Obviously,

---

[24] In Belleforest, the monarchy is elective only in the sense that the people choose their ruler by acclamation. Amleth insists throughout not only that he is the rightful successor but also that he is, in fact, legal king. Shakespeare omits any suggestion that Hamlet is acting as a legal ruler empowered to execute a traitorous subject.

[25] Critics have pointed out, quite correctly, that the Fortinbras parallel in the first scene establishes that the Polish monarchy is elective. Nevertheless, I agree with Dover Wilson that no audience would catch the subtle references and thus automatically expect the Danish mon-

the court would have elected Hamlet if it had known the truth. Obviously, too, appeal to this particular court is impossible. The only character in the play who might be classified as a "principal officer of the state" is senile and blind. And whether Claudius is called a tyrant or not, he has gained the crown by regicide and he uses his power illegally, to serve his own vicious ends. We surely sense that, in some way, Hamlet must remove him from the throne. He is incited to action by compelling motives. There is no hint anywhere in the play that political arguments demanding passive obedience to an elected king are, or should be, relevant to Hamlet's dilemma.

My own feeling is that all political arguments—whether for rebellion or obedience—are irrelevant to the play.[26] In fact, the issue of Hamlet's right to the crown is so thoroughly ambiguous as to suggest that we are to ignore political implications altogether. We expect Hamlet to be the legal heir, but see Claudius comfortably installed with full consent. Next we learn that Claudius is a regicide and possibly to be regarded as a usurper, but Hamlet speaks of his "ambition," not his "right." In the middle of the play we are told that Claudius "stole" the crown, but later Hamlet tells us that Claudius "popp'd in between the election and my hopes." We are never allowed a settled political perspective.

In the absence of any counter-evidence in the play itself, we should take our cue from Hamlet. In the Court Scene, we are likely to sense that something is wrong with the succession, but when Hamlet is at last alone on stage and can tell us what that something is, he makes no mention of the crown. His attention, and ours, is directed elsewhere. When we struggle with political issues, are we not diverted from the real issues of the play?

---

archy also to be elective. The 1936 debate between Wilson, J. P. Malleson, and others in the *Times Literary Supplement* remains fascinating (Jan. 4, 11, 18, 25, Sept. 26, Oct. 3, 10, 17) even after E. A. J. Honigman's recent thorough argument for the elective nature of the Danish monarchy in *Hamlet* in "The Politics in 'Hamlet' and 'The World of the Play,' " in *Stratford-upon-Avon Studies* 5 (1963). I grant the validity of all Honigman's evidence but doubt that the "mystery of the Danish succession" is really an element of suspense in the theater.

[26] For an illuminating discussion of this and other points, see Matthew N. Proser, "Hamlet and the Name of Action," *Essays on Shakespeare,* ed. Gordon Ross Smith (University Park, Pa., 1965).

# Index

# Index

Plays by Shakespeare and anonymous works are listed by title; all other works are listed under the author's name.